Canada Among Nations 2007

Canada Among Nations 2007

What Room for Manoeuvre?

EDITED BY
JEAN DAUDELIN
AND DANIEL SCHWANEN

Published for the Norman Paterson School of
International Affairs, Carleton University, in cooperation
with The Centre for International Governance Innovation

by McGill-Queen's University Press
Montreal & Kingston • London • Ithaca

© McGill-Queen's University Press 2008
ISBN 978-0-7735-3396-7 (cloth)
ISBN 978-0-7735-3397-4 (paper)

Legal deposit second quarter 2008
Bibliothèque nationale du Québec

Printed in Canada on acid-free paper that is 100% ancient forest free
(100% post-consumer recycled), processed chlorine free

This book has been published with financial support from the
Norman Paterson School of International Affairs, Carleton University,
and The Centre for International Governance Innovation.

McGill-Queen's University Press acknowledges the support of the Canada
Council for the Arts for our publishing program. We also acknowledge the
financial support of the Government of Canada through the Book
Publishing Industry Development Program (BPIDP) for our publishing
activities.

Library and Archives Canada has catalogued this publication as follows:

Canada among nations.
    Annual.
    1984–
Produced for the Norman Paterson School of International Affairs
at Carleton University
in cooperation with The Centre for International Governance Innovation.
Publishers varies.
Each vol. also has a distinctive title.
Includes bibliographical references.
ISSN 0832–0683

ISBN 978-0-7735-3396-7 (bnd)
ISBN 978-0-7735-3397-4 (pbk)

    1. Canada – Foreign relations – 1945–   – Periodicals.
    2. Canada – Politics and government – 1984–   – Periodicals.
    3. Canada – Politics and government – 1980–1984 – Periodicals.
    I. Noman Paterson School of International Affairs.

FC242.C345   327.71   C86–031285-2 rev

This book was typeset by Interscript in 10/12 Sabon.

Contents

Foreword

What Room for Manoeuvre? raises a question that has haunted Canadian policy-makers and citizens since Confederation: how free is the country to pursue what its various governments consider to be most proper and advantageous course in the world outside Canada? A preoccupation with an independent foreign policy has always been present but it has ebbed and flowed over time. However, such concerns have become acute since the signing of a free trade agreement with the United States in 1989 and the addition of Mexico to NAFTA in 1994. As was made clear by public debates and demonstrations surrounding the trilateral summit at Montebello last August, worries about the consequences of integration have not abated over almost twenty years of functioning free trade.

After a general introduction in which the editors carefully lay out the problem of "room for manoeuvre" and outline the many ways in which the book explores its facets, Wendy Dobson sets the tone by forcefully warning against complacency and by outlining the key areas where efforts are needed if what policy space there remains is to be captured. She calls in particular for clarity regarding what is to be done with that room to manoeuvre.

The rest of the book looks at the problem from a variety of angles. A full section explores "the Ottawa game," especially the elbow room that the main foreign policy bureaucracies have carved for themselves. Many of the analyses presented challenge currently fashionable views. The overwhelming weight of the Centre, namely the Prime Minister's and Privy Council Offices, is put in historical perspective by John Noble, who shows it to be at once not as severe as is often said, nor particularly new. Danford W. Middlemiss and Denis Stairs similarly bring down to size the "Hillier scare" by suggesting that the Afghanistan policy of the Canadian government would be little different without the Chief of Defence Staff's noisy antics before the media. Stephen Brown's chapter on CIDA, by contrast, will further worry those who see it as an ever weaker agency, increasingly devoid of autonomy. The section closes with chapters on Alberta and Quebec, two provinces whose governments have apparently been 'punching above their weight' on particular foreign policy issues, in particular Kyoto for Alberta and Afghanistan for Quebec. Here again, however, those widely shared impressions are challenged: Christopher J. Kukucha and Tom Keating wonder if Canada as a whole was indeed ready to implement Kyoto, and Jean-Christophe Boucher and Stéphane Roussel if Canada was that gung-ho about waging war in Afghanistan. Both chapters end up suggesting that these provinces may well have simply defended views that are in fact quite broadly shared in the country.

This defiant tone is maintained as the book moves to "the global game," where the challenges are traced less to external factors than to missed opportunities, lack of vision, contradictory positions, and under-investment in capacity. The discussion starts at one of the frontiers of international governance, namely intellectual property rights. Jeremy de Beer and Michael Geist suggest that a lot could be gained though a much more assertive and, most properly perhaps, creative stance. Robert Wolfe shows that the relative marginalization of Canada in the current multilateral trade negotiation processes is slightly different: while it indeed reflects Canada's declining influence on the agriculture issue that is the centre of contention, it also results from contradictory stands for which the pragmatism of its attitude and the quality of its representatives simply cannot compensate. In the following chapter, the issue of capacity is shown by Trevor Findlay to be central to Canada's declining visibility and influence on the nuclear proliferation discussion. These chapters suggest in sum that while Canada is certainly a "taker" of global trends, it does not adequately exploit many an opportunity to be a trend "maker" too.

The contributions of the last section are devoted to North America, which the editors have dubbed "the trenches" because this is where the strongest constraints appear to lie. What is striking here is how complicated the problem is in practice and how ambiguous the implications of North American integration are to Canada's room for manoeuvre. The big free trade debate appears in fact to be breaking down into a series of smaller ones, each with its own peculiarities and implications. Carol

Wise first outlines the challenges that North American economic dynamics and current U.S. trade policy pose for Canada, especially the pressures that again threaten to confine Canada to the provision of primary products to our immediate neighbour. She identifies clear options, however, involving a much more serious engagement with other hemispheric partners, arguably very much the direction in which Prime Minister Stephen Harper's America policy appears to be heading. By contrast, in his overview of the Security and Prosperity Partnership, Stephen Clarkson sees a much more constraining environment and, in what is probably the most pessimistic take on Canada's room for manoeuvre, contemplates with gloom the ever-deepening "constitutionalization" of North American integration. The last two chapters are more in keeping with the generally confident tone of the rest of the book, although at the same time extremely critical of the current failings of our North American policy. Looking at the nitty-gritty of Canada-U.S. relations, Colin Robertson outlines a strategy to better manage the constant challenges of bilateralism, with a more effective exploitation of Canada's human resources on the ground and through the leveraging of the interdependence that exists between the two countries. Debora VanNijnatten draws a portrait of lost opportunities and invasive mediocrity in the field of environmental management, where a lack of boldness leads either to poor results or to a convergence to which Canada should not be doomed.

All in all, and perhaps optimistically, most authors seem to agree with the editors that there is still much foreign policy room for Canadian decision-makers to manoeuvre. Most even argue that, with some boldness, Canada could easily expand that space through carefully crafted measures, touching especially on national capacity, both in government as well as in business and education organizations.

This edition of *Canada Among Nations*, the 23rd installment of the series, crowns the third year of close and extremely fruitful collaboration between the Norman Paterson School of International Affairs and The Centre for International Governance Innovation. We thank John English and Daniel Schwanen, as well as their dedicated team, and look forward to the next chapters of our partnership with CIGI.

Fen Osler Hampson
Director
The Norman Paterson School of International Affairs
Carleton University
Ottawa
November 2007

Acknowledgments

The 23rd edition of the *Canada Among Nations* series, *What Room For Manoeuvre?*, is for the third year in a row the product of a joint effort by the Norman Paterson School of International Affairs (NPSIA) and The Centre for International Governance Innovation (CIGI).

Like each volume in the series, this year's compilation is the outcome of a demanding process whose tight deadlines impose unusual pressures on its team of contributors. Beginning last spring, during a lively and exceptionally rich meeting in Niagara-on-the-Lake, they have responded with a marvellous mixture of skill, diligence, and enthusiasm. In spite of the diversity of backgrounds, professional expertise, and outlooks of its members, and without much prodding from the editors, the group has been able to draw a remarkably cogent and quite original picture of the challenges that confront contemporary Canadian foreign policy. We thank them all warmly for their contribution.

Through NPSIA and CIGI, the project was able to draw from a remarkable pool of expertise, experience, resources and networks. At NPSIA, Director Fen Osler Hampson and Associate Director Dane Rowlands have been constant sources of guidance and support. At CIGI, Executive Director John English and Associate Director Andrew F. Cooper have been steady and encouraging advisors. We would also like to thank Katherine Graham, dean of the Faculty of Public Affairs and Management at Carleton University, for continuing to support the *Canada Among Nations* series. We are indebted to the leadership of Jim Balsillie, chairman of CIGI's Board of Directors, for without his enormous support projects like this would not be possible.

Over the past year, the CIGI staff has provided superb project management. Kelly Jackson once again led the project team, organizing the Author's Workshop and coordinating the chapter revision process, duties she performed with efficiency and grace. Our thanks also to Andrew Schrumm, who was on board for another year and who excelled at multiple tasks, often on short notice. We also would like to acknowledge the help of Matthew Bunch with constructing the index, and of Ray Froklage and James Munro for their thorough fine-tuning of the manuscript.

Finally we would like to thank all the people at McGill-Queen's University Press who worked efficiently to turn the manuscript into a book along demanding deadlines. Of particular note in this regard we acknowledge with gratitude the efforts of Philip Cercone, Joan McGilvray, and Brenda Prince. Additionally, the production and marketing teams have been of great assistance in compiling and publicizing the many volumes of this series.

Jean Daudelin
Daniel Schwanen
Ottawa/Waterloo
November 2007

Abbreviations

9/11	11 September 2001
ACO	Alberta China Office
ADMS	associate deputy ministers
AFPA	Alberta Forest Products Association
ANZUS	Australia/New Zealand/US
ASEAN	Association of South East Asian Nations
Auto Pact	Canada-US Automotive Products Agreement
BIRPI	the Bureaux Internationaux réunis pour la protection de la propriété intellectuelle
BMD	Ballistic Missile Defence
BNA	British North America
BSE	Bovine Spongiform Encephalopathy
CANDU	Canadian Deuterium Uranium
CAP	Common Agricultural Policy
CBD	Convention on Biological Diversity
CCCE	Canadian Council of Chief Executives
CCME	Canadian Council of Ministers of the Environment
CD	Conference on Disarmament
CDS	Chief of the Defence Staff
CEC	Commission for Environmental Cooperation
CEO	Chief Executive Officer
CF	Canadian Forces
CIDA	Canadian International Development Agency
CIR	Canada-India Reactor
CNN	Cable News Network

CNSC	Canadian Nuclear Safety Commission
CO$_2$	Carbon Dioxide
CTBT	Comprehensive Nuclear Test Ban Treaty
CTBTO	Comprehensive Nuclear Test Ban Treaty Organization
CUSFTA	Canada-US Free Trade Agreement
CWS	Canada-wide Standard
DDT	Dichloro-Diphenyl-Trichloroethane
DFAIT	Department of Foreign Affairs and International Trade
DHS	Department of Homeland Security (US)
DMCA	Digital Millennium Copyright Act
DND	Department of National Defence
DPS	Defence Policy Statement
EC	European Community
EFTA	European Free Trade Association
ENDC	Eighteen-Nation Disarmament Committee
EPA	Environmental Protection Agency (US)
EU	European Union
FAO	Food and Agriculture Organization (UN)
FBI	Federal Bureau of Investigation
FDI	Foreign Direct Investment
FLQ	Front de Liberation du Quebec
FMCT	Fissile Material Cut-Off Treaty
FRG	Federal Republic of Germany
FTA	Free Trade Agreement
G7	Group of 7
G8	Group of 8
GATS	General Agreement on Trade in Services
GATT	General Agreement on Tariffs and Trade
GDP	Gross Domestic Product
GHG	greenhouse gas
GNP	Gross National Product
HEU	highly enriched uranium
IAEA	International Atomic Energy Agency
ICANN	Internet Corporation for Assigned Names and Numbers
ICT	information and communications technology
IFOR	Implementation Force in Bosnia and Herzegovina
IIMs	inter-sessional intergovernmental meetings
IJC	International Joint Commission
IMCO	Instituto Mexicano para la Competitividad
INF	Intermediate-range Nuclear Forces
IPC	Intellectual Property Committee
IPS	*International Policy Statement*
ISAF	International Security Assistance Force in Afghanistan

ISPs	Internet service providers
ISROP	International Security Research and Outreach Program
JCANZ	Japan, Canada, Australia, New Zealand
KEDO	Korean Peninsula Energy Development Organization
KFOR	Kosovo Force
MOX	mixed oxide
MP	member of parliament
MTCR	Missile Technology Control Regime
NAAEC	North American Agreement on Environmental Cooperation
NAALC	North American Agreement on Labour Cooperation
NACC	North American Competitiveness Council
NAFTA	North American Free Trade Agreement
NAMA	Non-Agricultural Market Access
NARAPs	North American Regional Action Plans
NATO	North Atlantic Treaty Organisation
NDP	New Democratic Party
NEG-ECP	New England Governors-Eastern Canadian Premiers
NEP	National Energy Program
NGOs	non-governmental organizations
NORAD	North American Aerospace Defense Command
NOx	Nitrogen Oxide
NPRI	National Pollutant Release Inventory
NPT	Nuclear Non-Proliferation Treaty
NSG	Nuclear Suppliers Group
NWS	nuclear weapon states
ODA	Official Development Assistance
PAROS	Prevention of an Arms Race in Outer Space
PCDA	Provisional Committee on Proposals Related to a WIPO Development Agenda
PCO	Privy Council Office
PCBs	Polychorinated-Biphenyls
PEMA	Pollution Emission Management Area
PMO	Prime Minister's Office
PNWER	Pacific Northwest Economic Region
PRT	Provincial Reconstruction Team
PRTR	Pollutant Release and Transfer Registry
PTBT	Partial Test Ban Treaty
PTP	Powering the Plains
R&D	research and development
RCMP	Royal Canadian Mounted Police
RGGI	Regional Greenhouse Gas Initiative
ROC	Rest of Canada

SALT II	Strategic Arms Limitation Talks
SFOR	Stabilization Force in Bosnia and Herzegovina
SPP	The Security and Prosperity Partnership of North America
TNCs	Transnational Corporations
TPA	Trade Promotion Authority
TPMs	Technological Protection Measures
TRI	Toxic Release Inventory (U.S.)
TRIPS	Trade-related Intellectual Property Rights
UN	United Nations
UNDC	UN Disarmament Commission
UNESCO	United Nations Educational, Scientific and Cultural Organization
UNSCOM	UN Special Commission
UNMOVIC	UN Monitoring, Verification and Inspection Commission
UPS	United Parcel Service
US	United States
USTR	United States Trade Representative
VOCs	volitile organic compounds
WHO	World Health Organization
WIPO	World Intellectual Property Organization
WTO	World Trade Organization

Canada Among Nations 2007

1 Room for Manoeuvre and the Paradox of Globalization

JEAN DAUDELIN

AND DANIEL SCHWANEN

The Canadian government sharpened its foreign policy focus between mid-2006 and 2007 by pronouncing Canada an "energy superpower," announcing specific geographic priority areas for Canadian engagement, and adopting an ostensibly less sceptical and more proactive international stance on the question of climate change (see Harper 2006; 2007). Cross-cutting a number of policy areas, there has been a surge of interest in the Arctic region as an international waterway by the government and many other Canadian and international political actors, scientists and commentators.[1]

During the same period, the forces of the global economy relentlessly continued to shape the landscape confronting Canadian private businesses and government policy-makers. Indian and Chinese economic growth continued unabated and pushed up the price of many Canadian natural resources – thus providing some buffer against the impact of a rising Canadian currency against its US counterpart and attendant shrinking employment in the manufacturing sector (Hodgson 2006; Anwar and Argitis 2007).

While understandably much ink has been spilled over North American integration since the landmark Canada-US Free Trade Agreement of 1988 and its successor the North American Free Trade Agreement (NAFTA) in 1994 it is not always appreciated how the global economic integration juggernaut is, in many ways, overtaking the continental trend. Thus, Canadian direct investments outside of the United States now vastly exceed those in that country (Canada 2007a, Table 5.3), and while the United States continues to be the dominant (if noticeably less so these days) destination for Canada's merchandise exports, some 40 per cent of Canada's fast-growing commercial services exports are sold outside of the NAFTA zone. Meanwhile, merchandise imports into Canada from non-NAFTA sources continue to surge (Canada 2007b, Figure 3).

Not only global economic forces, but also the security and humanitarian problems thrown up by state fragility and a dire environmental situation around the globe, have engaged the attention of Canadians. They have put into sharper relief the debate over the future role and makeup of traditional international global institutions, to which Canada has made major contributions over the past sixty years. Canada has often played a trusted, constructive role within these institutions, which has allowed it to "punch above its weight" on international matters. But with the emergence of new global challenges and players, came a rich but possibly ominous agenda of institutional renewal. Will Canada's ability to influence the world we live in be maintained within a renewed institutional framework?

The issues that these trends raise for Canada also mirror those that confront every country. It has become commonplace to hear that the activities of government are increasingly constrained, that their range of feasible options is ever narrower and that, as a result, their ability to autonomously shape the world is weakened and possibly broken beyond repair. This mantra is all the more powerful as nobody seems to escape this condition. The US remains the largest military power in the world, by a huge margin, but it cannot pacify poor and devastated Iraq. China's economic power is rising fast, but managing environmental degradation and weaning its economy from export and foreign investment dependency, in the face of a rapidly ageing population, are daunting challenges even for that most resourceful nation (Economy 2004). Everywhere, nations confront the fact that with integration in the global economy and a slew of global issues requiring international cooperation, also come constraints that may be unwelcome by many domestic constituencies, including agencies within governments themselves.

Were it true that international constraints are increasingly binding, this would be most consequential. In essence, it would imply that societies are being gradually deprived of what has for centuries been their main handle on themselves and on the world: their national governments. This in turn, could be a disaster for democracy, which would be made irrelevant, and a disaster also for human and social agency itself, which would now be confined to muddling through an environment of impersonal forces over which it has no control, and to coping in the face of challenges it has no means of preventing.

The problem may seem to be especially acute for Canada. Quickly going down the various scales of powers, from absolute economic weight to relative military capability, the country is perceived in many quarters as a fading power (Cohen 2004; Hillmer and Molot 2002), as too small and weak a player to have much impact on a game which, anyway, nobody dominates anymore. Canadian hockey fans will recognize this as the predicament of once proud clubs struggling not only with the weight of past expectations, but with new constraints that seem to make sustained team-building itself a thing of the past, even in larger markets.

This is the broad issue that we want to address in this book. We look at it through two different lenses: first by assessing the room for manoeuvre that various players and agencies involved in foreign policy-making enjoy; and second by examining the extent, nature and uses of the space that Canada still has in the world at large, and more specifically within North America.

The book's various chapters show that pessimism should not be the dominant mood. By opposing TIPA (There Is Plenty of Alternatives) to the more popular TINA (There Is No Alternative) buzzword, York University's Daniel Drache (2005) has neatly encapsulated our main message: Things are more complicated and for that very reason less discouraging than they appear. This book shows that the problem of freedom and space in foreign policy design and implementation involves many contradictions and paradoxes that open up the range of options available to actors. Many of these options, as we will see, are being acted upon, and many opportunities remain to be seized.

By moving somewhat away from the series' normal thematic focus, this edition is at the same time modest and ambitious. We felt that the fluidity of the moment, deriving from the Canadian government's minority status at the time of writing, and whose implications were well explored last year (Cooper and Rowlands 2006), but also from the volatility of the international environment, made it difficult to find a thematic focus that would not be obsolete in a few months. That very fluidity, and the resulting search for focus in the country's foreign policy, however, also suggest that pessimism about Canada's room for manoeuvre may not be justified after all. This was true of the recent past and there is no reason to think it will not be in the future: the government did not have to take as strong a pro-Israel stand last year over the conflict in Lebanon (CBC 2006); Prime Minister Stephen Harper's overture to Colombia (Bronstein 2007) came as a surprise to most, as was the affirmation that Latin America was now a priority (Ljunggren 2007; Daudelin 2007); and the Conservatives' calculated reconsiderations of climate change policy and the Afghanistan mission were not necessarily in the cards at the start of the year.

The questions explored in this book therefore go beyond the fact of the mere existence of room for manoeuvre: How does one define and gauge it in today's world? Is it expanding in some areas and not in others, and for whom? Is Canada using its room for manoeuvre effectively to advance national interests and values in an otherwise increasingly constrained world? And if so, what conditions would ensure the preservation and growth of this asset?

Before getting to the specific ways in which the issue was broached by our contributors, we want to explore at some length the concept of room for manoeuvre, with a systematic overview of its nature and foundation, of its importance to contemporary debates, and of its use in foreign policy.

THE PROBLEM

Defining the room countries have to manoeuvre speaks essentially to the choices that are open to their citizens, both in terms of public policy direction and private pursuits. What might be defined as "room for manoeuvre" is likely not the same for a country as a whole as for political actors within that country. And room for manoeuvre from a foreign policy angle is only a subset of a wider challenge that encompasses domestic choices, for example concerning fiscal or educational policies, that can have a very significant long-term impact on the country's position in the international marketplace.[2]

More specifically, it is important to distinguish between different elements that can affect a country's room for manoeuvre. Here we list six such elements: 1) an effective, general and democratic acceptance of the constraints that constitute a condition of membership in a broader entity, in exchange for wider opportunities within this entity; 2) the imposition by a foreign polity or by certain elements within a country, of constraints that prevent the government from instituting policies that would be beneficial to all; 3) the credibility that a country acquires in its dealings on the world stage and that allows it to influence global events that affect its citizens; 4) a country's own past internal policy choices, such as investment or lack thereof in infrastructure and education, or the accumulation of public debt, that give it more or less ability to deal with external challenges; 5) aspects of the socio-economic environment that are not typically under the control of any democratic government, such as the availability of new ideas or technologies and; 6) aspects of the policy environment that normally cannot be changed by a peaceful government acting alone, such as geography, or some types of external threats.

The first two sources of constraints define more visible limits to room for manoeuvre and they may be more or less contested within the country that confronts them. The middle two constitute short or mid-term constraints but very much remain within the ability of governments to influence over the longer-term, whereas the latter two must typically be taken as given. This taxonomy of constraints is important to keep in mind for policy purposes. As we will see below, different perspectives on whether a country has room for manoeuvre or not, where it lies, whether it is being used well, and how to acquire it or increase it, often depend on where the constraints are perceived to stem from.

A Global Issue

Issues that may now be termed "global," such as pandemics, climate change, and humanitarian and security issues linked to the increased worldwide mobility of people, is one set of reasons why room for manoeuvre for individual states appears to be shrinking. These issues belong to the last class of constraints identified above. Once the issue is out there, it must be taken as given by policy-makers. Increasingly, to the extent that their domestic constituencies want these problems to be addressed, governments, even the most powerful, are forced to realize that they cannot do so on their own. It is not so much that state sovereignty – its formal room for manoeuvre – has diminished, but that the global or trans-national scope of the problems has increased.

An apparent paradox results: for countries to deal more effectively with global challenges, being party to international agreements that are formally constraining on members may in fact increase their room for manoeuvre, by enhancing the collective ability to deal with the issues. As a result, there is likely to be a movement for more and better reasoned international institutions and linkages to deal with these issues. Thus, to the extent that "clubs" such as the current Group of Eight (G8) industrialized nations were formed to collectively address global issues, strong pressures now exist to bring other large players, whose cooperation is necessary, into the tent, in the hope of making the institution more effective (see Hajnal 2007; Cooper 2007; Bradford 2005).

The role that the increased availability of new ideas and technologies within each country plays, in limiting or enhancing countries' room for manoeuvre, is hotly debated, relative to the role played by more formal constraints such as trade agreements. In particular, thanks to technological advances and greater ease of circulation of people and ideas, distance (physical, cultural, or institutional) is less powerful in isolating a country from economic realities in others. In that sense, the world has simply been getting smaller, and that is what we mean by globalization. But, in the words of Thomas Friedman (2005), is it getting flatter? The answer seems to be, "no," as convincingly demonstrated by UCLA's Edward Leamer in his magisterial review of Friedman's thesis. The location of economic activity and benefits in this smaller world will depend on the same old generic factors: the power of positive externalities generated by agglomeration, the costs of delivery, and the distribution across space of consumers and their preferences (Leamer 2006, 6).

But, in a "smaller" world, the distribution of income within a country is much more influenced by what is going on in the outside world than it would in a "larger" one. Innovators, creators and intellectual workers – essential contributors to economic growth – have access to the global marketplace much more easily, which allows them to benefit from increased economies of scale that enhance the value of their investment in research and development, their talent, or their education. Conversely, these individuals with rising incomes can now more easily buy, from anywhere in the world, any type of good or service not requiring sophisticated skills, unique talents or a particularly close physical relationship between buyer and seller. This has meant that certain types of business and occupations have faced increased competitive pressure from lower-income individuals around the world that sell easily comparable generic skills or products. The result, both among and within countries, has been a tendency toward a widening distribution of incomes (Schwanen 2001; Leamer 2006).

When surveying a country's room for manoeuvre in foreign policy, one should thus ask how much influence governments have over these changes. What we do know is that trade and other agreements between governments that facilitate economic integration, also ease the emergence of the "smaller world" described above, along with its inevitable consequences on domestic distributions of opportunities and income. There has been an explosion of such trade agreements in recent decades, indicating a willingness of governments to accept the rewards and bear the costs of more open markets.

However, some groups of citizens in various countries have stopped seeing international economic agreements as legitimate constraints and feel that they are not adequately compensated by a parallel expansion of economic opportunities abroad. These groups associate these agreements with the more nefarious class of constraints on room for manoeuvre, which benefit an international economic elite and large corporate players, enabling them to capture globalization's benefits at the expense of the broader public good (see Barlow 2005; Klein 2002).

Thus, policy processes in areas once seen as self-contained, technical and even arcane, and as such legitimately delegated to technical experts, are now denounced as undemocratic and overly constraining (Wade 2003; Ciuriak 2007). Governments that already have difficulties dealing with the pace of change facilitated by trade agreements are said to be constrained by those same agreements in their ability to address, for example, pressing environmental or development issues to which trade is certainly linked.

This implies that the lines between room for manoeuvre on foreign policy and room for manoeuvre on domestic policy are becoming more blurred. The rise of "intermestic" issues is upon us, in turn highlighting the question of democratic engagement and room for manoeuvre for democratic institutions vis-à-vis international institutions, treaties and groupings.

Why Is It a Problem for Canada?

The question of margin for manoeuvre can become especially acute for countries whose economic and military weights, like Canada's, have been shrinking globally, yet that have become ever more open to global winds. Canada's particular position in North America, with all its advantages, also limits the options available for dealing with shifts in these winds. Thus, while some countries have chosen to strengthen and deepen regional economic and political ties in order to better confront international forces and assert global influence, Canada is somewhat "stuck" with the current NAFTA formula. Interest in the United States Congress to deal with pressing economic challenges in concert with its immediate neighbours is limited (Anderson and Sands 2007), a large proportion of Mexicans are generally disillusioned with NAFTA (as demonstrated in the disputed 2006 general election), and Canadians know full well that, if greater formal regional integration was pursued in a way that entailed more common policies and harmonization of rules on a North America scale, the risk is that these rules would be made in Washington rather than trilaterally (Wolfe 2003).

While, as mentioned above, Canadian trade and investment with other countries has recently increased faster than with the United States, there is no question that Canadian dependency on a secure and economically vibrant North America has increased substantially in absolute terms since the initiation of bilateral free trade in the late-1980s (Beaulieu 2007). Canada-US-Mexican trade remains vastly different from Canada's trade with the rest of the world, with a high intensity of materials and semi-finished products and parts crossing the North American borders back and forth on their way to become a finished manufacturing product. The value chain depends critically on the borders' offering the least impediment possible to these movements, and this certainly must inform Canadian policies.

The question is: does this reality merely suggest or does it dictate the adoption of certain policy tools? And beyond the choice of policy tools, does it mean Canada must choose goals it would rather not adopt? Take for instance the fact that the United States Department of Homeland Security has reportedly scuttled important talks with Canada on a cargo pre-clearance scheme because of concerns that Canada's Charter of Rights might prevent the application of tough security measures (Ibbitson 2007; see also Schneiderman 1996). This clearly goes to the heart of the question of maintaining the integrity of Canada's institutions, while satisfying both physical and economic security imperatives. In the meantime, dependency on a large, inward-looking and sometime insecure polity south of the border remains a fact of life. The challenge of securing Canadian room for manoeuvre in North America lies in the need to forge deeper ties within the United States that emphasize the mutual benefits derived from the relationship, while finding effective yet flexible solutions to common problems that respect each country's needs, values, and priorities.

Beyond North America, Canada's position is bolstered by its position as an important supplier to an ever more resource-hungry world, and also by its relatively enviable socio-economic record, notably in terms of fiscal room for manoeuvre and its capacity to cope with the challenges of an ageing population. Nevertheless, more thought needs to be given to our international role. While our vast fossil energy reserves make us an energy power of some import, will Canada's international credibility suffer because developing this resource means that we are not an effective partner in the effort to reduce greenhouse gas emissions? Regarding the large emerging economies of China and India, and the countries of the western hemisphere, what exactly are Canada's specific areas of interests and where can solid linkages be built that will engage their own interest? Being prepared to address these questions is an important way to ensure an intelligent use of our room for manoeuvre, compensating perhaps for our waning global economic and military weight.

WHAT DOES ROOM FOR MANOEUVRE MEAN IN PRACTICE?

The Role of Government

In the face of globalization, are we really pushed to harmonize, converge and shut up? Or does globalization merely open up exciting new opportunities for beneficial engagement and exerting influence beyond one's borders? Between these two extremes, how do countries define their room for manoeuvre?

A striking aspect of the debates in each country surrounding the practical policy aspects of room for manoeuvre in the face of globalization is how they transcend the typical left-right divide on how proactive governments should be on economic and social issues. For example, some economic conservatives see Canada's room for manoeuvre as being very limited vis-à-vis the United States, and on that basis urge Canada to adopt a policy of more widespread harmonization in order to facilitate integration (Hart 2006). But there are also many on the "right" that see the challenge in terms of how a country can create advantages for itself even in a more integrated economic environment, through forward-looking policies that actually distinguish it from those of other countries (Mintz 2007).

Similarly, feeling that Canada's choices are limited, many on the "left" decry what they see as the "constitutionalization" of Canada's external relationship, in particular through trade agreements such as NAFTA. Evoking the existence of a new constitutional order of sorts, as Stephen Clarkson does in this volume, emphasizes how such agreements lock Canada into a number of obligations that would be difficult to escape from, and so diminish existing and future governments' room for manoeuvre.

But others on the left reject the "myth of the powerless state" that the discourse of constitutionalization encourages. Australia's Linda Weiss (1999) has shown that while globalization is often being used as an argument for compelling governments to accept international obligations and the domestic economic reforms that accompany them, governments have much potential to remain free to manoeuvre. She suggests that a "different kind of state" will be emerging in the world arena, and emphasizes the link between the ability of countries to use and leverage emerging international alliances and the strength of their own domestic institutions. Weiss consequently foresees heightened rather than diminished differences among states' ability to act in a more integrated world.

Ultimately, the extent and nature of countries' room for manoeuvre is an empirical issue. It is sometimes disheartening to the researcher to see arguments about the impact of globalization and its manifestations (increased cross-border trade, investment, or movement of people, for example) reduced to a list of worst-case legal possibilities or anecdotes or, worse still, simply being described as an abdication of the state's responsibility to protect its residents against alien forces. These views suggest not only a loss of control by citizens over their own affairs, but also a malignant evolution toward some lower common denominator in terms of quality of life for those who partake, willingly or not, in the process. While this may ring true for some actors in some situations, the overall empirical reality may well be very different, as emphasized by Debora L. VanNijnatten in this volume with respect to North American environmental issues.

It may well be that, in the words of Daniel Gitterman (2002), the economic integration process that is part of globalization looks likely to be accompanied by a "march to a minimum floor" on certain standards rather than a race to the bottom. This would be natural in a world in which a key to partnering with other states is to demonstrate your bona fide, for example in terms of health, safety, security, and basic democratic and legal rights. Globalization has certainly changed the mix of potential costs and rewards of certain policies for actors within the state, requiring a fresh look at a number of policies within each country. Nevertheless, adopting common minimum standards, as the price to pay to partake in the benefits of wider arrangements, and the need to rethink certain policies in order to maintain social cohesion in the face of new economic challenges, do not necessarily reflect a diminished ability of governments to pursue high standards in the search for both better economic performance and quality of life.

Room for Manoeuvre as an Intrinsically Valuable Asset

At one formal extreme, room for manoeuvre can be defined as the ability for governments to engage in any behaviour that they may decide upon as a sovereign state. Of course, room for manoeuvre to such an extent does not exist in practice, if only because of the weight of past actions and objective international and national constraints.

A more workable assessment might ascribe a higher profile to the process of give-and-take in creating room for manoeuvre, and would thus incorporate the idea of tradeoffs in the definition. Often, by relinquishing the right to, say, discriminatory trade measures, Canada is able to gain similar protection abroad. In a world in which many growth opportunities exist outside of Canada, is this good or bad? In such a world, the formalism of an independent position is less important than the ability to deal with constantly shifting interdependencies. Many of the chapters in this volume emphasize the constraints, be they material, political, intellectual, legal, or even reputational, that impinge on the autonomous ability of governments to address shifting international issues. These constraints make clear that since absolute room for manoeuvre does not exist, it may be wise to consciously manage what freedom one really possess as a precious resource, allowing it to be reduced in some area, while building it up in another, more critical, area.

In this vein, it may be useful to envisage room for manoeuvre as a portfolio of resources and actions, a form of capital representing the power or ability to act when needed. Formal "sovereignty" would only be one element of this portfolio – and possibly not the most important one. Analytical capabilities, good reputation, an informed citizenry, material resources, flexibility and effectiveness in allocating scarce resources to international issues, ability to meet standards and perform useful roles within valued alliances, would be some of the others. On that view, in foreign policy as in other areas, defining, building and maintaining room for manoeuvre as an asset that can be called upon to support national objectives would become one of the core challenge of Canadian policy-making.

Where Does It Lie?

To paraphrase international theorist Alex Wendt's (1992) most famous statement, room for manoeuvre is what states make of it. There is no denying the existence of rigidities in the international environment, but they do not structure the whole field of action of state actors. In fact, rigidities themselves can be a significant source of power and autonomy.

Three main such "exploitable" rigidities are emphasized in the case studies of this book. The first is the deep interdependence that exists between Canada and the United States. The interpenetration of our economies, production chains and investment circuits, and the way in which these weave together both our countries' interests and security preoccupations is probably without equal, even among much more formally integrated European countries. North American interdependence, admittedly, is severely asymmetric. Total trade between Canada and the United States represents 49 per cent of our GDP but about 1 per cent of theirs (DFAIT 2007; authors' calculations). The nature of much of that trade, however, belies the superficial impression of one-sided economic dominance that raw trade numbers convey. About three-quarters is intra-industry and over one-third is intra-firm (Emerson 2007), much of which is concentrated in the auto sector, which remains a core component of American industry, and one whose integrated North American structure makes it completely dependent on the free circulation of goods between the two countries. A significant part of Canada-US trade is also made up of oil exports from Alberta. The province is in fact the US's largest foreign source of energy, and certainly the most stable, politically and economically, and as a result possibly the most reliable (see Kukucha and Keating, this volume). Similar situations are found in other sectors.

A similar interdependence exists on the security front, where raw numbers are even more discrepant and even less a reflection of the reality of mutual supportiveness. We have been an important part of the

American defence infrastructure during the Cold War and, were relations with Russia do deteriorate further – not as far-fetched a possibility as one would hope – we would be forced back into that position. This inescapable reality has never been lost on the US defence establishment, however, and it explains why Canada could afford to fight the Cold War on the cheap, not quite as a free rider, but admittedly, as RMC's Joel Sokolsky (2004: 11) has put it before, as an "easy rider." Over years and decades, the billions of dollars saved there have no doubt made it easier for our government to reach the fiscal health that today makes Canada the envy of the Organisation of Economic Cooperation and Development. The stark reality that asymmetric interdependence still means significant US dependence on us has not been lost on our decision-makers and in many ways it underpinned our ability to say no to participating in the invasion of Iraq and National Missile Defense, without having to pay too dearly for it.

There is a flip side to Canada's deep integration into a single North American economic and security space: our "hard" stakes in the rest of the world and in its crises are lessened, making us freer to make "disinterested" forays (Daudelin 2004), a marvellous asset to have. It is not clear however that we have made much of that freedom until now, or that such liberty of action has not morphed into moody unpredictability. Trevor Findlay's contribution to this book suggests that a case in point could be our largely folding the tent on nuclear non-proliferation to take on a central role in the landmines and now the small arms files, ditching much of a massive amount of expertise and credibility to jump for a few years into a sexier and faster-moving vehicle. The undeniable success of that involvement should not obscure the damage made to our ability to contribute to what is shaping up to be a central security issue of the coming decades.

Another aspect of the silver lining of North America's deep interdependence is that it builds and relies on a healthy and remarkably congenial mutual relationship. Interdependence and asymmetry basically ruling the day for all, there could be worse partners than the US to manage – just ask Europeans how they feel about their own gas dependence on Russia. US support has indeed been critical to our joining the G7 and the Quad, and it will help again in the future.

One last characteristic of the Canada-US relationship puts into relief the opportunities created by the very rigidities that also constrains the government's options: its institutions, from the North American Aerospace Defense Command and NAFTA to the International Joint Commission. As Colin Robertson points out in his chapter, a few spectacular trade disputes – softwood lumber and recently beef – makes us forget how remarkably efficient and lean institutions have enabled us to smoothly manage that monster of a relationship. Perhaps, as Robertson but also Carol Wise and Wendy Dobson suggest, the time might have come to strengthen them. But this very need underlines how Canada's interests are served by such institutions, not only in spite of, but *thanks to* the constraints that they impose to their participants, something that rings true beyond North America as, from Canada's perspective, international regimes have as a rule proven much more to be levers than shackles.The environmental saga, which Daniel Schwanen explored at length in last year's edition of *Canada Among Nations*, takes us beyond the clever instrumentalization of existing rigidities into another basis of a state's room for manoeuvre, namely, its international legitimacy, which flows in turn from the credibility of its commitments and the consistency of its engagements. Indeed, while Stephen Harper has to shoulder much of the public blame for Canada's disastrous inability to honour its commitment, the latter clearly derives from the recklessness of the previous Liberal government, which never quite factored in how challenging Kyoto compliance could be.

A similar fate has befallen the human security agenda, where bloated rhetoric was not matched by corresponding investments and, in the absence of a significant increase in capacity, could beckon for our (once again) newfound interest in the Americas. A clear measure of what is at stake, of one's ability to sustain an effort in a given area, and a talent for letting other take the lead might just as well bolster a reputation for credibility. This might be a key inference of Robert Wolfe's examination (this volume) of Canada's somewhat diminished role at the World Trade Organization (WTO): accepting that key aspects of this particular game are for others to play might not diminish at all our benefits from its successful completion, while cementing a well-deserved reputation for seriousness and pragmatism.

Wolfe's analysis, however, clearly shows that credibility also flows from technical competence, including diplomatic and negotiation skills, how good Canadian trade experts have been and continue to be, and how much of an impact this has on the role that Canada plays in global trade negotiations. Credibility, and the legitimacy that flows from it, are indeed not just a matter of consistency – the quality of one's contribution matters a lot too. This is probably the most broadly shared theme in this book: Canada's room for manoeuvre in the world depends to a striking extent on knowledge and technical expertise, and the latter does not grow on trees. Trevor Findlay shows in the case of nuclear proliferation how easy it is to destroy world class capabilities. John J. Noble, after many others including the Auditor General, makes a plea for a re-investment in Canada's diplomatic capacity and the Department of Foreign Affairs and International Trade (DFAIT) more specifically. Wendy Dobson and Colin Robertson also call for an effort to develop sorely lacking academic expertise on the United States. Robertson's chapter, along with Debora L. VanNijnatten's also show how the expertise that already exists or that needs to be developed or consolidated lies in a variety of federal government departments and also in provincial and even local governments. For North America, Stephen Clarkson's piece points to the significant weight of the private sector in that capacity and in the management of existing North American integration. Significant capacity already exists in sum, but building it up cannot be done in a narrow, DFAIT-focused, way.

At the same time, the federal government's specialized international capacity remains critical. Contributions to this book highlight two apparently contradictory facets of that problem: first, the need for spare capacity and redundancy; and second, the paradox of resources abundance.

Evoking another legend of Canadian diplomacy, Allan Gotlieb (2003, 31) has reminded us how intrinsically unpredictable foreign policy can be: "When asked to define Canadian foreign policy, Lester Pearson, was reported to have replied, 'Ask me at the end of the year and when I look back at what Canada has done, I'll tell you what our foreign policy is.'" The international environment is a key source of uncertainty. It is hard to know where the next crisis will be or what turn old crises can take: Israel's invasion of Lebanon was a surprise to most, and nobody quite knows what may happen in Iraq or in Iran, for that matter, over the next two or three years. To such externally-induced uncertainty one must add the changing moods and whims of the government itself, especially the prime minister. The crowd of people within the Canadian International Development Agency (CIDA), the Department of National Defence (DND) and DFAIT, for whom Afghanistan is now the main file can certainly attest that prior to September 2001, Afghanistan did not rank even on the periphery of Canadian international priorities. Similarly, though on a lesser scale, the sudden rediscovery of Latin America has come from nowhere, albeit in this case, significant capabilities and a depth of knowledge has survived from previous bouts of interest. However, the point remains here: the people brought together in 2007 to develop a Latin American policy were taken off other files and, in many cases, had not been involved recently with the Americas, if at all.

Flexibility is obviously a critical asset, but it cannot substitute for real knowledge, thick personal networks and field experience. Uncertainty calls for spare capacity and for the kind of knowledge whose immediate relevance may be marginal. Learning from scratch, re-jigging bureaucracies, re-creating divisions that have been dismantled, re-opening consulates where they had been closed, or closing them a few years after their inauguration, not only damages a nation's credibility, it directly weakens its ability to act in the world. The volatility of international affairs, in other words, implies that efficiency cannot be assessed narrowly and in the short-term. There is no evidence presented in this book or in recent writings on Canadian foreign policy to suggest that cutting DFAIT's budget further, or keeping most of our diplomats in Ottawa, makes much sense.

That being said, an increase in resources does not necessarily imply increased room for manoeuvre. As discussed in this book, the recent experience of DND (see Middlemiss and Stairs) and especially of CIDA (see Brown) suggest in fact that more money could sometimes mean a tighter leash held by the Prime Minister's Office (PMO) or the Privy Council Office (PCO) and less ability to fulfill broad departmental mandate. It is admittedly very early to measure the impact of the Afghan adventure on those departments, but it has yet to be shown that they will emerge stronger politically or institutionally from the massive increases in their budget that has come with the war. Their full instrumentalization by the "centre," as reflected by the weakness of their respective ministers, possibly has tactical advantages, but the strategic implications of such subordination, both for the department themselves, and for the government's foreign policy capability, is far from clear.

AN OVERVIEW OF THE BOOK

The Ottawa Game

Room for manoeuvre in Canadian foreign policy is a multifaceted problem. The various contributions to this book have been organized around three of them. The first explores the "Ottawa game," or more specifically the relationship between the various entities that make up the "foreign policy apparatus" (PMO, PCO, DFAIT, DND, CIDA), and the influence of two very vocal provincial governments, Alberta and Quebec, on the national foreign policy-making process. A second section looks at the recent evolution of Canada's room for manoeuvre in three key global regimes: intellectual property rights, international trade, and nuclear non-proliferation. Finally, a series of case studies examine the fate of Canada's room for manoeuvre in "the trenches" – the space where it appears to be most directly challenged, namely North America. The various contributions of that section look at the challenges of focus and capabilities, at strategic and tactical options, at the Security and Prosperity Partnership (SPP), at sub-national environmental cooperation, and at hemispheric trade policy beyond NAFTA.

The book opens with a broader discussion of the purpose to which Canada's room for manoeuvre should be put to use. For Wendy Dobson, sustained growth in living standards must be the ultimate goal. This calls for a long-term effort at "raising our game," and an ability to look beyond the features that currently seem to define our world. She outlines a strategy that moves boldly on North American integration, that takes full account of the emergence of a self-conscious Asian region, and that re-invests, albeit selectively, in international institutions. Canada has options and assets. It needs a clearer view of which of those options will still make sense in fifteen years, and of where exactly those assets should be invested.

Ottawa remains the place where such a strategy must be developed and implemented, and where the bureaucratic and political game will be played out. John J. Noble examines the key players in that game and the evolution of their relationship. He reminds us how much the recent emphasis on the weight of the "centre" in foreign policy is old news or even no news at all. For Noble, the prime minister has always been the key player, and the departments his instruments. He particularly notes the dangers of exaggerating the weight of institutional tensions and competition, for instance between the PMO or the PCO and DFAIT. His analysis of the various summit sherpas and of the many incarnations of international advisors to the prime minister cleverly shows how much work is done by diplomats crossing and straddling organizational boundaries. At the same time, however, he argues convincingly that foreign policy development and implementation needs to be coherently and capably managed, something that only a well-staffed and well-funded foreign policy apparatus can do. In the face of the Harper government's increasingly numerous and strong international commitments, Noble's plea for significant reinvestment in DFAIT, which echoes the Auditor General's, is eminently reasonable.

The Ottawa game, however, is not confined to DFAIT and "the centre." The massive reinvestment in DND and CIDA, largely tied to Canada's involvement in Afghanistan is sometimes perceived to be reshaping quite drastically the foreign policy-making landscape. Some have suggested, in fact, that the growing place that Afghanistan occupies in the country's external agenda has, perhaps for the first time ever, made DND a central foreign policy player. Danford W. Middlemiss and Denis Stairs' careful examination of recent development finds little support for such a "DND ascendant" thesis. Their analysis in fact outlines a kind of paradox of plenty, whereby increased resources, driven primarily by the country's political leadership's commitment to Afghanistan, appears to have led to a tighter subordination of DND and the Canadian Forces and to less autonomy in the establishment of their priorities. As defence issues became more prominent, and as billions of dollars were invested in new equipment and personnel, politicians appear to have become ever less willing to leave the file to the military. Through that lens, the prominence of the Chief of Defence Staff, General Rick Hillier, should thus be seen as one more instrument of the centre, not as the symbol of DND and the Canadian Forces' growing influence over foreign policy.

The paradox of plenty looks even starker in the case of CIDA, and more consequential too. In an analysis that echoes several other contributions to this book, Stephen Brown chronicles the tightening of the centre's grip over development policy, in step with the government's significant reinvestment in development aid. Once again, Afghanistan looms large in those developments. CIDA is a key contributor to the "whole of government" approach to that country, but it does not seem to have much say in its design. Brown argues in fact that CIDA has been put "under the gun" in Afghanistan, becoming little more than a weapon in the government's counter-insurgency armoury. This is significant not only because Afghanistan is now Canada's main recipient of foreign aid, but also because the Afghan mission, beyond the investment of new resources, involves as well the reallocation of personnel and funds from other areas. Perhaps even more consequential, the nature of CIDA's activities in Afghanistan does not mesh well with current understanding of aid effectiveness and of the conditions for sustainable development. Under attack for its ineffectiveness in Africa, and bedevilled by weak representation in cabinet, the Agency might not be able to resist its full instrumentalization by the government. Were this to happen, it is CIDA's specific mandate – to support sustainable development ... in order to reduce poverty and to contribute to a more secure, equitable, and prosperous world – that could be in jeopardy.

These four chapters suggest that there is not much room for manoeuvre for Ottawa's institutional players: the prime minister rules, while additional resources can be a mixed blessing. Beyond Ottawa however, and even before looking at international constraints, what checks are there to the prime minister's freedom? Two chapters tackle that question, looking at apparently obvious sources of constraints for the federal government – the ever confident provinces of Alberta and Quebec. Once again, the answers are less clear and probably more interesting than could be expected.

Christopher J. Kukucha and Thomas Keating look at the space that Alberta occupies in foreign policy, both directly and through its government's attempts to influence Ottawa. Youthful and booming

Alberta has often been painted, inside and outside of the province, as distinct from the rest of the country, especially central Canada. It's seen as having a special attitude, special interests and special needs, barely recognized in Ottawa and certainly not well reflected in federal policies, domestic or foreign. Kukucha and Keating's measured analysis of the province's influence on Canadian foreign policy suggests that this image if not very faithful to the reality, rhetorical flourishes notwithstanding. Energy and environmental issues rightfully dominate their discussion, but what they show belies all the noise on distinctiveness and alienation. Energy is now so big for the Canadian economy that there is little to choose between Alberta's supposedly special interests and Canada's national interest. Similarly, and perhaps most surprisingly for out-of-province readers, Albertans' take on the environment is not very different from that of other Canadians: Alberta's policy debate, in sum, is very much Canada's, and the arrival of the "bad boys" in Ottawa does not wreak much havoc in the capital's tidy policy debates.

Quebec is something else altogether – or is it? Anti-American fortress of pacifism, core haven of anti-Israel sentiment in the country, and above all, the main bulwark of opposition to Canada's military involvement in Iraq and Afghanistan, the province seems to punch well above its weight, literally hijacking the country's policy on Iraq, Afghanistan and towards the US. To this "Quebecistan" narrative Jean-Christophe Boucher and Stéphane Roussel oppose a reading of recent events in which Quebec is the bearer of a very Canadian tradition in foreign policy – one that is guarded towards the US, and also quite willing to support the use of military force. Far from it being Quebec that is out of line, it is Canada's current policy and its most forceful advocates that betray such a tradition. For Boucher and Roussel, in today's debate, Quebec becomes a scapegoat for the pro-US and pro-war camps, a way to deny the profound divisions that exist everywhere in the country on those issues. At the same time, it also stands as the symbol of a deeply *Canadian* point of view on the same issues, a return to which would likely resolve current tensions. From their standpoint, Quebec opinion is less the driver of foreign policy towards the US, Iraq or Afghanistan than the clearer expression of an increasingly strong national movement, which is the main force behind current reconsiderations of Canada's policy orientations.

The Global Game

What will be Canada's stand in what Jeremy de Beer and Michael Geist characterize as "the most significant intellectual property matter to confront the international community," namely the World Intellectual Property Organization's (WIPO) development agenda? That agenda seeks to redress a perceived imbalance between a "maximalist" approach to intellectual property protection and development priorities, an imbalance that exists at the expense of the latter (and of public policy priorities more generally). The authors contend that, in practice, intellectual property protection can sometimes be excessive, acting as a barrier to action on legitimate policy concerns in a number of fields, such as health, and to the emergence of groundbreaking technologies and business models. Intellectual property rules applicable to a hierarchical industrial model era are becoming a serious anachronism in the growing networked information economy.

The authors characterize Canada's position on intellectual property in various forums over the past decades as having not always been well thought out. Fortunately, they observe signs of change in this respect, with Canada seemingly uniquely placed to provide leadership in transcending the traditional developed/developing country divide on intellectual property. A well devised Canadian model could be used as a template in the WIPO's technical assistance programs, they argue. Canada's global room for manoeuvre is, in this case, directly related to the room for manoeuvre it has at home in implementing international regimes. Using the field of copyright law, de Beer and Geist show that such domestic room for manoeuvre is, in fact, considerable, including in the way Canada transposes international regimes into domestic law. Canada thus has the room for manoeuvre to adopt a leadership position toward a balanced global intellectual property regime.

As eluded above, the chapter by Robert Wolfe puts in historical and logical context the view that Canada's influence at the WTO is waning. Canada is not as vital as it once was in brokering global trade deals, particularly on agriculture and industrial tariffs. With agriculture central to the overall success of the Doha Round, it is therefore not surprising that the focus has shifted toward those countries that are crucial for achieving a breakthrough in this area. However, Wolfe also submits that one of the reasons Canada's importance has diminished somewhat is the intellectually contradictory position we are presenting to the world on agricultural protection – a barefaced case of "having our cake and eating it too" that undermines our credibility and ability to effect compromise. In this case, international room for manoeuvre is diminished because domestic room for manoeuvre is in short supply.

Canada nevertheless remains one of the few players that can contribute ideas and expertise across the whole range of WTO issues and forums. This is important in the world described by Wolfe: one in which informal meetings, technical know-how, analytical capacity and the existence of many small manageable formal or informal groups or "clubs," remain essential to solving issues in the wider forum. Thus, while Canada is objectively not as central as it might have been in brokering a future WTO deal, its room for manoeuvre to influence the outcome remains considerable.

Trevor Findlay's piece evokes the very complex and continuously evolving context in which Canada's policies on such a crucial global matter as nuclear non-proliferation, and by extension on other issues, must be built. The main lesson that emerges from his chapter is that by being active, creative and consistent, Canada can choose to build capacity and credibility that allows it to wield genuine influence over important global outcomes. This becomes particularly useful when other, often more powerful players are in need of such capacity and credibility to conclude agreements they work towards.

In this context, Findlay singles out Canada's "invaluable" contribution on technical issues, notably verification. Not only in the nuclear field, but also with respect to biological and chemical weapons, conventional armed forces reductions and limiting arms in outer space. On all these issues, technically-based compromises are an essential component of successful negotiations. As Findlay reminds us, Canada did not have to be active in this field: it chose to be. In the case of nuclear arms non-proliferation, the chapter also illustrates how this choice is linked to the Canadian interest in the spread of peaceful use of nuclear energy as an issue of domestic economic significance.

But the chapter also reminds us that Canada's foreign policy does not operate in an unconstrained world, either in terms of the shifting political situation of its main partners, or in terms of the time, intellectual capital, or other resources that it is willing to put in maintaining its capacity and credibility in a particular area. On the nuclear non-proliferation file, Canada's ability to exert influence will depend on the windows left open by other partners, above all the United States. And to the extent that putting our weight behind one priority at the expense of others deemed more important by key partners, Canada's credibility and thus influence is at risk. The upshot is that credentials have to be kept up to date and reduced involvement comes at a cost.

The North American Game, or "The Trenches"

American scholar Carol Wise begins the last section of the volume with a sober assessment of the evolution of the trade game in Washington and the available policy inroads. For Canada, part of the context is also the fact that, beyond its undisputed benefits, the dynamic shortcomings of NAFTA have also become evident. Canada's ability to not just become a trade "spoke" in a system of trade agreements of which the United States is the "hub" is continuously challenged by US "strategic" bilateral negotiations with smaller states in the western hemisphere. While at the same time would-be geographically wider arrangements such as the Free Trade Agreement of the Americas and the Doha Round of WTO negotiations flounder.

Canada's main trump card in this game, according to Wise, is the international heft that its resource base commands, but to the extent that this masks its inability to catch up to the United States on a number of economic indicators, in spite of the NAFTA, is worrisome for Canada's standings in the Americas, as is the extent to which the US is able, through bilateral agreements, to craft its own regional regulatory framework in the region that only incidentally addresses Canadian interests. Wise recommends that Canada, alongside Mexico, support an incipient Regional-12 initiative that would link, through additional trade agreements, countries of the hemisphere that already have trade agreements with the United States. Even if without participation of bigger countries such as Brazil, Argentina or Venezuela, this initiative would open the door to more dynamic trade relations in the hemisphere by simplifying the current complex structure of bilateral deals, and offer greater room for Canada to manoeuvre as it re-engages with the hemisphere.

Stephen Clarkson offers a concise but wide-ranging history of the SPP between Canada, Mexico and the United States, and of the prospective opportunities of the still-nascent SPP for Canada's room for manoeuvre. He roots the SPP within a well-developed analytical perspective: that of a more general trend toward the "constitutionalization" of Canada's external relationships.

In turn, two key questions seem to emerge from his chapter. First, the concept of "room for manoeuvre" applies not only to the elected governments, but also to actors in the private business sector and to civil society actors. Tradeoffs can and do develop between the room for manoeuvre afforded these various actors, including between legislatures and executive arms of governments, between federal and sub-federal levels of governments, and so on. Thus, trying to define Canada's "room for manoeuvre" quickly becomes an exercise in asking: "room for manoeuvre for whom?" Second, what does a Canadian room for manoeuvre mean, when the United States can essentially not only define what its paramount interests are, but also ensure that Canada acts in line with these priorities, be they related to security from physical harm or to questions of economic security?

Thus, the "constitutionalization" of Canada's external relationships becomes a question of defining the proper navigation tools for Canadian actors in an environment defined first and foremost by US priorities. As Clarkson makes clear, there are within this constitutional framework many opportunities for Canada to forge intelligent navigation tools for itself, and even pick its own navigation route. Clarkson's rich analytical and historical framework allows the reader to form his or her own conclusion on how effective – and for whom – Canada is using its room for manoeuvre in this context. But for the author, it is apparent that the cost of greater overall room for manoeuvre for Canadian business within North America is declining relevance of the Canadian state, combined with some relative marginalization of non-business groups within a possibly emerging North American executive decision process.

Writing on the basis of his wealth of experience in the United States, Colin Robertson offers an engaging perspective whereby new tools and new approaches, including the internet and advertising, can be mobilized to create room for manoeuvre for Canada and Canadians in the United States. In the face of the reality of the highly decentralized political processes in the US affecting trade and other issues of vital interest to Canadians, and realizing more than ever that "security is a currency that the Americans understand," Canadian diplomatic activity should respond accordingly. Canadians must not only lobby Congress, but "be there" to ensure that Americans are informed of Canada's contribution to their well-being, and that ultimately Canada's "brand" is seen as being of the highest quality, in a world where perceptions of reliability are increasingly as important as the reality.

Robertson notes in this respect that Canadians like their governments to cooperate in order to get results, and that genuine cooperation between the federal and provincial levels of government, on practical issues involving our Canada's "intermestic" relationship with the United States, creates added room for manoeuvre for both levels of government within the complex US maze. He also notes the importance of maintaining our understanding of the importance of the US relationship fresh, rather than repeating shibboleths. As a result, he calls for a Task Force that would do Canada's "domestic homework" on the challenges of North American integration and of globalization more generally speaking, and would report ahead of the inauguration of a new President in January 2009.

The final chapter by Debora L. VanNijnatten elucidates three important facets of Canada's room for manoeuvre on environmental policy within North America, in a way that strongly complements findings by other authors in this volume analyzing other policy arenas.

First, in spite of economic integration and even of new mechanisms to facilitate environmental cooperation, the regulatory environment continues to differ between Canada and the United States – with little evidence of convergence in the choice of policy instruments, if not of stated objectives. Second, whatever Canada's room for manoeuvre is in the field of environmental policy vis-à-vis its neighbour can and has been misused in some cases, and so Canada's autonomy in policy matters does not necessarily ensure a better objective outcome for Canadians. In turn, poorer outcomes in Canada may induce Canadian governments to look more toward US-style policy instruments, a sign of convergence, but one of Canadians' own choosing.

Finally, as environmental issues increasingly ignore borders, just as security or economic issues do, effectively dealing with them requires a greater degree of cross-border cooperation. But this may engage certain actors, whose room for manoeuvre would thus appear enhanced, at the expense of others, whose effective room for manoeuvre may thus seem constrained. In the case of environmental policy and of climate change policies in particular, the search for greater policy efficiency through greater voluntary integration and cooperation with the United States seems so far to have involved the use and expansion of provincial room for manoeuvre, perhaps at the expense of that of the federal government.

Can one draw some general conclusions about Canada's room for manoeuvre from this review of the articles in this volume? It appears that while both the manifestations and the intrinsic value of a country's room for manoeuvre are subject to many vagaries in an increasingly complex and integrated international system, it is something that is far from irremediably diminishing. It is thus worth exploring in some detail the realistic and contemporary approaches through which such room for manoeuvre can be assessed, maintained and put to more efficient use for the benefit of Canadians.

NOTES

1 For a detailed examination of the debate on Arctic sovereignty, see McRae (2007).
2 For an earlier exploration of the interplay between economic integration and domestic policy choices, see Courchene (1999).

REFERENCES

Anderson, Greg, and Christopher Sands. 2007. *Negotiating North America: The Security and Prosperity Partnership*. *White Paper* (Summer). Washington, DC: Hudson Institute.

Anwar, Haris, and Theophilos Argitis. 2007. "Canadian Dollar Trades Equal to US for First Time Since 1976." *Bloomberg*, 20 September. Available at: <http://www.bloomberg.com/apps/news?pid=20601082&refer= canada&sid=awhVMIymbXow>

Barlow, Maude. 2005. *Too Close for Comfort: Canada's Future within Fortress North America*. Toronto: McClelland and Stewart.

Beaulieu, Eugene. 2007. "Has North American Integration Resulted in Canada Becoming Too Dependent on the United States?" *Policy Options* 28, no. 09 (October): 97–102. Montreal: Institute for Research on Public Policy.

Bhalla, Surjit S. 2002. *Imagine There's no Country: Poverty, Inequality, and Growth in the Era of Globalization*. Washington DC: Institute for International Economics.

Bradford, Colin I. 2005. "Global Governance for the 21st Century." Mimeo. Washington, DC: Brookings Institution. Available at: <http://www.brookings.edu/views/papers/20051024bradford.pdf>

Bronstein, Hugh. 2007. "Canada steps into void left by US-Colombia rift," Reuters, *Edmonton Journal*, 16 July. Available at: <http://www.canada.com/edmontonjournal/news/story.html?id=341612a3-fae8-42e1-89f4-39d24599e77a&k=81856 >

Canada. 2007a. *Canada's State of Trade: Trade and Investment Update*. Ottawa: Department of Foreign Affairs and International Trade.

– 2007b. *International Merchandise Trade: Annual Review*. Ottawa: Statistics Canada.

CBC. 2006. "PM's rhetoric hurts Canada's peacemaking chances: opposition," *CBC News*, 18 July. Available at: <http://www.cbc.ca/story/canada/national/2006/07/18/graham-israel.html>

Ciuriak, Dan. 2007. "The State of the Trading System, the WTO, and the Doha Round." Conference Report. Waterloo: The Centre for International Governance Innovation.

Cohen, Andrew. 2004. *While Canada Slept: How We Lost Our Place in the World*. Toronto: McClelland & Stewart.

Cooper, Andrew F. 2007. "The Logic of the B(R)ICSAM Model for G8 Reform." *Policy Brief in International Governance*, no. 1 (May). Waterloo: The Centre for International Governance Innovation.

Courchene, Thomas J. 1999. *Room to Manoeuvre? Globalization and Policy Convergence*. The Bell Canada Papers on Economic and Public Policy, vol. 6. Kingston: John Deutsch Institute, Queen's University.

Daudelin, Jean. 2004. "Bubbling Up, Trickling Down, Seeping Out: The Transformation of Canadian Foreign Policy." In *Canada Among Nations 2004: Setting Priorities Straight*, edited by David Carment, Fen Osler Hampson and Norman Hillmer. Montreal and Kingston: McGill-Queen's University Press, 103–23.

– 2007. "Canada and the Americas: A Time for Modesty" *Behind the Headlines* 64, no. 3 (May). Toronto: Canadian International Council.

Drache, Daniel. 2005. "The Political Economy of Dissent: Global Publics after Cancun." In *Reforming from the Top: A Leaders' 20 Summit*, edited by John English, Ramesh Thakur and Andrew F. Cooper. Tokyo: United Nations University Press.

Economy, Elizabeth C. 2004. *The River Runs Black: The Environmental Challenge to China's Future*. Ithaca: Cornell University Press.

Emerson, David L. 2007. Address by the Minister of International Trade to the Council of the Americas, Washington, DC, 2 May.

Friedman, Thomas L. 2005. *The World Is Flat: A Brief History of the 21st Century*. New York: Farrar, Straus and Giroux.

Gitterman, Daniel P. 2002. "A Race to the Bottom, a Race to the Top of the March to a Minimum Floor?" In *Dynamics of Regulatory Change: How Globalization Affects National Regulatory Policies*, edited by Daniel Vogel and Robert Kagan. Berkeley, CA: University of California Press.

Gotlieb, Allan. 2004. "Romanticism and Realism in Canada's Foreign Policy." C.D. Howe Institute Benefactors Lecture, Toronto, 3 November. Available at: <http://www.cdhowe.org/pdf/benefactors_lecture_2004.pdf>

Hajnal, Peter I. 2007. *The G8 System and the G20: Evolution, Role and Documentation*. Aldershot, UK: Ashgate.

Harper, Stephen. 2007. Address by the Prime Minister to the APEC Business Council, Sydney, Australia, 7 September.

– 2006. Address by the Prime Minister to the Economic Club of New York, New York, NY, 20 September.

Hart, Michael. 2006. "Steer or Drift? Taking Charge of Canada-US Regulatory Convergence." *Commentary*, no. 229 (March). Toronto: C.D. Howe Institute.

Hodgson, Glen. 2006. "The Economic Outlook: Well Positioned for Growth." Presentation by the Conference Board of Canada Chief Economist to the 2006 International Livestock Congress, Calgary, 14 July.

Ibbitson, John. 2007. "Homeland Security: The Next Threat to Canada." *Globe and Mail*, 16 August, A13.

Klein, Naomi. 2002. *Fences and Windows: Dispatches from the Frontlines of the Globalization Debate*. Toronto: Vintage Canada.

Leamer, Edward E. 2006. "A Flat World, A Level Playing Field, a Small World After All, or None of the Above?" Review of Thomas L. Friedman, *The World is Flat*. Los Angeles: Anderson Center, UCLA. Available at: <http://uclaforecast.com/reviews/Leamer_FlatWorld_060221.pdf>

Ljunggren, David. 2007. "New Canadian focus on South America puzzles some," Reuters, 11 July. Available at: <http://www.canada.com/topics/news/national/story.html?id=021e862b-0a04-4850-b398-7b8bdaca450d&k=27025>

McRae, Donald. 2007. "Arctic Sovereignty: What is at Stake?" *Behind the Headlines* 64, no. 1 (January). Toronto: Canadian International Council.

Mintz, Jack M. 2007. "2007 Tax Competitiveness Report: A Call for Comprehensive Tax Reform." *Commentary*, no. 254 (September). Toronto: C.D. Howe Institute.

Molot, Maureen Appel, and Norman Hillmer. 2002. "The Diplomacy of Decline." In *Canada Among Nations 2002: A Fading Power*, edited by Norman Hillmer and Maureen Appel Molot. Toronto: Oxford University Press.

Schneiderman, David. 1996. "NAFTA's Takings Rule: American Constitutionalism Comes to Canada." *University of Toronto Law Journal* 46, no. 4 (Autumn): 499-537.

Schwanen, Daniel. 2001. "Trade Liberalization and Inequality in Canada in the 1990s." In *The Review of Economic Performance and Social Progress*, edited by Keith Banting, Andrew Sharpe and France St-Hilaire. Montreal and Ottawa: Institute for Research on Public Policy and Centre for the Study of Living Standards.

– 2004. "Deeper, Broader: A Roadmap for a Treaty of North America." In *The Art of the State II: Thinking North America*, edited by Thomas J. Courchene, Donald J. Savoie and Daniel Schwanen. Montreal: Institute for Research on Public Policy.

Sokolsky, Joel J. 2004. "Realism Canadian Style: National Security Policy and the Chrétien Legacy." *Policy Matters* 5, no. 2 (June). Montreal: Institute for Research on Public Policy.

Wade, Robert. 2003. "What strategies are viable for developing countries today? The World Trade Organization and the shrinking of 'developmentspace'." *Review of International Political Economy* 10, no. 4 (November): 621-44.

Weiss, Linda. 1998. *The Myth of the Powerless State: Governing the Economy in a Global Era*. Cambridge, UK: Polity Press.

Wendt, Alexander. 1992. "Anarchy is what states make of it: The social construction of power politics." *International Organization* 46, no. 2 (Spring): 391–425.

Wolfe, Robert. 2003. "See You in Washington? A Pluralist Perspective on North American Institutions." *Choices* 9, no. 4 (April). Montreal: Institute for Research on Public Policy.

PART ONE
The Ottawa Game

2 Raising Our Game:
Canada among Nations

WENDY DOBSON

The "room for manoeuvre" theme of this volume prompts the question, "to do what?" To the economist, the answer is a straightforward one. The central economic goal in any market economy is to ensure sustained growth in living standards – a goal that many Canadians take for granted. Canada's real gross domestic product (GDP) per capita relative to the United States has hovered around 80 per cent since the early-1990s, recovering slightly in recent years. However since 2000, the efficiency with which we use labour to produce that output has deteriorated – both in relation to US productivity performance, and more troubling, in relation to our own performance in the late-1990s (Cotis 2006). Correcting GDP for other indicators of wellbeing does not change the rankings that much. Yet Canada is extraordinarily well endowed and well situated in the world. Indeed, a bright future is ours to lose. We have lots of room for manoeuvre if we are focused and imaginative, anticipate change, and prepare to seek new sources of growth if old ones flag.

Taking advantage of our room for manoeuvre requires raising the level of our game. A transformation of historic proportions is underway in the world economy. Hungry new competitors have appeared in world markets, new technologies are being created and new industries and jobs as a result, requiring new thinking and institutions to address future opportunities. In this short chapter, I suggest five priorities for Canada's international economic policy that anticipate and respond to the turbulent and rapidly changing international economic environment.

Yet, Canada currently lacks an international economic strategy beyond the November 2006 *Advantage Canada* blueprint for what we should do at home to respond to the changing global economy.[1] This lack may matter little in the short-term. Canadians are net beneficiaries of economic openness as measured by the dramatic growth in demand for and prices of our natural resources. The latter has resulted in strongly positive terms of trade which reflect healthy prices for our exports relative to the declining prices of imports. Canadian growth and employment has largely escaped the US slowdown as job losses in manufacturing due to technological change and import competition are offset by job gains in natural resource sectors and construction. Wage and salary shares of national income have declined somewhat but corporate profits have recovered from lows in the late-1990s.

Benign short-term prospects may help to explain the sense of complacency. It may also result from the reluctance of a minority government to define Canadian interests in a strategic framework. But it could also be that we suffer the complacency of the "lucky" country, perceiving the global transformation as merely opening windows of opportunity for us.

When the time frame is extended to 2020, a lot can change. A strategy is required that anticipates and mitigates risks in the long-term outlook and that positions Canadians for challenges as well as opportunities. At least three sources of change could bring challenges. One factor in the long-term outlook is slower growth in China. The Chinese government is determined to slow economic growth in the next five years, to 7.5 per cent from recent unsustainable 10 per cent rates. Policy is being refocused on rebalancing the economy – away from export dependence to domestic demand.[2] A second factor is changes in political perceptions in the United States of its role in the world. The attacks of September 2001 and failure in Iraq have left it wounded, its people fearful and inward looking, and its administration with marginalized legitimacy both at home and abroad. Access to US markets is not assured despite the North American Free Trade Agreement (NAFTA) and the fact that the US market takes more than 80 per cent of our exports. Mounting congressional concerns over security and the country's "porous borders" are raising the cost of bilateral trade, just like a tariff would do. Another terrorist attack or catastrophic health event in either country would undoubtedly result in border closure. A third factor is the changing ways in which business is being done. The information and communications technology (ICT) revolution is making the world economy increasingly networked and disaggregated; competitive advantage is driven by knowledge and talent embodied in people. The rapid evolution of cross-border services trade through increasingly tightly integrated networks and flows of technical people and ideas make this change apparent. Yet we persist with industrial-era thinking, hierarchies and policies.

WHAT SHOULD WE BE DOING?

The first priority is the bilateral relationship with the United States. Canada's place in the world is influenced by, but not entirely attributable to, our proximity to the world's richest and most innovative economy. As a nation, our top priority should be to improve the management of the bilateral political and economic relationship while preserving our political independence and distinctiveness. NAFTA was concluded in the industrial era when goods trade was the priority, and indeed the unfinished business of NAFTA includes burdensome rules of origin that raise transactions costs for goods flows. But border and regulatory barriers increasingly interfere with business networks and the movement of low-risk technical people. Governments are addressing some of these issues, but in a slow incremental fashion that lacks concerted attention at the top. Thus, more radical approaches to improving North American efficiency are not considered, such as eliminating border barriers and negotiating a common external tariff.[3]

Another deficiency in the bilateral relationship is our own failure to manage it in a sustained professional manner. Public displays of recrimination hurt no one but ourselves – they merely confirm our failure or inability to competently manage it. Instead, we should be doing just the opposite: being smart about leveraging our unique proximity to the US market to make a difference (Mintz 2001) to promote domestic growth and productivity and to increase our competitiveness in third countries. Indeed, the second priority, discussed next, should be the catalyst for a major effort to create a barrier-free common economic space in North America.[4]

The second priority is our relationships with China and India, the world's two most populous countries whose economic emergence is shifting the center of global economic gravity. I have spent much of the past fifteen years teaching about and studying the economic integration of the East Asian economies in collaboration with partners throughout the region. For thirty years, China's economy has been doubling in size roughly every eight years; India is now on a more modest growth trajectory, but the size of its economy is likely to double between 2003 and 2012. China's decisions to negotiate a free-trade agreement with the Association of South East Asian Nations (ASEAN) and to discuss one with India are powerful signals of another new era. An East Asian community is unlikely by 2020 but a regional consciousness is developing in which the United States and Europe are "over the horizon." It is possible to spend weeks in the region with news of North America being crowded out by dynamic regional developments and trends. Deeper integration among the main Asian economies will require much adjustment in the region but this will be facilitated by growth rates that range from 5 per cent a year in most of the smaller economies to 10 per cent in China. East Asians outside of Japan are shifting their angle of vision in a dramatic way and Beijing (not Tokyo) is becoming Asia's economic leader.

There was a time when Canada had a unique standing with the Chinese because of our own leadership initiatives. Those days are gone but not forgotten as Canada's international interests and institutional capabilities fade in relevance. We have done little to maintain our unique standing, choosing rather to spread our diplomatic and business resources thinly throughout the region. Yet it is in our long-term interest to participate in both China's and India's re-emergence onto the world stage. Both will play expanding regional roles; both are already affecting global economic performance and will have eventual impacts on global institutions and world order.

We should adjust to the emergence of China and India by refocusing our domestic priorities (see Dobson 2004; 2006). There is a tendency to think of these countries mainly in terms of large potential market sizes, or in terms of labour-cost arbitrage. Indeed we are living through a major labour supply shock as nearly 250 million people of labour force ages from these countries alone enter the world economy between 2000 and 2010 (one of the main reasons for declines in labour's share of national income). But this shock will pass by 2020, largely because of accelerating aging of the Chinese population. What we should be focusing on is their potential talent. Large numbers of people with technical and science backgrounds are being trained in both countries but few currently have marketable skills.

As both countries continue to invest heavily in building their human and other technical capabilities, we will see competitive challenges in our knowledge based industries, not just in manufacturing. This means our priority should be the development of our own talent by reshaping skills and productive structures to produce what both countries want to buy and what they cannot (yet) produce themselves. Their demand for our natural resources has temporarily improved our terms of trade; but it is quite possible that this robust demand, particularly for fossil fuels, will not continue. For example, compulsory targets in China's 11th five year plan (2006–10) are to increase energy efficiency by 20 per cent and reduce pollutants by 10 per cent. Raising domestic research and development (R&D)

intensity to 2 per cent by 2010, measured by R&D expenditures as a share of GDP, is another significant plan target (Zhang 2006).[5]

The third priority – a strategic one for any rich and privileged nation – should be to focus on the world's poorest countries that are on the periphery and not yet integrated into this new networked world. Our official development institutions have strayed from their original mandates of development, poverty reduction and capacity building, to transferring resources to Canadian academics, consultants and businesses, and more recently, to areas of conflict. Canadian aid should be focused on the provision of public goods – basic health and education programs – primarily in the poorest countries that are prepared to reform themselves and integrate into the world economy.

The fourth imperative is to invest in selected international institutions that reflect this changing world. Most of these institutions exist – some are in need of reform and updating, but Canada's participation has not kept pace. As our relative economic clout declines, our value added lies in focusing on the issues and providing quality ideas and proposals. All too often our contribution to quality and commitment reflects a particular personality in a leadership position rather than a strategic commitment to multilateralism; one that endures despite changes in political regimes or personalities. A more effective high-level inter-governmental mechanism for managing the Canada-US relationship tops the list. But raising our game in evolving Asian cooperative forums comes a close second. We should also invest in regime maintenance at the global institutions governing trade, capital and environmental protection. Efficient functioning of the interdependent world economy depends heavily on agreed and enforced rules of the road. The Bank of Canada has been one of the respected voices in the reform of the International Monetary Fund as that institution struggles with its future in a world dominated by private capital flows. But our voice has faded at the World Trade Organization, and this should be a source of alarm for a country as trade-dependent as Canada.

The final priority is to invest in our stock of expertise in international economics and international relations. Public resources should be re-focused and increased to enable Canada's educational and research institutions to invest in building deeper international relationships and expertise. A systematic competitive and peer-reviewed funding program, such as exists in both Australia and the United States, structured along the lines of the centres of excellence program in the natural sciences is needed to replace heavy reliance on the aid program and ad hoc public investments, fired like grapeshot into a variety of institutions and foundations to serve passing political fancies.

In conclusion, Canada has much room for manoeuvre in international economic policy, particularly if we raise the level of our game, beginning with a focused strategic framework. The priorities identified here are given varying preference throughout the volume, reflecting the many perspectives on and great interest in sustaining and enhancing Canada's competitive global position.

NOTES

1 The full name of the document is *Advantage Canada: Building a Strong Economy for Canadians*. The publication was part of the November 2006 Economic Update by the Minister of Finance, setting out the government's policy agenda to achieve that goal.
2 The rebalancing of performance criteria for Communist Party cadres – adding to the traditional growth goal targets for health, education and environmental protection – are further evidence of determination to implement changes going forward.
3 But not a common commercial policy.
4 This concept was among the recommendations of a three-country independent task force convened by the Council on Foreign Relations (2005).
5 The R&D intensity target is indicative of a country's desire to build long-term domestic capacity.

REFERENCES

Canada. 2006. *Advantage Canada: Building a Strong Economy for Canadians*. Ottawa: Ministry of Finance.

Cotis, Jean-Philippe. 2006. "Benchmarking Canada's Economic Performance." *International Productivity Monitor* 13, no. 3 (Fall): 3–20 Ottawa: Centre for the Study of Living Standards.

Council on Foreign Relations. 2005. *Building a North American Community*. Independent Task Force No. 53. New York: Council on Foreign Relations.

Dobson, Wendy. 2006. "The Indian Elephant Sheds its Past: Implications for Canada." *C.D. Howe Institute Commentary*, no. 235 (June). Toronto: C.D. Howe Institute.

– 2004. "Taking a Giant's Measure: Canada, NAFTA and an Emergent China." *C.D. Howe Institute Commentary*, no. 202 (September). Toronto: C.D. Howe Institute.

Mintz, Jack. 2001. *Most Favored Nation: Building a Framework for Smart Economic Policy*. Policy Study no. 36. Toronto: C.D. Howe Institute.

Zhang, Yongsheng. 2006. "To Achieve the Goals of China's 11th Five-Year Plan through Reforms." Presentation to the Tokyo Club Foundation for Global Studies, Tokyo, 6 December. Available at: <http://www.tcf.or.jp>

3 PMO/PCO/DFAIT:
Serving the Prime Minister's Foreign Policy Agenda

JOHN J. NOBLE

This chapter deals with the relationships between the Prime Minister's Office (PMO), the Privy Council Office (PCO) and the Department of Foreign Affairs and International Trade (DFAIT) in the determination of Canadian foreign policy and the margin for manoeuvre which exists among them. After extensive research including interviews with many of the actors in those three organizations,[1] it is clear that the prime minister always has been the key player in the determination of Canadian foreign policy from the time of Sir John A. MacDonald to Stephen Harper. In fact the PMO, PCO and DFAIT largely complement each other to serve the prime minister's foreign policy agenda both in its establishment, direction and implementation. This does not mean that creative tension does not exist between or indeed within these bodies. But all three have to be working together to achieve the prime minister's foreign policy goals.

Formulating Canadian foreign policy has become much more complicated than it was under Louis St. Laurent and Lester Pearson and requires a whole-of-government approach which cannot emanate solely from the PMO, the PCO or DFAIT, but then again I am not sure it ever did. This is not a tale of woe or a lament for a non-existent "golden age" when some make-believe DFAIT and other foreign ministries were the centres of the foreign policy universe. I doubt that was ever true either. DFAIT's main role has been to support the Canadian prime minister from the time it was formed in 1909. Indeed from then until 1946, the prime minister was also the minister for external affairs, so the reporting relationship was more direct than it is today. Some senior officials believe that to accomplish diplomacy in the twenty-first century DFAIT should again become a ministry in the prime minister's portfolio, an idea which harkens back to Allan Gotlieb's claims in the 1970s that DFAIT was a "central agency" because it had to coordinate the activities of many other government departments in foreign activities. I think that Gotlieb was right, but he failed to convince the then clerk of the PCO, or other central agencies like Treasury Board of his case. Whatever role is given to DFAIT in the coordination of Canadian foreign policy, its over-stretched and under-funded capacity cannot be depleted anymore. In this respect, I want to issue a clarion call for the Canadian government to rectify the serious under-investment in DFAIT by successive governments, which has resulted in the rusting out of its far flung physical empire and serious staffing shortfalls highlighted recently by the auditor general (Canada 2007b). The priority given by the prime minister to restoring an assertive and effective foreign policy cannot be achieved without addressing those financial problems in the near future or else through real retrenchment from some of our global activities.

THE PRIMACY OF THE PRIME MINISTER IN FOREIGN POLICY

The prime minister is head of government and appoints his cabinet, the clerk of the PCO and deputy ministers; the latter usually on the advice of the clerk of the PCO. This means that deputy ministers, who are the senior public servants in each department, have a dual loyalty to both the prime minister and their respective minister as well as to the clerk of the PCO, in terms of their current jobs and future job prospects.

From the time the Department of External Affairs was established in 1909 until 1946, the prime minister was the minister for external affairs. Key issues relating to Canada getting full representation at the Versailles Treaty negotiations and a seat at the League of Nations were directed by Prime Minister Borden, who headed the Canadian delegation in Versailles (MacMillan 2001, 44–49, 93). Even after the Statute of Westminster and full independence in 1931, it would be another fifteen years, including the entire period of the Second World War, before a separate minister for external affairs was appointed in the person of Louis St. Laurent in 1946.

Canadian prime ministers can only focus on a certain number of foreign policy matters and have to leave other files to their ministers. The choice of which files they lead on is theirs alone. As a G8 country and member of a wide range of international organizations, some of which have also developed annual or biannual summits at the head-of-government level, the prime minister needs to be constantly advised about a wide range of developments that may help or hinder his policy objectives both at home and abroad. While that information may be channelled through the Prime Minister's Office or the Privy Council Office, or both, it often originates from DFAIT or one of its missions abroad. In turn DFAIT has to work with many other government departments to achieve many of the government's foreign policy objectives and also to keep informed about the many activities of other domestic departments whose activities have an increasing international perspective. The same thing goes for provincial activities, where a high degree of cooperation with the federal government, coordinated through DFAIT, is necessary and usually works, depending on the political atmosphere prevailing in federal/provincial relations.

THE PRIME MINISTER'S OFFICE (PMO)

No important policy decision can be taken without the concurrence of the prime minister and in today's world heads of government are much more involved in foreign policy than many of them ever thought would be the case.[2] The PMO is made up of the prime minister and his key political advisors. Its members come and go with each prime minister, indeed some may not remain through even one mandate of a prime minister, while others may remain throughout the entire term of office. The key person in the PMO, aside from the prime minister, is the chief of staff, who is responsible for ensuring that the government stays on track on its priorities and messages and keeps the prime minister out of trouble.

Pierre Trudeau had a senior foreign policy advisor in his PMO, Ivan Head, who was involved in anything related to foreign policy in which the prime minister was to be involved (Head and Trudeau 1995, 8). Many commentators have attributed a Foreign Affairs' perceived fall from its role of prominence in foreign policy to the existence of the Head position and Trudeau's general dislike of diplomats (Granatstein and Bothwell 1990; Andrew 1993; Cohen 2003; Noble 2003). However, while dislike of diplomats has been a common theme of most prime ministers since Trudeau, none have had a foreign policy advisor within the PMO, but all have relied mainly on the PCO position of "assistant secretary to Cabinet for foreign and defence policy," upgraded during the Chrétien years to "diplomatic advisor" and in the Martin and Harper governments to "foreign and defence policy advisor to the prime minister" (FDPA) and "deputy secretary to Cabinet" (Canada 2007g). That position has almost always been filled by a career foreign service officer.[3] Other players in the PMO can still be involved in foreign policy decisions, as Derek Burney, James Bartleman, Hugh Segal, and Eddie Goldenberg make clear in their recent books (Burney 2005b; Bartleman 2007; Segal 2006; Goldenberg 2006).

PRIME MINISTERS' PRIVATE NETWORKS

Prime ministers who stay in office for some time develop an extensive network of international contacts which they use for direct discussions on many issues and for keeping abreast of fast breaking stories where analysis from DFAIT may be slower than needed by the prime minister. That was certainly the case for Mulroney and Chrétien, and Martin had an international network stemming from his long time as minister of finance. Prime Minister Harper has already started to develop such a network, which will expand the longer he stays in office. Indeed in June 2007 he suggested he had been comparing notes with other leaders about their experiences with their foreign ministries. Harper told a Toronto audience that "every government in every country – all the leaders I've talked to – complain to me that their foreign service wants to do what it believes is foreign policy, not what the government of the day's foreign policy is. It is a universal problem" (Woods 2007).

LIMITS ON PRIME MINISTERIAL POWER

Contrary to some prevailing views about the omnipotence of prime ministers, they do not always impose their will on Cabinet or the caucus. Indeed in some areas there may be constitutional constraints or other legislative restraints. In their collective memoir on Canadian foreign policy from 1968–1984, Trudeau and Ivan Head cited pressure from Cabinet leading to a fisheries line proclamation in the Arctic "in spite of the contrary position of Trudeau and Sharp (his foreign minister)" (Head and Trudeau 1995, 63). Eddie Goldenberg says that "it was rare that Chrétien imposed his authority as prime minister against the wishes of most of the caucus and the Cabinet" (Goldenberg 2006, 383).

THE PRIVY COUNCIL OFFICE

The Privy Council Office (PCO) is staffed by public servants, who must remain aware of the wishes of their political master, the prime minister, but also true to defending the institutions such as the Constitution, the rule of law etc. and are responsible for providing non-partisan advice to the prime minister. The day he assumed office, Prime Minister Harper reversed a series of decisions by his predecessor that had rapidly expanded the numbers and role of the PCO in day-to-day operations, including the establishment of a secretariat on Canada-US relations. These changes were done while Alex Himelfarb was still clerk. Two years earlier Himelfarb had put together the large expansion package in the PCO in part because of electoral commitments by Paul Martin. According to Kevin Lynch, the current clerk of the PCO, who is also effectively the deputy minister to the prime minister,

> [the] PCO establishes the priorities of the government and then should let departments do their jobs, based on those priorities and complemented by a rigorous challenge function. It serves no one's interest for central agencies to micro-manage or co-manage files. This is why secretariats and teams that existed in PCO to advance work on cities, aboriginal affairs, smart borders, official languages, smart regulation, policy research, science advice, regulatory affairs and regional communications have been re-assigned to those departments with the clear mandate to deliver in these areas. In so doing, we have shrunk the number of PCO secretariats considerably, reduced its overall size by about fifteen per cent and refocused the efforts of the PCO secretariats on their core functions. Central agencies must add value, not layers, to the process of policy and decision-making and government operations. (Lynch 2006)

Nevertheless, if the prime minister is micro-managing his cabinet, as is sometimes said of Prime Minister Harper for example, then his deputy minister, i.e. the clerk, has to keep on top of the same files in even more detail than his boss. When the government is in a minority situation and some of the most difficult and politically sensitive files it faces have a foreign policy component, (for example, with the Harper government, the major military and reconstruction efforts in Afghanistan, and the government's response and *volte face* on climate change), the result may be micro-management and reduced access to the prime minister by the foreign policy advisor. Difficulties may be compounded in these situations if Foreign Affairs is perceived as not reacting with sufficient alacrity to changes of emphasis on foreign policy priorities.

Be that as it may, Harper downsized the number of PCO staff engaged in foreign policy including the dismembering of the Canada/US Secretariat. The current size of the Foreign and Defence Policy Secretariat in PCO is more in keeping with traditional numbers and it very much relies on advice and support from DFAIT, DND, CIDA, and other departments involved in international issues. The relationship between several clerks and DFAIT has been rocky since the time of Michael Pitfield in the 1970s, but none of the four ex-clerks I interviewed raised it as a serious problem in the formulation or delivery of foreign policy. Three of them went on to become "heads of mission" abroad[4] and perhaps had a better opportunity to appreciate the constraints under which Canadian diplomats and DFAIT operate, while the other had been a head of mission some time before becoming clerk.

THE ROLE OF CLERK OF THE PCO

The clerk and deputy minister have to balance the ephemeral considerations of the government with interests that are permanent. As head of the public service, the clerk has to ensure a healthy bureaucracy is ready to serve future governments, while, as cabinet secretary, he or she has to ensure that the decision-making processes of cabinet are followed.

"In a sense he is the counterweight to the political impetus in the short run. The individual has to be someone who looks over the horizon and thinks about the issues of the country, not just the issues of the government," said one person well acquainted with the job.

The personal dynamic between prime minister and clerk is crucial for successful government, but it goes beyond that. The clerk must also be able to "tell truth to power" and most successful prime ministers have wanted that characteristic in their clerks.

KEYS TO RELATIONSHIPS BETWEEN PRIME MINISTERS AND PUBLIC SERVANTS

I have always felt that personalities and personal compatibility are the keys to successful relationships between prime ministers, ministers and senior public servants. But as one former clerk pointed out, personalities are only one part of such relationships. When it comes to the clerk and deputy ministers, the other two important elements in their relations with the prime minister and ministers are respect for the constitution and the rule of law and the situation in which you find yourself at a particular point in time (your karma). Another former clerk stressed that, in the end, values, people and clarity of vision are most important.

PCO ROLE IN FOREIGN POLICY

The PCO challenge role is not to supplant or second guess ministers or deputy ministers. However, on foreign policy issues the foreign and defence policy advisor has not been confined to simply passing on advice emanating from DFAIT, DND, CIDA and elsewhere, but may provide the prime minister with his/her own advice. That was certainly within the terms of reference for Jean Chrétien's "diplomatic advisors" (Bartleman 2007, 16). Because the foreign and defence policy advisor is in much more regular contact with the prime minister than most other government officials or indeed many ministers, he/she is often on the receiving end of messages for the prime minister from all over government, from ministers as well as senior officials.

THE ROLE OF THE DEPARTMENT OF FOREIGN AFFAIRS AND INTERNATIONAL TRADE

The formal mandate of the Department of Foreign Affairs and International Trade is set out in the Department of Foreign Affairs and International Trade Act (R.S. 1985, c. E-22). The 2003 decision by the Martin government to break the department into two separate departments was described by Derek Burney as "bone-headed" (Burney 2005a) and no one has ever claimed responsibility for the idea, which was quickly reversed by the Harper government on the day it was sworn in. However questions remain as to how the two departments have been put back together since; even the reunited departmental letterhead uses the bifurcated names "Foreign Affairs Canada" and "International Trade Canada" rather than the formal DFAIT name set out in the act, or even Foreign Affairs and International Trade Canada.

In his 2005 Simon Reisman Lecture Derek Burney noted "we have a department of highly trained policy specialists whose day job it is to analyze, plan, and advise the government on foreign policy. The task for the ministers involved and the prime minister is to choose, to decide, and to lead on the basis of this advice, and to articulate to Canadians compelling reasons for the courses selected" (Burney 2005a).

The restored DFAIT mandate consists of:

1 ensuring that Canada's foreign policy reflects true Canadian values and advances Canada's national interests;
2 strengthening rules-based trading arrangements and to expand free and fair market access at bilateral, regional and global levels; and
3 working with a range of partners inside and outside government to achieve increased economic opportunity and enhanced security for Canada and for Canadians at home and abroad. (Canada 2007c)

In mid-2007 the new deputy minister at Foreign Affairs, veteran diplomat and former deputy of international trade and agriculture, Len Edwards, the deputy minister of international trade, Marie-Lucie Morin, and Associate Deputy Minister David Mulroney led the department through an "alignment review" which produced three "key" priorities: i) Afghanistan; ii) North America and the Hemisphere; iii) Growing/emerging markets, with a focus on China and India.[5]

PUTTING THE PRIME MINISTER'S
STAMP ON FOREIGN POLICY

Incoming governments are sorely tempted to conduct a foreign policy review to demonstrate that their predecessors did not get everything right and they have something new and exciting to add to the definition of Canadian foreign policy. Trudeau, Mulroney, Chrétien and Martin, all made attempts to put their own imprint on Canadian foreign policy, but none of them fundamentally changed the basic objectives of promoting and protecting Canada's security, economic interests, and Canadians' core values (Noble 2005).[6] The means to achieve those objectives and the challenges faced by governments since Trudeau's time have changed significantly. We no longer face nuclear annihilation and a Cold War; our biggest security threat now comes from non-state actors against whom the traditional use of military force is proving to be problematic; we have a North American Free Trade Agreement which covers over eighty per cent of our trade; and climate change now looms in Harper's own words in June 2007 as "perhaps the biggest threat to confront the future of humanity today" (Canada 2007f). The challenges posed by globalization, HIV/AIDS and other pandemic diseases, terrorism, nuclear proliferation and regional conflicts cannot be dealt with unilaterally by even the United States. Increasing international co-operation is required across an ever growing number of issues. Expertise on these matters lies within not just DFAIT but within a large number of other domestic departments and has to be effectively coordinated to be more useful; a phenomenon whose extent, according to one ex-clerk, had not been fully appreciated by DFAIT.

HARPER'S FOREIGN POLICY

Foreign policy was not one of Prime Minister Harper's priorities during and after the 2006 federal election (Conservative Party of Canada 2006b).[7] Indeed he admitted publicly on a couple of occasions in the second half of 2006 that "one of the biggest surprises I've had in this job has been the degree to which foreign policy has really taken a lot of my time" (LARNACA 2006; Conservative Party of Canada 2006a). In February 2007 Prime Minister Harper elaborated a strategy for making the country stronger which included as its fourth priority "the restoration of an assertive foreign policy that serves Canadian values and interests" (Canada 2007e). One thing that Harper did not announce to help achieve that objective was another foreign policy review. The emphasis which Harper has put on values as well as interests has surprised some commentators and has been ignored by others who had criticized his predecessor Liberal governments for stressing values. But it comes from a longstanding Canadian tradition going back to at least the 1947 Gray Lecture by then foreign minister Louis St. Laurent (St. Laurent 1947).[8]

THE BRITISH EXPERIENCE WITH FOREIGN POLICY

Something which Pearson knew and Harper understands was reiterated recently in the British Parliament by long serving British diplomat Lord Hannay:

You cannot make foreign policy by blueprint. No single country, not even the United States, can say foreign policy is to be thus, thus and thus. It is made by a lot of tiresome foreigners out there who have different ideas about what their priorities are, and you have to respond to them. ... [Documents] will always be outdated fairly quickly, because events will come along that will drive you to find responses that are not laid down in such documents. (United Kingdom 2006a, 1)

At the same session Sir Jeremy Greenstock, another British diplomat, noted that "it is a trend of our age that as international affairs increasingly interlink with domestic affairs, the head of any Government should be closely and in a detailed way concerned with foreign policy." He went on to say that

the Government's capacity to handle international affairs is not just a matter of direct communication between the most senior members of government. It is the product of a wide-ranging amount of teamwork, built on the knowledge and understanding, the contact and communications, that the British Government have, through all their capillaries, with other people in other countries. You cannot, at the top, seal a deal that has not been thoroughly prepared further down the system. You cannot negotiate at a conference without knowing what everybody else with whom you are about to negotiate may be thinking or may be carrying in their suitcase. You cannot understand what is happening in a country without having on the ground people who know, who understand and who have analysed the roots of that change, that problem or that particular development. (United Kingdom 2006)

The Harper government appears to be learning the importance of having people on the ground but has yet to make the investment in foreign affairs capacity required for the kind of external representation associated with the status of being a G8 country.

Lord Hannay also observed that "Heads of Government are now much more involved in the day-to-day business of diplomacy. That has nothing to do with our country or the way in which our Government is organised; it is about the way in which the world, European Councils, G8 meetings and so on are organised" (United Kingdom 2006b, 1).

SUMMITRY HAS CHANGED
THE CONDUCT OF DIPLOMACY

The introduction of a variety of annual or biannual summit exercises [G8, Asia Pacific Economic Cooperation (APEC), Summit of the Americas, North Atlantic Treaty Organization (NATO), Commonwealth Heads of Government, Francophonie] and the rise of a number of challenges to national governments which can only be resolved through international co-operation ensure that heads of government have become more and more directly involved in foreign policy as it becomes more and more entwined with what used to be considered domestic policy. The prime minister has to be ready to deal with issues at each summit, even if those issues are not high on his government's agenda. The PMO, PCO and DFAIT have to work through how the prime minister will handle these issues in the summit context. The general desire for politicians to show results from a summit means that the bureaucracy of each country is tasked in the preparations for such meetings to develop proposals which can show progress was made on some files.

The glaring anomaly in the panoply of summits in which the Canadian prime minister participates is the absence of a bilateral annual summit with the president of the United States, our most important partner in almost every sense. That should change with a new president in 2009, whichever party is in office in Ottawa at that time.

The links between domestic and foreign policy have been around a lot longer than some current practitioners or academics recognize. Mitchell Sharp in his memoirs (covering a period before the rise of summitry) had two chapters on his time as foreign minister in the 1970s, one about "External Affairs: The Domestic Side" and the other "External Affairs: Implementing Foreign Policy." He concluded the former by noting "the Canadian secretary of state for external affairs is at the very centre of 'internal affairs' – domestic politics" (Sharp 1994, 200).

HARPER'S KEY FOREIGN
POLICY DECISIONS

A brief overview of Harper's foreign policy decisions shows the extent to which the prime minister really runs foreign policy. At the same time he has tasked DFAIT with coordination responsibilities which normally would be handled in the PCO. If DFAIT is to coordinate a whole of government approach, it really then becomes a central agency. But DFAIT does not have all the levers of power needed to do this. Harper has yet to support his decision with investment of the resources necessary to ensure DFAIT's success. Furthermore, in the case of Afghanistan, the resources required cannot be furnished by Canada alone.

Several of the Harper government's most controversial decisions have centred on foreign policy decisions which were not taken initially with an eye to public opinion polls: making Afghanistan Canada's number one foreign policy priority (at least until 2009); an alleged tilt in support for Israel and a corresponding change in our "balanced" approach to the Middle East;[9] giving the cold shoulder to China because of its human rights abuses; and the rejection of Canada's commitments in the Kyoto Accord followed by a subsequent reversal of position with respect to climate change and the acceptance of the need for some real reductions in Canadian emissions and an emphasis on more participation by the major global polluters.

AFGHANISTAN

Afghanistan has proved to be a difficult file to manage for the prime minister who decided in early 2007 to shift overall coordination for it from the PCO to Foreign Affairs. He appointed his foreign and defence policy advisor, David Mulroney, as associate deputy minister of foreign affairs with a specific mandate to coordinate the government's approach and implementation of policies in Afghanistan (Canada 2007d). While some questioned whether this job could be better done in Foreign Affairs, which has no mandate to coordinate the activities of DND or CIDA, the prime minister and the clerk of the PCO, Kevin Lynch, have in fact indicated that this is part of how they believe the government should be run.[10]

Attempts at co-ordination of policy in Afghanistan hit a rocky patch in the spring of 2007 over the question of the handling of detainees captured by Canadian soldiers. A variety of conflicting statements by ministers and finger-pointing by un-named officials in DFAIT and DND, suggested the government did not yet have its act together on the matter.

A NEW FOCUS ON
THE WESTERN HEMISPHERE

In February 2007, reflecting on his first year in office, Prime Minister (PM) Harper announced that Canada "will seek to re-engage relationships throughout the Americas, with our partners in Mexico, the Caribbean, and Central and South America" (Canada 2007e).

In mid-April 2007 DFAIT announced the appointment of the then ambassador to Cuba, Alexandra Bugailiskis, as a new assistant deputy minister and executive coordinator of the Americas Strategy. She is to be responsible for the provision of strategic guidance and direction on the comprehensive whole-of-government Americas Strategy for Canada's relations and activities in the region and supporting the prime minister's engagement in the region (Canada 2007a). Creating a new assistant deputy minister (ADM) position in DFAIT for a specific region of the world is a reversal of a previous decision, forced upon DFAIT by budgetary cuts in 2003–2004, to eliminate all geographic ADMs with the sole exception of one for North America and one for the rest of the world. It was not an appropriate solution for a G8 country to put responsibility for bilateral relations with the rest of the world on the shoulders of one ADM no matter how competent an individual. DFAIT also needs to restore bilateral ADMs for Asia/Pacific, Africa and the Middle East, and Europe but will have difficulties selling this idea to the Treasury Board and others. Indeed it is clear that the new priority on the Americas does not come with any new money to fund new initiatives and DFAIT is in an "alignment review" to see how it can rearrange its existing resources to better reflect the government's priorities (Canada 2005; Canada 2007h).

At the G8 Heiligendamm Summit in Germany in June 2007, in response to criticisms about lowering the level of the promised increase in Canadian aid funds to Africa, the prime minister noted that Africa is not Canada's "sole focus" because there are also development challenges in the Americas (*The Record* 2007).

One of the co-editors of this book, Jean Daudelin, who is a specialist on Latin America, suggested in a Canadian International Council *Behind the Headlines* booklet published in late May 2007 that it should be a "time of modesty" for Canada in the Americas because, with the exception of the Caribbean, what Canada does in the Americas "has little bearing on Canadians" (Daudelin 2007). On the basis of past experience by several Canadian governments, the "rediscovery" or "re-engagement" of Canada with the hemisphere is something which is dusted off periodically but never really takes off. Whether this time will be different is still an open question.

KEY FIGURES IN CANADIAN FOREIGN POLICY

In examining the players driving the above foreign policy decisions the prime minister looms as the key figure. Harper's initial stance on climate change was the one which led his first environment minister up a dead end alley with Canadian public opinion ultimately forcing him to reverse course, replace the minister, and accept climate change as a threat to the "the future of humanity" (Canada 2007f). Similarly his positions on Afghanistan, China and the Israel/Palestine conflict very much bear his stamp.

Conventional wisdom about Prime Minister Harper is that he runs a tight ship and tries to control everything from policy to communications from the PMO and PCO. That may well be true. However in foreign policy he has tasked DFAIT with clear responsibilities to coordinate a whole-of-government approach to his major foreign policy priority, Afghanistan and also to coordinate a whole-of-government approach to a newly prioritized Strategy of the Americas.

He has not delegated responsibility for setting the agenda – no prime minister ever does – but has tasked DFAIT with this coordination responsibility. That was one of the roles which the Martin government also assigned to DFAIT in the 2005 International Policy Statement. It was a traditional role for DFAIT throughout my 35 years of service there and much of my time dealing with Canada-US issues, international security matters or multilateral issues involved extensive and on-going cooperation with other government departments in Ottawa as well as provincial and territorial governments in the development and implementation of Canadian foreign policy objectives. Yet, it is a role that after years of budget cuts, DFAIT appears increasingly unable to fulfill.

THE FOREIGN AND DEFENCE POLICY ADVISOR

The position of foreign and defence policy advisor to the prime minister was described by one former clerk as being one of the four most important senior bureaucratic positions in the federal government along with the deputy ministers of finance, inter-governmental affairs and foreign affairs. Traditionally the incumbent has regular and direct access to the prime minister both in Ottawa and on all trips abroad. There is a clear need for the incumbent and the clerk to work out a *modus operandi* in terms of keeping each other informed on matters of mutual interest, particularly where a particular foreign policy issue is likely to become a major preoccupation of the government (such as Afghanistan or climate change).

Another important function of the FDPA is to take notes of all conversations between the prime minister and foreign leaders either during face to face meetings or in telephone conversations and to ensure the prompt distribution of a record of the discussions to those that need to know. The FDPA is the one to wake the prime minister up in the middle of the night in the event of an international crisis or a phone call from a foreign head of government.

The FDPA also has an established network of back-channel contacts into the White House and the chanceries of other heads of government which permits direct contact (Bartleman 2007, 41). Eddie Goldenberg claims in his book that Chrétien's decision on Iraq was not conveyed to the Americans until it was announced in the House by the prime minister (Goldenberg 2006, 1–8). However, I have had it confirmed that Chrétien did instruct his diplomatic advisor to speak to US secretary of state, Condoleezza Rice, prior to his announcement in the House and that he did do so.[11]

The fact that the FDPA is a career diplomat means that he or she knows most of the foreign and defence establishment and almost all incumbents have developed direct relationships not just with deputy ministers in DFAIT, DND and CIDA, but with other officials throughout those departments. Several previous clerks, not necessarily the ones I interviewed, had little or no interest in foreign policy or time for it because of other priorities and were quite content to have the foreign and defence policy advisor taking the lead, always with the caveat of "no surprises" and the need to keep them fully informed of any advice submitted to the prime minister or discussions with him. This is something which varies with prime ministers and clerks and the increased interest of the current clerk in foreign affairs may also be due to the increasing overlap between domestic and foreign policy.

DFAIT SUPPORT FOR G8 AND OTHER SUMMITS

Mr. Harper has continued the tradition, started after the departure of Ivan Head in 1978, of having as his main advisor for the G8 Summit (called the sherpa), the deputy minister of either Foreign Affairs or International Trade.[12] In February 2007 following the retirement of Peter Harder as deputy minister of Foreign Affairs and previous G8 sherpa, the prime minister appointed the new associate deputy minister of foreign affairs, David Mulroney, to be his sherpa for G8 Summits in addition to co-ordinating the government's efforts in Afghanistan. The political director (ADM level) in DFAIT also serves an important function in the G8 preparatory process with respect to international political issues.

Other Foreign Affairs officials serve "sherpa" type roles for the prime minister for other summit processes: the Francophonie; the summit of the Americas and annual summits of the Security and Prosperity

Partnership of North America; the Commonwealth Heads of Government; APEC; and NATO. These officials work meticulously with the PCO and PMO and representatives of other government departments and other governments to ensure that the prime minister's objectives for these summits are achieved.

Most other G8 countries do not use someone from their foreign ministry to act as the G8 sherpa. Rather he or she may come from the equivalent of the PCO or the PMO.[13] Prime Minister Mulroney used Derek Burney as his G8 sherpa when Burney was our ambassador in Washington (immediately after having served as Mulroney's chief of staff), with backup from DFAIT. Burney also had extensive experience with the G8 summit process from his time in DFAIT. In his last two years in office, Mr. Chrétien had Robert Fowler, then Canadian ambassador to Italy as his sherpa for the Kananaskis Summit and then his foreign and defence policy advisor, Claude Laverdure for his last summit, both with backstopping from DFAIT. A 2003 recommendation from Gordon Smith, a former DFAIT deputy minister and G8 sherpa, that the G8 sherpa position be filled by the foreign and defence policy advisor in PCO was not followed by either the Martin or Harper governments (Smith 2003). Several former FDPAs that I spoke with felt that it would not be a good idea for them to have been sherpa given their other responsibilities.

THE ROLE OF THE G8 SHERPA

The role of the original G8 sherpas has been described as

creating a powerful informal entity whose advice to leaders was derived at least in part from views they reached collectively. That these views could have crystallized despite national interests that might have acted as a barrier to collegial thinking is a reminder of how much the global economic system owes to a small group of men and one woman who brokered, cajoled, negotiated, briefed, advised and eventually succeeded in bringing about one successful economic summit after another. (Ryten 2004, xv)[14]

Summits are no longer simply "economic" but the work of the sherpas in ensuring some degree of success cannot be underestimated.

A new dynamic was created with the advent of the Africa permanent representatives (APRs or "African sherpas") at the Genoa G8 Summit in 2001.The Genoa Communiqué created APRs and handed the preparation of a response to the New Partnership for Africa's Development immediately to Canada as host of the next summit. Prime Minister Chrétien asked Robert Fowler to take on both the sherpa and APR

functions for the Kananaskis Summit. Fowler retained the latter function with PMs Martin and Harper until his retirement in October 2006.
It was suggested to me that having one person chair both groups
worked best (even if its never been duplicated), as it integrated the
thinking and product of both groups while avoiding most of the subsequent rivalry. The selection of APRs also caused structural difficulties.
Some were clearly senior to their respective sherpa (i.e. ministers from
the UK and Germany, a former governor of the Bank of France and
former managing director of the IMF from France) and some were distinctly junior and/or subservient to their country's G8 sherpas [the case
with US, Japan, European Union (EU), Russia, and Italy]. With the creation of APRs, summitry changed significantly: i) Africa became a main
agenda item for every summit since Genoa (2001); ii) "Outreach"
changed from a few non-G8 visitors around the margins of the meeting
to a number of African leaders (and –latterly, others) being invited inside the tent; and iii) a very different and much wider public interest in
summit proceedings was generated.

Within Canada the access which the G8 sherpa has to the prime minister on an on-going basis (the preparatory process has become a year
round business) provides the deputy minister or associate deputy minister of DFAIT with the opportunity to become better acquainted in a direct manner with the prime minister's views and approach to foreign
policy and to better gain his confidence. At the G8 summit meetings the
only official in the room with the prime minister is the sherpa, no one
from PMO or PCO is there (they certainly accompany the prime minister's delegation but have to remain in the Canadian delegation office).

POLITICIANS' DISTRUST OF BUREAUCRATS

The mistrust of the senior public service as being out of sync with incoming governments has existed since the time of John Diefenbaker
and Prime Minister Harper himself mentioned it during the 2006 federal election when he said that if he won the election, "the reality is
that we will have for some time to come a Liberal Senate, a Liberal civil
service, at least senior levels have been appointed by the Liberals and
courts that have been appointed by the Liberals" (*Ottawa Citizen* 2006).
Those comments were a blow to the integrity of bureaucrats who pride
themselves on being neutral, impartial and non-partisan. They also
raised the spectre of a Harper government gutting the senior ranks and
replacing them with their own political appointees, something which
did not happen either in Ottawa (more on this below) or with respect
to most diplomatic appointments where Harper has been much more
parsimonious in the number of non-career appointments than any of

his predecessors. The Harper government did replace five "political" diplomatic appointments made by the Martin government in a low-key manner, but with one exception the replacements were not "political appointees."[15]

Paul Wells has chronicled the Harper government's attitude to bureaucratic changes in his recent book:

"We made a decision early on – like very early on, before the election began – that in the event of victory we would not get involved in a complicated rejigging of the machinery of government," one senior Conservative said. "That was considered and rejected, basically for the reason that if you start to reorganize the machinery of government, kiss your productivity goodbye for the next two years as everyone figures out who reports to whom."... Everything else he left much as he found it – with two key exceptions.

... Very rapidly, Lynch and Harper implemented a major facelift of the senior public service. The machinery didn't change, but there were plenty of new machinists. Deputy ministers are the top bureaucrats figures in a permanent government that does not change just because the party in power changes. But this new government made a point of changing deputies. By June there would be new deputy ministers at Finance, Industry, Human Resources, International Trade, Environment, Indian Affairs, Citizenship and Immigration, Natural Resources, Intergovernmental Affairs and Public Safety. (Paul Wells 2006b, 283–5)

Harper clearly wanted to put his imprint on the senior public service without rocking the boat too much.

HARPER'S FRUSTRATIONS WITH DFAIT

Harper's early frustrations with DFAIT are also chronicled by Paul Wells, who reported that Harper found a DFAIT draft on the results of the election in Belarus so bland that he penned his own text and suggested DFAIT learn from it (Wells 2006a).[16]

Harper's continuing frustrations with DFAIT surfaced in the *Toronto Star* in late June 2007 which reported, "Harper says he is being undermined by public servants who are uncomfortable with the Conservative government's aggressive approach to foreign policy matters" (Woods 2007). The article went on to say that Harper had indicated that the way to overcome resistance is "to provide very strong direction" (Woods 2007). Columnist Jeffrey Simpson opined that "the government, however, just doesn't care for Foreign Affairs and always wonders about its advice" (Simpson 2007). Harper made a clarification of his comments in the *Hill Times* in early July 2007 stating that, "the support we get from the bureaucracy was generally pretty good." The

PMO also released a partial transcript of the comments on which the *Star* article was based which was much more nuanced than reported by the *Star* (*The Hill Times* 2007, 4).

DFAIT AND THE "CENTRE"

Summitry has changed the role of the prime minister in day-to-day foreign policy formulation both in Canada and elsewhere. The resulting increased influence of the "centre" in foreign policy decision-making is not strictly a Canadian phenomenon. The same phenomenon has happened in the United Kingdom, the country which most resembles the decision-making process at the federal level in Canada.[17] Furthermore, the charges about centralization apply not just to foreign policy but to almost every other aspect of domestic policy.[18]

Many commentators have suggested that contemporary foreign ministries in the West, including DFAIT, suffer from at least three major faults: i) they have no idea of how their own government works, but they know how the systems work abroad in Paris, London or Tokyo; ii) they have a terrible reputation on management issues; and iii) rightly or wrongly they suffer from the reputation of living the luxury life abroad, which generates difficulties with Canadian politicians and with Ottawa bureaucrats.[19] In some respects therefore DFAIT has been the author of its own misfortune by not having paid sufficient attention over the years to playing the bureaucratic game with other key players in Ottawa and in not paying sufficient attention to effective management both at home and abroad. One former clerk expressed surprise that DFAIT could still operate in a pre-Glasgow Royal Commission manner (that Commission examined financial management and accountability and recommended extensive reform in the administrative practices of the public service in Canada in 1979).

While the Harper government has promised to increase its spending on defence and official development assistance, it has not done so with respect to Canadian diplomacy, despite proclaiming that it wants an assertive foreign policy. DFAIT experienced a cut of C$64 million in 2006 while a domestic department with a similar size budget, Agriculture Canada, had just a C$2 million cut (clearly there are a lot more votes in agriculture than in foreign affairs). Four Canadian Consulate Generals in G8 countries were closed (Milan, Italy; St Petersburg, Russia; Osaka and Fukuoka, Japan). A large chunk of the public diplomacy program, which had been a key element of the concept of a twenty-first century foreign ministry espoused by Deputy Minister Peter Harder in 2005, remained unfunded and there were cuts to the promotion of Canadian culture.

DFAIT'S FINANCIAL, PHYSICAL, AND PERSONNEL CHALLENGES

In October 2006, then Deputy Minister of Foreign Affairs Peter Harder outlined some of the constraints and challenges being faced by DFAIT in a speech to the Retired Heads of Mission Association (RHOMA) (Harder 2006). These included: a new round of cuts in the fiscal year 2007/2008 of C$46.4 million; increased representation abroad from other government departments (OGDs) in DFAIT accommodation which is no longer capable of expansion (in the 05/06 fiscal year, OGDs added 53 new positions abroad); the risk of suffering a death by a thousand cuts; DFAIT had 349 of 4,559 employees acting in higher-level positions for periods beyond a year; 455 rotational vacancies and 747 non-rotational positions were open; twenty-eight missions are at the highest hardship levels, designated dangerous and/or difficult; more than 40 missions require armour-plated vehicles for security of Canadian personnel serving there; from 2001 to 2005, there were 16 mission evacuations involving over 200 Canadian staff and dependents.

Many of the above personnel deficiencies were highlighted in a May 2007 report by the auditor general (Canada 2007b). The political class in Canada does not recognize the extent to which the on-going cut backs in DFAIT have impacted negatively on its ability to continue to deliver a G8 level foreign policy on an over-stretched and under funded budgetary base.[20] The same mentality appears to drive the new Strategy of the Americas: "do it without any new money."

DFAIT IS STILL A KEY PLAYER IN CANADIAN FOREIGN POLICY

Notwithstanding all of the problems and shortcomings being experienced by DFAIT, the prime minister and the PCO continue to rely on its expertise in almost all aspects of foreign policy especially in terms of delivery and inputs and analysis in policy development. Successive prime ministers seem to have had much better relationships with individuals from DFAIT than with the bureaucratic machine which is DFAIT. One of the former clerks mentioned that during the 1990s DFAIT took the decision to cut back its policy formulation capability when major cut-backs were imposed on all government departments. Other departments did not choose the same route and for several years the Department of Industry has been taking the lead role in policy research with respect to various aspects of Canada-US relations and trade policy issues both of which should be the primary responsibility of DFAIT.

AN ASSERTIVE FOREIGN POLICY
REQUIRES NEW MONEY FOR DFAIT

If the prime minister is serious about pushing ahead with a more assertive, value-laden and interest-driven foreign policy, then he is going to have to make some real investment in DFAIT to restore its capabilities, albeit at a much lower level of expenditure than he has invested in the Canadian Forces. To date that has been a major disconnect with the clear objectives for foreign policy which he has established.

THE ROOM FOR MANOEUVRE

In terms of the margin for manoeuvre which PMO, PCO and DFAIT have, much depends on the direction in which the prime minister wants to move and what he wants to achieve within the context of a minority government. The direction and priorities come from the prime minister and the prime minister has made clear he has been providing "strong direction." The Strategy for the Americas, the changes in policy towards Afghanistan and climate change have been developed at the direction of the prime minister. The prime minister's speech to the United Nations General Assembly in September 2007 also promises to unveil more with respect to his perception of Canada's priorities abroad.

On climate change and other issues, apart from the key driver of Canadian public opinion, being part of the G8 process and all of the other summit processes serves as a driver for the development and modification of Canadian policy in anticipation of what is going to happen at those events. This prime minister is very much results driven and wants to be able to show concrete actions resulting from his participation in international meetings.

This was perhaps one of the reasons why the prime minister moved on climate change when he did. In November 2006 he avoided a meeting with Finland, the country then holding the EU presidency, reportedly because of fears of being criticized for his position on climate change. Six months later he could not avoid Chancellor Merkel of Germany, whose country was simultaneously hosting the G8 summit and holding the EU presidency in 2007. He could also see the winds of change blowing south of the border and wanted to avoid a common dilemma faced by Canadian governments: being led out on a limb by the Americans, who then change position and leave us out there or even worse, saw off the limb.

Events inside and outside Canada can often affect the direction of the government. One of DFAIT's ongoing roles is to constantly analyze how events outside Canada impact on Canadian interests either negatively or positively. In this process DFAIT also has responsibility to identify, often with assistance from other departments, possible Canadian responses to these external developments. The responses can either be defensive or involve new initiatives. Such initiatives can only be undertaken with political direction. In this government that means the PMO with the advice of the PCO. Harper's first foreign minister, Peter MacKay, did not have the margin for manoeuvre with Stephen Harper that Lloyd Axworthy had with Jean Chrétien. However that does not mean that all new policy initiatives will emanate from either PMO or PCO. DFAIT has a responsibility to the government to be suggesting possible new initiatives and ensuring that agreed policy is implemented.

The realignment exercise conducted by DFAIT in mid-2007 resulted in just three key priorities, one of which elevated relations with the (western) hemisphere to the same level as that of relations with the United States. The emphasis on the Hemisphere is clearly a prime ministerial priority and did result in the creation of the new senior position in DFAIT previously mentioned. Other less charitable observers might suggest that giving equal ranking to the United States and the rest of the hemisphere downgraded relations with the United States to the level of relations with the rest of our hemispheric partners. From my perspective, relations with the United States are far more important than with any other country of the hemisphere. Equally with the prospect of a change of course on Afghanistan by 2009, this foreign policy priority could well slip to the back burner regardless of who wins the next federal election. It is not yet clear whether DFAIT's realignment exercise will result in a real reallocation of financial, human and physical resources together with a further closure of posts abroad. It is always easier to close a consulate than an embassy or high commission because the latter implies a downgrading of relations with a country as a whole rather than just one part of it. Given the diverse nature of Canadian society, any attempt to close an embassy or high commission is likely to draw political protests in at least one or more federal ridings, none of which can be ignored in the context of a minority government.

The room for manoeuvre in terms of relations with the United States is not great given the changing moods in Washington and the anti-American complex promoted by the three opposition parties. But this is too important an issue to be left to "knee-jerk anti-Americanism." Two former Canadian diplomats, Derek Burney and Paul Heinbecker, who are not known for a commonality of view with respect to the management of Canada's relations with the United States, have both come to a similar conclusion. For Burney "the ultimate measure of foreign policy is relevance and influence. To be relevant you must be engaged. To be influential you need to establish a basis of trust with your counterpart anchored more by tangible commitment than by simple rhetoric" (Burney 2005b, 189). Paul Heinbecker has been criticized as being an Axworthy idealist (Granatstein 2007, 50–57). But he too has recently concluded, unlike the prescriptions in Lloyd Axworthy's book (2003),[21] or in the more recent book by Axworthy protegé Michael Byers (2007) that "to be effective abroad, we need to be influential in Washington. To be influential in Washington, we need to be effective in the world. Between this yin and yang of international relations, there will always be ample room for Canadians of vision, principle and purpose" (Heinbecker 2007).

CONCLUSION

All in all, Prime Minister Harper has demonstrated a much more authoritative tone to his foreign policy than might have been expected in a minority government. He has set the tone and the policy priorities in every aspect of his government and makes all the major announcements. He is ably seconded by the clerk of the Privy Council who is immersed in all aspects of the government's operations including foreign policy. However on foreign policy the prime minister has tasked DFAIT with responsibility to coordinate and deliver on two of his top priorities: Afghanistan and the Strategy for the Americas. He relies on DFAIT advisors for advice on the plethora of international meetings he has to attend. He wants to conduct an assertive foreign policy but will not be able to do so for long unless there is recognition of the need to restore DFAIT's capacity to deliver those foreign policy goals, through a serious injection of cash to its base budget.

NOTES

1   I have interviewed former chiefs of staff to prime ministers, former clerks of the PCO, former assistant secretaries to cabinet for foreign and defence policy, former officials who served as the sherpa for the G7/8 Summit process, and former under secretaries (now deputy ministers) of External/Foreign Affairs and International Trade. I have also drawn on the memoirs of Lester Pearson and Pierre Trudeau and his foreign policy advisor Ivan Head, as well as those of former foreign ministers Mitchell Sharp, Mark MacGuigan and Lloyd Axworthy. Recent books by Derek Burney, who served as chief of staff to Prime Minister Mulroney from 1987–89, Eddie Goldenberg, who was Prime Minister Chrétien's senior policy advisor throughout his governments, and James Bartleman, who was Prime Minister Chrétien's foreign policy advisor from 1994–1998, contain much relevant information and insight with respect

to the key players in the formulation of Canadian foreign policy and its delivery as does Allan Gotlieb's "Washington Diaries."

2 See Canadian Press report of PM Harper's remarks to press in Larnaca, Cyprus on July 21, 2006, and his speech to the B'nai Brith on October 6, 2006; Tony Blair "What I've Learned" in *The Economist*, May 31, 2007 edition; and James Bartleman (2007, 39).

3 Incumbents of the position from 1978 on have been: Jacques Roy (1978/70), Allan Sullivan (1979/80), Robert Fowler (1980–86), Reid Morden (1986–88), Ernest Hébert (1988–89), Anne Marie Doyle (1989–90), Paul Heinbecker (1990–92), James Judd (1992–94), Jim Bartleman (1994–98), Michael Kergin (1998–00), Claude Laverdure (2000–03), Jonathan Fried (2003–06), David Mulroney (2006–07), Susan Cartwright (2007–present).

4 Jocelyn Bourgon as ambassador to the OECD in Paris; Mel Cappe as high commissioner to the United Kingdom and Alex Himelfarb as ambassador to Italy.

5 The six "strategic" or "ongoing" priorities are: i) a safer, more secure and prosperous Canada within a strengthened North American partnership; ii) greater economic competitiveness for Canada through enhanced commercial engagement, secure market access and targeted support for Canadian business; iii) greater international support for freedom and security, democracy, rule of law, human rights and environmental stewardship; iv) accountable and consistent use of the multilateral system to deliver results on global issues of concern to Canadians; v) strengthened services to Canadians, including consular, passport and global commercial activities; vi) better alignment of departmental resources (human, financial, physical and technological) in support of international policy objectives and program delivery both at home and abroad. See <http://lbp.dfait-maeci.gc.ca/panorama/2007/06/0621-SCM-PFM-Alignmentupdate-en.asp>

6 PM Harper's three policy objectives in the western hemisphere revolve around these same themes.

7 See the Conservative Party of Canada (2006b). Foreign and trade policy are covered in the last three pages of a 46 page platform.

8 See St. Laurent (1947). He listed the 5 fundamental principles of Canadian foreign policy as: i) our external policies shall not destroy our unity; ii) the concept of political liberty; iii) respect for the rule of law; iv) some concept of human values; v) a willingness to accept international responsibilities.

9 See for example Michael Byers (2007, 53–61).

10 See Kevin Lynch (2006). See also David Mulroney's DFAIT Panorama message (Mulroney 2007).

11 See also Bob Woodward (2004, 373).

12 The list of Canadian officials who have served as G-7/8 sherpa after Ivan Head 1976–77, is as follows: 1978–79 Robert Johnstone; 1980 Klaus Goldschlag; 1981 Allan Gotlieb; 1982–83 De Montigny Marchand; 1984–88 Sylvia Ostry; 1989 James H. Taylor; 1990–92 Derek Burney; 1993–94

Reid Morden; 1995–97 Gordon Smith; 1998–2000 Don Campbell; 2001
Gaetan Lavertu; 2002 Robert Fowler; 2003 Claude Laverdure; 2004–06
Peter Harder; 2007 David Mulroney.

13 When I served in France (1994–98), I was in regular contact with the French
   sherpa for President Mitterrand, the Deputy Secretary General in the Elysée,
   Anne Lauvergon and the sherpa for President Chirac, his Diplomatic Advisor,
   Jean-David Levitte.

14 See also Derek Burney (2005b).

15 Prior to his election Mulroney had a "hit-list" of public servants who should be
   replaced prepared by Erik Neilson. The list is contained in Annex "A" to Peter
   C. Newman (1995; 2005, 440–444).

16 From Paul Wells (2006a): "Harper took one look at the proposed release,
   swore, took out a pen and paper and drafted his own version. 'Just put it out.
   Don't even tell Foreign Affairs. They can read it later. Maybe learn something,'
   he told his staff. What they read was pretty blunt. The election 'was not free or
   fair,' began the communiqué, which went out in Harper's name. 'I am shocked
   that a dictatorial and abusive regime such as this one can continue to exist in
   today's Europe.'"

17 See Lord David Owen (2006) and his testimony to the UK Select Committee on
   Foreign Affairs November 8, 2006.

18 See Donald J. Savoie (1999; 2003) and Jeffrey Simpson (2001). Several of those
   interviewed highly contested Donald Savoie's thesis and denied the concentration of policy formulation and decision-making at the centre.

19 James Bartleman notes: "the perception had taken root in the greater public
   and in the public service that Foreign Affairs personnel had become pampered
   fat cats who enjoyed a lifestyle abroad that other Canadians could only dream
   about. The reality that the majority of staff worked most of their careers in un-
   healthy, difficult, and often dangerous environments was overlooked in the
   rush to condemn the handful who abused the system" (Bartleman 2007, 27).

20 A senior official with Citizenship and Immigration (CIC) noted that CIC's operations abroad are being negatively affected by DFAIT's inability to lodge CIC officers in exiting embassies. CIC officers in Moscow are doubled up in cramped
   offices which probably don't meet Ontario's Occupational Health and Safety
   requirements. The same problem exists at many other embassies abroad.

21 See also my review of this book: Noble (2004).

REFERENCES

Andrew, Arthur. 1993. *The Rise and Fall of a Middle Power: Canadian
   Diplomacy from King to Mulroney.* Toronto: J. Lorimer.
Axworthy, Lloyd. 2003. *Navigating a New World: Canada's Global Future.*
   Toronto: Alfred A. Knopf.

Bartleman, James. 2007. *Rollercoaster: My Hectic Years as Jean Chretien's Diplomatic Advisor, 1994–1998*. Toronto: Douglas Gibson Books.

Burney, Derek. 2005a. "Foreign Policy: More Coherence, Less Pretence." The Simon Reisman Lecture in International Trade Policy, Ottawa, 14 March. Available at: <http://www.carleton.ca/ctpl/pdf/conferences/2005 reismanlectureburney.pdf>

– 2005b. *Getting It Done: A Memoir*. Montreal and Kingston: McGill-Queen's University Press.

Byers, Michael. 2007. *Intent for a Nation: What is Canada for? A relentlessly optimistic manifesto for Canada's role in the world*. Toronto: Douglas & McIntyre.

Canada. 2005. "Aligning the Department with Priorities." Administrative Notice, 14 May. Department of Foreign Affairs and International Trade. Available at: <http://lbp.dfait-maeci.gc.ca/panorama/2007/05/0514-USS-DMT-DMA-ExecComRetreat-en.asp>

– 2007a. "Appointment of Alexandra Bugailiskis as Assistant Deputy Minister and Executive Coordinator for the Americas Strategy (RLX)." Messages from Ministers and Deputy Ministers, 18 April. Department of Foreign Affairs and International Trade. Available at: <http://lbp.dfait-maeci.gc.ca/panorama/2007/04/0417-USS-DMT-Bugailiskis-en.asp>

– 2007b. *Human Resource Management, Foreign Affairs and International Trade Canada*. 1 May. Report of the Auditor General. Available at: <http://www.oag-bvg.gc.ca/domino/reports.nsf/html/20070503ce.html>

– 2007c. "Mandate and Priorities." 20 July. Department of Foreign Affairs and International Trade. Available at: <http://geo.international.gc.ca/department/about_us-en.asp>

– 2007d. "Prime Minister Announces Changes in the senior ranks of the Public Service." Press Release. 26 January. Prime Minister's Office. Available at: <http://www.pm.gc.ca/eng/media.asp?category=1&id=1508>

– 2007e. "Prime Minister Harper outlines agenda for a stronger, safer, better Canada." Press Release. 6 February. Prime Minister's Office. Available at: <http://www.pm.gc.ca/eng/media.asp?category=2&id=1522>

– 2007f. "Prime Minister Stephen Harper calls for international consensus on climate change." Press Release. 4 June. Berlin: Prime Minister's Office. Available at: <http://www.pm.gc.ca/eng/media.asp?category=2&id=1681>

– 2007g. "Privy Council Office." Organizational Chart. June. Ottawa: Privy Council Office. Accessible at: <http://www.pcobcp.gc.ca/docs/Org/OC-June-2007_e.pdf>

– 2007h. "The Alignment Review – An Update." 21 June. Ottawa: Department of Foreign Affairs and International Trade. Available at: <http://lbp.dfait-maeci.gc.ca/panorama/2007/06/0621-SCM-PFMAlignmentupdate-en.asp>

Cohen, Andrew. 2003. *While Canada Slept: How We Lost our Place in the World*. Toronto: McClelland & Stewart.

Conservative Party of Canada. 2006a. "Speech to B'nai Brith at the Award of Merit Dinner." Ottawa, 18 October. Available at: <http://www.pm.gc.ca/eng/media.asp?category=2&id=1365>

– 2006b. "Stand Up for Canada: Conservative Party Platform 2006." Available at: <http://www.conservative.ca/media/20060113-Platform.pdf>

Daudelin, Jean. 2007. "Canada and the Americas: A Time for Modesty." *Behind the Headlines* 64, no. 3 (May). Toronto: Canadian International Council.

Goldenberg, Eddie. 2006. *The Way It Works: Inside Ottawa*. Toronto: McClelland & Stewart.

Granatstein, J.L. 2007. *Whose War Is It?* Toronto: HarperCollins Canada.

Granatstein, J.L., and Robert Bothwell. 1990. *Pirouette: Pierre Trudeau and Canadian Foreign Policy*. Toronto: University of Toronto Press.

Harder, Peter. 2006. "Remarks by V. Peter Harder Deputy Minister to the Retired Heads of Mission Association (RHOMA)." Department of Foreign Affairs, 18 October. Available at: <http://www.international.gc.ca/department/dm_speeches/deputyminister-speeches-2006–10-24-en.asp>

Head, Ivan, and Pierre Trudeau. 1995. *The Canadian Way: Shaping Canada's Foreign Policy, 1968–1986*. Westminster, Maryland: McClelland & Stewart Ltd.

Heinbecker, Paul. 2007. "The Davey Lecture." University of Toronto, Victoria College, 29 March. Available at: <http://www.heinbecker.ca/Speeches/DaveyLectureCanadianForeignPolicyPH.pdf>

The Hill Times. 2007. "The Question that Prompted PM's Response on Foreign Service, Civil Servants." 2 July.

LARNACA. 2006. *Cyprus (CP)*. 21 July.

Lynch, Kevin. 2006. "Making Public Service Renewal Real." Remarks by the Clerk of the Privy Council and Secretary to the Cabinet at the 2006 APEX symposium, 30 May. Available at: <http://www.pco-bcp.gc.ca/default.asp?Language=E&Page=Clerk&Sub=ClerksSpeeches&oc=20060530_apex_e.htm>

MacMillan, Margaret. 2001. *Paris 1919: Six Months that Changed the World*. Toronto: Random House.

Mulroney, David. 2007. "Introducing the new Afghanistan Task Force: more colleagues, new structure and a clearer mandate than ever." DFAIT. 16 May. Available at: <http://lbp.dfait-maeci.gc.ca/panorama/2007/05/0516-DMA-AfghanTaskForce-en.asp>

Newman, Peter C. 2005. *The Secret Mulroney Tapes: Unguarded Confessions of a Prime Minister*. Toronto: Random House Canada.

– 1995. *The Canadian Revolution: From Deference to Defiance*. Toronto: Penguin Books Canada.

Noble, John J. 2003. "Overestimating Canada's Decline in the World." *Policy Options* 24, no. 09 (October): 78–9. Available at: <http://www.irpp.org/po/archive/octo3/noble.pdf>

– 2004. "Circumnavigating America in Axworthy's world of soft power." *Policy Options* 25, no. 02 (February): 94–5.

– 2005. "Do Foreign Policy Reviews Make a Difference?" *Policy Options* (February).

Ottawa Citizen. 2006. "Harper's suspicions of PS hint of rocky relations to come: Bureaucrats feel their integrity impugned." 17 January. Available at: <http://www.uofaweb.ualberta.ca/govrel/news.cfm?story=42156>

Owen, David. 2006. "The ever growing dominance of No 10 in British Diplomacy." Lecture delivered at the LSE, the London School of Economics, 8 October.

The Record. 2007. "Canada blamed for diluting G8 aid deal." 9 June. Available at: <http://www.therecord.com/home_page_front_story/home_page_frontstory_1066268.html>

Ryten, Jacob. 2004. *The Sterling Public Servant: A Global Tribute to Sylvia Ostry*. Edited by Jacob Ryten. Montreal: McGill-Queen's University Press.

Savoie, Donald J. 2003. *Breaking the Bargain: Public Servants, Ministers, and Parliament*. Toronto: University of Toronto Press.

– 1999. *Governing from the Centre: The Concentration of Power in Canadian Politics*. Toronto: University of Toronto Press.

Segal, Hugh. 2006. "The Long Road Back: The Conservative Journey 1993–2006." Toronto: HarperCollins.

Sharp, Mitchell. 1994. *Which Reminds Me ... a Memoir*. Toronto: University of Toronto Press.

Simpson, Jeffrey. 2007. "Civil servants can 'Speak Truth to Power', but will they be heard?" *Globe and Mail*. 12 July. Available at: <http://www.theglobeandmail.com/servlet/story/RTGAM.20070712.wcsimp13/BNStory/Front/home>

– 2001. *The Friendly Dictatorship: Reflections on Canadian Democracy*. Toronto: McClelland & Stewart.

Smith, Gordon S. 2003. *Managing Canada's Foreign Policy*. May.

St. Laurent, Louis. 1947. "The Foundations of Canadian Policy in World Affairs." *Department of External Affairs*. The Duncan & John Gray Memorial Lecture, Toronto, 13 January. Accessible at: <http://www.geocities.com/Athens/Forum/2496/future/stlaurent.html#s2>

United Kingdom. 2006a. *Select Committee on Foreign Affairs Minutes of Evidence*. Testimony of Sir Jeremy Greenstock. 8 November. Parliament. Available at: <http://www.publications.parliament.uk/pa/cm200607/cmselect/cmfaff/167/6110802.htm>

– 2006b. *Select Committee on Foreign Affairs Minutes of Evidence*. Testimony of Lord Hannay of Chiswick GCMG, CH, Sir Jeremy Greenstock

GCMG and Matthew Kirk. 8 November. Parliament. Available at: <http://www.publications.parliament.uk/pa/cm200607/cmselect/cmfaff/167/6110802.htm >

Wells, Paul. 2006a. "Harper's first 100 days: taking charge." *Policy Options* 27, no. 03 (November): 83–7.

– 2006b. *Right Side Up: The Fall of Paul Martin and the Rise of* Stephen Harper's New Conservatism. Toronto: Douglas Gibson Books.

Woods, Allan. 2007. "PM, public servants at odds over policy." *Toronto Star.* 25 June. Available at: <http://www.thestar.com/News/article/229056>

Woodward, Bob. 2004. *Plan of Attack*. Toronto: Simon & Schuster.

4 Is the Defence Establishment Driving Canada's Foreign Policy?

DANFORD W. MIDDLEMISS
AND DENIS STAIRS

The purpose of this chapter is to assess the proposition – held in some quarters with intensifying conviction – that the Department of National Defence (DND) and the Canadian Forces (CF), taken together, are now the ascendant drivers of Canadian foreign policy. While the argument presumably applies mainly to decision-making in the polit-ico-security issue area, it is sometimes claimed that DND/CF priorities have become central to the government's performance in other fields as well, and most notably in the context of Canada's overall bilateral rela-tionship with the United States.

CAVEATS AND OTHER HESITATIONS

The authors cannot claim that the analysis that follows is definitive, if only because a fully persuasive assessment would require far more information than is currently available on what has been happening in-side the government apparatus and behind the scenes. While suggestive snippets of evidence surface from time to time, and while clues can be obtained from gossip and anecdotes recounted in the media or circu-lated informally among interested *cognoscenti*, the details of who said what to whom, when and with what effect are still largely hidden from the public domain. Serious students of bureaucratic politics, like seri-ous students of history, know that "the facts" will eventually "come out," but only with the passage of time. Patience on matters of this kind is therefore required. A rush to judgment, even if it ultimately proves to be premature, can still perform a useful service in clarifying the issues and nourishing public debate, but those who do the rushing are wise to conduct themselves in modest spirit and in the company of caveats.

Even if the supply of information were wholly adequate to the task, the interpretive problem would still be very complicated, if only because many different players are involved in both foreign and defence policy decision-making, and because their interactions with one another come in variously overlapping combinations and through a constantly evolving series of communications processes. In such circumstances, the real flow of influence – obscured by ganglion "feedback loops" and by the invisible effects on behaviour of "anticipated reactions" – can be hard even to trace, much less to measure.[1]

In the present case, there is a further problem in that the governmental defence establishment, even if "defence" is here understood in traditional military terms, is composed of two organizational hierarchies, not one – namely, the civilian apparatus associated with the DND on the one hand, and the uniformed CF on the other. The two have different perspectives and are guided by different cultures. Different priorities can result. In such cases, conflict inevitably ensues. To treat the two together, therefore, as if they comprise a homogeneous bureaucratic entity, can be seriously misleading. The task of uncovering the politics – thereby exposing the dominant locus of influence – may thus call for a more intricate and finely tuned analysis than is commonly assumed.

This analytical task is rendered more daunting still by the imprecision of the term "foreign policy" – by the fuzziness, that is, of what political scientists have been known to call the "dependent variable." Hence, the answer to the question, "Is the defence establishment driving Canadian foreign policy?" obviously depends in part on what the questioner means to include in the phrase "Canadian foreign policy." Clearly, for example, neither the DND nor the CF is the driver of Canadian policy in response to the Kyoto Accords, even though it can be argued that this is a "foreign policy" (as well as domestic policy) issue. Even in fields that are unambiguously concerned with politico-security affairs, moreover, there are many areas of activity in which the traditional defence establishment plays at most a marginal role and sometimes no role at all (as in the case, for example, of policies designed to facilitate cooperation with the Americans in pursuing both Canadian and American security interests at the Canada-US border).

Finally, it may be worth observing that the foundational premise of the question before us – namely, that in some circumstances "defence policy" *can* drive foreign policy – seems a little odd on its face. At first blush, after all, the CF appears to be an *instrument* of foreign policy (like the government's cadre of diplomatic representatives abroad, or the executors of its overseas propaganda initiatives,[2] or those in charge of its development assistance establishment[3]) and therefore ought not to be confused with the policy itself. The contents of the toolbox do not tell the carpenter what to make. They only give him options. (By virtue of their limitations, of course, they may deny him options, too.) Particularly in a liberal-democratic society, in which the supremacy of the political leadership over the military is jealously guarded, it seems odd to think that either the armed forces themselves, or the civilian public servants in DND with whom they work, might be dominating foreign policy decision-making in the larger sense.

In attempting to explain why some observers might nonetheless be drawn to this argument, a brief discussion of the broader context may be warranted.

THE CONTEXT AND ITS ORIGINS

Paradoxically, the issue before us has developed against a backdrop of several years of public discussion and debate that have been fostered by the perception that Canada's influence and reputation in world affairs has significantly declined.[4] Not all the reasons for this development have been subject to Canadian government control. Some, for example, are related to changes in the distribution of power in the world more generally, changes linked among other things to the rise of new and important players in the international hierarchy and to the recovery of some older ones. But Canada's presumed loss of place is commonly thought to derive also from decisions that Canadian governments themselves have made – decisions emerging above all from budget processes that have resulted in fewer assets being available for the conduct of foreign affairs. Recent initiatives designed to repair some of the damage wrought in this way by the deficit-reduction efforts of the 1980s and 1990s, while winning plaudits in some quarters, have had the paradoxical side-effect of raising the question of whether the custodians of the military toolbox, in particular, are now exerting a greater influence than they did before over the purposes for which their tools are being used and how they are being deployed.

This issue has acquired greater significance – certainly greater political salience – as a result of the intensification of Canadian military operations abroad, which have increasingly entailed combat activities as well as the performance of traditional peace-observation (surveillance), peace-keeping and related confidence-building functions. The strengthening of the military arm, when coupled with evidence that it is now being more robustly used, has thus generated a suspicion that the two may be inversely linked. The implicit thesis is not that the government has started to reinvigorate the military because it perceives a foreign policy need to do so, but that the military itself is autonomously exploiting its refurbished muscle – and hence its influence – to pressure the government into making more intensive use of its capabilities.

The issue of who is driving whom (and what) has also become a subject of topical interest because the argument for co-ordinating and integrating the government's operational enterprises abroad, particularly where multi-dimensional initiatives and programmes are involved, has become a widely accepted doctrine (even if faith in it has faded a little in some quarters as a result of experiences in Afghanistan). The idea was manifested in the "3D" notion (diplomacy, defence and development)[5] that came to underlie much of the policy argumentation in the Martin government's *International Policy Statement: A Role of Pride and Influence in the World*, or IPS (Canada 2005a), especially in relation to the perceived need to respond to security problems thought to be posed by so-called "failed and failing states." A very similar conceptualization was echoed in the "3-block war" vocabulary that developed in parallel inside DND, and it could be discerned as well in the fashionable buzz-phrase references in Ottawa to "whole of government" operations abroad.

The lead department in the writing of the IPS was supposedly Foreign Affairs Canada.[6] The reality was much more complicated, not so much because of problems between the Pearson building and the DND, but because the Canadian International Development Agency (CIDA) proved to be a defensively resistant bureaucratic player, and because the orchestration attempts of Foreign Affairs were repeatedly challenged by inconvenient interventions from the Privy Council Office (PCO) and the Prime Minister's Office (PMO). It was not long before it seemed sensible to ask which of the supposedly cooperating departments was really the dominant one – in effect, to raise the question posed repeatedly during Senate committee hearings on Canada's post-9/11 national security policy: "Who's driving the bus?" (Canada 2003, 15:40 and 15:55).

Once again the question – in theory, at least – had practical political salience, if only because it could be hypothesized that an integrated strategy that was dominated, *de facto* if not *de jure*, by a newly muscled DND/CF would lead to reliance on a more robustly "military" set of foreign policy stratagems abroad. This in turn would collide with traditional peacekeeping approaches, as well as with international "development" priorities and with conflict-resolution diplomacy of the kind often associated (accurately or otherwise) with the Canadian Foreign Service at its best.

In the context of their discussions of these matters, different observers have inevitably displayed different preferences, and their respective preoccupations therefore warrant at least a little elaboration here.

THE CASE FOR
THE "DND-ASCENDANT" THESIS

To provide perspective, it should be observed at the outset that the notion that Canada's foreign policy (in the politico-security issue-area, at any rate) has been dominated by the defence establishment is not a novel phenomenon, and the vigilance of Canadian political leaders in protecting the principle of civilian supremacy even as long ago as the first half of the twentieth century has been reviewed and documented with particular care by James Eayrs (1961, 70–102). Somewhat later, during the early years of the first government of Pierre Elliott Trudeau, the new political leadership was fond of asserting that Canada's foreign policy had become overly rigid and constrained by the requirements of its defence policy. In effect, a mere "instrument" of foreign policy was having the effect of determining the policy itself. In more concrete terms, the suggestion was that Canada's long-standing commitments to the North Atlantic Treaty Organisation (NATO) and the North American Aerospace Defense Command (NORAD) had locked Ottawa into a set of arrangements that diminished its capacity for creative innovation in a world jeopardized by the Cold War. In an earlier version of a similar argument, analysts like James M. Minifie had asserted that Canada's defence-oriented alliance relationships were depriving it of the opportunity to pursue a policy of non-alignment, a policy that they thought would yield a far more promising foundation upon which to base a constructive contribution to the de-escalation of East-West tensions (Minifie 1960; 1964).

NATO, of course, had been fabricated by diplomats, but NORAD was unquestionably the result of bilateral pressures emanating from the United States and exerted largely through military channels. Its purpose was to enhance the efficiency with which Canada and the US could cooperate in the defence of North America. Ultimately, in 1957, the chairman of the Chiefs of Staff Committee, General Charles Foulkes, almost single-handedly convinced the newly-ensconced prime minister, John Diefenbaker, to accept the proposed arrangement – notwithstanding the reservations of the foreign service, whose concerns had led the immediately preceding government of Louis St. Laurent to postpone the making of a final decision on the issue during its last months in office (Foulkes 1961, 112–25; Robinson 1989, 17–23).

The NORAD arrangement was itself the culmination of a long series of measures designed to promote Canada-US defence cooperation going back to the late 1930s. The military's generic support for this sort of initiative is manifested even to this day in the enhancement of various "interoperability" arrangements with American forces as well as in the pressure – so far unsuccessful – to work closely with US authorities on the development and eventual deployment of new technologies for defence against ballistic missiles. The combination of geographical contiguity with the United States and the inherent obligation of the military establishment to maximize its prospects for successfully defending Canada in the event of major military attack from abroad, generates, from the point of view of the CF, a perpetually unassailable argument in favour of continental defence cooperation.

But the principal military preoccupation in all these contexts has been the desire to optimize the CF's operational capabilities in the North American theatre (as well as in joint operations overseas), and nothing more. While such arrangements can have implications for foreign policy down the road (Middlemiss and Stairs 2002), they are not really about control over the substance and conduct of foreign affairs in the larger sense. They may *reflect* foreign policy, but they do not really *drive* it. As policies, they are controversial only to the extent that there are disagreements over whether the security threats – as defined – are credible or not, and whether the defensive strategies adopted in response to them are efficacious or not. It is true that they can exact certain political and diplomatic costs. Canadians at home, for example, may see them in symbolic terms as manifestations of an undignified want of autonomy, and observers abroad may interpret them as evidence of a kind of pro-American partisanship. The arrangements at issue, moreover, do clearly presuppose a shared Canada-US interest in continental security. But in themselves they do not dictate foreign policy behaviours outside the continental defence domain, narrowly conceived.[7]

In practice, disagreements over whether such cooperative defence strategies are well-advised or not; whether they will ultimately prove counterproductive or not; or, whether they reflect American imperial and hegemonic dominance or not. These disputes and others like them often flow from fundamental differences over how best to promote international security in general, and Canadian security in particular. That this is so has a bearing on the rhetoric of the debate under consideration here, since the claim that foreign policy is being dominated by the defence establishment is essentially a way for critics to argue that an inappropriate policy is being followed because it is being made under the influence of the wrong people. The argument about the bureaucratic origins of the policies in question thus becomes a proxy for an argument about whether the policies themselves are good or bad.

This pattern certainly seems to be evident in the current discussion, in which the assertion that the DND is ascendant in the making of Canada's international security policy amounts to a way of explaining why that policy (particularly but not solely in relation to Afghanistan) is militarily more robust than the policy favoured by the critics. At the overtly political level, this position is most obviously represented by the New Democratic Party (NDP), but also by pressure groups and think-tanks like The Council of Canadians (for whom Steven Staples [2006] has advanced the military dominance argument in its most explicit form), the Polaris Institute (Staples and Robinson 2005) and Project Ploughshares (Regehr and Whelan 2004). Latterly, the argument has often been pegged more specifically to the personal influence of the Chief of the Defence Staff (CDS), General Rick Hillier. Given Hillier's visibility and popularity, and given also the superficial persuasiveness of arguments that attribute complex developments to the influence of individual personalities (arguments that are easily understood) rather than to more complicated and abstract forces (e.g., the interactions of competing bureaucracies), this is not surprising. It has, however, the inevitable side-effect of weakening somewhat the "bureaucratic politics" version of the critique (that is, the argument that the DND and CF are winning the policy game in their capacity as bureaucratic institutions). It also fails to accommodate the awkward reality that not everyone in the DND, or even in the uniformed services themselves, agrees with the position that their most senior military commander has taken.

All such complicating factors aside, however, it is still possible – hypothetically, at least – that the DND and the CF, jointly or separately, have become such dominant forces in government decision-making that they are now the principal players in determining Canada's foreign policy outputs in the politico-security field. This possibility is what underlies our assignment here.

MODE OF ANALYSIS

Given the complexities of the problem as outlined at the start of this discussion, it is useful to begin by asking what indicators should be used as measures, or tests, of bureaucratic ascendancy in the real world of government. Among the possibilities, five come most obviously to mind:

1 the evidence provided by the origins and substantive content of official policy statements;

2 the allocations of public funds among the alternative instruments of foreign policy, and the trend lines they reveal;
3 the patterns of policy action (or implementation) – that is, what actually seems to be happening in the field;
4 the impact of "real world" circumstances as a determinant of policy [as opposed to the exercise of autonomous will in a context in which imperatives (for Ottawa) are absent, and where an existential capacity to choose among competing options is clearly present]; and
5 the exogenous impact of the autonomous preferences of the political leadership and their influence on the decision-making process relatively to that of other players, including most obviously in the current case that of the DND and the CF.

We will discuss each of these indicators in turn.

I. OFFICAL POLICY STATEMENTS

Soon after taking over as prime minister in December 2003, Paul Martin promised a new, comprehensive review of Canadian foreign and security policy. He made it clear that he intended to re-orient Canada's foreign policy, in *all* of its dimensions, with a view to responding more effectively to the growing problems of political and economic instability overseas, and most notably in Africa. In this context, he observed that "merely re-building Canada's armed forces on old models [would] not suffice" (Regehr and Whelan 2004, 2). Substantial changes in the defence establishment therefore seemed to be in the offing.

Online foreign policy "consultations" with the Canadian public at large, complemented by a series of "town meetings" in various urban centres, had been completed under the auspices of the Chrétien government, but they had produced little of real value from the policy-generating point of view. This time, the intention was to have various departments and agencies – Foreign Affairs, International Trade, DND, the PCO and CIDA most obviously among them – conduct a more holistic and integrated review, with Foreign Affairs playing the leading role. The documents that ensued – like "green papers" in the traditional parlance of parliamentary government – would then be made available to the relevant parliamentary committees for purposes of public discussion and debate. Concrete policy decisions would be taken at the end of this process.

The review, however, was soon in serious difficulty. In-fighting quickly broke out among the various bureaucratic players as they sought to protect their respective turfs (Blanchfield 2004, A11). By the end of 2004, the international policy *review* had been transformed into an international policy *statement*, with no provision for public input. The prime minister at this stage was still unhappy with what he was reading.

In the meantime, his new defence minister, Bill Graham, was reported as having rejected as "dreadful dreck" the traditional, separate, service-oriented approach being taken in the early drafts of the DND's own contribution to the policy review process. "You want me to go out and demand more money for the status quo? It's not going to happen," he is reputed to have told his advisers. "We've got to get a new chief (of defence staff) in here now" (Thorne 2005a, A10). In search of a team of advisers more sympathetic to the government's orientation, he introduced General Hillier to the prime minister, who promptly agreed that Hillier should be appointed as the new CDS. Ward Alcock was similarly appointed as the DND's new Deputy Minister, and he and Hillier were to become the key architects of an innovative "top-down" vision of a transformed CF. With his recent experience as the commander of the 34-nation NATO International Security Assistance Force in Afghanistan (ISAF), Hillier in particular had impressed both the minister and the prime minister with his bold conception of how best to redesign the Forces to deal with the new challenges of a post-cold war and post-9/11 world (Campion-Smith 2005b; Thorne 2005b, 3).

With the *International Policy Statement* still subject to bureaucratic flux and confusion late in 2004, its various departmentally-contributed components, including that of DND, were sent back to their respective departments to be re-drafted as separate annexes to the broader IPS that was eventually to emerge under the imprimatur of the prime minister himself. As a result, a small inner team of civilian defence officials was created to try to mesh the defence review with the prime minister's covering document. The team completed its task very quickly, and was ready with the result by early 2005. Since there had been little input from the various environmental commanders, however, the process had generated some apprehension among the individual services. The IPS was constantly changing, and all of the services wanted to be sure that the rationales they were mounting to support their respective roles and equipment preferences were adjusted as necessary to mesh with the *Statement*'s account of what kinds of capabilities would ultimately be required. The hope throughout this period was that all the policy documents would be completed prior to the February budget, presumably to give at least the appearance that "policy" decisions were guiding the funding priorities (confidential interviews).

As it turned out, however, this aspiration was frustrated by other developments. The minority status of the Paul Martin government following the 2004 election was a general and continuing source of distraction. It was compounded in the defence field by controversies over the somewhat belated reaction to the 26 December 2004 tsunami disaster in the Indian Ocean (which called into question the very same "rapid-response" capability that was to be at the core of the new defence policy), and by the government's fitful and somewhat contradictory announcement in February 2005 that Canada would *not* be joining the US Ballistic Missile Defence (BMD) project. Defence issues were thus receiving a lot of attention, but not in the systematic, orderly fashion originally envisaged for the review process.

Even before the IPS had been completed, moreover, the new CDS appointed four high-level working groups – or CDS "action teams," as they came to be called – to begin implementing the department's own Defence Policy Statement (DPS). These were soon working aggressively on some key implementation issues, notably command and control; force generation and employment; force capabilities and development; and organizational reform and re-structuring (confidential interviews; Thorne 2005b, 827–8).

Finally, on 19 April 2005 the government unveiled its sweeping new plan for transforming the Canadian military. Central to the Martin-Graham-Hillier vision was the notion of a larger, better-equipped, more responsive and ultimately more effective CF at home and abroad, all within an ambitious, five-year time frame (Canada 2005b). The underlying purpose was to enhance Canada's international influence, and to gain more credit for its military contributions. As Hillier put it, "I think the world does need more Canada; it needs more of Canada in a leadership role. But you only get those leadership roles and the chance to influence things when you have a big enough commitment into a specific mission" (Campion-Smith 2005a, A06). This, however, implied a need to concentrate on fewer, more focussed operations, rather than scattering Canadian military contributions in small dribs and drabs over a wide array of missions, as had been the typical pattern in the era of traditional Canadian "peacekeeping." Meaningful contributions would entail larger CF contingents, and this in turn would require a more flexible, combat-oriented military establishment. "Let's pile on in a significant way," Hillier has been reported as saying. "Afghanistan is a perfect case in point where we had the opportunity to have real effect and we did," adding, "We cannot be everywhere" (Ibid.).

From the purely military point of view, the potentially attractive side-effect of this more focussed approach was that it would generate visible demonstrations of Canada's importance overseas. That, in turn, could translate into more influence for the DND and the CF where (they assumed) it counted most – namely, with the people of Canada, whose support might then have a favourable impact on budget calculations in the cabinet.

Having said that, it should be noted here that the real origins of the change of policy – implementation details aside – lay with the political leadership and not with the DND or the military. Hillier, for example, was appointed CDS over the heads of more senior officers because his ideas meshed in the first instance with those of the minister. Graham recognized in turn that they would also appeal to Paul Martin, and he therefore ensured that the prime minister and the general would meet. In effect, the political leadership was looking for a military commander who could – and would – do the job they wanted done, and they found him in Hillier. The general has a forceful and engaging personality, and he soon became a media favourite. He pursued his mandate, moreover, with the expected zest and vigour. But if his policy orientation had clashed with that of the political leadership, he would not have been given even the opportunity to try. He was able to lead, in short, only because politicians in high executive office, agreeing with his ideas, wanted him to do so.

Finally, it should also be understood that there was nothing in the IPS – or for that matter in the DPS – that pre-supposed a dominant DND/CF role in any particular context. It was clear, presumably, that operations conducted in combat-prone theatres would be particularly dependent on CF involvement, since little could be accomplished in such circumstances unless reasonable levels of security were established. But the policy model advanced by the IPS and recognized by the DND was multi-dimensional, involving the integration of inputs from a variety of government departments and agencies. The implication was that some players would be dominant in some circumstances, and others in different circumstances, and in practice the emphasis might well shift from one area of endeavour to another as any particular intervention progressed through different phases of implementation over time. All the elements involved were regarded as essential, and their combined effectiveness would depend on their being mutually supportive. The whole would thus be more than the sum of the parts. Neither the DND nor the CF, therefore, would be automatically ascendant, although their role would obviously be more important in some cases than in others, and there might well be situations in which they could exercise a veto (e.g., if they concluded that an operation was not militarily viable, or posed too great a danger to life and limb).

It could obviously be argued that, under the "whole of government" operational concept, this occasional capacity to veto would be more commonly available to DND than to other core actors. CIDA, for example, can be told to shift its resources from (a) to (b), whether it likes it or not.[8] Similarly, the Department of Foreign Affairs and International Trade (DFAIT) can be instructed by the political leadership to take initiatives of which it does not approve. It is very difficult, however, for politicians to override military commanders who assert – which they naturally hate to do – that a proposed operation is not militarily feasible.

The exercise of a veto power is not, however, what those who argue the case for DND/CF ascendancy actually have in mind.

II. BUDGET ALLOCATIONS

Policy pronunciamentos aside, the first concrete indicator that the DND's fortunes were on the rise came in the much-anticipated federal budget announcements of 23 February 2005. Pledging some C$12.8 billion in additional funding over the next five fiscal years, the budget signified the government's recognition that the Forces had reached a state of crisis in their operational readiness and capabilities – a fact that even the most jaded of Canadian observers had long since acknowledged, given the almost endless parade of reports and other studies issuing from various parliamentary committees, the Auditor General of Canada, university research centres and other reputable organizations with an interest in Canadian defence. While most commentators welcomed the intent of the proposed defence increases, however, few, if any, were confident that the promised funding would be sufficient to remedy the deficiencies of the present, let alone cover the requirements of the new DPS. Few were confident, either, that the Martin Liberals would still be in office to honour their financial pledges when the real spending was scheduled to begin – that is, in the last two years of the budget forecast (Thorne 2005b, 828–30).

Nevertheless, the promised infusion of significant new monies, from DND's vantage point, was not only a welcome change, but also provided at least symbolic reinforcement for the vision of a more muscular Canada taking on a more active leadership role in world affairs. This was a helpful encouragement to the change process inside both the DND and the CF, and in the longer term it could lead to a significant enhancement of Canada's capacity to "make a difference" overseas.

The central question, however, was whether the new trend-line would continue under the next government. When the "new" Conservatives were elected to office early in 2006, the initial answer appeared to be, "Yes." During the election campaign, Stephen Harper exploited the opportunity provided by an alleged Liberal error in airing media advertisements which cast aspersions on the military to vigorously defend the Canadian Forces. To the surprise of many, moreover, he whole-heartedly embraced the Liberals' increasingly controversial mission in Afghanistan, with all the political and financial baggage that it was threatening to attract. Later, in its first budget, the new government promised to top up the Liberal defence allocation by an additional C$5.3 billion during the same five-year period. By the budgetary test, therefore, defence truly seemed to be ascendant.[9]

While many of the foregoing observations are necessarily speculative, the underlying conclusion seems clear enough: defence expenditures have increased quite substantially since 2004, but this has been a reflection more of the political assessments – in both the domestic and international contexts – of the civilian leadership than of influences autonomously generated by the DND or the CF. Latterly they have also been stimulated by imperatives emanating from combat experiences in the Afghan theatre – imperatives that in the end may actually divert resources away from the longer-term development strategies of both the department and the military leadership. If the Afghanistan initiative begins to display quagmire characteristics, there is even a strong possibility that it will backfire in the domestic political environment, thereby rendering current military aspirations politically unrealistic. Once again, political forces and the political process, not the military establishment, emerge as the final arbiters of "policy".

One other observation is required here. It is clearly the case that the DND/CF budget, by Canadian standards, is very substantial in absolute terms, and it outweighs by far the budgets of other departments pertinent to the present discussion. But care has to be taken in concluding that this reflects a correspondingly pre-eminent DND influence inside the government apparatus. The reality is that the minister of national defence – except, perhaps, under wartime conditions of the "world war" variety – is not normally regarded as one of the more important members of cabinet. The size of the defence budget is a reflection of something else, which is the fact that some of the tools in the foreign policy toolbox are inherently more expensive than others. Programme agencies (like CIDA) often require more money to do their job than regulatory, administrative or representational departments like DFAIT, for example, or even more obviously the so-called "central agencies" (e.g., the PCO, the Department of Finance, and the Treasury Board). But no one would argue that CIDA has more influence in Ottawa than Finance. If major budget increases are granted to DND, therefore, this does not necessarily mean that greater influence over policy decisions will follow. It can certainly mean that more options will then be open to the government abroad. Somewhat paradoxically, it may also make it harder for the CF to exercise the veto option discussed earlier. The main point, however, is that the correlation between size of budget and departmental influence is uneven and heavily dependent on exogenous circumstances and the political pressures that they generate. Even where there *is* a connection, moreover, the flow of causation may be more a matter of "having the influence and therefore getting the money" than of "having the money and therefore getting the influence."

III. POLICY IMPLEMENTATION

The clearest and most dramatic evidence that we have on the role of the CF relatively to other players at the level of policy implementation is provided by the experience in Afghanistan, but more circumstantial indicators can also be found within the DND itself.

In the case of Afghanistan, it is certainly true that the armed forces are carrying the lion's share of the load, and the deployment in the field of personnel from other agencies (DFAIT, CIDA, RCMP, Justice and the like) is minuscule by comparison. In large measure, however, this circumstance is a function of realities *in situ*, especially given the instabilities typical of the particular zone of operation (Kandahar) to which the bulk of Canadian forces have been assigned, and given also the immediate operational objective (which is to defeat the "Taliban" and their diversely composed cohorts). The premises of the operation itself, which originate with NATO but ultimately reflect the post-9/11 preoccupations of the United States, can be debated, but whatever their merits, the fact that the operation entails combat activity is indisputable, and combat is a function that only the CF can perform.

Also relevant in this context is the apparent failure of both the DND at home and the CF in the field to control the behaviour of CIDA, which has focussed primarily on developing governance capacity in Kabul while leaving the CF-led Provincial Reconstruction Team (PRT) to fend largely for itself on the front line in Kandahar. The need to improve the calibre of Afghan public administration is hardly open to challenge, and there is certainly a case for giving it a high priority. It is not, however, the only priority, and it is certainly not the one that military personnel in the field would choose. Recently there have been attempts to resolve the problem, in effect, by going around CIDA and allocating more reconstruction funds directly to the military for its own use in Kandahar itself. The Agency has certainly complied with the insistence of both the Martin and Harper governments that it give Afghanistan pride of place in its funding allocations, but it appears to have been remarkably successful – albeit at the price of attracting some criticism – in ensuring that neither the DND nor the CF would determine how it would execute its responsibilities in the Afghan theatre.

At home, critical commentary from organizations like the Polaris Institute would argue that DND/CF attempts to enhance the "interoperability" of the Canadian Forces with those of the United States are further indicators of military ascendancy. As indicated earlier, however, the operational advantages of interoperability arrangements have given them a very long history in Canadian defence policy, and recent drives to take them further have clearly resulted not so much from new-found influence in the CF and the DND as from requirements defined by new developments in military technology on the one hand, and the experience of joint operations in "coalitions of the willing" on the other. These are perceived to be largely technical matters, affecting the selection of communications equipment and the like, rather than "policy" issues in the larger sense.

A much more revealing indicator of the real locus of power and influence is provided by the already-mentioned decision of the Martin government not to participate in BMD, which ran directly contrary to DND/CF preferences, and was a manifestation instead of pressures emanating from the Liberal Party caucus and from the domestic constituencies to which its members were particularly sensitive.

Yet another "policy implementation" test of DND/CF influence can be found within the DND itself, as represented by the fate of the so-called "Canada First" Defence Strategy. We lack the space to explore this matter in detail here. Suffice it to say that, while the Conservatives were prepared to live with much of the 2005 Liberal defence plan while in Opposition, they campaigned on a defence policy described as "Canada First." Guided by the "national interest," it would entail a re-ordering of CF roles and missions to place the primary emphasis on "sovereignty protection, domestic defence, and North American shared defence." Only secondarily would a Conservative government "also support international peace and security missions as well as humanitarian assistance." In concrete terms, the Conservatives would increase the size of the CF to at least 75,000, and would initiate simultaneous increases in the Reserves. There would be an immediate injection of "significant funds" into the DND budget to address capital, personnel, operating and maintenance shortfalls, and to implement their policy, "annual increases" would "follow throughout [their] mandate" (Conservative Party of Canada 2005a, 40–1).

As their campaign platform evolved, further details were added. A Conservative government would recruit 13,000 additional regular forces personnel and 10,000 additional reservists. CF spending would increase by C$5.3 billion over five years beyond currently projected levels of funding. The CF's capacity "to protect Canada's Arctic sovereignty and security" would also be increased and a regular army presence would be established in British Columbia. The former would involve among other things the construction of three armed, naval, heavy icebreakers capable of carrying troops, a military/civilian deep water docking facility at Iqaluit, and sundry new training, surveillance and search and rescue facilities and establishments in the far north, along with new strategic and tactical airlift, and new territorial defence battalions to be stationed in or near several major urban centres across Canada (Conservative Party of Canada 2006, 45; 2005b; 2005c).

While the merits of these proposals could be, and were, debated, it was clear that Harper and the Conservatives intended to give far greater emphasis to the "home game" in contrast to the Liberals' preference for missions overseas – the "away game." The prime minister indicated, moreover, that the increased funding required for these measures would be "allocated within a new, detailed 'Canada First' defence strategy to ensure our national security" (Conservative Party of Canada, 2005c).

Once in office, however, the Conservatives were apparently faced with strong opposition from General Hillier, whose transformation priorities, with their emphasis on expeditionary capabilities, were quite different from the "Canada First" orientation of the prime minister and the new Minister of National Defence Gordon O'Connor (himself a former army general with an imposing personal demeanour). Confronted with Hillier's personal vision for Canadian defence, the realities of minority government, and the all-consuming priority of the Afghanistan mission, O'Connor soon found that his promise of an early completion of the "Canada First" Defence Strategy, initially "by the end of the summer" of 2006 (Canada 2006, 22–4), would have to be broken. The deadline was eventually moved back to Christmas (Akin 2006). By the spring of 2007, it had been subsumed even more vaguely under the phrase, "in the coming months" (Canada 2007, 15). At the time of writing (June 2007), it seems to have become an object of indefinite delay.

As this cursory account suggests, the underlying causes of the diversion of the DND's attention have been primarily circumstantial, but they have been compounded by a contest of wills within the DND/CF leadership that the prime minister himself has not seen fit to resolve. A resolution of the internal disagreement has been impeded as well by the usual inter-service rivalries, with the Navy being especially unnerved by what it perceives as an Army-centric concept of defence transformation, and the Air Force not being very happy with the high priority assigned to airlift (e.g., to transport, as opposed to aerial combat) capacity. In these circumstances, both services are inclined to assume a posture of "wait and see" rather than play a constructive role in facilitating a settlement that might work substantively to their disadvantage.

It is important here to take special notice of the impact of these various internal divisions on the defence establishment's overall position. It is speaking with several voices, not one, and given that the available resources, at whatever level, are bound to be finite, some of these voices are not only different, but incompatible. There is not even agreement at the top – that is, between the minister of national defence on the one hand, and the CDS on the other. Meanwhile, the perception in many quarters is that the prime minister has effectively "ticked the box" on the defence file, and has shifted his attention elsewhere. One of the consequences is that the minister of national defence is left unsupported in the contest. Another may turn out to be that the funds that would be necessary to implement the "Canada First" strategy will never materialize at all.[10] In any case, whatever the "reality" described by the foregoing observations, it hardly accords with the ascendancy model. Life in the real world of government is far more complicated.

We now turn finally, but more briefly, to the parts played respectively by circumstance and by political leaders in limiting the influence of the defence bureaucracies – civilian and uniformed alike.

IV. CIRCUMSTANCE AS A POLICY DETERMINANT

Treated in detail, the interplay between those in public affairs who make policy decisions on the one hand, and the exogenous circumstances they have to take into account in doing so on the other, is an extraordinarily complex subject, and its intricacies cannot be explored here. Even if the problem is considered in more cursory style, however, it should be obvious from the discussion thus far that circumstances in the domestic and international environments have had a major steering effect on many of Ottawa's most important decisions recently in the defence field, and that they have frustrated the ambitions of at least some of the key players within the supposedly "ascendant" defence establishment. Under the Martin government, the IPS document itself was the product partly of the perception that the concerns of informed observers at home over the decline of the armed forces had reached the point at which further neglect might have negative political consequences, and partly of an assessment of the hazards being generated abroad by conditions in so-called "failed and failing states." The popular alienation resulting from the latter could be exploited – and clearly *was* being exploited – by transnationally-organized "terrorist" organizations that had malevolent purposes in mind. Had the evidence actually pointed to the arrival of a more benign world, then a more complacent evaluation – and a more relaxed policy – would have ensued irrespective of what the most influential players in the DND and the CF might have preferred.

More particularly, the involvement in Afghanistan was driven by the encouragement of the UN, the active engagement of NATO, and the desire of the political leadership to mend broken fences with the Americans. As it turned out, there was vigorous military (and para-military) resistance in some parts of the theatre – Kandahar notably among them – and this dictated an increasingly robust military response. The wisdom of that response is open to debate, but there can be little doubt that, if conditions in the theatre had been more receptive to what was intended as an externally-guided modernization enterprise, the military involvement would have been conducted on a smaller scale and with much less emphasis on active combat. There might then also have been an even greater focus on the non-military elements of the intervention as a whole. What made the combat activity seem so essential was that the intervening foreigners – well-intentioned though they might be – were under military attack.

It is, of course, true that the CF senior command "chose" in this instance not to exercise its latent veto power, but rather to advocate an escalation in Canada's involvement. The CDS in particular seems to have regarded the prospect of a robust engagement as an opportunity for building support for an expansion of Canada's expeditionary force capabilities. But his position was not universally supported within the CF. Once the expanded Canadian contingent began operations in the theatre, moreover, the circumstances that ensued soon developed a momentum of their own. Politically, as the inimitable argot of DND headquarters now has it, the Afghanistan enterprise became a "no-fail mission" (confidential interviews). It gobbled up resources, and in so doing threatened other options – some of the more expensive elements of the Harper government's Canada First strategy almost certainly among them. [The Treasury Board, as the rueful denizens of DND headquarters like to put it, is now reduced in this connection to saying simply, "Show us the money" (confidential interviews).] Thus, in this area of public policy as in others, it is often easier for governments to get things going than to see them through. Unforeseen circumstances have an inconvenient habit of getting in the way.

Much the same might be said of the decision earlier on BMD. This is a particularly interesting example because the DND and CF were strongly supportive of a modest Canadian participation in the programme, and they had reason to believe that Prime Minister Martin himself had concluded that co-operating with the Americans at a low-cost level would be in the national interest, particularly given the importance of the Canada-US relationship overall, the need to moderate some of the tensions that had built up under the previous Liberal government, and the fact that the United States would obviously proceed with the programme whether Canada signified its support or not. In the event, the defence establishment was stunned when the prime minister actually moved in precisely the opposite direction – presumably in response to political opposition not only in the country at large (and not least of all in Quebec), but also in his own caucus, and particularly among Liberal MP's from both Quebec and Ontario.

The point here is not to suggest that the government's defence decisions were entirely "determined" by exogenous factors, or that circumstances were such as to deprive it of any genuine capacity to choose. Choices were clearly made. But they were made in the light of evolving conditions at home and abroad, and were profoundly affected by them. In the weighing of the various considerations that had to be taken into account, it could hardly be said that the DND was always the winner or that the CF were routinely the victors – much less that they had actually driven the pertinent policy decisions.

V. POLITICAL LEADERS AND "LAST-SAY" DECISION-MAKING

This observation leads to a few short comments on the last of our five indicators. In fact, the most powerful argument in opposition to the "DND/CF ascendancy" thesis rests on the obvious point that the most important policy decisions on these matters have not, in practice, been made by the department bureaucracy or the armed forces at all. They have been made instead by political leaders, Liberal and Conservative alike, who in the process have taken their own preferences, along with certain practical political calculations (both national and international), carefully into account.

There is, of course, a lengthy literature exploring the interactions between political leaderships and their permanent public service advisers in the context of British-style parliamentary government. More than one erstwhile cabinet minister has testified to the difficulty of overriding the determined opposition of highly experienced and technically well-informed senior civil servants, except in cases where political imperatives are clearly on the minister's side. In the late-1960s and early-1970s, such concerns animated much of the management style of the Trudeau government, and Conservative prime ministers have routinely – if not always fairly – suspected the Canadian public service of harbouring anti-Conservative loyalties and inclinations. The renowned British television series entitled *Yes, Minister* found a rich mine of comic inspiration in the tension between the amateurs who occupy ministerial office and their professional public service advisers. And there can be no doubt that on matters of detail, and on many other matters, too, the political leadership must rely heavily on the advice it collectively receives from the senior civil service.

But in the case of defence policy, there are factors at work that ensure that the political leadership's performance as the "last say" decision-maker on matters of general policy is not merely cosmetic, but real. Three of these stand out.

The first is the size of the defence budget, which makes it a matter of great interest to all members of cabinet who have other programme proposals that they think are well worth funding. In the final analysis, the government's defence policy is defined by its defence budget, and particularly in a country whose security challenges often seem both in-direct and far-removed, it will be jealously watched by all those – inside government and out – who have other ideas for spending money.

Secondly, there is a sense in which defence policy is a matter of polit-ical judgment that most moderately well-briefed lay people can com-prehend. Complex technical issues can certainly be involved, and there are cultural and other "human resource" issues that can befuddle those who are unfamiliar with the military world. But most of these consider-ations play themselves out at lower levels. For the most part, the larger policy issues are reasonably accessible to amateurs (again, both inside government and out), and in consequence they are less easily subordi-nated to the power represented by professional public service expertise.

Thirdly, the use of the military instrument invariably raises issues of principle whose resolution no responsible leadership in a liberal demo-cratic society can delegate to others. In combat situations, it involves the destruction of life, limb and property. Under many non-combat as well as combat circumstances, it can require as well the deliberate plac-ing of young, healthy and dedicated citizens in harm's way as a matter of carefully calculated "public policy." These are not decisions that can be taken lightly, even if the uniformed personnel involved are volun-teers, and even if they and their senior commanders are "willing" to the point of being "gung-ho." Ministers are therefore expected to give them close attention, and they do.

In sum, deputies and commanders advise, but cabinets and prime ministers decide. The latter, moreover, are inclined to change their advisers if they are unhappy with the advice they receive, searching as they do (and as in the case of the Hillier appointment) for persons of like, or at least compatible, mind. In the case of the Harper govern-ment, moreover, the dominant position of the political executive has been reinforced by the prime minister's determination to keep central-ized political control over the entire government agenda. Even during the Chrétien government some analysts were beginning to argue, in effect, that far from the bureaucracy imprisoning the politicians, the bureaucratic professionals were themselves being overwhelmed by amateur and often untutored politicians and their aides in the PMO (Savoie 1999). Under the Conservatives, however, this process appears to have been taken to new levels, arousing frequently critical commentary in the press.[11]

Those who argue the case for the ascendancy of the defence establishment would doubtless be tempted to counter this interpretation with evidence in particular that General Hillier single-handedly convinced the Martin government at a meeting on 21 March 2005 to expand the forthcoming deployment of the 250-person PRT in Kandahar to include a battle group composed of roughly 1,000 troops. In this discussion, it is true, the CDS had to overcome opposition, but he also had bureaucratic support from Foreign Affairs, and he is reputed to have "won the room by appealing to the Martin government's desire to be a global player, especially where it could assist the US war on terror" (Staples 2006, 5). His recommendations – even if they were rooted partly in his own agenda – were thus in line with the prime minister's preferences, and presumably with his expectations at the time he authorized the Hillier appointment as CDS in the first place.

CONCLUSION

A close analysis of the DND/CF ascendancy thesis shows that it neglects the complexity of the factors that really impinge on defence policy decision-making, and that the most important decision-makers are really the ones in the political leadership. In the defence context, therefore, the principle of responsible government should be regarded as a working reality. If critics dislike what the government is doing in the politico-security field abroad, they should hold the prime minister and the cabinet to account, rather than assuming that policy is somehow under the nefarious control of the DND or the armed forces.

NOTES

1 It should be noted, in any case, that the power of bureaucracies in Ottawa, like the power of states in the international community, is always relative. Even if it were to be established that the DND had somehow become "ascendant" in certain foreign policy issue areas, this might be a reflection more of the relative decline in the influence of DFAIT and CIDA – as the Auditor-General and others have recently suggested – than of an absolute increase in the power of the DND

itself. Such slippery realities make it easy to assert, but hard to prove, who is "up" and who is "down," and harder still to know why.

2 Some Canadians may think Canada does not engage in propaganda activity. If so, their assumption is probably based on the view that propaganda is deceitful, and Canada does not degrade itself (in peacetime, at least) by performing wilful acts of deceit. Deception in such matters, however, is akin to beauty residing most often in the eye (or the ear) of the beholder. From the purely analytical point of view, in any case, propaganda is defined by its purpose and auspices, and not by the veracity or otherwise of the messages and images of which it is composed. If the government subsidizes the National Ballet to enable an overseas tour, it has "image-building" objectives in mind. No insult is intended by the thought that in such a case the ballet company is performing a propaganda function and has been mobilized as an instrument of foreign policy. Those who are not persuaded by this example, however, might prefer to think instead of the International Service of the CBC.

3 The most committed supporters of overseas development assistance programming, including those who manage the CIDA often resist the notion that development assistance should be guided by foreign policy purposes, believing that it inevitably weakens the performance of the developmental function in favour of diplomatic objectives. Hence the recurrent turf wars between CIDA and other government agencies, DFAIT and DND included. But it is hard to deny that most Canadian development assistance programmes perform politico-diplomatic as well as developmental purposes.

4 This thesis has been advanced in a wide variety of quarters, and perhaps most vigorously by those who have been dismayed by the erosion of Canada's military capabilities. The issue was posed with particular clarity five years ago in another volume in the Canada Among Nations series (Hillmer and Molot 2002). Among many others, see also Cohen (2003), Rempel (2006) and Granatstein (2007).

5 The concept was sometimes expanded to include trade policy (labelled as "Commerce" in the IPS). Hence the occasionally deployed acronym, "3D+T."

6 Under Paul Martin's government (2003–06), the Department of Foreign Affairs and International Trade was divided into two departments, Foreign Affairs Canada (FAC) and International Trade Canada (ITC). Each of the two drafted a separate chapter for the IPS.

7 If anything, the linkage in recent years has gone entirely the other way. The most enthusiastic supporters of intensified continental defence integration have included observers who are mainly preoccupied with preserving reasonably free access for Canadian business to American markets. From that vantage point, intensified defence cooperation is one mechanism for responding to American security concerns, and thereby keeping the border open to Canada-US trade while minimizing the transactions costs that have to be absorbed by transborder traffic. Commercial policy is here driving (or attempting to drive) defence policy, rather than the other way round.

8 The Agency's capacity for evasion and obstruction in response to unwanted directives of this sort has proven over the years to be considerable, however, and the practice has earned it a certain notoriety both within the government and among outside observers.

9 This impression was reinforced by a spate of new equipment announcements – totalling some C$17.1 billion – in mid-2006 (Day 2006).

10 According to leaked accounts, the steadily rising defence funding curve DND was expecting is now projected to be considerably "flattened" over an extended number of years. If this proves to be true, then DND will have to defer some of its near-term procurement and personnel expansion initiatives and also reduce annual CF operations to some extent. General Hillier has already acknowledged that he has had "to take a bit of an appetite suppressant" with respect to some of his transformation projects (Pugliese 2007; confidential interviews). The "defence ascendant" thesis is not supported, either, by the "bare-bones" 2007 defence budget.

11 This is not a peculiarly Canadian phenomenon. It is evident most alarmingly in the United States – where it is systemically encouraged by the structure of government – but it has also surfaced in the United Kingdom and elsewhere. In foreign policy, it has been buttressed in many countries – Canada included – by the growth of "summit" diplomacy.

REFERENCES

Akin, David. 2006. "Feds earmark billions for military equipment." *CTV.ca*, 24 November.

Blanchfield, Mike. 2004. "Infighting stalls foreign-policy review." *Montreal Gazette*, 29 December.

Campion-Smith, Bruce. 2005a. "Top general plots bold new mission: Hillier envisions nimble task forces Vision for helping failing states." *Toronto Star*, 14 February: A06.

– 2005b. "More money helps overcome 'demotion.'" *Toronto Star*, 19 March: F01.

Canada. 2003. *Proceedings*. No. 15, 28 April. Standing Senate Committee on National Security and Defence.

– 2005a. *Canada's International Policy Statement: A Role of Pride and Influence in the World – Overview*. Ottawa: Department of Foreign Affairs and International Trade.

– 2005b. *Canada's International Policy Statement: A Role of Pride and Influence in the World – Defence*. Ottawa: Department of National Defence.

– 2006. *Proceedings*. No. 1, 8 May. Standing Senate Committee on National Security and Defence, 22–4.

– 2007. *Report on Plans and Priorities 2007–2008*. Ottawa: Department of National Defence.

Cohen, Andrew. 2003. *While Canada Slept: How We Lost Our Place in the World*. Toronto: McClelland & Stewart.

Conservative Party of Canada. 2005a. *Policy Declaration*. 19 March.

– 2005b. *Harper Stands Up for Arctic Sovereignty*, 22 December.

– 2005c. *Harper Calls for Boost to Canadian Forces*, 13 December.

– 2006. *Federal Election Platform 2006*.

Day, Adam. 2006. "Purchases Welcomed By The Military." *Legion Magazine*, September/October.

Eayrs, James. 1961. *The Art of the Possible: Government and Foreign Policy in Canada*. Toronto: University of Toronto Press.

Foulkes, General Charles. 1966. "The Complications of Continental Defence." In *Neighbors Taken for Granted: Canada and the United States*, edited by Livingston T. Merchant. Toronto: Burns and MacEachern.

Granatstein, J.L. 2007. *Whose War Is It? How Canada Can Survive in the Post-9/11 World*. Toronto: HarperCollins.

Hillmer, Norman, and Maureen Appel Molot, eds. 2002. *Canada Among Nations 2002: A Fading Power*. Don Mills, ON: Oxford University Press Canada.

Middlemiss, Danford W., and Denis Stairs. 2002. "The Canadian Forces and the Doctrine of Interoperability: The Issues." *Policy Matters* 3, no. 7 (June).

Minifie, James M. 1960. *Peacemaker or Powder-Monkey: Canada's Role in a Revolutionary World*. Toronto: McClelland & Stewart.

– 1964. *Open at the Top: Reflections on US-Canada Relations*. Toronto: McClelland & Stewart.

Pugliese, David. 2007. "Military shelves plans for expansion." *Ottawa Citizen*, 7 March.

Regehr, Ernie, and Peter Whelan. 2004. *Reshaping the Security Envelope: Defence Policy in a Human Security Context*. Waterloo, ON: Project Ploughshares.

Rempel, Roy. 2006. *Dreamland: How Canada's Pretend Foreign Policy Has Undermined Sovereignty*. Montreal and Kingston: McGill-Queen's University Press.

Robinson, H. Basil. 1989. *Diefenbaker's World: A Populist in Foreign Affairs*. Toronto: University of Toronto Press.

Savoie, Donald J. 1999. *Governing from the Centre: The Concentration of Power in Canadian Politics*. Toronto: University of Toronto Press.

Staples, Steven. 2006. *Marching Orders: How Canada abandoned peacekeeping – and why the UN needs us now more than ever*. Ottawa: The Council of Canadians.

– and Bill Robinson. 2005. *It's Never Enough: Canada's Alarming Rise in Military Spending*. Ottawa: The Polaris Institute.

Thorne, Stephen. 2005a. "Defence minister rejects review as 'dreadful dreck': Graham seeks bolder vision for Canadian military." *Winnipeg Free Press*, 12 February.

– 2005b. "Rick Hillier." *International Journal* 60, no. 3 (Summer): 824–30.

5 CIDA under the Gun

STEPHEN BROWN

CIDA IN THE NEW MILLENNIUM

The new millennium brought significant changes to the Canadian International Development Agency (CIDA). After almost a decade of decline, Canadian Official Development Assistance (ODA) rapidly rose from C$2.6 billion in 2000–01 to C$4.1 billion in 2004–05 (Canada 2006b, 1).[1] This dramatic budget increase, not seen since the early 1980s, provided CIDA with the financial means to improve not only quantitatively but qualitatively. In parallel, the government began revising its aid policies and changing its priorities and delivery modalities (Canada 2002; 2005a). Successive prime ministers each brought a new direction to foreign aid, usually building on his predecessor's achievements: Jean Chrétien reversed the decline in aid flows and designated Africa a priority; Paul Martin integrated aid more tightly with other foreign policy "instruments" (in what is known as the "whole-of-government" approach) and took steps to focus on a smaller number of countries and sectors; Stephen Harper sought to concentrate and integrate even further, focusing resources and innovative approaches on Afghanistan. In response to these changes, a number of researchers questioned CIDA's policy autonomy vis-à-vis other donors (Campbell and Hatcher 2004) and reacted critically to Canadian aid policy (Black and Tiessen 2007; Brown 2005; 2007a; Cameron 2007; Goldfarb and Tapp 2006; Stairs 2005).

This chapter examines how recent trends have affected CIDA in the context of changing motivations for foreign aid, greater integration of

Canadian foreign policy instruments and new pressures on the agency from other Canadian actors. It finds that increasing budgets and inter-departmental coordination have created a sort of paradox: as resources increase and the agency gains importance, CIDA's margin to manoeuvre is decreasing. Greater policy integration and the increased politicization of aid have reduced CIDA's autonomy and capacity to fight poverty and actually promote development. This could be because as CIDA's budget grows, it wields resources that are more attractive for "capture" by parties more interested in Canada's own security, diplomatic or commercial interests than in development assistance that actually focuses on poverty reduction. Alternatively, this may be explained by that fact that CIDA's policy subordination makes the government more willing to channel resources through the agency in order to achieve non-development-related foreign policy interests. If successful from the point of view of Canadian interests, increased politicization of aid could further increase CIDA's importance and reduce its autonomy. If current initiatives fail, CIDA could see itself marginalized from the rest of government, regaining autonomy but enjoying more modest financial resources.

THE BATTLE OVER AID MOTIVATION

The battle over the purpose of ODA lies at the heart of the current changes affecting CIDA. To a large extent, it is not new: the rationale for foreign aid has been hotly debated since its inception. On one hand, foreign aid can be conceptualized as a self-interested tool, designed to further donors' own political, commercial and security interests. "Realists" have long advocated such an approach. For instance, Hans Morgenthau (1962, 309) considered foreign aid an additional "weapon in the political armory of the nation." On the other hand, many "liberals" see aid as an expression of international solidarity and believe it should be provided out of ethical concern and compassion – for instance, David Halloren Lumsdain (1993) and Roger Riddell (1996). Cranford Pratt (2000) characterizes these two motivations as "international realism" and "humane internationalism" respectively. The two are however not always in opposition to one another. They can align, for instance, when Canada has an interest in presenting itself as a generous provider of ODA, be it at the United Nations, to developing countries or among its donor peers.

Since the inception of Canada's aid program, the two rationales have coexisted uneasily. In the words of a 1987 parliamentary report, Canadian ODA has been "beset with confusion of purpose" (Canada 1987, 7). While Canada's first foray into foreign aid in 1950 was designed to prevent the expansion of Soviet influence in South Asia, the Canadian government supplemented concerns over Western security with a desire, at least at the rhetorical level, to help the poor and promote social justice. Canada has thus simultaneously pursued a "trinity of motives" that combined development goals with Canadian foreign policy and commercial ones (Morrison 1998, 12–13).

The mix of the motivations has changed over time. In 2000, Cranford Pratt found that, over a 25-year period, government policy documents increasingly emphasized self-interest, at the expense of ethics and compassion (Pratt 2000). Following the events of 11 September 2001, the trend was accelerated, notably in Paul Martin's government's *International Policy Statement* (IPS) (Brown 2005, 2007a), much to the distress of Canadian non-governmental organizations (NGOS) that work in the field of development and other "humane internationalists." The tying of aid to the purchase of goods and services from the donor country is one indicator of donor self-interest. By this measure, Canada is the second most selfish donor of the 22 donor countries that belong to the Organisation for Economic Co-operation and Development. Though the proportion has decreased in recent years, in line with government commitments (Canada 2002, 21–22), Canada still tied over 40 per cent of its aid in 2005, compared to an average of less than 7 per cent (OECD 2007, Table 23).[2]

It is within this context that CIDA finds itself in the middle of a tug-of-war that is closely related to motivations. This is not just a theoretical debate, since motivations help determine the choice of recipients and the size of their programs. Humane internationalism suggests a focus on poverty reduction and the poorest countries, as well as disaster relief; commercial interests favour focusing aid on important trade and investment partners, which tend to be middle-income countries; while security interests advocate concentrating resources on strategically important partners, for instance in the "global war on terror." This struggle has the potential of radically affecting CIDA's future and is closely related to the question of policy integration and the relationship among government departments.

POLICY INTEGRATION AND INTER-DEPARTMENTAL STRUGGLES

CIDA began as an office with the then Department of External Affairs. Since it became a separate entity in 1968, it has maintained an often tense relationship with what is now called the Department of Foreign Affairs and International Trade (DFAIT). According to one close observer of CIDA, "every effort to enhance CIDA's autonomy ...

provoked a strong reaction, aimed at putting the Agency under the thumb of External/Foreign Affairs and harnessing aid more fully to commercial and foreign policy priorities" (Morrison 1998, 401). In the 1990s, there was even discussion of an attempted DFAIT "takeover bid of CIDA" (Pratt 1998).

Conflict over "turf" is not unusual between departments, but CIDA's relationship with DFAIT is not limited to bureaucratic squabbles. The two bodies have a fundamentally different philosophical approach to foreign aid. According to the CIDA website, "the purpose of Canada's Official Development Assistance is to support sustainable development in developing countries" (Canada 2007f), suggesting an altruistic approach, while DFAIT concentrates on the self-interested objective of "advanc[ing] Canada's national interests" and "achiev[ing] increased economic opportunity and enhanced security for Canada and for Canadians" (Canada 2007g). They converge only when Canadian interests are interpreted to include a robust development assistance program.[3]

In recent years, the government has increasingly emphasized the policy integration of the various departments involved in the international arena. This was initially presented as the "3D approach" (referring to diplomacy, defence and development) and then "3D+T" (when trade was added). This morphed into the "whole-of-government" approach, which was at the centre of the 2005 *International Policy Statement*. The IPS assigned DFAIT the lead role in coordinating integrated strategies (Canada 2005b, 30), as well as additional responsibilities for intervening in "failed and fragile states" (creating a Stabilization and Reconstruction Task Force) and stabilizing and rebuilding countries in crisis (managing a Global Peace and Security Fund), thus strengthening DFAIT's primacy in international policy and potentially expanding DFAIT's responsibilities into what was considered CIDA's bailiwick.

Policy integration is a method to achieve objectives, rather than an objective in and of itself. The whole-of-government approach can be used as a "fig leaf" to justify a particular policy and hide the actual goals themselves. It can also refer to a range of forms of inter-departmental cooperation, from information sharing and coordination to full hierarchical integration (Canadian Council for International Co-operation 2006, 1–2). In the past, according to one analyst, "CIDA has never had significant influence on the trade or other foreign policies of the Canadian government" and "[t]he pursuit of development objectives by CIDA has been tempered from the start by commercial and international political considerations" (Pratt 1999, 83). CIDA's closer collaboration with the government's other international policy actors, mainly DFAIT and the Department of National Defence (DND), carries the strong risk that development objectives will be subordinated to security and commercial interests, rather than the other way around (Brown 2007a).

Though the Martin government's *International Policy Statement* included a chapter on development, Stephen Harper's Conservative government has provided very little policy direction of its own on foreign aid. Initially, CIDA retained the development contents of the IPS, merely rebaptizing it the Agency Transformation Initiative. However, within a year, the initiative was quietly dropped. With a low-profile minister (Josée Verner, who had no international development experience before becoming minister of international cooperation) and a decision-making process highly centralized in the Prime Minister's Office, CIDA does not seem to play much role in setting priorities. The case of Afghanistan provides a key illustration.

IS AFGHANISTAN THE NEW AFRICA?

While in office, Liberal Prime Ministers Jean Chrétien and Paul Martin advocated increasing Canada's foreign aid focus on Africa, most prominently at successive G8 summits. Indeed, Canada was part of – and had helped shape – a consensus among donors that priority should be placed on Sub-Saharan Africa, including a shared commitment to doubling aid to the continent between 2003–04 and 2008–09 (Canada 2005a, 7, 23). In contrast, Africa was seen as a Liberal issue by the incoming Conservative government and placed on the backburner (see Brown 2008). Under Prime Minister Harper, the government's attention appears to limit itself to only one country (other than the United States): Afghanistan. Foreign Minster Peter MacKay (2007a) has called the Afghanistan mission "the number-one priority for the Government of Canada in its foreign policy."

The prime minister repeatedly announces new funds for development assistance to that country, but not all such announcements constitute new funding. In other words, CIDA's budget is not always increased by a corresponding amount. At times, CIDA has to cut aid to other countries, such as Bangladesh, to be able to meet the commitments made by the prime minister. In total, CIDA has spent about C$600 million on Afghanistan since the Taliban were overthrown in 2001, a figure that is expected to reach almost C$1 billion dollars by 2011 (Canada 2007d).

Though Afghanistan is not among the 25 countries identified as Canada's priority "Development Partners," it has become the top recipient of Canadian ODA. As of March 2007, CIDA's Afghanistan Task Force is headed by a vice-president, the first time such a senior manager has been put in charge of a country desk. This kind of emphasis placed on a single country is unprecedented in CIDA's history. Many officials consider the resources being allocated to Afghanistan and the close cooperation with DFAIT and especially with DND and Canadian Forces on the ground to be an experiment or laboratory for a new form of policy integration. If successful, it could potentially be replicated elsewhere, with Haiti being a prime candidate (see Canada 2006a).

The inter-departmental partnership in Afghanistan has, however, not been an easy one. Though Prime Minister Harper gave Associate Deputy Minister David Mulroney and DFAIT the role of coordinating Canadian activities in Afghanistan in January 2007, DND remained the most active Canadian player, led by Chief of Defence Staff Gen. Rick Hillier. The difficulties of carrying out development activities where fighting is still occurring coupled with a slow-moving bureaucracy have meant that CIDA has not been able to spend quickly the funds earmarked for Afghanistan in its own development projects. Large sums have been turned over to multilateral donors, such as the World Bank, various United Nations agencies and the Asian Development Bank. The lack of public third-party reporting has made it more difficult to determine the impact of these contributions. This was widely reported in the media in 2006, after law professor Amir Attaran's access-to-information requests were met with government stonewalling. Since then, CIDA and the Canadian government more generally have placed a lot more emphasis on Canada's assistance to Afghanistan, publishing glossy brochures and building an important web presence, including on CIDA's homepage and through a dedicated website hosted by DFAIT, entitled "Protecting Canadians / Rebuilding Afghanistan" (www.canada-afghanistan.gc.ca).

Other parties are interested in taking advantage of CIDA's Afghanistan "pot of gold."[4] A recent Senate report complained that CIDA's work was not visible in Kandahar, the province where Canada is focusing its activities. As part of a strategy to "win hearts and minds" ("when our military is seen to be there to assist rather than conquer"), it recommended that "CIDA provide from its budget C$20 million directly to the Canadian Forces for their use in local development projects" in Kandahar, until security could be established (Canada 2007e, 9, 26). This was precisely the kind of securitization of aid that NGOs and other critics had been warning against. Using aid for military purposes, including as a reward for anti-Taliban collaboration, betrays the basic philosophy of development and the fundamental principle of neutrality of humanitarian assistance, potentially in breach of the Geneva Conventions and international humanitarian law. It also puts humanitarian workers' lives at risk by associating them with one side in the armed conflict, actually leading the NGO Médecins Sans Frontières/Doctors Without Borders to cease its operations in Afghanistan in 2004.[5]

CIDA's work in Afghanistan was criticized by other actors as well. In 2006, a retired Canadian military officer attributed the "failure" of the 3D approach in Kandahar province to insufficient contributions from

CIDA and DFAIT (Lehre 2006). In 2007, an international think tank reported that "Canada's development, aid and counter-narcotics strategies remain incoherent and limited in their capacity to impact positively on even the basic needs of Kandahar's people" and that these were "compromising the entire Canadian mission and the international community's primary objective [of] preventing the return of extremism to the region" (Senlis Council 2007, 8–9). It recommended a massive increase in development assistance to over C$1 billion per year (equivalent to more than a quarter of Canada's total ODA), as well as transferring CIDA's responsibilities to a special envoy in Kandahar mandated to "maximise Canada's development, diplomatic, military and civilian volunteer resources" (Senlis Council 2007, 16).

By mid-2007, it appeared that the whole-of-government approach had reached its limits in Afghanistan. Not only was CIDA under attack from various parties, notably Canadian military, for a lack of presence and results, especially in Kandahar province; the media also reported on squabbles between DND and DFAIT over the blame for the transfer of prisoners to Afghan authorities, who then gravely mistreated them – another possible breach of international law. Rather than policy integration increasing effectiveness, the main players were seen to have a dysfunctional, even conflictual relationship.

Why did CIDA decide to place such emphasis on Afghanistan? The country was not one of Canada's 25 priority "Development Partners" and many other countries had similarly high levels of poverty. Afghanistan did fall under the category of "failed and fragile states," which had been stressed in the IPS and could provide some degree of justification, but, again, many other countries with equal claim to the label were not selected. Furthermore, it is still not clear how much development work can be carried out in a war zone, though it is understood to cost more and be less effective, which contradicts the government's emphasis on aid effectiveness.

In fact, it was not CIDA that decided to concentrate on Afghanistan, but other government bodies, notably the Prime Minister's Office. The true reason depends closely on the association of Afghanistan with the Taliban and by extension with Osama bin Laden and al-Qaeda. Countless speeches by the prime minister and his cabinet colleagues evoke the tragedy of 9/11 and link Canadian security to the pacification and reconstruction of Afghanistan. A February 2007 joint DFAIT/DND/CIDA progress report to parliament concludes that "Canadians can be proud of the sacrifices and contributions made by our forces and personnel in Afghanistan in 2006. We are a country standing up for our interest, a country actively protecting our security" (Canada 2007c, 19). Along the same lines, the minister of foreign affairs has stated, "We are there to protect the security of Canada and Canadians" (echoing the banner on the dedicated Canada-Afghanistan website referenced earlier), adding a mention of "implications for a wide range of Canadian interests – not only our security interests, but also our trade and investment activities" (MacKay 2007b). Though the benefits for Afghans are constantly evoked as well, they are insufficient to explain why intervention has taken place in Afghanistan rather than, say, Darfur. Instead, the priority that Canada places on Afghanistan responds to a security agenda, rather than a development one, and one actually more closely and directly related to the United States' security than Canada's. In this case, CIDA's resource allocation process has been subordinated to this broader objective.

PRESSURE ON OTHER FRONTS

In 2007, CIDA came under pressure on two other fronts. First, a scathing Senate report on Canadian aid to Africa attacked CIDA as "ineffective, costly, and overly bureaucratic" and described Canadian development assistance as "slow, inflexible, and unresponsive to conditions on the ground in recipient countries" (Canada 2007h, XI). Though deeply flawed in its assumptions, methodology and argumentation (Brown 2007b), the report's harsh assessment of CIDA's work led it to propose two possible remedies. Because "Africa has to be a central focus of our foreign policy and our African policy must be made more robust" (Canada 2007h, 97), the report recommended radical decentralization and policy integration. It advocated creating an Africa Office that "would incorporate all international development, international trade and foreign affairs personnel dealing with the African continent and would consult closely with the Department of National Defence" and "[d]ecentralizing a minimum of 80 per cent of the staff within the new Africa Office and decision-making authority ... to Canadian missions in the field in Africa" (Canada 2007h, 98). The other remedy was to either give CIDA a clearly defined parliamentary mandate or, failing that, abolish the agency and transfer its staff and functions to DFAIT. The latter possibility was not developed in the report, but nonetheless attracted a disproportionate amount of media attention, further feeding CIDA's public relations problems.

At the same time, a private member's bill, introduced by Liberal John MacKay in May 2006, was making its way through parliament. The bill, known as C-293 or the Official Development Assistance Accountability Act, aimed "to ensure that all Canadian official development assistance abroad is provided with a central focus on poverty reduction and in a manner that is consistent with Canadian values,

Canadian foreign policy, sustainable development and democracy promotion and that promotes international human rights standards," according to the version passed by the House of Commons (Canada 2007a).[6] By focusing aid on altruistic poverty reduction above all else, Bill C-293 has the potential to re-establish a clear sense of direction and purpose at CIDA. It would also reverse the trend towards greater whole-of-government policy integration, which injects far more Canadian self-interest into CIDA's programming. For those reasons, it was opposed by the minority Conservative government, but enjoyed unanimous support from opposition parties in the House of Commons. If it becomes law, it could however have some unintended consequences, discussed further below.

ASSESSING THE RESULTS

From the point of view of the Canadian state, the whole-of-government approach and CIDA's subordination to Canadian self-interest could be a positive step forward. Indeed, from the "realist" perspective, it strengthens the government's capacity to meet its objectives abroad. The greater centralization of decision-making and the strengthening of "the Centre" (bodies such as the Prime Minister's Office and the Privy Council Office) also has the potential of increasing Canada's prestige abroad, especially among allies. In particular, the integrated focus on Afghanistan could help improve relations with the United States, demonstrating for instance that, though Canada is not present in Iraq, it can be counted on to contribute significantly on another important front in the so-called "global war on terror."

The value of these changes depends on the actual success of policy integration on the ground. Results to date in Afghanistan indicate that the whole-of-government approach might actually wind up irremediably discredited. It remains to be determined – and may be impossible to do so – whether the main problems are poor communication and coordination, insufficient contributions on the diplomacy and development sides, or unrealistic expectations – especially of development projects in the midst of an undeclared war. It could also be that, as suggested above, the whole-of-government might have been an appropriate approach, but that the use of force will prove to have been the wrong means. Moreover, if instead of contributing to the defeat of the Taliban and a weakening of al-Qaeda Canada's involvement in Afghanistan makes it a more likely target of terrorist attacks, it would have ostensibly decreased rather than increased Canadians' security and proved contrary to national self-interest (illustrating the difficulties on some occasions of determining actual self-interest).

The erosion of CIDA's autonomy, while increasing its prominence as a foreign policy actor, has negative repercussions from the "humane internationalist" point of view. While ODA has never been allocated solely on an altruistic basis, recent changes have reduced the emphasis on development itself, including poverty reduction and the principles behind the Millennium Development Goals. If Canada and other donors restrict their aid to countries where they have security or other interests at stake, many other countries in need – especially in Africa – risk becoming "aid orphans" and then potentially collapsing or becoming "failed states." It also contradicts the notion of a human rights–based approach to development, which focuses on the rights of recipients instead of the interests of the donor.

As CIDA's budget has increased, the agency's margin to manoeuvre has shrunk. Yet it is unclear which is the cause and which the effect. Has an increase in financial resources caused other government bodies to seek to harness them? Or has increased subordination at CIDA made government decision-makers more willing to channel extra money through CIDA? It is likely that the two are too intertwined to be extricated and that they are mutually reinforcing. Moreover, though it is hard to determine to what extent, a range of international influences also came into play. In particular, "peer pressure" from the European members of the G8, and donor countries more generally, has also contributed to the government's decision to increase foreign aid.

The concrete result of joining up development with diplomacy, defence and trade will be to lessen the impact of Canadian aid on development indicators in developing countries. At best, it will help end conflict and rebuild post-conflict societies, which are important activities. However, if those are Canada's goals, other means might actually prove to be less costly and more effective. For instance, foreign troops may never be sufficient to quell the fighting in Afghanistan (or Iraq). Other means, such as a negotiated settlement that would include all major parties, could be more efficient and effective. Having sent troops on the ground to defeat the Taliban – whom Gen. Hillier has called "detestable murderers and scumbags" (Leblanc 2005) – Canada is unlikely to support the option of negotiating peace with them.

Though the whole-of-government approach reduces the autonomy of all parties involved, it theoretically creates new opportunities. CIDA does not however appear to have gained any influence on other agencies. As CIDA loses control of its own agenda-setting, there are no indications that other government agencies are changing their priorities to accommodate CIDA's mission to "support sustainable development in developing countries" (Canada 2007f). On the contrary, the pursuit of Canadian interests is evermore emphasized.

SIGNS OF THINGS TO COME

What policy turns CIDA will take in the future are far from clear. Recent indications of further shifts come from outside CIDA itself. The March 2007 federal budget expressed the goal of placing Canada "among the largest five donors in core countries of interest, in order to improve how we work" and promises to "put more of our staff in the field" (Canada 2007b, 262). The commitment to decentralize may have been triggered by the Senate report on aid, released the previous month, which lamented that over 80 per cent of CIDA staff work in the Ottawa area (Canada 2007h, XI, 92). However, it is not clear how the relocation of hundreds of employees (often accompanied by family members) to field offices around the world can be squared with the simultaneous commitment to "reducing administrative costs" (Canada 2007b, 262). The implications of the other goal left CIDA staff scratching their heads. Among the top 30 recipients of Canadian aid in 2004–05, Canada was among the top five bilateral donors in only eleven countries (Canada 2006b, 52–3, table T).[7] This seemed to imply that the list of 25 priority countries of assistance, announced in 2005, would be whittled down further, perhaps with some new ones added. It seems likely that the decision on which ones and according to what criteria would be made by Cabinet or more likely the Prime Minister's Office, rather than within CIDA. This commitment was later repeated by the minister responsible for CIDA, Josée Verner, who in an interview explained that a country-by-country analysis had to be carried out and "in some countries you can spend just a little more money to be in the top five" (Berthiaume 2007b). This suggested that only minor adjustments could be made to place Canada in the top five donors in many countries, which is not the case in numerous others. Also, it is unclear how being in the top five would *ipso facto* increase the impact of Canadian aid, especially if increasing funding by only a small amount would place Canada there. Instead, it suggests that the real motivation is prestige, being able to impress voters and taxpayers, as well as donor peers.

Further manifestations of coming changes came in June 2007, linked to the G8 summit in Heiligendamm, Germany. Prime Minister Harper admitted that though the government was respecting its commitment to double aid to Africa between 2003–04 and 2008–09, its contribution for the continent would rise to. C$2.1 billion, rather than C$2.8 billion, as promised by the previous government. He claimed that in spite of this C$700 million budget cut Canada was still meeting the letter of the commitment, even if it did not meet the dollar target previously announced, because actual expenditure on Africa in 2003–04 wound up being C$350 million less than expected. By using reduced generosity towards

Africa in the past to justify further cuts in the future, Harper gave an un-
mistakable indication that CIDA would be abandoning the priority it
previously placed on that continent. The highly critical Senate report on
"40 years of failure" in aid to Africa might have constituted the last nail
in the proverbial coffin. Though funds were being redirected to Afghanistan, Harper also announced at the summit that Canada's foreign aid
focus would shift to Latin America and the Caribbean, perhaps in part a
petulant response to high-profile critiques of the deficiencies of Canadian aid to Africa. This change of focus again came as a surprise to
most CIDA officials and others working in the field of foreign aid, as
until then it seemed that Canada was actually losing interest in Latin
America (Cameron 2007). Equally unexpected was CIDA President
Robert Greenhill's subsequent indication that Canada would focus less
on "failed and fragile states" such as Afghanistan and Haiti and increasingly emphasize countries where "we've actually seen real results"
(Berthiaume 2007a). As of July 2007, a comprehensive reorganization of
CIDA was expected to be announced imminently, though it would remain to be seen to what extent it would further detail the policy shifts to
which various high-level officials alluded and how many of the changes
would be more cosmetic than substantive.

Beyond the government's control is the fate of the Official Development Assistance Accountability Act. If Bill C-293 passes in the
Liberal-dominated Senate and is proclaimed, it would refocus Canadian development assistance on poverty reduction and render it less
subject to being used to further Canada's own foreign policy objectives. This would reinforce CIDA's identity as an institution dedicated
to helping poor people in poor countries. Such policy insulation could
however have the perverse effect of reducing the priority the government accords to foreign aid, causing it to cut CIDA's budget.

Irrespective of policy changes within CIDA, whole-of-government
efforts will increase the impact of Canadian foreign aid on development only if DFAIT and other government bodies reduce their emphasis on Canadian interests and privilege those of developing countries
instead or if they reconceptualise Canadian interests as depending
primarily on a much more just and equitable world – both highly unlikely scenarios. CIDA can therefore either sit at the table with bigger
players (mainly DND and DFAIT) and have its development agenda
overridden by Canadian self-interest, or it can try to insulate itself
from outside influence, risking in the process a dramatic decrease in
the resources it is allocated. Under current circumstances, CIDA is
unlikely to seek to dissociate itself from other government agencies.
If, however, the whole-of-government approach meets its Waterloo in
Afghanistan, the coming decade might bring about precisely that

scenario for CIDA. Future funding and priorities, however, like so much else, will depend on which party is in power.

Though the Conservative government has continued to increase ODA by 8 per cent per year in current dollar sums, in line with the earlier Liberal commitments, Canada's aid budget actually shrank slightly between 2005–06 and 2006–07, when expressed as a percentage of GNP, from 0.33 to 0.32 per cent (Berthiaume 2007b). Canada is far off course to reach its stated goal of 0.7 per cent, announced in 1970 and reiterated countless times since then. A large majority of Canadians believe in a "moral obligation to help poor countries"[8] and could thus be considered "humane internationalists." However, foreign aid is a low-ranked priority when contrasted with issues like health care or education among voters in Canada and other donor countries (Noël, Thérien and Dallaire 2004; Otter 2003). Foreign aid thus is unlikely to become an important issue in future elections and "realists" in decision-making positions can either continue to reduce CIDA's margin to manoeuvre and divert foreign aid to serve domestic interests or renege with impunity on prior commitments to step up the fight against poverty abroad. Parliament, and especially the Cabinet, currently lack strong and effective advocates for foreign aid. As long as the Conservatives are in power, their mantra of accountability to taxpayers could easily serve as a justification for further cuts – though this would imply an admission that their best efforts to improve the effectiveness of Canada's foreign aid had failed.

NOTES

The author would like to express his gratitude to those whose comments helped strengthen this chapter, especially David Black, as well as to Julia Williams for her excellent research assistance.

1 This 58 per cent increase in current dollars over only a four-year period corresponds to a significantly smaller increase – only 10 per cent – when expressed as a percentage of gross national product (GNP): from 0.29 to 0.32 per cent for the same two fiscal years.

2 The United States did not report its figures, but were likely to reflect a higher tying rate than Canada's.

3 Some Canadian interests can be relatively easily defined, such as the integrity of the country's borders or the physical safety of its citizens. Others are more open to interpretation and redefinition. For example, different governments can conceptualize self-interest in foreign aid differently. Under the influence of the "international aid regime," one could impute a Canadian interest in

providing a generous amount of ODA and setting certain priorities, such as aid to Africa (Black and Thérien with Clark 1996). Otherwise, Canada could lack credibility among its donor peers and with developing countries, which would reduce its international influence. Such an argument holds more sway with the multilateralist Liberals than fiscal Conservatives, who consider the billions of dollars spent annually on foreign to be more effectively used for other purposes.

4 CIDA's budget for 2007–08 was C$3.0 billion, compared to DND's C$16.9 billion and only C$2.0 billion for DFAIT, itself a 7 per cent reduction on the previous year's allocation (Canada 2007i, 1–14).

5 This decision followed the killing of five of its employees, which a Taliban spokesperson justified by stating that "Organizations like Médecins Sans Frontières work for American interests and are therefore targets for us" (Weissman 2004: 7).

6 As of July 2007, the bill was awaiting third reading in the Senate, whose Standing Committee on Foreign Affairs and International Trade was reportedly stalling because the bill contradicted the recommendations of its own report on aid to Africa to focus on investment and private sector development, rather than poverty reduction.

7 Namely Haiti, Iraq, India, Nigeria, Indonesia, Ethiopia, Bangladesh, Mali, Cameroon, Senegal and Pakistan (of which the latter seven were among Canada's 25 "Development Partners"). During that year, Canada ranked seventh among bilateral donors in Afghanistan, though the Canadian government later stated that it was among the top five donors (Canada 2007c, 5).

8 According to CDFAI (2007), 70 per cent of Canadians polled agreed with that statement and only 13 per cent disagreed.

REFERENCES

Berthiaume, Lee. 2007a. "CIDA Boss Hints at Shift to Stable Nations." *Embassy*, 27 June.

– 2007b. "Josée Verner Outlines Her Foreign Aid Agenda." *Embassy*, 6 June.

Black, David R., and Jean-Philippe Thérien with Andrew Clark. 1996. "Moving with the crowd: Canadian aid to Africa." *International Journal* 51, no. 2 (Spring): 259–86.

Black, David R., and Rebecca Tiessen. 2007. "The Canadian International Development Agency: New Policies, Old Problems." *Canadian Journal of Development Studies* 28, no. 2 (June): 191-212.

Brown, Stephen. 2005. "Achieving the Development Objectives of Canada's International Policy Statement." *McGill International Review* 6, no. 1: 52–5.

– 2007a. "'Creating the World's Best Development Agency'? Confusion and Contradictions in CIDA's New Development Policy." *Canadian Journal of Development Studies* 28, no. 2 (June): 213-28.

– 2007b. "Le rapport du Sénat sur l'aide canadienne à l'Afrique: une analyse à rejeter." *Le Multilatéral* 1, no. 3 (July/August): 1, 6–7.
– 2008. "L'aide publique canadienne à l'Afrique: vers un nouvel âge d'or?" In *L'aide canadienne au développement: bilan, défis et perspectives*, edited by François Audet, Marie-Eve Desrosiers and Stéphane Roussel. Montreal: Presses de l'Université de Montréal, forthcoming.

Cameron, John. 2007. "CIDA in the Americas: New Directions and Warning Signs for Canadian Development Policy." *Canadian Journal of Development Studies* 28, no. 2 (June): 229-49.

Campbell, Bonnie and Pascale Hatcher. 2004. "Existe-t-il encore une place pour la coopération bilatérale? Réflexions à partir de l'expérience canadienne." *Revue Tiers Monde* 45, no. 179: 665–87.

Canada. 1987. *For Whose Benefit? Report of the Standing Committee on External Affairs and International Trade on Canada's Official Development Assistance Policies and Programs.* Ottawa: House of Commons of Canada, SCEAIT.

– 2002. *Canada Making a Difference in the World: A Policy Statement on Strengthening Aid Effectiveness.* Hull: Canadian International Development Agency.

– 2005a. *Canada's International Policy Statement: A Role of Pride and Influence in the World: Development.* Gatineau: Canadian International Development Agency.

– 2005b. *Canada's International Policy Statement: A Role of Pride and Influence in the World: Diplomacy.* Ottawa: Department of Foreign Affairs and International Trade.

– 2006a. *Canada's International Policy Put to the Test in Haiti: Report of the Standing Committee on Foreign Affairs and International Development.* Ottawa: House of Commons of Canada, SCFAID.

– 2006b. *Statistical Report on Official Development Assistance. Fiscal Year 2004–2005.* Gatineau: Canadian International Development Agency.

– 2007a. *Bill C-293 – An Act respecting the provision of official development assistance abroad.* Passed 28 March 2007. Ottawa: House of Commons Canada. Available at: <http://www2.parl.gc.ca/HousePublications/Publication.aspx?Language=E&Parl=39&Ses=1&Mode=1&Pub=Bill&Doc=C-293_3&File=24#1>

– 2007b. *Budget 2007: A Stronger, Safer, Better Canada.* Ottawa: Department of Finance.

– 2007c. *Canada's Mission in Afghanistan: Measuring Progress.* Report to Parliament. Ottawa: Government of Canada.

– 2007d. *Canadian Development Assistance in Afghanistan.* Canadian International Development Agency. Available at: <http://geo.international.gc.ca/cip-pic/afghanistan/library/econ_soc-en.asp>. Last accessed 6 June 2007.

– 2007e. *Canadian Troops in Afghanistan: Taking a Hard Look at a Hard Mission*. Ottawa: Senate of Canada, Standing Senate Committee on National Security and Defence.

– 2007f. *Mandate*. Canadian International Development Agency. Available at: <http://www.acdi-cida.gc.ca/CIDAWEB/acdicida.nsf/En/NIC-5493749-HZK>. Last accessed 6 June 2007.

– 2007g. *Mandate & Priorities*. Department of Foreign Affairs and International Trade. Available at: <http://geo.international.gc.ca/department/about_us-en.asp>. Last accessed 6 June 2007.

– 2007h. *Overcoming 40 Years of Failure: A New Road Map for Sub-Saharan Africa*. Ottawa: Senate of Canada, Standing Senate Committee on Foreign Affairs and International Trade.

– 2007i. *Part I – The Government Expenditure Plan*. 2007–2008 Estimates. Treasury Board of Canada Secretariat. Available at: <http://www.tbs-sct.gc.ca/est-pre/20072008/me-bd/part1/ME-001_e.pdf>

Canadian Council for International Co-operation. 2006. "The Whole-of-Government Approach in 'Fragile States': Part 2 of 3." Discussion Paper. Ottawa, December.

Canadian Defence and Foreign Affairs Institute. 2007. Poll on Foreign Aid Conducted by *Innovative Research Group*. February. Calgary: CDFAI. Available at: <http://www.cdfai.org/PDF/Poll%20on%20Foreign%20Aid.pdf>

Goldfarb, Danielle and Stephen Tapp. 2006. *How Canada Can Improve Its Development Aid: Lessons from Other Aid Agencies*. Commentary no. 232. Toronto: C.D. Howe Institute.

Leblanc, Daniel. 2007. "JTF2 to hunt al-Qaeda: Canada's top soldier announces mission to root out 'murderers' in Afghanistan." *Globe and Mail*, 15 July: A1.

Lehre, Eric. 2006. "Is the 3-D Construct at work in Kandahar or are we kidding ourselves?" *The Dispatch: Newsletter of the Canadian Defence and Foreign Affairs Institute* 4, no. 3 (Fall). Available at: <http://www.cdfai.org/newsletters/newsletterfall2006.htm>

MacKay, Peter. 2007a. Notes for an Address to the Standing Committee on Foreign Affairs and International Development, Ottawa, 20 March. Available at: <http://w01.international.gc.ca/minpub/Publication.aspx?isRedirect=True&publication_id=384997&Mode=print>

– 2007b. Notes for an Address to the Vancouver Board of Trade. Ottawa, 11 April. Available at: <http://w01.international.gc.ca/minpub/Publication.aspx?isRedirect=True&publication_id=385073&Mode=print>

Morgenthau, Hans. 1962. "A Political Theory of Foreign Aid." *American Political Science Review* 56, no. 2: 301–309.

Morrison, David R. 1998. *Aid and Ebb Tide: A History of CIDA and Canadian Development Assistance*. Waterloo, ON: Wilfred Laurier University Press.

Noël, Alain, Jean-Philippe Thérien and Sébastien Dallaire. 2004. "Divided Over Internationalism: The Canadian Public and Development Assistance." *Canadian Public Policy* 30, no. 1 (March): 29–46.

Organisation for Economic Co-operation and Development. 2007. Statistical Annex of the 2006 Development Co-operation Report: Tying Status of ODA by Individual DAC Members. Table 23, 2005. Available at: <www.oecd.org/dac/stats/dac/dcrannex>. Last accessed 7 June 2007.

Otter, Mark. 2003. "Domestic public support for foreign aid: does it matter?" *Third World Quarterly* 24, no. 1 (January): 115–25.

Pratt, Cranford. 1998. "DFAIT's Takeover bid of CIDA." *Canadian Foreign Policy* 5, no. 2: 1–13.

– 1999. "Greater Policy Coherence, a Mixed Blessing: The Case of Canada." In *Policy Coherence in Development Co-operation*, edited by Jacques Forster and Olav Stokke. London and Portland, OR: Frank Cass, 78–103.

– 2000. "Alleviating Global Poverty or Enhancing Security: Competing Rationales for Canadian Development Assistance." In *Transforming Development: Foreign Aid for a Changing World*, edited by Jim Freedman. Toronto, Buffalo and London: University of Toronto Press, 37–59.

Riddell, Roger C. 1996. "The moral case for post–Cold War development aid." *International Journal* 51, no. 2: 191–210.

Senlis Council. 2007. *Canada in Afghanistan: Charting a New Course to Complete the Mission*. Ottawa: Senlis Council.

Stairs, Denis. 2005. *Confusing the Innocent with Numbers and Categories: The International Policy Statement and the Concentration of Development Assistance*. Calgary, AB: Canadian Defence and Foreign Affairs Institute.

Weissman, Fabrice. 2004. "Military humanitarianism: A deadly confusion." *Activity Report 2003/2004*. Paris: Médecins Sans Frontières, 7–9.

6 Of "Bad Boys" and "Spoiled Brats": Alberta in Canadian Foreign Policy

CHRISTOPHER J. KUKUCHA
AND TOM KEATING

"The West has wanted in. The West is in now. Canada will work for all of us."

Stephen Harper on election night 2006

Much was made of the turn in Canadian politics when Stephen Harper's Conservatives won the 2006 federal election and formed a minority government with a plurality of seats. A minority Conservative government with a prime minister from Calgary, backed by 27 Conservative members of parliament (MPs) from Alberta led many commentators to maintain that there was a new locus of power in Canada. Alberta had its third prime minister while the majority of Albertan MPs were on the government side of the House for the first time since the early 1990s, and the provincial government shared party labels with its federal counterpart. The popular view was that Alberta would now assume its rightful place at the apex of Canadian political power and that years of neglect from central Canada would be overcome. "The geological plates of Canadian life have changed and the shift in power is towards the West – economic power, population and resources," said David Taras, a political analyst at the University of Calgary. "It ratifies a major shift that has taken place over the last 10 or 15 years" (Seskus and Fekete 2006, A3). "[Alberta] will have significant influence," said Ted Morton, an unsuccessful candidate to replace Ralph Klein as the province's premier, who belongs to the so-called "Calgary school" that helped shape Harper's political views and authored the "firewall" letter. "You have a prime minister from Alberta who understands Alberta and Alberta's interests and how they fit in Confederation, and you're going to have several cabinet ministers from here as well and the most experienced core of MPs" (Walton 2006, A20). Roger Gibbins of the Canada West Foundation concluded "'It's a very important turning point and possibly a point of political maturity, the bringing together of economic wealth and political power.' The net result, at least initially, should be that the Alberta government will feel less threatened by Ottawa and more relaxed in federal-provincial relations" (Savada 2006, A4).

There were a few voices of caution. Defeated Liberal candidate and former cabinet minister the Honourable Anne McClellan said that the Conservative Party "is probably viewed – rightly or wrongly – as an Alberta-based party, so [Harper] will have to be extra careful and cautious in his dealings with Alberta. Everything will be looked at in other parts of the country as: 'Is this a special favour for Alberta? Is this a reflection of something the rest of the country does not accept or share?'"(McLean 2006, A5). Barbara Yaffe reminded her readers that "for all the influence Alberta is about to enjoy in Ottawa, the Harper Conservatives owe their current good fortune to, not Alberta, but Ontario" (Yaffe 2006, A11). Harold Jansen also took a skeptical view: "There's going to be heightened expectations that Alberta's influence is going to increase, and so I think the potential for disappointment and frustration is equally great as well" (Walton 2006, A20). He also reminded readers that "It was under the Mulroney government with 21 MPs from Alberta that the Reform Party formed, and so I don't think that just because there is solid Alberta representation in the government caucus that we can write the obituary for western alienation" (Ibid.).

A popular theme in conservative circles in Alberta, "western alienation" has been around for a long time and persists regardless of the changing fortunes the province has experienced in recent decades. It had even infected Mr. Harper, who was among those Albertans who called for a "firewall" to protect Albertans from their rapacious neighbours and central government. David Bercuson suggested more than twenty years ago that "some of the grievances that stimulate the growth of regional feeling ... exist in the mind only. Attitude itself has created and sustained alienation and regionalism in the West" (cited in Ford 2006, 215). Much of this alienation is directed at the federal government for failing to represent Alberta's interests in both domestic and foreign policy. On the foreign policy front, commonly held views suggest that the federal government gives a low priority to Alberta's interests abroad or that it fails to represent the opinions of Albertans in formulating foreign policy. With a prime minister from Alberta and added representation from Albertan MPs around the cabinet table, it would be hard to argue that Ottawa is still not listening. The selelection of a new premier also raised the possibility that Alberta might be moving beyond its paranoia phase into a more constructive relationship with the rest of the country, one where its economic clout would be matched by more significant levels of political power. Yet this was not to be.

Shortly after the federal election, the provincial Conservatives began to look for a new leader as Ralph Klein was forced to retire sooner than expected. As candidates began to cue up to be his replacement, establishing one's anti-Ottawa credentials became a part of the process. Klein had perfected this approach, making it part of the ritual of the premier's political toolkit. The pressure, or perhaps temptation, to take on Ottawa and the rest of Canada has been too great for Klein's replacement to resist. Ed Stelmach has repeatedly set out his Alberta-first credentials, even as he has been forced to demonstrate a more environmentally responsible approach to future economic development. Intergovernmental Affairs Minister Guy Boutlier went a step further in stating that Alberta would assume its proper place in federal politics. "We're kind of the bad boys of Confederation," Boutilier said. "What Albertans understand is this: they contribute immensely to this country of ours, but also we want to be able to benefit from it" (Fekete 2007, A14). But the most forceful message was delivered by Ted Morton who wasted little time in challenging the federal government and the rest of the country as predatory interveners in Alberta's good fortune. Such views, however, were not shared by all Albertans and were not well supported by the evidence. In response to the claims of Ottawa's voracious attack on Alberta's vulnerable wealth, Paul Boothe (2007, A21) tried to set the record straight, pointing out that many of Alberta's problems in areas such as revenue shortfalls and immigration stem not from federal measures, but from poor planning and policy development at the provincial level. Still, the sentiments of Morton and others strike a popular chord in the hearts of many Albertans, convinced that their place in Confederation has consistently been undermined by federal governments of whatever stripe in Ottawa. The reality, of course, is that Alberta has not only the highest incomes in the country and an enviable public account, but that it has often been able to exercise real influence over the direction of Canadian policy in areas vital to the interests of the province. An examination of the Alberta government's efforts to shape the direction of Canadian foreign policy demonstrates that the provincial government has had considerable influence in those areas of most concern to the provincial economy and the province's place in Confederation. The record also reveals that the province has been, next to Quebec, the most consistently active government in promoting its interests at home and abroad. In reviewing Alberta's place in Canadian foreign policy, this chapter examines two principal questions. First, what are Alberta's foreign policy interests and how are they promoted and defended, both in Ottawa and in other countries? And second, when Alberta's interests diverge from those of other parts of the country or from the national interests as defined by Ottawa, what is the province's impact on the final foreign policy outcome?

The view that Alberta has somehow been left out or ignored in the development of Canadian policy is commonly held in the province. The sense of alienation that has persisted in Alberta has had little to do with the economic position of the province, however, as Albertans have enjoyed a significant period of economic growth, despite years of Liberal rule in Ottawa. In fact, the provincial economy has expanded at a rapid rate, leaving much of the rest of the country behind in its dust and CO_2 emissions. As the following summary from the Alberta government attests, the provincial economy grew at unprecedented rates that far exceeded other Canadian provinces in the decade before the election of the Harper government:

1 Over the past decade, Alberta had the highest rate of economic growth in Canada at 4.3 per cent.
2 Alberta's exports of goods and services more than tripled between 1995 and 2005 to C$87.8 billion.
3 Between 1995 and 2005, manufacturing shipments more than doubled to C$60.3 billion.
4 In 2005, Alberta investment per capita was C$18,403, more than twice the national average. A total of C$60.3 billion was invested in 2005, almost triple the 1995 level.
5 Average annual employment in the province in 2006 increased by 86,300 over 2005. Approximately 465,600 new jobs were created between 1996 and 2006.
6 Alberta's average unemployment rate in 2006 was the lowest in Canada at 3.4 per cent.[1]

A significant piece of provincial economic growth came in the private sector, with corporations such as EnCana Corp reaping record profits. The impressive economic growth was matched by an equally impressive environmental toll as the oil and gas industry recorded a 51 per cent increase in CO_2 emissions between 1990 and 2004. The province also led the country in industrial green house gas emissions. The economic boom has also raised concerns about the quality of life and the longer term sustainability of the provincial economy and its environment as concerns over such issues as skilled labour shortages and high housing costs increase. The mayor of Fort McMurray (the community most directly affected by the oil sands development) complained about the "apathy on the part of industry or government to address our municipal challenges involving population infrastructure, costs, housing and debt will lead to a substantially reduced quality of life for residents" (cited in Layton 2007, A17). Former Premier Peter Lougheed expressed similar concerns, citing labour shortages, inflation and environmental pressures as major challenges for the province (Thomson 2006, A18).

The debate on Alberta's place in the Canadian confederation and its influence over national policy resonates on foreign policy, in no small part, because of the foreign policy agenda that now places matters of provincial interests and jurisdiction in a priority position. Bilateral and multilateral trade and the environment have been prominent foreign policy concerns. They are also significant issues for the province of Alberta. In considering the province's role in Canadian foreign, trade and environment policies have been the areas where the province has attempted to exercise the most influence. Other foreign policy issues sometimes appear on the provincial radar, such as former Premier Klein's remarks supporting the American invasion of Iraq, but even these seem closely tied to the overwhelming interest of maintaining a favourable trade relationship with the United States. Energy, trade and now environmental policy also stand (along with the long-standing issues of equalization) as the principal issues that have fueled the flames of alienation in the province. As discussed below, however, allegations of federal neglect of provincial interests, lack of provincial influence or deep policy difference between Alberta and central Canada over national policy and priorities have been grossly over stated. The gap between provincial interests and federal policy in the areas of trade and the environment are not as wide as popular stereotypes suggest. The evidence indicates that Alberta's principal interests have certainly been supported in Canadian trade policy since the 1980s and that the province has worked (albeit not always successfully) to secure a provincial role in the development of policy in this area, including representation abroad. It also suggests that in the areas of conflict between provincial and federal environmental policy, that the conflict has been moderated in part by the election of the Harper government and its initial rejection of Kyoto that alleviated provincial fears, but also because of the new provincial government's attempt to anticipate pending federal regulations with more modest regulations of its own and because of growing public concern with environmental conditions that bring Alberta public opinion in line with the rest of Canada. Thus provincial activity in the areas of trade and the environment provide little support for the argument that Alberta has been neglected in Canadian foreign policy.

ALBERTA'S FOREIGN RELATIONS

The Alberta government's interest in foreign policy has been motivated almost exclusively by its desire to protect and advance the province's economic interests and to protect the province's position in the federation. Even though the province occasionally offers its views on non-material foreign policies (such as the American invasion of Iraq), its motivations for such interventions appear to be shaped by economic considerations. Examining Alberta's foreign policy activities over a range of issue areas highlights both where and how Alberta has altered not only Canadian foreign policy but also the evolution of international norms and standards. By implication, this will also demonstrate where Alberta's position has not had an impact, or policy areas where the province does not perceive these objectives as vital to its self-interest. Alberta has a very narrow and well-established range of sectoral priorities (and markets) that have not been dramatically altered by increasing liberalization of trade and/or international agreements. These have remained constant over the past three decades and directly influenced all areas of Alberta's foreign policy. Alberta has adeptly advanced its interests in key sectors such as energy and agriculture. It has also been a leader in federal-provincial relations related to Canadian foreign policy. Tangible outcomes are also evident in matters of environmental policy. In terms of other sectoral issues, such as trade promotion or Canada-US relations, however, there is less evidence of provincial impact.

TRADE POLICY

An understanding of Alberta's approach to foreign policy requires an examination of the province's economy, and especially its export situation. The economic picture for Alberta is strikingly clear and straightforward – it rests on selling energy to the American economy. The situation has become even more extreme in recent years, as Table 6.1 demonstrates. Energy exports to the American market overwhelm all other sectors of the provincial economy. In fact, no other Alberta export to the United States exceeds 5 per cent of the province's total bilateral trade. For the most part, the "mineral fuels" category consists of crude petroleum and liquefied petroleum or hydrogen. Alberta exported roughly equivalent amounts of each product to the US until 1999 – but in 2000, both sectors increased trade significantly. By 2005 exports of liquefied petroleum exceeded C$32 billion, whereas figures for crude petroleum equaled C$24.5 billion. Maintaining secure access to this market is the overriding concern of the provincial government.

Table 6.1
Alberta's Exports to the United States, Percentage of Total by Sector

Sector	1997	1998	1999	2000	2001	2002	2003	2004	2005	2006
Mineral Fuels	68.9	61.5	62.2	69.6	71.5	69.4	77.6	77.4	79.7	78.6
Plastics	2.3	2.0	2.1	1.6	2.5	2.6	3.2	3.6	3.7	4.2
Boilers, Machinery, Mechanical Appliances	1.7	2.7	2.1	1.7	2.0	2.4	1.8	1.8	1.8	2.2
Organic Chemicals	2.4	2.9	2.4	2.5	2.6	2.7	1.7	1.8	1.8	1.9
Wood and Articles of Wood	3.3	4.2	4.7	2.4	2.3	2.7	2.4	3.1	2.1	1.5
Electrical Machinery	.8	5.4	6.4	8.6	5.0	3.8	2.1	1.7	1.2	1.4
Meat/Edible Offal	2.7	3.5	3.8	2.4	2.7	3.0	1.8	2.1	1.8	1.1
Live Animals	2.7	3.1	1.8	1.2	1.6	1.6	0.5	0.1	0.4	1.0

Note: Categories are general HS2 product chapters.
Source: Industry Canada (2007).

Related to this is a strong interest in maintaining a favourable climate for foreign (principally American) investment in the provincial economy.

The data also demonstrates that the province is exceedingly reliant on the United States for its other primary exports (see Table 6.2). During the past ten years, for example, Alberta has consistently shipped over 80 per cent of its goods and commodities to American consumers. Historically, Alberta's second largest export market is Japan, although trade has declined from a maximum of C$1.8 billion in 1995, to just over C$1.2 billion in 2006. Provincial exports to Japan are currently dominated by three sectors, rape or colza seeds and meat of swine (over C$200 million in 2005), and chemical wood-pulp (approximately C$150 million). Alberta's trade with China, driven by exports of sulfur and acyclic alcohol, has also increased from sales of approximately C$430–480 million in the late-1990s to C$2.1 billion in 2006. Exports to South Korea, on the other hand, are dominated by chemical woodpulp, which totaled over C$180 million in 2002. Finally, Table 6.2 makes it clear that Alberta has not capitalized on Mexico as a primary export market, with trade reaching a high of only 1 per cent in 2004. In fact, bilateral trade with Mexico is dominated by one sector: "live animals," specifically "meat of bovine animals." This product has grown from less than C$10 million in 1998 to over C$260 million in 2004.[2]

Table 6.2
Alberta's Top Five Export Markets, Percentage of Total

	1997	1998	1999	2000	2001	2002	2003	2004	2005	2006
United States	80.4	81.4	83.9	88.0	88.8	87.6	89.3	87.7	89.2	88.5
China	1.2	1.5	1.6	1.3	1.5	1.7	1.6	2.8	2.5	2.6
Japan	5.0	4.3	3.8	2.4	2.2	2.5	1.8	1.9	1.6	1.5
Mexico	0.6	0.9	0.7	0.6	0.8	0.9	0.6	1.0	0.6	0.7
South Korea	1.6	1.4	1.4	1.0	0.8	0.9	0.7	0.6	0.6	0.5

Source: Industry Canada (2007)

Table 6.3, which identifies Alberta's top five import partners, illustrates similar patterns. Once again, the United States is dominant, but not to the same level as exports. Only one sector, however, consistently exceeds 20 per cent of imports (that which includes machinery and mechanical appliances). During the past five years, other consistent imports include: motor vehicles, trailers and bicycles; mineral fuels and oils; aircraft; articles of iron or steel; and electrical machinery and equipment. Purchases from China, however, have dramatically increased during the past decade and now total approximately 7 per cent of provincial imports. Only two product classes, however, are consistently at or near the 20 per cent level (electrical machinery and equipment, and boilers, machinery, mechanical appliances and nuclear reactors).[3] All other imports are below 10 per cent. This suggests that China's expanded presence is due to increased volume of trade, as opposed to a significant shift in its import profile. In contrast to exports, Mexico has increased imports to Alberta from 1.7 per cent in 1997 to 3.9 per cent in 2006. In doing so, Mexico has established itself as the province's third largest source of imports. Mexico's trade with Alberta is dominated by one sector, electrical machinery and equipment, which totaled 33.7 per cent in 2005. Other product codes above 10 per cent in 2006 included: motor vehicles, trailers and bicycles; articles of steel; and boilers, machinery, mechanical appliances and nuclear reactors. As with China, Mexico's increased import presence is due to growth in already established import sectors.

These market realities demonstrate that Alberta's export economy has not dramatically shifted despite the increasing liberalization of international trade and the implementation of trade agreements, such as the Canada-United States Free Trade Agreement (CUSFTA), the North American Free Trade Agreement (NAFTA), or the World Trade Organization (WTO). Specifically, the scale of trade has increased but not the

Table 6.3
Alberta's Top Five Sources of Imports, Percentage of Total

	1997	1998	1999	2000	2001	2002	2003	2004	2005	2006
United States	77.9	80.1	73.8	74.1	75.0	72.4	72.5	70.3	70.1	68.4
China	0.8	0.8	1.0	1.3	1.5	2.5	3.0	4.3	6.8	6.7
Japan	2.1	1.5	1.9	1.6	1.3	1.3	1.4	1.1	1.3	1.1
Mexico	1.7	1.6	2.6	3.3	3.5	3.8	3.7	3.9	3.6	3.9
South Korea	0.8	0.7	1.0	1.0	1.0	0.8	0.9	0.8	0.9	0.9

Source: Industry Canada (2007)

diversification of exports. Therefore, specific sectors are consistently prioritized in the province's international relations. Energy has been an obvious priority for the province, but in terms of trade policy in this sector most of the "battles" were fought in the 1980s as Alberta was successful in including guaranteed levels of energy exports in CUSFTA and NAFTA. Specifically, Alberta was a key supporter of a free trade agreement with the United States due both to its opposition to the National Energy Program (NEP) and Premier Peter Lougheed's preference for enhanced cross-border economic linkages. These objectives were also adopted by Lougheed's successor, Donald Getty (Doern and Tomlin 1991, 133–4). In terms of NAFTA, Alberta envisioned potential opportunities related to Mexico's constitutionally protected oil and gas industry but it was not a priority for the province. For the most part, its market-based objectives in the energy sector were achieved with the CUSFTA. These measures stand as a clear example where the province had a significant influence on Canadian trade policy and international norms and standards in this area.

Agriculture is an additional area of concern, but provincial interests have drifted over different issues, primarily red meats and grains. Historically, and in trilateral and multilateral trade negotiations on agricultural products, the Alberta government ensured that its important export markets remained open and were not sacrificed in exchange for protectionist dairy and poultry sectors in central Canada. More recently, and as an extension of these initiatives, the provincial government has become a vocal advocate for market-based reforms, through such measures as the elimination of marketing boards for barley and wheat. On this matter, Alberta seems to have found a supportive voice in Ottawa, as the Harper government appears sympathetic to the further liberalization of this sector.

The Bovine Spongiform Encephalopathy (BSE) crisis that started in 2003 with the discovery of an infected cow in Alberta and led to the closure of the US border to beef imports, was also a major source of frustration for the provincial government, which maintained constant pressure on Ottawa for both temporary assistance to farmers and diplomatic efforts to re-open the border. The data presented in Table 6.1, however, demonstrates that Alberta's impact on international trade can also be based on political, as opposed to strictly economic reasons. Specifically, since 1997 shipments of "meat/edible offal" and "live animals" have never exceeded 3.8 per cent of provincial exports. The relevance of cattle to the provincial economy is further clarified when it is understood that relevant HS2 product "chapters" include pork and other animals. In fact, when trade statistics are examined using more detailed HS4 product "group" codes two conclusions are clear. First, "meat of bovine animals – fresh or chilled" dropped from 2.7 per cent of Alberta's exports in 2002 to 1.6 per cent in 2003 and 1.9 per cent in 2004 but at no point was bilateral trade completely suspended. This is due to the fact that Washington re-opened the American border to limited exports in specific types of beef, namely Canadian boneless beef from cattle under 30 months, shortly after the discovery of BSE. And second, trade in "live bovine animals," however, remained closed and exports dropped from 1.4 per cent in 2002 to 0.3 per cent in 2003 and 2005. No live cattle from Alberta were shipped to the United States in 2004.

Therefore, cattle ranchers in Alberta suffered greater economic losses than provincial beef processors due to BSE. Compared to trade in energy, however, these figures clarify that Alberta's beef and cattle industry is not a "sacred cow," at least to the same degree as mineral fuels. Despite this reality, it is important to acknowledge that trade in live cattle, based on 2006 HS4 data, was still one of Alberta's top five exports to the US despite levels of less than 1 per cent. Therefore, Alberta's position during the BSE crisis was based on both economic and political reasons, especially due to the Conservative's long-time support from rural farmers. It should also be pointed out that Alberta was not the only province pushing for these measures. Comparatively, Saskatchewan's exports of live cattle to the US exceeded five per cent in 2002, and Manitoba's totaled 3.1 per cent in 2001. Regardless, Alberta's impact was not insignificant in terms of Ottawa's international and domestic response to BSE.

Another area of concern in trade policy has been the negotiations over subsidies and countervailing measures in the WTO. Here the province has been less than successful, though it has tried to push its position forward. Alberta joined all Canadian provinces in opposing US pressure to alter Article 2.2 of the subsidies and countervail measures agreement of the General Agreement on Tariffs and Trade (GATT) during the Uruguay Round of negotiations. Alberta proposed a "net subsidy" approach, but this was rejected by Ottawa. In other areas of multilateral trade negotiations, provincial influence is more difficult to discern. In terms of services, Alberta has been pushing for specific changes to WTO's General Agreement on Trade in Services (GATS) regarding Mode IV access for environmental and engineering services. This has now become part of Canada's negotiating position, but at this point no changes to international norms have been achieved.

Alberta's role in the ongoing softwood lumber dispute has been rather low-key in comparison. Alberta exports approximately 7 per cent of Canada's total shipments to the US, compared to British Columbia whose exports are closer to 56 per cent of the total. As a result, there was considerably less at stake for the province. Nonetheless the provincial government supported the Alberta Softwood Lumber Council (part of the Alberta Forest Products Association [AFPA]) that vocally opposed the recent softwood lumber agreement. In the end, the Alberta government accepted the agreement as an "acceptable compromise." The AFPA has continued to criticize the deal and it now appears the industry association is targeting the provincial government for assistance. In this area, in part as a result of its limited interests, the provincial government had little real impact on Canadian policy or international developments.

Perhaps Alberta's most significant influence on Canadian foreign policy has been its leading role in advancing the international priorities of provincial governments within Canadian federalism. This is an area where Alberta has had significant impact dating back to the 1970s when the provincial government first pushed for expanded provincial involvement during the Tokyo round of GATT. It was an Alberta proposal that helped "regularize" federal-provincial consultation on the CUSFTA – this process subsequently became known as the CFTA, CNAFTA and now CTrade. Under CTrade there are regularized federal-provincial meetings on trade policy, four times annually. Alberta's influence in advancing these procedural norms has been due to its bureaucratic expertise in the area and its self-proclaimed goal of "protecting provincial rights." Additional efforts by Alberta – and Quebec – to push for a more formalized federal-provincial process on trade policy, both in terms of consultation and participation, has been less successful to date.

TRADE PROMOTION

Historically, Alberta has been among the more active Canadian provinces in working abroad to promote trade, investment and tourism.

This has been facilitated by its relative wealth and its level of distrust over what has been perceived as a centrally dominated approach to trade and investment. For a number of years, however, the provincial government limited its foreign offices to London (opened in 1948); Los Angeles (1964) and Tokyo (1970). In contrast, Quebec and Ontario had opened (and closed) foreign offices and trade commissions prior to the 1930s. Following the Second World War, provinces began to re-visit the idea of foreign delegations. In 1945, Ontario re-opened its London office and established a further presence in Chicago (1953), New York (1956), and Los Angeles and Cleveland (1967). The province also opened offices in Europe and Asia, including Milan (1963), Stockholm (1968), Brussels, Vienna and Tokyo (1969), Frankfurt (1970) and Mexico City (1973). Quebec, on the other hand, posted a delegation in New York in 1941 and added several offices in subsequent years, including Brussels (1972), Tokyo (1973), Mexico City (1980) and Buenos Aires (1998). Therefore, Alberta's historic efforts, at least comparably, reflected an "idiosyncratic" approach to overseas representation, similar to British Columbia, Manitoba, Saskatchewan, Nova Scotia and New Brunswick.

More recently, however, the province has expanded its presence – usually as part of Canadian consulates. Among the offices established by the province are ones in Beijing, Hong Kong, Tokyo, Seoul, Taipei, Mexico City and European postings in London and Munich. For the most part, these offices focus on trade, investment, immigration and education considerations. In China, for example, the Alberta China Office (ACO), located in the Canadian embassy in Beijing, coordinates provincial interests. The ACO was founded in 1999 and oversees Alberta's Hong Kong Office, established in 1980, as well as the China-Alberta Petroleum Centre, and the province's presence in Taipei. Most other offices, including Mexico City (2002), were opened during the past five years. Ultimately, Alberta's foreign offices exist for two main reasons. One motivation is the transparent pursuit of international trade and investment. The second, however, is Alberta's perceived role for itself as a provincial leader in international affairs within Canadian federalism. In fact, many of these initiatives were announced as Quebec expanded its foreign presence during the 1990s and Ontario announced plans to open a series of new offices in 2001.

The premier (and at times other ministers) has also had an active travel schedule, mainly to promote trade and investment. Among the priorities have been repeated trips to Asia, and especially China. Premier Klein made his first trade mission to Asia in 1993, and made subsequent trips to China in 1997, and to China and Korea in 2004. Despite these initiatives, and Alberta's offices in China, Japan and

South Korea, provincial officials are not overly optimistic about future expansion of Alberta's Pacific trade options, beyond a small number of sectors, due to a lack of railway infrastructure to British Columbia and capacity problems in coastal ports. The reality is also that Alberta does not have a wide range of "attractive" exports. This is substantiated by the narrow sectoral trade with China and its steady or declining rate of trade with Japan and South Korea.

The us is the key focus of the province's trade promotion efforts. At the institutional level, the government's primary attention has been directed to its mission in Washington, dc – opened in March 2005 with former provincial cabinet minister Murray Smith as the provincial representative. The decision to establish an office in Washington, while connected to the Canadian embassy, reflected a concern for more effective representation of the province's interests in the us at a time when the bilateral relationship between Canada and the us had hit a rocky patch. Policy differences over the war in Iraq, missile defence and softwood lumber, threatened to disrupt Alberta's expanding energy market. There were also concerns about the continuing bse fallout. This is another example of Alberta being in front of other provinces trying to have an impact in the us – the key measure being access to Congress and the executive branch. The Martin government responded by establishing a "secretariat" in the Canadian embassy so all provinces would have an institutionalized processs of lobbying us officials. Alberta was the only province that acted – and this is how Murray Smith ended up in Washington. Alberta always called it an "office," and Ottawa has not really challenged this in the Harper era (Blanchield 2004, A5). Insuring that the Americans heard the Alberta government's voice became an important concern. The mission's explicit purpose has been to protect energy and agricultural interests. The premier has also been active in the us undertaking visits to Washington, dc, and Boston (2005); New York (2005); Alaska (2006); and, back to Washington (2006). In 2006, the Alberta government was quick to respond to an opportunity to use the Simthsonian's Folklife Festival to do some high level lobbying. For twelve days in the summer of 2006, the provincial government wooed Washington personalities. The premier and ten cabinet ministers visited Washington and participated in four conferences. Meetings were also held with Vice President Cheney; Senate Energy Committee Chair Pete Domenici; House Agriculture Committee Chair Bob Goodlatte; and Canadian Ambassador Michael Wilson. For a couple of weeks, a large truck from the Alberta oil sands was also parked in front of the Smithsonian, as a friendly reminder to Americans from where their automotive fuel originated.

Canada-US relations are an obvious priority for Alberta, as seen in the province's direct representation in Washington. The province is also a member of numerous cross-border organizations, although at this time these exist primarily as forums of sub-federal discussion with only limited functional relations being formalized. Alberta, for example, has ties to numerous associations including the Western Governor's Association, the Council of State Governors-West, the Pacific Northwest Economic Region (PNWER), the Rocky Mountain Trade Corridor, the Montana-Alberta Bilateral Advisory Council and the CanAm Border Trade Alliance, and these forums have addressed questions of border access. To date, it is not clear if these initiatives will have any long-term impact on Alberta's ability to influence trade and investment relations, although some progress has been made on cross-border transportation issues. Discussions within PNWER have focused on CANAMEX, a proposed trade corridor through Alaska, the Yukon, BC, Alberta, Montana, Idaho, Utah and Nevada to the Mexican border. Post-9/11, PNWER also focused on preventing the disruption of cross-border shipping and business travel, most notably with Intelligent Transportation Systems and Joint Use Vehicle Inspection Stations. States and provinces also made a commitment to promote joint-permitting of trucks and streamlining other cross-border activities. Most of this, however, is an extension of federal initiatives, such as the Canada-US Shared Border Accord. Many of these developments have also been in response to "crisis" issues (such as BSE) or resulted in sub-federal agreements between Canada and the US that are primarily functional in nature (such as the Governing the Siting and Permitting of Interstate Electric Transmission Lines in the Western United States agreement).

ENVIRONMENT

Years ago, the provincial government recognized the importance of environment policy in defining federal-provincial relations which led it to play an active role in trying to shape federal environmental policy for more than a decade. Alberta and Quebec, for example, were actively involved in advising the federal government during the negotiation of the side deals on labour and the environment as part of the NAFTA negotiations. Annex 41 of the North American Agreement on Environmental Cooperation (NAAEC) and Annex 46 of the North American Agreement on Labour Cooperation (NAALC) are a direct result of provincial input – both of which focus on specific issues related to the compliance of Canadian provinces. (There were no similar sections re: US or Mexican states.) Ottawa subsequently set out to negotiate compliance agreements with Canadian provinces. Only a small number of provinces have signed these agreements, but Alberta was a major supporter of these compliance mechanisms and was the first to sign both agreements. Although provincial involvement at that time was based more on interests within Canadian federalism, Alberta did contribute to aspects of this international agreement. It is important to point out, however, that this was not due to specific environmental concerns, but rather with a view to defining federal-provincial relations in this and other areas. Specifically, Alberta believed these could be the first steps to formalizing intergovernmental relations in this and other areas of foreign policy – specifically trade policy. In this way, the Alberta government did help to establish international procedural norms, but the substantive impact of these arrangements has been minimal.

More recently, however, procedural interests have shifted to substantive ones, and there is evidence to suggest that Alberta's interests are having an impact on the environmental policies of Stephen Harper's Conservative government, particularly in the area of greenhouse gas emissions. The environment has become an important consideration for both the federal and provincial governments. Nationally, concern over both the image of Canada abroad (in light of the Conservatives formal abandonment of its Kyoto commitments and because of the substantive impact of climate change for the country) has forced environmental issues onto the federal government's agenda. Provincially, the Alberta government has also been forced to face environmental issues, largely because of its position as the principal source of industrial pollutants in the country and increased concerns within the province over the environmental consequences of its natural resource-based economy.

Provincial activity on environmental issues intensified during the debate on the ratification and implementation of the Kyoto Accord, which the Chrétien government signed in 1997 and ratified in 2002. Form the very start of negotiations, the Alberta government opposed the agreement and actively promoted a "made in Alberta" solution. Alberta's opposition to the Accord was both reinforced and exacerbated when the US government announced its intention of not signing Kyoto in 2001. The provincial government took its lead from a number of energy companies who threatened disinvestment if environmental regulations to meet Kyoto targets were to be imposed. The dire economic consequences have been challenged by observers who note the lack of sound evidence for the scale of economic dislocation being advanced by some corporate interests (Urquhart 2005). Premier Klein, however, reiterated and legitimated these threats in a speech to the Global Business Forum in Banff in October 2002. The Klein government even went as far as threatening a constitutional challenge of the agreement – not surprisingly, this became a negative influence on relations between Klein and Chrétien.

Alberta's persistent opposition to Kyoto appeared to have paid off with the election of Conservatives in 2006. Almost immediately after coming to office, the Harper government expressed its reservations about Kyoto. Then-Environment Minister Rona Ambrose, a junior minister from Alberta, was given the task of removing Canada from its Kyoto commitments, a move that stood in stark contrast to Canada's traditional support for pledged international undertakings. While perhaps realistic in noting the unlikely prospects of Canada actually meeting its commitments under the accord, Ambrose and the government sent a clear message to Canadians and the international community that it would publicly disassociate Canada from the accord. The reaction from environmentalists from around the globe was scathing, while many foreign leaders took the opportunity to criticize Canada. The shift in policy and its delivery also generated much opposition at home, and the government was forced into a partial retreat. The messenger was booted out, as Ambrose was reassigned to another portfolio, and a new minister, John Baird, began to deliver a more environmentally friendly message. Meanwhile, in Ambrose's home province and especially in the Alberta government, backing away from Kyoto was viewed favourably. It would, however, be a mistake to conclude that all Albertans were enamoured by the Kyoto withdrawal and the move to a "made in Canada" approach. Groups such as the Pembina Institute took issue with the change in policy and increasing numbers of Albertans, expressed their concerns about environmental issues. Research scientists in the province also questioned the foundations of the government's position (Smith 2002). A slim majority of Albertans polled in 2006 supported "stricter emission standards (for the province), even if it means a significant increase in the cost of producing oil and gas" (D'Aliesio 2007). In a later poll released by the Pembina Institute on the eve of the Harper government's announcement of new environmental measures, over 70 per cent of Albertans favoured actual cuts in emissions by the provinces industrial producers even if it meant increased costs to the provincial economy. Attitudes were changing in the province and the Alberta government looked for a way to respond.

The provincial government, for its part, under Premier Stelmach has not been silent on environmental concern, but has chosen a more industry-friendly path in promoting intensity-based emission. In March 2007, in anticipation of new federal measures, the provincial government announced new standards for slowing the growth of greenhouse gas emissions in the province. Under the regulations, large scale industries were asked to lower the amount of energy used per unit of output. The effect would be to reduce the rate of growth, rather than the actual amount of greenhouse gases being emitted. Indeed as energy production increases, Alberta's greenhouse gas emissions are expected to continue to grow. This will ensure that Alberta, which now produces about 40 per cent of the country's greenhouse gases, will retain its place as the largest source of industrial greenhouse gases in Canada. The provincial policy was taken both to establish its jurisdictional credentials in case of constitutional challenges down the road, but also to send a strong signal to the federal government of the province's main priorities.

Provincial concerns over the possibility of federal regulations that would force energy producers in the province to curtail emissions have generated the inevitable references to the NEP and cries of federal encroachment on the province's principal source of wealth (Gutner 2007). The complaints intensified after the selection of Stéphane Dion as the leader of the Liberal party (given the priority that environmental issues played in his successful campaign) and the prime minister responded by initiating his own green credentials. Alberta's Premier Ed Stelmach "warned Ottawa ... that any environmental tug-of-war over conflicting emission standards will see his government pursue Alberta's best interests. 'We're the trustees. The ownership of those resources belong to Albertans, and Albertans are the ones that will decide the best way to approach this issue'" (D'Aliesio and Fekete 2007). In pre-empting the federal policy, the Stelmach government had also made clear that it was not interested in revising its policy to meet different federal guidelines. In the end, the "call to arms" was unnecessary, as the province's approach was closely mirrored in the federal plan released at the end of April 2007. In putting forward intensity-based reductions the federal plan imposed no ceiling on greenhouse gas emissions and protected Alberta's lucrative oil sands producers from having to undertake actual reductions in greenhouse gas emissions for the foreseeable future. The provincial and federal plans were so close that there was little room for either the province or the private sector to raise objections. The federal policy was even more favourable to provincial commercial interests, as it excluded oil sands from the new regime of regulations that were brought into place. It also left a three year open window in which new investments were to be protected from meeting standards. While the industry breathed a sigh of relief, other Albertans were more concerned about the quality of the air they would be breathing in the future.

CONCLUSION

Based on this review, it is not exactly clear what this mingling of economic and political power would lead to in the way of foreign policy changes for Canada. The implication may have been that foreign policy will look different now that Alberta is "in". Yet Alberta's foreign policy interests reveal little about how such policy might actually change. The principal areas of concern raised by the Alberta government in the past have been more in the way of unfounded threats to Alberta's interests rather than of specific policies on which there has been a difference between Edmonton and Ottawa. Clearly energy policy and energy trade have been the foremost concerns, but here there is little difference in policy approach between Alberta and Ottawa. Both governments have been anxious to secure Canada's position as the principal energy supplier for the American market. This policy was locked in as part of the NAFTA and despite the periodic fear-mongering coming from Calgary and Edmonton, the federal government has done nothing to challenge this commitment. There have been some comments by those not in power – opposition parties, environmentalists, public research groups, etc. – that the government should reconsider its policy of "fuelling" the North American economy. Others have at times suggested using energy as a way of putting pressure on the US government to change its policy on, for example, softwood lumber. Yet these suggestions have never come close to policy officials and had no support under previous or present governments. It is quite evident that while the Harper government will support the maintenance and expansion of Canadian energy exports, this will be a continuation of past practice rather than a new departure.

Political pressure for stronger environmental measures both in the rest of Canada and in Alberta seems unlikely to abate. Despite threats of disinvestment from domestic and foreign investors and the Alberta government's reiteration of such threats, public concerns about environmental degradation continue to grow not only in the rest of Canada, but also within Alberta. In the face of such concerns, it will be more difficult for governments at both levels to resist undertaking changes to address the threats that unregulated pressures on the environment pose for both the quality of life and the longer-term sustainability of the provincial economy.

This review of provincial activity in selected foreign policy issues has found little reason for fears of "western alienation." This is especially true since the election of the Harper government, but Canadian foreign trade policy has long been working in support of provincial government objectives and Canadian environmental policy, even during the years of rhetorical support for Kyoto posed no threat to provincial economic interests, despite the protestations of Premier Klein. The existing alignment of provincial and federal political forces provides considerable potential for Alberta to take a greater leadership role in the direction of Canadian policy at home and abroad. It has the potential to forge trade and environmental policies that balance sustainable economic growth in a manner that not only respects the environment, but are attentive to the long-term sustainability of the economy and the social network needed to support it. To do so, however, the provincial government should recognize that it does not exist in isolation from the rest of the country nor from the rest of the world.

Alberta's leaders should heed the advice of keen observers such as Boothe (2007) who cautions that the Stelmach government's persistent anti-Ottawa stances are simply "following the time-honoured Alberta tradition of diverting attention from [the province's] real problems like runaway spending, a dangerously overheated economy, and a looming environmental crisis. Instead of the 'bad boy' of Confederation, Alberta is looking more and more like the 'spoiled brat'."

NOTES

1 These figures obtained from the Alberta Government, at http://www.alberta-canada.com/economy/economicResults; accessed on March 20, 2007.
2 Trade statistics elaborating on basic HS2 product "chapters" is taken from HS4 product "groups." This information is also available at Industry Canada 2007.
3 While the goods in that formal category include nuclear reactors, Alberta does not in fact import any from China. These "tariff items" classes (HS 84 and HS 85), as the WTO and its members formally call them, are quite broad.

REFERENCES

Blanchfield, Mike. 2004. "Alberta Drove New US Policy, Documents Show." *Ottawa Citizen*, 13 December: A5.

Boothe, Paul. 2007. "Picking fights should no longer be in the cards." *Calgary Herald*, 19 January: A21.

D'Aliesio, Renata. 2007. "Alberta keeps emitting unabated." *Calgary Herald*, 7 March: A4.

– and Jason Fekete. 2007. "Greenhouse gas emitters will get grace period: Alberta staggers new climate regulations." *Calgary Herald*, 10 March: A6.

Doern, Bruce G. and Brian W. Tomlin. 1991. *Faith and Fear: The Free Trade Story*. Toronto: Stoddart Publishing.

Fekete, Jason. 2007. "Alberta won't shy away from a scrap: 'Bad boys of Confederation' are prepared to ruffle feathers, Boutilier says." *Edmonton Journal*, 6 January: A14.

Ford, Catharine. 2005. *Against the Grain, An Irreverent View of Alberta*. Toronto: McClelland & Stewart.

Gunter, Lorne. 2007. "Dion reveals hidden agenda for Alberta: Liberal leader's about-face on carbon tax would have same effect as the hated NEP." *Edmonton Journal*, 4 March: A18.

Industry Canada. 2007. *Trade Data Online: Trade by Product (HS) – HS Codes*. Available at: <http://strategis.gc.ca/sc_mrkti/tdst/tdo/tdo.php?lang=30&headFootDir=/sc_mrkti/tdst/headfoot&productType=HS6&cacheTime=962115865#tag>. Last accessed 1 July 2007.

Layton, Jack. 2007. "Greening the elephant: Real leadership can bring sustainability to the oilsands." *National Post*, 23 February: A17.

Markusoff, Jason. 2007. "Inflation won't keep premier from spending: Annual fund earmarked for municipalities will reach $1.4B in 3 years." *Edmonton Journal*, 17 January: A3.

McLean, Archie. 2006. "Another run not out of the question: Taking break after losing Edmonton Centre to Tory rival." *Edmonton Journal*, 25 January: A5.

Sadava, Mike. 2006. "Ottawa about to get more Alberta friendly." *Edmonton Journal*, 24 January: A4.

Seskus, Tony and Jason Fekete. 2006. "Harper leads power shift to West." *Calgary Herald*, 24 January: A3.

Smith, Ryan. 2002. "Scientists offer advice to Klein on climate change." *University of Alberta Express News*, 25 October. Available at: <http://www.expressnews.ualberta.ca/article.cfm?id=3252>

Thomson, Graham. 2006. "Time is not on our side as Alberta struggles to cope with this boom." *Edmonton Journal*, 11 November: A18.

Walton, Dawn. 2006. "Albertans harbouring list of great expectations; Even with a PM from a Calgary riding, 'Tory Glory' may not bring hoped-for clout." *Globe and Mail*, 24 January: A20.

Yaffe, Barbara. 2006. "'West Wants In' is code for what Alberta now has a shot at." *Vancouver Sun*, 31 January: A11.

7 From Afghanistan to "Quebecistan": Quebec as the Pharmakon of Canadian Foreign and Defence Policy

JEAN-CHRISTOPHE BOUCHER
AND STÉPHANE ROUSSEL

In a liberal democracy, public opinion is certainly one of the principal internal constraints on policy-makers, especially when the government does not possess a legislative majority that would enable it to manoeuvre without constantly being at the mercy of the opposition parties. This problem appears to be exacerbated when public opinion is divided along marked socio-political cleavages.

This is precisely the case of Stephen Harper's present Conservative government. The prime minister, probably quite pleased (and maybe surprised) with the election of ten conservative Members of Parliament (MPs) in Quebec during the 2007 federal election, appears to anticipate future substantial gains in this province; enough, perhaps, to obtain a majority government. Thus, Canadians sense that a strong operation to seduce Quebec is being conducted by the Conservative party – one that visibly extends to the execution of foreign policy. However, this is a minefield for the Conservatives and if foreign policy issues become a key political theme in the next federal election (Hébert 2007), Quebec's idiosyncrasy could frustrate the Conservative's political agenda.

The events of 2006 give a general impression of the debates and complications that may present challenges to Stephen Harper's electoral ambitions. All year long, both Quebec's provincial government and public opinion have put pressure on the federal government in the hopes that it will comply with the Kyoto objectives on greenhouse gas reductions. Conservatives are also on the defensive on the Afghan mission, especially since they pushed through the House of Commons a motion to extend the mission until 2009, in spite of the fact that the population's support for the mission is in continuous decline. Furthermore, the apparent ideological proximity between the Harper government and the George W. Bush administration, the latter of which Quebecois are extremely suspicious if not to say totally allergic, could convince many voters to rejoin the ranks of the Liberal Party of Canada or the Bloc Quebecois.

Obviously, Quebecois do not hold a monopoly on critical perspectives toward these issues. Most opinions voiced by Quebecois actually resonate in English Canada. But the determination of Conservatives to win votes in Quebec, coupled with the fact that Quebecois are particularly sensitive on these issues, confers greater visibility of the province when these themes are picked up by the media. The constraints imposed on the conduct of foreign policy are amplified by the fact that on others issues, there seems to be a chasm separating Quebecois and other Canadians. This was the case when Quebec was accorded a seat in the Canadian delegation at the United Nations Educational, Scientific and Cultural Organization (UNESCO) and during the 2006 Israeli intervention in Lebanon, events which we will discuss later in this chapter. In this general social and political context, it is appropriate to examine the commonly accepted notion that Quebecois have cultivated a different understanding in matters of defence and foreign policy – one that is notably underpinned by a strong pacifist leaning – and that they exercise more influence on decision-making on these issues than other Canadians.

In the first section of this chapter, we examine the debates that, in 2006, appeared to have exacerbated the division between the country's Francophone and Anglophone communities. The second section attempts to call into question certain myths regarding the attitudes of Quebecois toward defence and foreign policy issues, and demonstrate that the differences separating the "two solitudes" are not as important as they may initially appear. Finally, the last section presents an explanation of the persistence and functionality of these myths. On the one hand, according to more conservative commentators, analysts and politicians, Quebec's influence and opinions are poisons that eat away and paralyze Canadian foreign policy. Quebec's positioning thus becomes a justification for inaction, either as a policy outcome (or non-outcome for that matter) or as a plausible scapegoat. On the other hand, by continuously maintaining and insufflating social-democratic values, Quebec – in concert with other progressive elements in the Canadian federation – assists in preserving the distinctive and integral character of Canada. We compare Quebec's function in Canadian foreign policy with the Pharmakon ritual of Ancient Greece. Meaning both a poison and a remedy depending on the use and dose of the substance, the

Pharmakon was usually a symbolic scapegoat invested with the sum of the corruption of a community. Seen as a poison, it was subsequently excluded from a community in times of crisis as a form of social catharsis, thus becoming a remedy for the city. We argue that, in many ways, Quebec can be both a poison and a remedy in terms of Canadian foreign policy.

FROM UNESCO TO "QUEBECISTAN," PASSING BY KYOTO AND AFGHANISTAN: QUEBEC SOCIETY AND DEBATES ON CANADIAN FOREIGN POLICY

When Stephen Harper's government came into power following the 2006 January federal election, many expected to fight rear-guard battles on certain issues held dear by the Conservative party such as fiscal policies or the fight against crime. However, the strongest political winds came from themes associated with foreign policy. More often than not, Quebec society was pitched, or pitched itself, right into the middle of the storm.

Three controversies in particular shed a revealing light on how Quebec positions itself on foreign policy issues and on the ensuing reactions that emanate from parts of English Canada. The first debate revolves around the inclusion of Quebec's provincial officials in the Canadian delegation at the UNESCO. The second one occurred in the summer of 2006 when Israeli troops launched an assault on Hezbollah militants inside Lebanon's territory. The third, more disseminated, debate questions the influence of Quebec on foreign and defence policies in Canada.

Since the end of the 1990s, Quebec's provincial governments have requested a seat at any international negotiation forum in which their specific constitutional jurisdictions are addressed, most notably at the World Trade Organization and at the UNESCO. Although strongly disputed by federal officials, this interpretation of the constitutionality of provincial international capacities has always been contended by sovereignist and federalist governments in Quebec. First stated by the Parti Quebecois government,[1] the demand regarding Quebec's representation in international organizations was reaffirmed by the provincial Liberals in 2004 and received positive support from Prime Minister Paul Martin during the 2005 federal election campaign. Nonetheless, it was not until 2006 that the Conservative Party inscribed the issue in their electoral platform and acted on it with the signing of a formal agreement between Quebec and Ottawa in May 2006 (Paquin 2007b). It is not really the reactions that followed this relatively benign gesture that are revealing, but rather the ones that preceded it in the fall of

2005. As Paquin has noted (2006–07), the reaction of some English newspapers were particularly virulent. Editorials published in the *National Post* (2 September 2005), the *Ottawa Citizen* (5 October 2005) and the *Globe and Mail* (5 October 2005) denounced the project as a genuine risk to Canada's international influence. "Canada must speak with one voice" was the message that was largely accepted in English Canada (see also Hébert 2007, 175–6; Granatstein 2007, 159–61).

The July 2006 crisis, in which Israeli forces used a land and aerial offensive to neutralize Hezbollah insurgents, which had been using the cover of Lebanon's territory to attack Israel, was more serious. If the immediate attention was on the problems linked with evacuating thousands of Canadian nationals living in Lebanon, the debate was "imported" to Canada when Prime Minister Harper recognized the right of Israel to defend itself against aggression and described the Israeli reaction as "measured." This official standpoint was highly criticized in Quebec, in part because of a genuine sympathy for the prominent Lebanese community living in Montreal, but also because of a basic disagreement with the prime minister's moral evaluation of the Israeli intervention. This standpoint polarized commentators, each accusing the other of being misinformed and conducting biased analyses, sometimes in words far from eloquent. For example, Brigitte Pellerin (2006) did not hesitate to point out that Quebec has an anti-Semitic past and expressed fear that Quebecois "will punish Mr. Harper at the polls in the next election for standing clearly against a second Holocaust."

The controversy rapidly degenerated when, on 6 August 2006, many artists and politicians in Quebec – of both federal and sovereignist allegiance – participated in a public anti-war demonstration in Montreal. The presence of a marginal number of more radical demonstrators who brandished Hezbollah flags and posters with slogans hostile to Israel, incited strong reactions and revived the debate regarding attitudes in Quebec society toward violence and the Middle-East conflict. According to Montreal Gazette columnist Don MacPherson (2006): "It's finally becoming respectable again in Quebec to express support for terrorists." Barbara Kay, of the National Post, went even further, affirming that:

Left-wing Quebec intellectuals and politicians (Pierre Trudeau being an obvious example) have always enjoyed flirtations with causes that wrap themselves in the mantle of "liberation" from colonialist oppressors – including their very own home-grown Front de Liberation du Quebec (FLQ), which gave them a frisson of pleasure as it sowed terror throughout Canada in the late '60s with mailbox bombs, kidnappings and a murder. Their cultural and historical sympathy for Arab countries from the francophonie – Morocco, Algeria, Lebanon –

joined with reflexive anti-Americanism and a fat streak of anti-Semitism that has marbled the intellectual discourse of Quebec throughout its history, has made Quebec the most anti-Israel of the provinces, and therefore the most vulnerable to tolerance for Islamist terrorist sympathizers. (Kay 2006a)

The rationale behind Quebec's attitude was presented as residing both in the persistence of an anti-Semitic discourse and an immigrant population where the proportion of Middle-Eastern Francophones is higher than in the rest of Canada. According to MacPherson (2006) and Kay (2006b), one of the political consequences of an independent Quebec would be an inherent tolerance toward Islamic terrorist movements, hence the "Quebecistan" moniker. Furthermore, this attitude is accused of preventing the Canadian government (being sensitive to Quebec's electoral mood swings) to take a firm and clear stance in favour of Israel and against terrorism, such as the one illustrated by Stephen Harper's declaration (Pellerin 2006).

These attacks fostered strong reactions amongst Quebecois, both sovereigntists and federalists. If some thought that the politicians participating in the 6 August demonstration lacked judgment (Roy 2006; Pratte 2006a), they nevertheless rejected the analysis of their colleagues and responded to the "Quebecistan thesis." First, it is a genuine attachment to peace and a rejection of war as a political solution that the majority of Quebecois were expressing during the Lebanon crisis. In judging the Israeli reaction as disproportionate, Quebecois were making a moral judgment on means, not necessarily on objectives. As such, they were conveying an opinion held by most European governments. Second, Quebec does not have a monopoly on anti-Semitic history or on anti-American reflexes. However, attributing these deviances to Quebec shadows similar ideas, either pacifist, anti-Semite or proto-terrorist, promoted elsewhere in Canada. Third, commentaries like the ones made by MacPherson and Kay are perceived in Quebec as manifestations of intolerance toward Quebec society and any different opinions that it might uphold. If the target is the sovereignist movement, such commentaries nonetheless have an impact on Quebec's population in general, as most Quebecois commentators acknowledge. Finally, one of the consequences of this particular debate is that it reveals and reinforces English Canada's misconceptions about Quebecois (Boivert 2006a; Boivert 2006b; Pratte 2006a; Pratte 2006b; Legault 2006; Sansfaçon 2006). It is revealing that few voices were heard in English Canada that called into question the opinions expressed by the likes of Pellerin, MacPherson and Kay.[2]

The third debate, which is more discrete, touches directly on the question of the Canadian government's room for manoeuvre in matters of foreign policy. More precisely, it deals with the capacity of Quebecois and their political leaders to influence foreign policy orientations and decisions. Ted Morton (2003) and Jack L. Granatstein (2004, 193–4; 2006, 150–1) have largely contributed to the promotion of the idea that Quebecois are given a disproportionate influence in this process and are thus "deforming" Canada's foreign policy. This phenomenon was supposedly at work in determining the outcomes of recent events such as the decision of the Chrétien government not to participate in the Coalition of the Willing against Iraq in March 2003, or the failure of Paul Martin's government to support the American missile-defence program.

The principal political consequences of this alleged influence is the imposition on the rest of Canada (ROC) of a foreign and defence policy that essentially reflects pacifist ideas and, in the recent years, the anti-Americanism prevalent in Quebec. This influence apparently originates from the disproportionate electoral weight of Quebec (especially in a minority government context) and by the fact that these ideas are easily associated with Quebec's politicians in Ottawa, including those that, from 1968 to 2006, served as prime ministers. In this perspective, Quebec is, at least in part, responsible for the hardships of Canadian foreign policy.

This idea is echoed by some Francophone commentators that highlight mostly the positive consequences of Quebec's influence on Canadian foreign policy. According to Stéphane Paquin (2007a):

Without Quebec, Canada would be in Iraq and would be participating in anti-missile defence. Without Quebec, the FTA and NAFTA would never have seen the light of day. Without Quebec, Stephen Harper would have dropped Kyoto and is now obligated (by Quebec) to revise his position. Without Quebec, Canada would have probably voted "NO", with Australia and the United States, to the Convention on cultural diversity.

In sum, Quebec's political culture, federalist or sovereigntist, fundamentally influences Canadian foreign policy beyond its demographic weight and, in my opinion, essentially for the good ...

Chantal Hébert makes a similar argument, albeit in a more implicit fashion, when she recalls the discussions that took place on the protection of cultural diversity (2007, 175–6). Contrary to the analysis offered by Granatstein, she depicts Quebec as the protector of Pearsonian orthodoxy and the principle guardian of progressive policies and Canada's good conscience. In short, according to these commentators, Quebec serves as the "Jiminy Cricket" of Canada.

All of these crises are interrelated. For example, the debate about "Quebecistan" gave a second wind to the argument about Quebec's capacity to speak with its own voice (Bernard 2006; Pratte 2006). Furthermore, the debate over the extent of Quebec's influence on Canadian foreign policy appeared in the discussions about the reaction to Harper's policies towards Israel and the Middle East. In general, all are a symptomatic of a growing discomfort between Francophones and Anglophones on foreign policy. If Chantal Hébert is right in her prediction that Canada's major internal conflicts of the 21st century will spin around issues such as the environment or security (Hébert 2007, 300), these questions need to be examined more closely.

QUESTIONING THE ASSUMPTIONS

The image of the "two solitudes" still resonates forcefully to any Canadian observer of Quebec and its relations with the rest of Canada vis-à-vis international relations. We can best explain the persistence of the "pacifist myth" by the fact that commentators from both linguistic communities often employ it in their arguments. The discussion above actually points toward this conclusion. Canadian nationalists, such as Granatstein, use this myth to denounce Quebec's influence on Canadian foreign policy decision-making, while nationalist Quebecois draw on it to exemplify Quebec's distinctiveness. In fact, the "pacifist myth" benefits from a double-foundation, stemming from the claims of both Canadian and Quebecois nationalists, which greatly amplify its force and its persistence.

The current debate revolves around three empirically unverified assumptions. First, that Quebecois[3] are effectively pacifists, opposing any Canadian participation in foreign military operations short of United Nations (UN) peacekeeping ones. The second, more implicit argument posits that this specifically Quebecois attitude toward the use of force is significantly different from the attitudes of other Canadians. Last but not least, it is widely assumed that Quebecois have more influence on Canadian international behaviour than do other members of the confederation. These assumptions build upon and reinforce each other. However, to shed light on Quebec's distinctiveness regarding foreign policy issues and, hopefully, to encourage a more "empirically driven" debate, we must explore them all individually. Any attempt to ascertain or take a stance in the debate on Quebec's influence on foreign policy should, first and foremost, try to understand Quebec's attitude toward foreign policy and its alleged differences with public opinion in the rest of Canada. These three assumptions constitute the essence of the "myth" of Quebec's particularism on Canadian foreign policy.

QUEBEC'S ALLEGED PACIFISM

The conventional wisdom asserts that when it comes to defence and security policies, Quebecois are essentially anti-militarists, if not outright pacifists (Rioux 2005). The perception in Canadian's collective conscience is that Quebec's public opinion is generally hostile to the deployment of the Canadian Forces on foreign soils, and that any deployment should and must be circumscribed within peacekeeping operations supported by the UN. However, the empirical data to support such an analysis is slim at best. Few empirical studies conducted after the Cold War actually demonstrate a clear link between Quebec society and pacifism. The principal line of argumentation supporting the conventional wisdom appeals to negative historical experiences, such as the Patriotes rebellions of 1837 and 1838, the Henri Bourassa "nationalist" admonition during the Boer war in 1899, the conscription crises of 1917–18 and 1942–44 and the October crisis of 1970, in which French-Canadians clearly opposed the militaristic policies promoted first by Colonial British administrations and later by Ottawa itself. (Mongeau 1993; Granatstein 2007, 141–8; Robitaille 2004) Simply linking pacifism and Quebec through the use of an historical causal explanation has been the easy way out of actually studying the contemporary attitudes of Quebecois toward peace, war and everything in between. For a good example see Légaré-Tremblay (2005).

Two studies[4] that actually tried to empirically substantiate this perception are worth mentioning. First and most notably, J.I. Gow in 1970 attempted to compare French and English public opinions[5] between 1945 and 1960 on defence and security issues (Gow 1970). At the time of his study's publication, Gow noted an evolution in Quebec's public opinion concerning the use of force abroad and situated this development in the context of a more general attitudinal change towards international relations. Compared to their past attitudes, by 1960 "Quebecois were more inclined to see Canada play an active role in the world. Compared to other Canadians, they were however still more hesitant regarding the deployment of Canadian forces abroad, conscription, the Commonwealth and the pacific coexistence" (Gow 1970, 120–1). Establishing a causal link between this evolution and the Quiet Revolution, Gow contemplated in his own conclusions the real possibility of a Quebec society in full identity mutation which encouraged a more internationalist attitude.

Second, in his 2005 study, Jean-Sebastian Rioux argued that the "pacifist myth" had some empirical substance. Analyzing the overall coverage of leading French-Canadian (*La Presse*, *Le Soleil* and *Le Devoir*) and

English-Canadian newspapers (the *Montreal Gazette* and the *Ottawa Citizen*), Rioux concluded that the English language newspapers were more concerned about military issues than their French counterparts on an average proportion of 2.07. Overall, English-Canadians were better informed on defence and security topics than were their French counterparts. However, the link between the divergence of topic salience and the actual effects on public opinion has yet to be made. In his conclusion, Rioux acknowledged that "[there] is no obvious pattern or lessons or rule of thumb to allow us to state with empirical certainty that Quebecois are in favour of certain kinds of deployments; for example, depending on if they occur within the UN context or if they involve Francophone countries, although more in-depth analysis is needed to ascertain why some deployments find support in Quebec, and why some do not" (Rioux 2005, 23).

Exploring empirically Canadians' and, more specifically, Quebecois' attitudes toward defence and security issues is a frustrating endeavour. As many authors before us have noted (Rioux 2005; Munton and Keating 2001), the Canadian track record of scientific polling on international issues is dreadful. Major pollsters for whom methodology is not an issue – such as Gallup, Angus-Reid, Ipso-Reid and Decima – do not execute any systematic sounding out of Canadian attitudes on foreign and security policy. Even within the relatively limited time-frame (1990–2007) that is of most interest to the arguments in this chapter, pollsters do not annually examine Canadian public opinion on defence and security matters and rarely ask the same question in a repeated fashion, thus failing to capture potential fluctuations in attitudes.[6] We have collected "snapshots" of public sentiment towards some of the most important military interventions of the last 17 years, such as: the various UN missions of the mid-1990s (Bosnia, Rwanda and Somalia); NATO's multiple missions [Implementation Force in Bosnia and Herzegovina (IFOR), Stabilization Force in Bosnia and Herzegovina (SFOR), Kosovo Force (KFOR) and International Assistance Force in Afghanistan (ISAF)]; and ad hoc multilateral interventions such as those in 1991 and 2003 in Iraq and in Afghanistan in 2001. In all, more than thirty polls were collected that focused generally on defence issues and specifically on the level of public support for Canada's involvement in these interventions.

For the purpose of this particular chapter, our analysis concentrates on assessing attitudes toward Canada's participation in non-UN missions since 1990. This was done for two main reasons. First, the conventional wisdom about Quebec's attitude toward the use of force holds that Quebecois are generally highly sympathetic to UN-led missions. There is no point of contention here: being supportive of UN peacekeeping operations is not, in itself, reflective of an "anti-militarist" stance. However, one could argue that participation in more "force-heavy" international interventions (such as the SFOR in Bosnia and Herzegovina or the ISAF in Afghanistan) could have been met with strong anti-militarist opposition from the Canadian public and, according to conventional wisdom, even more so from Quebecois. Second, and more importantly, Canada's participation in UN deployments has plummeted since 1997. Although still priding itself on its UN track record, Canada has been far from an active UN troop contributor for the last decade. From 3137 military personnel deployed within various UN missions in 1996, comprising 67 per cent of Canadian troop deployment in that year, the average percentage of Canadian Forces' personnel allocation to the UN since 1997 as been around 5 per cent.[7] For the last ten years, Canada's contribution to international interventions has been heavily concentrated within NATO-led or ad hoc multilateral interventions (such as the American operation Enduring Freedom in Afghanistan). Consequently, polls analyzing Canadian public support for UN missions have been non-existent since 1997.

As one can see from the data presented in Graph 7.1, Quebecois have been generally sympathetic to Canada's military involvement throughout the post Cold War period. Such missions as the stabilizing force in Haiti in 1994, the IFOR/SFOR in Bosnia after 1995, the Kosovo operation in 1999 and the Afghanistan ISAF experience in Kabul were all supported by a majority of Quebecois. Furthermore, these were international interventions (except perhaps Haiti) where the use of force exceeded UN peacekeeping caveats and where the rules of engagement were the least stringent. As many authors have previously observed (Martin and Fortmann 1995; Nossal and Roussel 2001), the Kosovo case was particularly interesting since it did not benefit from the UN cloak of legitimacy and was still met in Quebec with continuous support. These results confirm Gow (1970) and Rioux's (2005) studies which acknowledge an internationalist sentiment in Quebec and an openness to the use of military force. They also indicate that classifying Quebecois as pacifists is somewhat of an oversimplification.

However, there is one aspect of the "pacifist myth" that still rings true: a genuine reticence among Quebecois to participate in military operations where immediate Canadian interests seem to disappear behind American imperatives. This attitude is similar to the one held by French-Canadians in the 19th and 20th century (most visibly in 1899, 1917 and 1944) when they were clearly opposed to Canadian participation in British-led military interventions. Still today, Quebecois are reluctant to shed Canadian blood for what is perceived as foreign

Graph 7.1
Quebec's Support to Canadian Participation in Non-UN Missions (1991–2006)

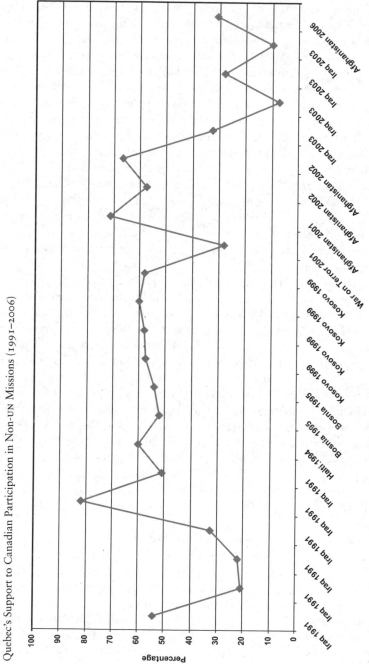

Source: Various public opinion polls, 1990–2007. Compiled by authors.

interests. In short, Quebecois agree with John Manley that if Canada wants to sit at the big table in international forums, it can't always go to the washroom when the check comes in (Molot and Hillmer 2002, 1–2). That being said, sitting at the big table doesn't necessarily mean that they are willing to pay somebody else's bill.

QUEBEC'S "DISTINCTIVENESS" IN CANADIAN DEFENCE POLICY?

As we have tried to briefly show, asserting that Quebecois are against the use of military force is problematic at best. The conventional wisdom, held dearly on the two banks of the Ottawa River, is not entirely supported by recent (that is post-1990) public opinion polls. Notwithstanding the methodological difficulties of comparing various polls across time and across issues, Quebecois have been generally supportive of Canadian military participation around the world – especially when these missions where conducted within a multilateral framework. However, some could argue that Quebecois are generally less internationalist than other Canadians, and hence more critical of international participation – especially if this action would take on military colors. In short, the key question is whether there is a fundamental difference of public opinion between Quebec and the rest of Canada on the use of force and Canadian participation in military interventions abroad.

When comparing Quebecois and ROC public opinion on diverse defence-related issues, the disparity between the two solitudes appears to be more a question of intensity than opposition. On a multitude of questions related to military operations abroad – be it UN-led, NATO-led or other ad hoc multilateral interventions – Quebecois are essentially Canadian. That is to say, they along with their ROC counterparts are highly supportive of the use of the Canadian Forces when these missions are conducted within a multilateral setting, and not necessarily only within a UN framework. When we analyze the differences between Quebecois and ROC public opinion supporting or opposing Canadian military participation in non-UN missions from 1990 to 2007, we must conclude that the distinction (taking the margin of error into account) is negligible. As illustrated in Graph 7.2, the "pacifist myth" is supported here only by a 2 per cent to 8 per cent discrepancy between Quebecois and other Canadians in most cases. In other words, it seems far-fetched to particularize Quebec's attitude toward the use of force solely on the basis of its theoretical "pacifism." At best, in light of these results, the claim can only be made that the distinction between the two solitudes is one of intensity, and not necessarily of opinion.

Graph 7.2
Difference, with Margin of Error, Quebec's and ROC's Support to Canadian Participation to Non-UN Missions (1991–2006)

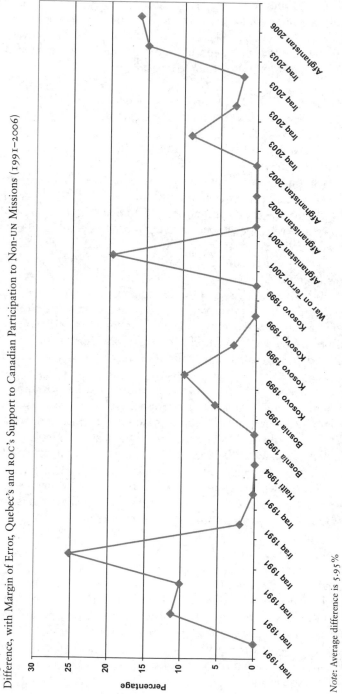

Note: Average difference is 5.95 %
Source: Various public opinion polls, 1990–2007. Compiled by authors.

Nevertheless, there are only four times since 1990 when Quebec's and the rest of Canada's public opinion diverged beyond a ten per cent margin: the 1991 invasion of Iraq; the first Afghanistan mission (more specifically, Operation Apollo) in 2001–2002; the Iraq war in 2003; and the 2006–2007 Afghan mission. There is a significant difference between Quebec and the rest of Canada when the country participates in foreign military operations closely undertaken with the United States or that are seen to be strongly in line with American interests. Opposition to the use of force, therefore, appears to be an insufficient condition in explaining Quebecois' attitude toward Canadian military deployments. If it was an influential element, it would be difficult to explain why Quebecois were highly supportive of military missions in Bosnia (IFOR/SFOR), Kosovo and the brief 2003–2006 ISAF Kabul mission in Afghanistan.[8] In this light, the use of force appears to be an insufficient condition to explain Quebecois' attitude toward Canadian military deployments.

Quebec's anti-American sentiment, exacerbated by the tenure of the G. W. Bush administration, is often disregarded when explaining why Quebecois feel so strongly about certain defence issues. Although many authors have recently acknowledged its influence on Quebec's public opinion on foreign policy issues (Rioux 2005; Martin 2005; Haglund 2006; Balthazar 2005; Coulon 2005), we still do not have a clear idea on the extent and influence of anti-Americanism in Quebec. What seems clear however is the mounting of a general uneasiness among Quebecois to the Bush administration's radicalization of US foreign policy.[9] For example, a 2005 SES Canada Research survey revealed that 44 per cent of Quebecois wished to have more distance in terms of Canada's relationship with US on defence cooperation, while only 28 per cent of other Canadians were of the same opinion. All recent foreign policy decisions in which Canada-US defence cooperation was a factor (that is Afghanistan 2001 and 2005–2007, Iraq 2003, the ballistic-missile defence (BMD) initiative in 2005 and even the Lebanon crisis in 2006) were influenced by Quebec's anti-Americanism.

Quebecois are favourable to the use of force abroad when accomplished within missions associated with international organizations such as the UN and NATO, but are suspicious when these military adventures echo perceived American interests or influence. Thus, anti-Americanism seems to be the intervening variable influencing Quebec's public opinion on defence issues. As Rioux explains: "For Quebec, therefore, as long as Ottawa designs defence policy that meet Canadian foreign policy objectives – as opposed to American or European interests – that respects Canadian values and priorities, there may exist ample political capital for supporting defence issues" (Rioux 2005, 25).

One other element highlighted by our study of public opinion polls is the relative harmony of the trends in Quebec and the ROC public opinion curves. In other words, in spite of the various particular events that cause fluctuations in the public perception of Canadian missions abroad, the difference in public opinion between Quebec and ROC remains reasonably stable. This is surprising when contemplating the Afghanistan intervention between 2006 and 2007 and Canadian involvement in the Kandahar region. As one can see from Graph 7.3 which represents the evolution of Canadian public opinion toward the Kandahar mission, (and notwithstanding the various methodological deficiencies of the Strategic Counsel polls) public opinion in Quebec, Ontario and Western Canada appears to respond similarly to particular events. While Quebecois are more opposed than other Canadians to this particular mission, the difference between the levels of opposition is constant, ranging between 18 per cent and 20 per cent. Of course, with only the polls as limited evidence, it is not possible to identify all of the stimuli that cause these "mood swings" in Canada, but it is safe to say that Quebec and the ROC sing in unison in their response to the Kandahar mission.

In retrospect, our data seems to reveal that the attitudes of Quebecois compared with those of other Canadians toward military deployment abroad are not overly dissimilar in the post-Cold War period. Quebecois, as Canadians, have in general largely supported Ottawa's decisions to use the Canadian Forces in international interventions. As such, it seems that the internationalist sentiment is perhaps as strong in Quebec City and Montreal as it is in St. John's, Toronto, Calgary and Vancouver. Thus, accusing Quebecois of being too "pacifist" seems a moot point as this value is shared by other Canadians as well. However, as our results indicate, Quebecois are more critical of Canadian deployments that appear to match American interests and where national values and interests are not clearly palpable.

QUEBEC'S INFLUENCE ON CANADIAN FOREIGN POLICY?

What are the limits, if any, imposed by Quebec's idiosyncrasy on Canadian foreign policy? As we have seen, some authors, like Morton (2003) or Granatstein (2004; 2005a; 2007) have argued that Quebec has literally hijacked Canadian foreign policy for better or for worse. Although we have tried to show that Quebecois are not necessarily "pacifists" and are not overly different from other Canadians in respect to their support for military interventions abroad, this question of Quebec's influence on Canadian international policies still needs to be addressed.

Graph 7.3
Distinction between Public Opinions in Quebec, Ontario, and Western Provinces on Canada's Participation to the Canadian Mission in Afghanistan (2006–07), Total Opposed

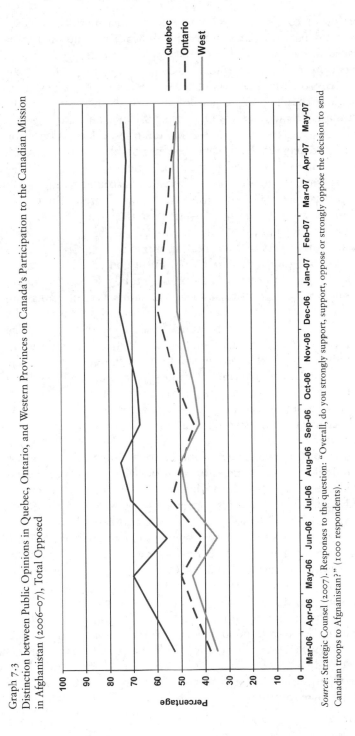

Source: Strategic Counsel (2007). Responses to the question: "Overall, do you strongly support, support, oppose or strongly oppose the decision to send Canadian troops to Afghanistan?" (1000 respondents).

In the period of 2003–2007, the Quebec "pacifist myth" and ensuing widespread debates in Canadian political, academic and media circles resurfaced in light of Canada's decisions in three separate events: non-participation in the 2003 Iraq invasion, non-participation in the American BMD program in 2005 and the extension of the Afghan mission in the Kandahar region until 2009. Although these are not the only case studies at hand to assess Quebec's influence on Canadian foreign policy, they all share important communalities: a strong rejection of participation/extension by Quebecois; a notable military aspect; clear ties to Canada-US defence cooperation; and a general perception that Quebec is playing a major role in Ottawa's decision-making.

The Chrétien government's decision not to participate in the US-led Iraq invasion in 2003 is often attributed to the strong opposition within Quebec to the operation. The fact that 150,000–250,000 Quebecois marched the streets of Montreal at minus 26 degrees Celsius in February 2003 to demonstrate their opposition compared to a maximum turnout of 30,000 people in Toronto certainly strikes the imagination. While 81 per cent of Quebecois disapproved of Canadian participation in the US military intervention in Iraq, 62 per cent of the ROC were of the same opinion (Environics Research Group 2003). The combination of a strong anti-Bush reaction in Quebec and the need to curry favour in the face of a provincial election characterized by the prospect of a sovereignist government coming to power were key parts of the equation when it came to the Chrétien government's decision.

Whether staying out of Iraq does not seem like such a bad idea now four years later in 2007, Ottawa's decision not to follow Washington's lead in this matter should not be attributed solely to Quebecois attitudes. First, a majority of Canadians were opposed to any involvement in Iraq (though admittedly to a lesser extent than Quebecois). Support for Canadian participation in the US-led Iraq invasion never rose above 45 per cent. Second, Jean Chrétien and his entourage's anti-Bush sentiments are well documented. From Raymond Chrétien's support to Al Gore's candidacy in the US elections of 2002 to Chrétien's Communications Director, Francoise Ducros' allegation that Bush was a "moron," Ottawa did its part to exacerbate tensions between Canada and the US Last, the opposition to the Iraq invasion was not the "appanage" of Canada: Washington's unilateralist position on the Iraq issue was highly controversial at the time and anti-war protests were held around the globe, most notably in Western capitals such as Paris, Berlin, London and Rome. All of these factors played a role in Canada's refusal to get involved in Iraq and Quebec's public opinion only played a minor one.

The Martin government's decision to forgo partaking in the US ballistic-missile defence program in 2005 is another case in which the alleged weight of Quebec's opinion on the formulation of national policy was highlighted by many. Pierre Martin's (2005) short but concise text analyzing whether Quebec was at "fault" for this decision is probably the best effort that has been made to understand the influence of Quebec on Ottawa's decision-making. At face value, the relatively weak position of the Martin minority government, especially in the midst of the sponsorship scandal, had emphasized Quebec's electoral importance for the prospect of the next federal election. Quebec's public opinion was opposed to Canada's contribution to BMD – 63 per cent of Quebecois agreed with the government's decision not to participate in the US plan (Decima 2005) – and political leadership in Quebec (especially from the Bloc Quebecois) clearly expressed its disagreement with the prospect of joining BMD. Martin could ill afford to lose any further seats in the province in an upcoming federal election and this political calculation probably boosted the strength of Quebec's voice on the BMD decision.

However, simply blaming Quebec for having single-handedly "forced" the Martin government is far from a complete explanation. First, many pockets of political opposition, aside from Quebec's public opinion, were campaigning for a rejection of Canada's participation in BMD. As Pierre Martin noted: "In [Prime Minister Paul Martin's] own caucus, the most vocal opponents of BMD were from outside Quebec and expressed their opinion with passion" (Martin 2005). Second, Paul Martin's lack of leadership in clearly asserting his decision on the matter and subsequently defending it contributed to the strength of those in opposition to Canadian participation in BMD. Last but not least, the Bush administration's attempts to bully Canada into joining BMD, epitomized by various public declarations from both countries' officials, painted both parties into corners. Again, if Quebec was a factor in Martin's decision not to participate in the BMD plan, it was a small one and its influence was solely based on the federal circumstances at the time.

Despite strong reactions in Quebec and elsewhere in Canada criticizing the Harper government's position on the Canadian Forces' deployment in Kandahar (Quebecois have opposed the Afghan mission by an average majority of 68 per cent), clearly these concerns did not lead to policy changes in Ottawa. The Harper government is actually dealing with a unique political context. First, although leading a minority government, the Conservatives are not currently overly threatened by any other federal parties. Contrary to the Martin government, who had to work with an effective and credible opposition (the Conservatives and the Bloc Quebecois) and deal with a national scandal (sponsorship program), Stephen Harper benefits from the frailty of his political adversaries. Second, the political leadership in Quebec (again looking to the

Bloc Quebecois) is far from opposed to Canada's participation in Afghanistan. The Bloc's official position is, in fact, quite nuanced:

The Bloc Quebecois insists on the importance of a rapid rebalancing of this mission in favour of its humanitarian aspect. In May 2006, the Bloc Quebecois voted against the prolongation of this mission until February 2009 in its actual form. However, the moment it got involved, we think that Canada must respect its commitment and should maintain its military effort with the International Security assistance force (ISAF) in Afghanistan. A sudden disengagement would comprise severe consequences for the Afghan population. This gesture, would moreover, be irresponsible toward our allies that count on Canadian collaboration.[10]

Third, the Conservatives' flirtation with Quebec seems to be based on a different strategy than that of previous Liberal governments. Contrary to the governments of Jean Chrétien and Paul Martin, the Conservatives appear to be waging a seduction campaign with Quebec based on domestic-oriented issues, such as the recognition of Quebec as a nation within the confederation or fiscal rebalancing in favour of provinces, while keeping a strong stance on foreign policy decisions. The Harper government probably has "some" room to manoeuvre in light of the particular political context.

When all is said and done, maybe Quebec has voiced its opposition more forcefully on these issues. Then again, it is not at all clear that it was heard in Ottawa. Quebecois are not as prominent and influential in foreign policy decision-making as some would think (Canadian nationalists) or wished (Quebecois themselves). However, the emphasis wrongfully put on Quebec-ROC's disagreement toward the use of force abroad hides another reality: there is no unified consensus inside the ROC itself on these issues. Contrary to what Canadian (such as Granatstein) or Quebecois (such as Paquin) commentators assume, Canadian opinion on the use of force is actually scaled on a wide continuum, ranging from Quebec's anti-Americanist influenced liberalism on the one hand to Alberta's and the Maritime provinces more "realist" understanding of Canada's place in the world. Simply put, there is no "rest of Canada" that could represent a unified counterpart to Quebec's stance on defence issues.

QUEBEC AS THE PHARMAKON OF CFP

The conventional wisdom debate along the "two solitudes" division obscures this simple fact. The Quebec "pacifist myth" projects the illusion that there is an homogenous English-Canadian attitude toward the use of force. The Strategic Counsel's repeated polling of public opinion on Canada's participation in the Afghan mission is a blatant example of this phenomenon. As shown in Graph 7.3, the Strategic Counsel establishes a distinction between three Canadian regions: Quebec, Ontario and the Western Provinces. As other sporadic polls published by Angus-Reid (April 2007) or Decima Research (June 2006) have shown, this division is highly problematic. For example, Alberta and B.C.'s public opinion diverge quite strongly on numerous international issues such as the Afghan mission and Kyoto. Another example of this divergence is seen in the June 2006 Decima Research report which revealed that 57 per cent of British Columbians opposed the decision to extend the mission of the Canadian troops in Afghanistan whereas 40 per cent of Albertans were of the same opinion (64 per cent of Quebecers opposed the decision). Additionally, in its April 2007 report, Angus-Reid's results show that 56 per cent of British Columbians agreed with the statement "Canada should withdraw its troops from Afghanistan before their mandate ends in February 2009" while only 27 per cent of Albertans offered a similar response (66 per cent of Quebecois agreed with the statement). These polls tend to show that B.C. and Quebec's populations were more of the same mind on these issues than were the "Western Provinces" as a group.

In other words, the pacifist myth creates a sense of Canadian unity and more specifically, a sense of ROC unity. This specific influence appears to be a "positive externality" of the pacifist myth debate.[11] René Girard's (1977) idea of the Pharmakon seems a good, if not perfect, intellectual ground upon which to understand the connections between myths, identity and communal scapegoating. Coined after the Ancient Greek term *pharmacos*, meaning either a poison or a remedy depending on the use and dose of the substance, the Pharmakon was a sacrificial victim (an animal, a person, etc.) which was invested with the sacred mission of cleansing a community of its corruption by being sacrificed or expelled. In times of crises in Ancient Greece, when important communal scissions threatened the social fabric of a city-state, a Pharmakon was chosen to represent the sum of the city's evil and corruption. The victim was then cast out of the city either by death or exile and this action was understood as cleansing the city of its sins.[12] According to Girard, the Pharmakon phenomenon was, in essence, a communal conflict catharsis or a social remedy that was and still is fundamental to human societies. The Pharmakon transposition helps to create a sense of unity in communities, especially in times of great disjunction between its members.

We could argue that Quebec appears to be playing a "Pharmakon" role by being both the poison and the remedy in contemporary Canadian foreign and defence policy. This analogy could help to reconcile the two main opposing views on Quebec's contribution to Canadian foreign policy, which can be depicted as two sides of the same coin. From the perspective of some Canadian nationalists, Quebec could be viewed as a poison since it represents the dissidents who are distracting the majority (that is the rest of Canada's majority) in its quest to achieve the national interest. The attitude of Quebecois is seen as an obstacle to reconciliation with the US (our data tends to show that they may be right on this point), to the constitution of robust military forces able to fight in "real" wars instead of safer (but now irrelevant) peacekeeping missions, and in the process of harmonious and rational decision-making regarding major issues. In its worst expression, Quebec represents a nest for extreme ideas, such as anti-Semitism or complicity with terrorism and "islamo-fascism" (Kay 2006b). Thus, from the perspective of some Canadian nationalists, Quebec would be a "poison" in the Canadian federation, especially in terms of foreign policy.

But the same arguments can also be used to support the idea of Quebec as providing a remedy to Canadian foreign and defence policy, and furthermore, from two perspectives. First, the constant discussion around the "two solitudes" is not only comforting to Quebecois by reinforcing their historical victim perspective toward military institutions and the "uniqueness" of their identity inside the Canadian federation, but it also serves English Canada's sense of unity through denying significant attention to its regional heterogeneity. By focusing and concentrating anger toward Quebec, some English Canadian commentators can more easily dismiss non-Quebecois who hold similar views to Quebecois regarding the use of force or Canada's role in international interventions. Second, Quebec can be perceived as the most reliable guardian of what is presented as the values par excellence of Canadian foreign policy: those that are against conservative and American worldviews (Paquin 2006–2007; Pratte 2006a). These values include, among others, a faith in the United Nations and international institutions, the primacy of peaceful conflict management methods to solve political problems, and the preservation of a distinctive cultural and social identity.

By its symbolic nature, the Pharmakon analogy also reminds us that the debate about Quebec's attitude or influence on Canadian foreign policy remains first and foremost a discourse. Like all political discourse, it is possible to identify some of the interests it serves. It is very tempting to draw some connections to the debate over national unity – a debate in which the discourse employed can serve those on each side of it very well. Quebec sovereigntists did not hesitate to use this discourse to point out how different Quebecois are; an observation which was then added to the rationale for sovereignty. Bernard Landry's famous words after the rally held in Montreal against a possible Canadian contribution to the "Coalition of the Willing" in February 2003 is a good example of this: "this means that there is really two nations in Canada. Those who didn't know can [now] see it clearly ... With all due respect, this shows that Quebecois are a nation and this nation should have international status" (Quoted in Robitaille 2004, 62). It is nevertheless revealing that, according to both Parti Quebecois and Bloc Quebecois political programs, a sovereign Quebec foreign and defence policy would be not very different from the Canadian one, at least from its Pearsonian expression (Roussel and Theorêt 2004). For the federalist camp, debates over issues such as the Middle-East conflict or BMD present a golden opportunity to recall how irresponsible (if not simply dangerous) separatists are, and then to draw apocalyptic scenarios for a sovereign Quebec.

Of course, the Pharmakon analogy has obvious limits. In Ancient Greece, the purification ceremony culminated by the death or the banishment of the Pharmakon. This is clearly not the fate awaiting Quebec here. It is a useful metaphor that articulates the dual nature (poison and remedy) of the "pacifist myth" in Canadian foreign policy. Those who find discomfort with what they perceive as Quebec's distinctive attitude place their hopes in the ability of some federal politicians to conclude another concordat with Quebec, as Louis St-Laurent did it at the beginning of the Cold War (Granatstein 2007, 147–8), or to uphold and defend the distinction "between a democracy and a gang of fanatical exterminationists," something that politicians in Quebec seems to have hard time doing, according to Kay (2006a). Nevertheless, if we think that Quebec has any unique influence on Canadian foreign policy, it is not the one of which we may first think. The evidence we have reviewed shows that a compelling argument about Quebec's influence on Canadian foreign and defence policy must relativize the importance of Quebec's distinctiveness and influence on these matters. However, the image of the "two solitudes" has its uses and influences on Canadian politics which cannot be overlooked.

CONCLUSION

Quebec's so-called "distinctive pacifism" is often presented as a constraint on Canadian foreign and defence policy, no matter if the outcome is perceived as having had a positive or negative impact. As argued in this chapter, this idea is, at the very least, debatable. Indeed,

Quebec's "pacifism" pertains more to "anti-Americanism" than to an-timilitarism or isolationism and the available data remains insufficient to make a definitive judgment about the width of the gap splitting the Quebecois and the ROC, although the evidence is robust enough to question the validity of the conventional wisdom. If the difference be-tween Anglophone Canadians and Francophone Quebecois is less sub-stantial than this conventional wisdom holds, then it is possible to talk of a "self-imposed constraint." As the war in Afghanistan goes on, such a delusion could be counter-productive and politically costly.

Further research on the political implications of the discourse over Quebec's distinctiveness and influence over Canadian foreign and de-fence policy is essential. Our hypothesis, based on our preliminary work, is that such a difference still exists, but that it is much narrower than commonly held. Beyond episodic peaks, the average difference observed in the polls on defence and security questions is around ten per cent. The curves of the two groups are parallel, suggesting that they are reacting similarly to the same stimuli. This seems to indicate that the trends observed by Gow in the early 1970s are continuing on: Quebecois are more "internationalist" than "pacifist" or "isolation-ist," and increasingly so. At the same time, differences among other Canadian provinces are becoming more visible, reducing the relevance of a comparison between Quebec and the ROC.

In this context, the most important task that remains is to explain why Quebecois are moving toward an internationalist agenda. What political, social or economic factors are at the origin of this shift? Moreover, if a difference remains (even a minor one), it also deserves an explanation. Carefully qualifying the factors at play is probably the only way to contribute positively to debates that are otherwise largely based on clichés, prejudices, or simplistic images borrowed at times from a distant past.

But trying to get a more accurate or nuanced image of the attitudes displayed by a society and their influence over political decision-makers is not enough. Discourses such as those about the legitimacy of Quebec's representation abroad, about the proper approach toward complex situations (such as those in the Middle-East), or about the value of Quebec's contribution to the shaping of Canadian foreign pol-icy cannot be settled by "facts and figures." Because they carry emo-tional charges and political meaning, it is also important to identify who is using such a discourse, what the underlying assumptions are and whose interests it serves. In this perspective, and even with its limited potential as an analytical tool, the Pharmakon analogy is a powerful reminder of the necessity to make a distinction between the substance and the symbol.

NOTES

The authors would like to thank Jean-Sébastien Rioux who was the initial instigator of this research program, but decided to pursue different challenges in the public service. The authors also highly benefited from the comments and corrections made by the editors of this volume as well as the editing skills of Kelly Jackson. Any shortcomings, either in form or in the general thesis of this paper are entirely the authors' responsibility.

1 The origins of this demand are contained in the 1965 Gérin-Lajoie Doctrine.
2 There are, of course, some notable exceptions, such as Abley (2006). MacPherson *et al.* are not the only ones to have expressed such an opinion. Jack Granatstein, mentioning this episode (2007, 155–156), writes: "some francophone commentators detected substantial anti-Semitism playing its part in shaping the almost unanimous public response against Israel's 'war crimes', including placards reading 'Juifs assassins' and quotes Jean Renaud and Jacques Brassard." Unfortunately, he does not reveal his sources.
3 The term "Quebecois," especially used in the current discussion, is ambiguous. Most pollsters do not differentiate between linguistic communities and our conclusions or thesis should hold for any person, be it Francophone, Anglophone or Allophone living in the Province of Quebec.
4 Martin and Fortmann's (1995 and 2001) studies on Canadian public support for Canadian Forces' deployments during the 1990s is another attempt to investigate empirically the role of public opinion on foreign policies. They conclude that "In general, we find public opinion to be resilient in its internationalism. This was particularly true in the case of support for Canada's participation in UN peacekeeping operations and support for joining NATO in Operation 'Allied Force'" (Martin and Fortmann 2001: 50). However, they do not assess the role of Quebec's public opinion and particularly on these issues and, thus, are of limited use for our present analysis.
5 Unfortunately at the time, public opinion polls did not discriminate between provinces, but only by the mother tongue of the respondents. Provincial demarcations within public opinion date actually only appear in the polls published after 1975. Gow assumes that most French speaking respondents were Quebecois. Methodologically erroneous as it may seems today, Gow had to work with the instruments available to him at the time.
6 One exception is the Strategic Counsel's analysis on public support of the Afghanistan mission since 2006. The Strategic Counsel is the only pollster consistently analysing the Canadian public by using the same question, permitting empirically verifiable research. However, its sampling size is insufficient (that is 1000 respondents across Canada) if one wants to compare provincial results. For example, only 240-odd respondents come from Quebec, pushing the margin of error to an unacceptable 6.3.

7 In 2001, that per centage was briefly augmented to 20 per cent of foreign troop allocation thanks to the Ethiopia-Eritrea mission.

8 We are indebted to Thomas Juneau for this counter-argument to our thesis. Although we will probably not convince him of the soundness of our conclusion, only a quantitative content analysis of speeches and media coverage could shed light on this matter.

9 As Stanley Hoffmann duly noted (2001), there are two forms of anti-Americanism. The first, being more pervasive and reductionist, is a general rejection of what Americans are and what they represent. The second, what Hoffman calls "ambivalent" anti-Americanism, is generally associated with a critical stance on the American way of doing things, especially in terms of foreign policy. It is sometimes difficult to differentiate between the two since being a "reductionist anti-American" necessarily brings you to formulate disapproving judgments on US behavior abroad, thus artificially inflating the "ambivalent anti-American" group.

10 The Bloc Québécois' official position on the Afghan mission is available at http://www.blocquebecois.org/fr/audiovisuel.asp?id=109

11 We are not arguing here that there is a conspiracy theory at work; the term "externality" is quite appropriate in the sense that it is an unforeseen consequence.

12 The death of Socrates could be seen in this light where, after the collapse of the Athenian campaign against Sparta at Syracuse, the Greek philosopher was accused and charged, among other things, of having corrupted the Athenian youth, and sentenced to death by drinking hemlock.

REFERENCES

Abley, Mark. 2006. "Sympathy for Lebanon widespread; But that doesn't make Quebecers anti-Semitic, writes Mark Abley." *The Toronto Star,* 19 August: F05.

Balthazar, Louis. 2005. "Cet empire d'où nous vient tout le mal." *Argument. Politique, société, histoire* 7, no. 2 (Spring-Summer): 12–21.

Bernard, Louis. 2006. "Le Québec sans voix. L'incapacité de débattre des questions internationales dans nos instances politiques québécoises est débilitante." *La Presse,* 21 August: A13.

Boisvert, Yves. 2006a. "Le Québecistan vous répond." *La Presse,* 16 August: A5.

– 2006b. "Writer's 'Quebecistan' label a cheap shot; Anti-Semitic current in province no worse than rest of Canada." *The Toronto Star,* 20 August: A17.

Coulon, Jocelyn. 2005. "Le nouvel antiaméricanisme." *Argument. Politique, société, histoire* 7, no. 2 (Spring-Summer): 48–55.

Girard, René. 1977. *Violence and the Sacred*. Baltimore: John Hopkins University Press.

Gow, James Ian. 1970. "Les Quebecois, la guerre et la paix, 1945–1960." *Canadian Journal of Political Science* 3, no. 1: 104–11.

Granatstein, J.L. 2007. *Whose War Is It? How Canada Can Survive in the Post-9/11 World*. Toronto: HarperCollins.

– 2005a. "Quebecers are at the Helm. It is bad for national unity to have Quebec setting agenda on the war in Iraq or a missile-defence program." *The Ottawa Citizen*, 1 November: A15.

– 2005b. *Canada, Quebec, Anti-Americanism and Our Leadership Vacuum*. Available at: <http://www.cda-cdai.ca/CDA_GMs/AGM68/GranatsteinI05.pdf>

– 2004. *Who Killed the Canadian Military?* Toronto: Harper Collins.

Haglund, David G. 2006. "Québec 'America Problem': Differential Threat Perception in the North American Security Community." *American Review of Canadian Studies* 36, no. 4: 552–67.

Hébert, Chantal. 2007. *French Kiss. Le rendez-vous de Stephen Harper avec le Québec*. Montréal: Les éditions de l'Homme.

Hoffmann, Stanley. 2001. "On the War." *New York Review of Books* 48, no. 17.

Kay, Barbara. 2006a. "The Rise of Quebecistan." *National Post*, 9 August: A18.

– 2006b. "Quebecers in denial: Counterpoint." *National Post*, 17 August: A16.

Légaré-Tremblay, Jean-Frédéric. 2005. "Le soleil à l'ombre de Gulliver." *Argument. Politique, société, histoire* 7, no. 2 (Spring-Summer): 40–7.

Legault, Josée. 2006. "Francophones unjustly labelled intolerant." *The Gazette*, 18 August: A21.

MacPherson, Don. 2006. "It's safe to support terrorists again: Politicians showed poor judgment on Sunday by associating with Hezbollah sympathizers." *The Gazette*, 8 August: A19.

Martin, Pierre. 2005. "All Quebec's Fault, Again? Quebec Public Opinion and Canada's Rejection of Missile Defence." *Policy Option* 26, no. 5 (May): 41–4.

– and Michel Fortmann. 2001. "Support for International Involvement in Canadian Public Opinion After the Cold War." *Canadian Military Journal* 2, no. 3 (Fall): 43–52.

– and Michel Fortmann. 1995. "Canadian public opinion and peacekeeping in a turbulent world." *International Journal* 50: 370–400.

Mongeau, Serge. 1993. "La tradition antimilitariste au Québec." In *Pour un pays sans armée*, edited by Serge Mongeau. Montreal: Écosociété, 81–9.

Morton, Ted. 2003. "A New Quebec Alberta Alliance?" *National Post*, 20 May. Available at: <http://www.tedmorton.ca>

– and Tom Keating. 2001. "Internationalism and the Canadian Public." *Canadian Journal of Political Science/Revue canadienne de science politique* 34, no. 3: 517–49.

Nossal, Kim R., and Stéphane Roussel. 2001. "Canada and the Kosovo War: the Happy Follower." In *Alliance Politics, Kosovo, and NATO's War: Allied Force or Forced Allies?* edited by Pierre Martin and Mark R. Brawley. New York: St. Martin's Press, 181–99.

Paquin, Stéphane. 2007a. *Communication pronounced at the Monterey University* (Mexico), 8 March.

– 2007b. "Bilan Charest: les relations internationales du Québec." *L'Action nationale* 97, no. 3: 101–10.

– 2006–2007. "La gouvernance à paliers multiples: un accent sur le cas de la Belgique." *Télescope*, ENAP: 82.

Pellerin, Brigitte. 2006. "Quebec's ugly little bias." *Ottawa Citizen*, 20 July: A16.

Pratte, André. 2006a. "The Myth of 'Quebecistan': Counterpoint." *National Post*, 16 August: A14.

– 2006b. "Kay contre Biz." *La Presse*, 17 August: A20.

– 2006c. "De Pearson à Duceppe." *La Presse*, 21 August: A13.

Rioux, Jean-Sébastien. 2005. *Two Solitudes: Quebecers' Attitudes Regarding Canadian Security and Defence Policy.* Calgary: CDFAI.

Robitaille, Antoine. 2004. "Quebecers: A Pacifist People?" *Inroads* 14 (Winter/Spring): 62–75.

Roussel, Stéphane and Charles-Alexandre Théorêt. 2004. "A 'Distinct Strategy'? The Use of Canadian Strategic Culture by the Sovereignist Movement in Quebec, 1968–1996." *International Journal* 49, no. 3 (Summer): 557–77.

Roy, Mario. 2006. "Les liaisons dangereuses." *La Presse*, 10 August: A16.

Sansfaçon, Jean-Robert. 2006. "Propos sous influence." *Le Devoir*, 17 August.

St-Laurent, Louis. 1947. "The Foundation of Canadian Policy in World Affairs." Gray Foundation Lectureship, Toronto. *Statements and Speeches* 47, no. 2, 13 January.

PUBLIC OPINION POLLS

Angus-Reid Strategies. 2007. "Canada in Afghanistan. Canadians Grow Impatient with Afghan Mission." Data collected between 19 April through 20 April 2007.

– 2007. "Kyoto Protocol and Climate Change. Canadians Reject Baird's views on Global Warming." Data collected between 24 April through 25 April 2007.

Decima Research. 2006. "More oppose than support extension of mission in Afghanistan." Data collected between 25 May through 28 May 2006.

– 2006. "Les Canadiens divisés sur l'Afhanistan." Data collected between
31 March through 4 April 2006.

– 2002. "Six Canadiens sur dix pensent que le Canada ne dépense pas assez
pour l'armée et la défense." Data collected between 13 December through
21 December 2002.

– 2001. "Canadians solidly behind the war against terrorism. But many
are concerned about their personal safety." Data collected between
18 September through 22 September 2001.

Environics Research Group. 2003. "Only One-Third of Canadians Approve of
Iraq War, Canadian Participation Without UN Sanction." Data collected
between 7 March through 27 March 2003.

Gallup. 2002. "The Gallup Poll: Opinion Polarizing on Military in
Afghanistan, but Majority Still Sees Right Amount of Canadian
Participation." Data collected between 15 January through 20 January
2002.

– 2002. "The Gallup Poll: Few Canadians See Not Enough Military
Participation in Afghanistan." Data collected between 11 February through
16 February 2002).

– 2001. "The Gallup Poll: Majority Sees Enough Canadian Participation in
Military Actions in Afghanistan." Data collected between 17 October
through 23 October 2001.

– 1999. "The Gallup Poll: Majority of Canadians Approve of NATO' Actions
in Kosovo." Data collected between 12 April through 18 April 1999.

– 1999. "The Gallup Poll: Canadians Approval of NATO's Actions in Kosovo
Declines." Data collected between 14 May through 23 May 1999.

– 1998. "The Gallup Poll: 80% Consider Iraq a Threat to World Peace,
Majority Would Favour Canada Joining Military Offensive." Data collected
between 18 February through 24 February 1998.

– 1995. "The Gallup Report: United Nations Losing Respect Among
Canadians." Data collected between 7 August through 13 August 1995.

– 1995. "The Gallup Report: 58% Agree with NATO Offensive in Bosnia."
Data collected between 6 September through 11 September 1995.

– 1995. "The Gallup Poll: Six in Ten Favour Canada Sending Troops to
Balkans." Data collected between 6 December through 11 December 1995.

– 1994. "The Gallup Report: Canada's Peacekeeping Role Assessed." Data
collected between 10 January through 17 January 1994.

– 1994. "The Gallup Report: Canadians Assess Country's Role in Haiti."
Data collected between 3 October through 8 October 1994.

– 1992. "The Gallup Report: Majority Support U.N. Intervention in Former
Yugoslavia." Data collected between 10 September through 14 September
1992.

– 1991. "The Gallup Report: Mulroney Applauded for Persian Gulf War
Performance." Data collected between 6 March through 9 March 1991.

– 1991. "The Gallup Report: Majority Favor Canadian Participation in Persian Gulf War." Data collected between 6 February through 9 February 1991.

– 1991. "The Gallup Report: Majority of Canadians Remain Opposed to War Against Iraq." Data collected between 2 January through 5 January 1991.

– 1990. "The Gallup Report: United Nations Gains Increasing Respect from Canadians." Data collected between 12 September through 15 September 1990.

– 1990. "The Gallup Report: Majority Favor Keeping Canadian Troops in Europe." Data collected between 10 January through 13 January 1990.

– 1990. "The Gallup Report: Canadians Approve of Sending Forces to Persian Gulf." Data collected between 12 September through 15 September 1990.

– 1990. "The Gallup Report: Majority of Canadians Opposed to War Against Iraq." Data collected between 5 December through 8 December 1990.

Institut canadien pour la paix et la sécurité internationales. 1990. "Les nouvelles conceptions de la sécurité: les attitudes du public canadien." Data collected in June and July 1990.

SES Canada Research. 2005. "Defence Relationship with the US." Data collected between 17 March through 22 March 2005.

Strategic Counsel. 2007. "Trusted Canadian Institutions, Afghanistan, and Foreign Ownership." Data collected between 14 May through 18 May 2007. Available at: <http://www.thestrategiccounsel.com/our_news/polls/2007-05-18%20GMCTV%20May%2014-17.pdf>

PART TWO
The Global Game

8 Developing Canada's Intellectual Property Agenda

JEREMY DE BEER
AND MICHAEL GEIST

Knowledge is now the most precious resource in the global economy. This valuable intangible profoundly affects commerce, culture, education, health, nutrition and other core economic, social and humanitarian issues. Access to and exchanges of all sorts of knowledge are, therefore, integral to all countries at any stage of development, including Canada.

Knowledge pertaining to revolutionary digital and biological technologies is currently governed by a global regime of institutions and agreements on trade, intellectual property and related topics. The last decades of the twentieth century were marked by an unprecedented convergence between intellectual property lawmaking and global trade policy. Bilateral and multilateral international agreements led to the harmonization of intellectual property standards throughout the world. International intellectual property policy was developed primarily as a response to the trade agendas of a few developed countries. The social and economic interests of developing countries were largely ignored.

The dynamic global economic landscape of the twenty-first century requires rethinking international intellectual property policies. New norms are challenging the substance of existing intellectual property rules, as the networked information economy offers previously unimaginable opportunities (Benkler 2006). The procedures for creating international intellectual property laws are changing, as emerging economic powerhouses insist upon equitable participation in negotiations with full information and without coercion (Drahos and Braithwaite 2002, 189–92). The forums for debating policies and making laws are proliferating, as intellectual property issues affect national, regional and international institutions and interests in a range of fields (May 2007, 96–8).

Canadians are well positioned to help shape emerging intellectual property paradigms. Canada has first-hand experience with what has become a template for bilateral or regional agreements in this area, the North American Free Trade Agreement (NAFTA), and was among the key players in negotiations over the single most important international instrument in the field, the 1994 Agreement on Trade-Related Aspects of Intellectual Property (TRIPs). At the same time, however, as a net importer of intellectual property, Canada struggles to preserve its independent cultural identity and shares many other intellectual property concerns with developing countries.

In this chapter, the new global intellectual property framework is explored in order to identify what room to maneuver exists for Canadian foreign and domestic policies. By taking advantage of flexibilities in existing international agreements and promoting progressive attitudes toward new international initiatives, Canada can advance its own interests while simultaneously facilitating social and economic development in other parts of the world. To seize this opportunity, Canada should leverage its technocratic expertise to positively influence global knowledge governance policies and implement domestic reforms as "middle-ground" models for the information society. Adopting the incisive strategies proposed here will secure a leadership role for Canada in the world's new knowledge economy.

BACKGROUND

The process of globalizing intellectual property standards began during the late nineteenth century. The first major multinational agreement regarding patents, trade-marks and industrial designs was the Paris Convention for the Protection of Industrial Property, approved and signed in 1883. Copyrights were first the subject of an international treaty in 1886, when the Berne Convention for the Protection of Literary and Artistic Works was formed. In 1891, the Madrid Agreement Concerning the International Registration of Marks became the first international instrument dealing with trade-marks. In 1893, the predecessor to the World Intellectual Property Organization (WIPO)[1] – the Bureaux Internationaux réunis pour la protection de la propriété intellectuelle (BIRPI) – was established to govern international patent, copyright and trade-mark conventions.

Underlying nineteenth century intellectual property agreements were controversies about the relationship between intellectual property and trade (May 2007, 14–19). Free trade liberals rejected intellectual property protections as an unjustified constraint on trade in goods. Representatives of industries that stood to gain from extended intellectual property protection, on the other hand, trumpeted the rights of authors and inventors and lamented "theft" and "piracy" by foreigners. As a result of declining enthusiasm for free trade generally, and to make domestic intellectual property systems more palatable, the views of the latter group grew dominant (May 2007, 16).

Throughout the twentieth century the BIRPI grew considerably in scope and in stature. New states were eager to join the organization and intellectual property exporters welcomed the expansion of their markets. Though all states did not share the same normative views on intellectual property, particularly about development-related issues, the BIRPI managed to marginalize differences of opinion among its members.

It did so in several ways. One was to rely on industry associations to evaluate proposals for development-friendly reform, as was done with a 1961 Brazilian resolution that bore a striking resemblance to WIPO's more recent and comprehensive Development Agenda (Koury Menescal, 2006). Similarly, BIRPI used the common practice of employing like-minded technical experts to minimize the influence of intellectual property critics. Another strategy was to promote international agreements that contained stronger and longer intellectual property protections but that preserved states' ability to tailor protections to their own circumstances. Good examples of this latter strategy are the Conventions of Berlin in 1908 and Rome in 1928 that addressed copyrights in the music and broadcasting industries respectively. More generally, during the early and mid twentieth century, countries were rarely forced to add new intellectual property rights or expand existing ones (Gervais 2002, 936–7). Instead, international agreements were premised on pre-existing domestic legislation and political consensus.

Flexible treaty obligations tended to preserve peace among countries with divergent domestic conditions. Christopher May (2007, 21–2) points out that developing countries were not the only ones to take advantage of flexibilities. For instance, countries such as Australia, where broadcasting is a public service connecting sparse populations across vast distances, were not comfortable extending private rights into that sector.

Because Canada is also such a country, unique in other ways as well, it stood on the sidelines of many international intellectual property initiatives during the early and mid twentieth century. Though Canada participated in periodic revisions of the Paris and Berne Conventions (Vaver 2000, 4), it did not vigorously pursue an international intellectual property agenda to suits its own interests. Maybe intellectual property was not perceived to be a priority issue. Perhaps this was because of Canada's colonial ties to the United Kingdom. Or perhaps it was assumed that our national interests mirrored those of other developed countries, especially the United States.

Canada's ties to the United States were particularly pronounced in the negotiations that led to the Agreement on Trade-Related Aspects of Intellectual Property. During the negotiations, Canada was part of a group known as "the Quad," which also included the United States, European Union (EU) and Japan. Building consensus among Quad members outside of the formal negotiation processes proved key to the eventual securing of a broader agreement in support of the US business agenda (Drahos and Braithwaite 2002, 117). Despite being part of the inner circle, however, Canadian officials played a small, if any, role in designing the new international intellectual property paradigm. Instead, the Intellectual Property Committee (IPC) essentially drafted the entire TRIPs agreement, leaving negotiators to do only the fine-tuning (May 2007, 28–9; Sell 2003, 107; Drahos and Braithwaite 2002, 123–5). This would not be extraordinary, except that the IPC was not a group of delegated officials, as its name might suggest. Rather, it was a lobbying association that included the heads of powerful US corporations, such as the chairs of Pfizer and IBM (Drahos and Braithwaite 2002, 118).

Daniel Gervais (2002, 947) calls the fact that a comprehensive agreement covering all forms of intellectual property was negotiated in a few short years "astonishing," especially given the sluggish pace and partial coverage of intellectual agreements negotiated over the previous hundred years. This incredible agreement exists in part because of concessions on developing countries' demands concerning textiles and agriculture exports (May 2007, 29; Drahos and Braithwaite 2002, 11).

But furthermore, some countries, particularly Japan and members of the European Union, had no reason to oppose a TRIPs agreement that mainly replicated their domestic laws or existing obligations under bilateral treaties or regional agreements. That was the situation Canada also found itself in. The TRIPs agreement resembles the intellectual property provisions contained in Chapter 17 of the 1994 NAFTA in most material respects. Since Canada had already agreed to the substantive requirements of NAFTA, no major amendments to domestic law were required to comply with TRIPs standards specifically.

For example, prior to NAFTA Canada had resisted adhering to revised versions of the Berne Convention but, under hard pressure from the US, altered its stance (Handa 2002, 398–9). NAFTA required compliance with (but not signature of) Berne, so Canadian law was amended to protect computer programs and require cable re-transmitters to pay royalties to US broadcasters. Canada did not ratify the revised Berne

Convention and the Rome Convention concerning copyrights for performers, sound recording makers and broadcasters until 1998, at least in part because a piecemeal amendment approach was used as a lever in trade negotiations (Handa 2002, 399).

Canadian policy has been to avoid formalizing relationships with other countries as long as Canada can reap the benefits of protection abroad while maintaining flexibility to implement protections that suited domestic needs (Handa 2002, 402). This attitude is reflected in documents prepared by and for the federal government over the past half-century, which demonstrate awareness that intellectual property protection can seriously affect Canada's trade deficit (Handa 2002, 400). One of the most notable was a 1977 report from Andrew Keyes and Claude Brunet in which the authors stated: "[T]he fully developed nations, largely exporters of copyright material, have a stronger voice in international copyright conventions, and a tendency has existed over the past half century for developing countries, including Canada, to accept too readily proffered solutions in copyright matters that do not reflect their economic positions." Thirty years later these remarks still ring true.

Sunny Handa (2002, 402) points out that Canada has been forced to capitulate on intellectual property issues, despite the consequential outflow of dollars which may not be in Canada's best interests. Pressure from the US has played a large part in Canadian policy-making. But Canada has not been the only country to face pressures.

Another reason many countries have agreed to higher intellectual property standards has been the US strategy of threatening and sometimes using bilateral trade sanctions pursuant to section 301 of the United States *Trade Act* of 1974 (Matthews 2002, 31–5; Drahos and Braithwaite 2002, 134–7). In 1993, the Office of the US Trade Representative commenced a section 301 investigation against Brazil, in 1994 it did so against China, and at various times has done the same against Thailand, India, Egypt, South Africa, Korea, Poland, Italy and others including Canada (Handa 2002, 425–6).[2] Though critics call this for what it is – bullying – sadly many countries find it preferable to negotiate with the US rather than create the risk of an investigation and sanctions under section 301 (Handa 2002, 426).

In this climate, one of the US negotiators' most notable accomplishments after TRIPs was the completion in 1996 of a pair of copyright-related treaties known as the WIPO Internet Treaties. The cornerstones of these agreements are prohibitions against tampering with technological protection measures (TPMs) that lock up electronic content, as well as bans on products that might be used for that purpose.

Canada signed these treaties, but has yet to ratify them. As such, it has no binding duty under international law to implement their provisions domestically through legislation. In the words of one copyright commentator, signing is to ratifying what dating is to marriage (Knopf 2006). Nevertheless, Canada now finds itself facing relentless pressure, primarily from US politicians and industry representatives, to act on its alleged international obligation (Geist 2007). Yet Canadian politicians and bureaucrats remain mired in confusion, without a clear vision of what direction they ought to take.

The present paralysis is directly attributable to a lack of foresight at the end of the twentieth century regarding intellectual property policy. Laws were designed to suit the outdated, hierarchical industrial models of information production, and are ill equipped to exploit the potential of the networked information economy (Benkler 2006). Yet Canada is now in the practical, though not legal, predicament of being bound to follow through on its ill-advised statements of support for now obsolete agreements like the WIPO Internet Treaties.

Though most countries have not ratified the WIPO Internet Treaties, and recent negotiations to establish a new Broadcasting Treaty have collapsed, it would be wrong to assume WIPO has been marginalized. The World Trade Organization's (WTO) challenge to WIPO's competence might be a manner of forum shopping, but May (2007, 33–5) points out that what is really happening is "forum proliferation."

Indeed, the WTO is not the only other forum where intellectual property is growing in importance. Since the WTO's 2001 Doha Declaration on the TRIPs Agreement and Public Health, which affirms that the TRIPS Agreement should not prevent WTO members from taking measures necessary to ensure the protection of public health, the World Health Organization (WHO) has increased its awareness of and involvement in intellectual property issues. Other agencies have a long history of intellectual property related activity, such as the United Nations Educational, Scientific and Cultural Organization (UNESCO), which has administered the Universal Copyright Convention since 1952. UNESCO's more recent Convention (2005) on the Protection and Promotion of the Diversity of Cultural Expressions addresses publications, movies and broadcasts, which are matters also dealt with under agreements governed by WIPO. WIPO worked with the Internet Corporation for Assigned Names and Numbers (ICANN) to develop a Uniform Domain Name Resolution Policy to address the intersection between trade-marks and domain names.

There is a Convention on Biological Diversity (CBD) that, with adequate support, could impact on patenting practices in the life sciences, as well as the traditional knowledge and genetic resources of indigenous communities. Another key agreement is the International Treaty on Plant Genetic Resources for Food and Agriculture, which is governed by the UN's Food and Agriculture Organization (FAO) and contains important provisions on intellectual property.

The involvement of these organizations reflects the breadth of social, cultural, medical, nutritional, scientific and economic issues affected by intellectual property issues. Trade, however, remains among the most influential considerations. And with the Doha Round stalled, negotiations are becoming increasingly bilateral rather than multilateral in nature.

The United States has vigorously pursued bilateral agreements containing "TRIPs-plus" standards, and has successfully completed such agreements with over a dozen countries.[3] One of the next bilateral challenges for Canada is to retain sovereignty over its intellectual property policy within the Security and Prosperity Partnership framework it has established with the US and Mexico. A special advisory body of representatives from large North American corporations – the North American Competitiveness Council – has the potential to exert significant influence on this process (Savage 2006). Canadians must be cognizant of this, so as not to repeat the experiences leading to the TRIPs agreement.

Canada is also exploring a number of other bilateral and plurilateral trade agreements. During upcoming negotiations with countries in Latin America and the Caribbean, for example, Canada should not seek to harmonize maximalist intellectual property protections. Far better would be to focus on impact assessments, information sharing, co-operative policy-making and other consultation mechanisms. Canada's recent agreement with the European Free Trade Association (EFTA) countries of Iceland, Norway, Switzerland and Liechenstein focused on tariff elimination rather than ratcheting up intellectual property standards. Though the lack of intellectual property provisions in this agreement might merely be attributable to high standards already in place, the parties have wisely avoided "the more, the better" mentality that often pervades international intellectual property lawmaking.

OPPORTUNITIES AT WIPO

Despite the engagement of the WTO, WHO, UNESCO, FAO, CBD and other agencies with intellectual property norm-setting and harmonization activities, WIPO remains active in this field. For example, members of WIPO are having serious discussions about harmonizing higher patent protections through a new Substantive Patent Law Treaty. Yet contradictorily, WIPO is facing mounting pressure to institute development-friendly reforms reflective of its role as a specialized agency of the United Nations.

This is a matter Canada must urgently act on if it is to become more proactive in twenty-first century intellectual property policy-making.

The WIPO Development Agenda is the most significant intellectual property matter to confront the international community certainly since TRIPs, and perhaps ever. The Agenda goes to the heart of WIPO's mandate and ongoing relevance in the global governance of intellectual property. It should have broad-ranging impacts on many aspects of international intellectual property law and policy-making in all sectors, from the life sciences to information communications.

The Agenda stemmed from a 2004 proposal submitted by Brazil and Argentina, and supported by a group of countries known as the "Friends of Development" and a contingent of civil society organizations. Like Brazil's 1961 resolution, the proposal sought to put a development-oriented focus on international intellectual property initiatives. May puts it this way: "The key demand of the Development Agenda is to re-establish, at the global level, the traditional public policy aspects of intellectual property, and specifically how public policy ends can be related to [intellectual property rights]" (2007, 79). Topics affected range from restating WIPO's mandate and reforming its governance structures to providing technical assistance and building capacity to modulating norm setting activities and promoting access to knowledge.

In response to a large number of proposals, the WIPO General Assembly constituted a Provisional Committee on Proposals Related to a WIPO Development Agenda (PCDA) and convened inter-sessional intergovernmental meetings (IIMs). During a series of meetings over the past several years, 111 initial proposals were catalogued, debated, organized and amalgamated into manageable lists of key issues. In September 2007, 45 recommendations will be put before the General Assembly (New 2007), but it remains to be seen what concrete actions might be taken after that.

Canada did not put forward any of its own proposals in respect of the Development Agenda. It did occasionally intervene with comments on others' proposals or on intellectual property issues generally. The Canadian Delegation has made some positive contributions to discussions about the Agenda. During the first IIM, it acknowledged: "In both developing and developed countries alike, effective balance and flexible intellectual property frameworks could serve to promote creativity and disseminate information to both users and developers, resulting in economic, social and cultural benefits for communities" (WIPO 2005a, para. 62). On the topic of intellectual property and anti-competitive practices, the Canadian Delegation indicated its common interests with developing countries, promised to share with the PCDA a series of studies commissioned by the Competition Bureau and Canadian Intellectual Property Office and suggested it could help broker linkages with an international network of competition agencies (WIPO

2007, par. 137). Canada followed up on its commitment by hosting a side event on this topic at the latest meeting of the PCDA.

At the second meeting, Canada pointed out it was important to remember that the interests of developing countries are not always uniform, and further noted that some of the concerns expressed by specific developing countries were shared by developed countries and their stakeholders (WIPO 2005b, par. 51). The impact of intellectual property on access to knowledge is one example of a shared concern. Yet despite Canada's earlier talk about access to knowledge, at the most recent meetings of the PCDA Canada was one of several countries that expressed concern about referencing this phrase as part of WIPO's norm-setting mandate (Love 2007). This attitude reflects Canada's alignment with a group of other developed countries that agreed to move forward with moderate reforms but resisted fundamental changes.

In many respects, Canada is ideally suited to break from the developed world pack to assume a leadership position on the development agenda. First, intellectual property laws have a heavy impact on a wide range of key societal issues, including health, education, agriculture, communications and culture. Cultural policy presents a particularly vivid illustration of the challenges faced by Canada as well as less developed countries. The intellectual property-trade dilemma here is that low protection for foreign cultural products may cause the population to consume more of them at the expense of domestic industries while high protection may cause a large outflow of royalty payments (Handa 2002, 406). It is difficult to strike an appropriate balance, so it is important that Canada, like developing countries, maintain sovereignty over intellectual property laws so that these trade-offs can be judged in light of domestic concerns, not be dictated by foreign special interests.

Furthermore, despite the fact that Canada is a signatory to virtually all major intellectual property treaties, it remains a net importer of copyrighted work and ranks toward the bottom of G8 nations for pharmaceutical research and development. In fact, the bulk of Canada's C$1.7 billion annual trade deficit in cultural goods (like books, CDs, films and paintings) and over half-billion dollar deficit in cultural services (including broadcasting, television, music and other royalty flows) results from trade with the United States (Canada 2006a, 2006b). According to Industry Canada, from 1992 to 2003, the Canadian trade deficit in pharmaceuticals grew from C$1.2 billion to C$5.6 billion.

We are not implying that Canada should reduce or eliminate protections to make knowledge available more cheaply *just* because it is a net importer of intellectual property. After all, one would not make the argument that Canada should not address climate change because it is a net exporter of fossil fuels. However, Canada's status as a net importer of intellectual property puts it alongside the developing and least developed countries facing pressure from the US to ratchet up standards of protection. Intellectual property proponents argue that Canada and other countries can become intellectual property exporters by increasing levels of protection.

Canada can demonstrate that this argument rests on a fallacy about the impact of intellectual property on development. Stronger intellectual property protections do not necessarily lead to economic, let alone social or cultural development. Canada's experience illustrates that intellectual property laws are important, but serve as only a small part of an overall policy designed to foster innovation, creativity and economic growth. Indeed, intellectual property protections can sometimes stifle development by propping up the monopolies of information industry incumbents at the expense of groundbreaking technologies and business models.

The foregoing discussion suggests that the dichotomy between developed and developing countries is often a false one. As Canadian delegates acknowledged during meetings of the PCDA, in many contexts Canada's interests are the same as those of developing countries. Domestic and international policy-makers, therefore, ought simply to strive for balanced intellectual-property policies that reflect sensitivity to the range of affected social and economic issues. While the government of Canada has set development assistance as a priority, committing significant new funding towards aid programs, other countries need more than just dollars. Canadian political support for alternative perspectives on intellectual property would carry long-term benefits that would extend well after the current round of aid funding is exhausted.

As the entire world strives to identify effective growth policies, the WIPO Development Agenda has the potential to play an important role in altering the current intellectual property framework. Though general consensus is that advancing proposals on the Development Agenda to the WIPO General Assembly is itself a sign of tremendous success, the litmus test will be whether or not recommendations are implemented in practice. Experts are optimistic, but acknowledge that opportunities could be squandered in implementation (Musungu 2007). For fundamental transformations to succeed, countries such as Canada must also become "friends of development."

DOMESTIC REFORMS

While Canada can establish a strong presence at international fora such as WIPO, its best opportunity for global leadership stems from enacting domestic reforms that can serve as a model for developed and developing countries worldwide. WIPO provides technical assistance to developing countries, but its programs do not support novel solutions to intellectual property problems (May 2007, 63). Canadian domestic models, if properly crafted, can be used as templates in WIPO's technical assistance programs. Canada can become a beacon for other countries looking for balanced, middle ground intellectual property solutions.

Canada has begun to take a leadership role by attempting to implement middle-ground models in some areas. It was the first country to act upon the spirit of the Doha Declaration on the TRIPs Agreement and Public Health. Through Bill C-9, part of former Prime Minister Jean Chrétien's "Pledge to Africa," the *Patent Act* was amended to allow generic pharmaceutical companies to obtain compulsory licences to manufacture and sell medicines to developing and least developed countries facing health crises. Norway, India, China and the EU all followed Canada's lead.

Critics have condemned the Canadian reforms as ineffective, though Rwanda just recently announced that it would import hundreds of thousands of doses of HIV/AIDS drugs manufactured under Canada's compulsory licensing scheme. Moreover, while the system could certainly be improved, Canada's action in this respect is an important demonstration of support for the principle that health and human rights are more important than patents and property rhetoric. The Access to Medicines Regime is currently undergoing an accelerated statutory review. Through this process, Canada can and should improve its regime to provide a positive example for other countries.

Canada should also implement progressive patent policies by amending domestic laws to address the problem of "biopiracy" – the misappropriation of biological materials without consent or compensation. To comply with the spirit of the CBD and the FAO's "International Seed Treaty," Canadian patent law should require applicants to disclose the origins of biological materials that are part of their claimed inventions. Canadian patent law should also mandate the equitable sharing of the benefits arising from the utilization of traditional knowledge and genetic resources from developing or least developed countries. Obviously, the same principles ought to be applied in the context of dealings with Canada's First Nations. Concerns over misappropriation go beyond patent policy to affect other areas of intellectual property, especially in respect of cultural issues.

And indeed, patent law is not the only area where Canada can adopt a leadership role. Much can be done in respect of Canadian copyright policy. We have chosen to focus the remainder of this chapter on copyright matters as an illustration of the specific ways in which Canada can exercise its room for manoeuvre vis-à-vis its intellectual property policies.

That opportunities exist for Canada to chart new ground within the confines of existing international copyright law has not escaped the attention of global intellectual property leaders. For example, in late March 2007, McGill University hosted an important conference on the future of copyright and the music industry, bringing together music notables such as famed producer Sandy Pearlman and New Democratic Party's Heritage critic, Charlie Angus. The most interesting – and surprising – comments came from Bruce Lehman, who served as the assistant secretary of Commerce in the Clinton administration and as the chief architect of the WIPO Internet Treaties and the US Digital Millennium Copyright Act (DMCA).

Reflecting on the decade since the WIPO treaties were established, Lehman (2007) acknowledged that "our Clinton administration policies didn't work out very well" and "our attempts at copyright control have not been successful." Moreover, he suggested that the world is moving toward a "post-copyright era" for music, a development that he believed was the result of the recording industry's failure to adapt to the online environment. Lehman followed his criticism of US policy by issuing a challenge to Canada, urging policy-makers and political leaders to think outside the box on future reform. Indeed, he argued that Canada was well positioned to experiment with new approaches consistent with international copyright law.

Given the Canadian marketplace realities and the Lehman recommendation to chart our own course on copyright, how might Canada respond on the domestic front? There are at least five issues that should be addressed to leverage emerging technologies and to chart a course that enables Canada to establish a world-leading, forward-looking model of intellectual property law.

i. Greater Creative Flexibility and Innovation – Expand Fair Dealing

In 2004, the Supreme Court of Canada issued a critically important copyright decision that has helped reshape the Canadian intellectual property landscape. The *Law Society of Upper Canada v. CCH Canadian*, a 2004 unanimous decision, involved a dispute between the Law Society – the body that governs the legal profession in Ontario – and several leading legal publishers. Unlike today's high profile cases that typically involve the Internet, this case centered on a distinctly old-fashioned copying technology – photocopiers.

The Law Society, which maintains the Great Library, a leading law library in Toronto, provided the profession with two methods of copying cases and other legal materials. First, it ran a service whereby lawyers could request a copy of a particular case or article. Second, it maintained several stand-alone photocopiers that could be used by library patrons. The legal publishers objected to the Law Society's copying practices and sued for copyright infringement.

The Law Society emerged victorious on most counts. The court ruled that it had neither infringed the publishers' copyright nor authorized others to do so. One of the most important long-term effects of the CCH decision was the Court's strong support for the fair dealing provision, which it characterized as a user right. The Court emphasized the importance of a broad and liberal interpretation to fair dealing, which covers a series of prescribed uses including research, private study, criticism and news reporting.

Unfortunately, the relatively rigid categorization of exceptions runs counter to the very notion of a broad and liberal approach. On this issue, the United States provides the ideal model since its "fair use" provision does not include such limiting language, thereby encouraging innovative, fair uses of existing work.

A full fair use provision – one that would amend the current Copyright Act so that the list of fair dealing rights would be illustrative rather than exhaustive – would help solve many difficult issues. Similarly, a shift to fair use would help bridge the gap on the use of the Internet in Canadian schools by rejecting both the blanket Internet exception for school use proposed by some education groups and the comprehensive Internet licensing scheme advocated by Access Copyright, a leading copyright collective. The change would clear the way for fair use that is not currently covered by the private study or research fair dealing rights, but also ensure that creators are compensated for uses that extend beyond what might reasonably be viewed as fair use.

Canada recognized the benefits of a fair use system in a landmark policy paper in the 1980s, yet failed to introduce legislation to implement the recommendation. With both Australia and the United Kingdom openly considering shifting their laws from fair dealing to fair use, this is the one issue on which Canada can ill-afford to be left behind since an overly restrictive fair dealing regime harms both innovation and creativity.

ii. A Canadian Model for WIPO Internet Treaties' Implementation

The WIPO Internet Treaties, which Canada signed in 1997, are frequently cited as a prime reason for Canadian digital copyright reform. Several of our trading partners, most notably the United States, are aggressive proponents of the treaties, which mandate new legal protections for technological protection measures.

While the treaties are indeed an important consideration in the policy process, it is important that Canadians separate fact from fiction. The myths associated with the treaties frequently focus on Canada's place in the international copyright world and the impact of WIPO Internet Treaties' ratification on Canadian creators and consumers. The arguments surrounding Canada's place in the international copyright world often imply that Canada has failed to meet its international copyright obligations, that signing the treaty in 1997 now compels Canada to ratify it, and that Canada has fallen behind the rest of the world by moving slowly on ratification.

None of these claims are true. Canada has not failed to meet its international obligations since it has no obligations under the WIPO Internet Treaties – under international law, obligations only arise once a country has ratified a treaty not merely signed it. Canada's decision to sign the WIPO Internet Treaties was simply a sign of support, and did not mean that Canada would have a legal obligation to ratify them. In fact, at the time Canada considered signing the treaties, then-Canadian Heritage Minister Sheila Copps was advised that "international convention is such that signing in no way binds Canada to ratify the treaties. It is a symbolic gesture" (Geist 2005).

The WIPO Internet Treaties' impact has been similarly exaggerated. Supporters argue that failure to ratify will result in diminished protection for Canadian artists outside the country and that ratification will not have an adverse impact on Canadian consumers. Once again, neither of these claims prove to be accurate under close scrutiny. Concerns about the protection of Canadian artists outside the country is based on the premise that Canadians will only enjoy stronger protections elsewhere if foreign artists benefit from equivalent protections in Canada. In reality, ratification of the WIPO Internet Treaties won't provide Canadian artists with any additional protections in countries such as the United States and Japan since these countries are already obligated to extend equal protection – known as national treatment – to local and foreign artists under existing trade agreements.

While WIPO Internet Treaties' ratification will not directly benefit Canadian artists in foreign jurisdictions, foreign artists will enjoy great benefits from ratification to the detriment of Canadian consumers, since formal ratification of one of the WIPO treaties would require additional changes to Canadian copyright law, most notably providing national treatment for the controversial private copying levy. As a result, Canada's private copying levy could double in size simply to support royalty payments to foreign artists.

Despite their shortcomings, Canada may ultimately decide to implement the WIPO Internet Treaties. In reaching that determination, policy-makers should be guided by the Canadian national public interest, not a series of myths that inaccurately imply that Canada has little choice in the matter.

iii. Striking the Property Balance – Protection for and from Technological Protection Measures

Owners of online databases and other digital content deploy technological protection measures to establish a layer of technical protection that is designed to provide greater control over their content. Some major record labels and movie studios have touted TPMs' promise for more than a decade, maintaining that technological locks could prove far more effective in curtailing unauthorized copying, distribution, performance and display of content than traditional copyright laws. While TPMs are frequently associated with encryption protection, TPMs encompass a broad range of technologies including more mundane approaches such as password protections. While TPMs do not provide absolute protection – research suggests all TPMs can eventually be broken – companies continue to actively search for inventive new uses for these digital locks.

Given the flawed protection provided by TPMs, lobbyists have asked for additional legal protections to support them, known as anti-circumvention legislation. Although characterized as copyright protection, this layer of legal protection does not address the copying or use of copyrighted work. Instead, it focuses on the protection of the TPM itself, which in turn attempts to ensure that the underlying content is only accessed and used as controlled by the copyright owner.

As Canadians consider implementing anti-circumvention provisions within domestic law, several lessons learned elsewhere bear repeating. First, anti-circumvention represents an entirely new approach to copyright law. While copyright law seeks to balance creator and user rights by identifying the rights and limitations on rights holders, TPMs, supported by anti-circumvention legislation, create new layers of protection that do not correlate with traditional copyright law.

In a 2002 Supreme Court of Canada decision, *Théberge v. Galerie d'Art du Petit Champlain inc*, Justice Binnie stated that "once an authorized copy of a work is sold to a member of the public, it is generally for the purchaser, not the author, to determine what happens to it." Anti-circumvention legislation challenges this premise, since activity that is lawful under traditional copyright law may be unlawful under certain anti-circumvention legislation.

Second, there is considerable flexibility in how a country implements its anti-circumvention obligations into national law. While the US Digital Millennium Copyright Act is the best-known implementation, the approaches in several European countries, as well as some in the developing world, indicate that a country can seek to maintain the copyright balance, avoid regulating technologies and foster a pro-competitive marketplace within the WIPO framework. Canada can implement a middle-ground solution.

Third, the US DMCA experience illustrates that the fears raised by critics of the US approach have come to fruition. In less than a decade, the DMCA has become a heavily litigated statute used by rights holders and non-rights holders to restrict innovation, stifle competition and curtail fair use. This has occurred in large measure due to the US decision to strictly regulate anti-circumvention devices and to downplay the connection between TPM protection and copyright.

Ottawa should ensure that the anti-circumvention provisions feature a direct connection to traditional copyright infringement by limiting the scope of a circumvention offence to users who circumvent for the purpose of committing copyright infringement. Copyright, competition and constitutional law analysis all support this approach (Geist 2005, ch. 4–7).

From a copyright perspective, failure to link anti-circumvention with copyright would alter the balance between creators and users as it would invariably lead to an expansion of the rights attached to copyright. The US experience provides ample evidence in this regard as courts have openly acknowledged that copyright compliant activity or devices are no longer sufficient, since anti-circumvention renders certain activity illegal that is legal under traditional copyright norms. Such an approach would run directly counter to recent Supreme Court of Canada pronouncements on Canadian copyright law that have emphasized the need for an appropriate balance to encourage creativity and innovation in the long-term interests of society as a whole.

The impact of non-linkage would extend the provisions well-beyond works typically associated with copyright. Provisions that open the door to using anti-circumvention provisions beyond traditional copyright norms risk generating uncertainty in the marketplace and the potential for lawsuits that restrain competition and limit consumer choice. This issue has not escaped the attention of many other countries including Germany and Denmark, which have implemented laws that link anti-circumvention legislation to copyright infringement.

Beyond the copyright and competition policy reasons for a direct connection between anti-circumvention and copyright, a strong constitutional law reason exists as well (de Beer 2005). The federal government's jurisdiction over copyright is .derived from s.91(23) of the *Constitution Act, 1867*. Anti-circumvention legislation that is closely connected with traditional copyright principles would be less likely to unconstitutionally entrench on provincial jurisdiction over matters of property and civil rights.

iv. A Robust Public Domain – Reject Copyright Term Extension

The 2002 *Théberge* decision, referenced above, involved a challenge by Claude Théberge, a Quebec painter with an international reputation, against an art gallery that purchased posters of Théberge's work and then proceeded to transfer the images found on the posters from paper to canvas. The gallery's technology was state of the art – it used a process that literally lifted the ink off the poster and transferred it to the canvas. The gallery did not actually create any new images or reproductions of the work since the poster paper was left blank after the process was complete. Théberge was nevertheless outraged – he believed he had sold paper posters, not canvas-based reproductions – and he proceeded to sue in Quebec court, requesting an injunction to stop the transfers as well as the seizure of the existing canvas-backed images.

Although the Quebec Court of Appeal ruled in favour of the seizure, the majority of the Supreme Court overturned that decision, finding that the images were merely transferred from one medium to another and not reproduced in a fashion contrary to the *Copyright Act*.

Writing for the majority, Justice Binnie emphasized the dangers inherent in copyright that veers too far toward copyright creators at the expense of both the public and the innovation process. He noted that "excessive control by holders of copyrights and other forms of intellectual property may unduly limit the ability of the public domain to incorporate and embellish creative innovation in the long-term interests of society as a whole, or create practical obstacles to proper utilization" (para. 32).

Canadian policy-makers are contemplating launching a public consultation to discuss the prospect for extending the term of copyright from the current life of the author plus fifty years to life of the author plus seventy years. A consultation is unnecessary; the government should simply undertake to meet the international standard of life plus fifty years eliminating any consideration of term extensions that provide no real additional incentive to create, yet hold the danger of keeping valuable works out of the public domain.

Indeed, if Canada wanted to lead on this issue, it might consider, as has Professor David Lametti of McGill University, the prospect of scaling back the length of the term of copyright for certain works (Lametti 2005). For example, the term of copyright for a software program, which is frequently outdated only months after its release, is the same as a novel or musical composition. Reconsidering copyright terms could yield varying term lengths depending on the type of work to provide more suitable terms of protection.

v. Establishing a Balanced System for Internet Service Providers

A critical aspect of digital copyright reform is the role of Internet service providers (ISPs), who serve as intermediaries for online activities. Certain rights holders have aggressively pursued the establishment of a "notice and takedown" system. Under notice and takedown, copyright holders have the right to notify ISPs that one of their subscribers has posted copyright infringing content (the notice). Depending on the system, ISPs respond to the notice by either notifying the subscriber (who may voluntarily take down the content), taking down the content themselves, or awaiting a court order (the takedown). In return for taking action, ISPs qualify for a safe harbour from liability.

The United States implemented a notice and takedown system several years ago. Canada has moved slowly on this issue, however, due in large measure to concerns arising from the US experience. Under the US system, computer generated notices have become the standard, with errors becoming the norm. For example, notices have been sent to take down a child's Harry Potter book report, a sound recording by a university professor mistakenly identified as a song by a well-known recording artist and an archive of public domain films.

In fact, one study of the US experience found that some ISPs receive tens of thousands of notices every month with only a handful actually relating to materials found on their networks (Geist 2004). Moreover, notices have also been used to suppress free speech and criticism. Diebold, an electronic voting equipment maker used the system to attempt to remove company memos detailing problems with its e-voting machines, while the Church of Scientology has used it to remove web sites critical of its activities.

Canadian policy-makers and parliamentarians should respond to this issue by opting for a "notice and notice" system that respects the rights of copyright holders, the privacy rights of users, the fairness of court review and the need to appropriately limit the burden placed on ISPs. Notice and notice is comprised of a four-step process. First, a copyright holder, having exercised appropriate due diligence in confirming an alleged infringement, sends a notice to the ISP. Second, the

ISP promptly notifies its customer of the allegation and leaves it to the customer to voluntarily take down the content. Third, if the customer refuses to take down the content, the copyright holder applies to a Canadian court to order its removal. The ISP serves as a conduit to ensure that the subscriber is aware of the court proceeding and can challenge if desired. Fourth, if the court issues an order, the ISP responds to the order by taking down the content. This approach would provide copyright holders with an efficient mechanism for removing infringing content, while also ensuring respect for subscriber privacy and free speech rights as well as granting ISPs limited liability.

CONCLUSION

The changing global economic landscape requires rethinking international intellectual property policies. Canada stood on the sidelines of many international intellectual property initiatives during the early and mid twentieth century as negotiators did not vigorously pursue an international intellectual property agenda to suit national interests.

In many respects, Canada is today ideally suited to break from the developed world pack to assume a leadership position on emerging intellectual property law and policies, such as the WIPO Development Agenda. Canada's own intellectual property position is closer to the developing world than some might think. Despite the fact that Canada is a signatory to virtually all major intellectual property treaties, it remains a net importer of copyrighted work and ranks toward the bottom of G8 nations for pharmaceutical research and development.

While Canada can establish a strong presence at international fora such as WIPO, its best opportunity for global leadership stems from enacting domestic reforms that can serve as a model for developed and developing countries worldwide. Canada should continue to implement progressive patent policies by amending domestic laws to address the problem of "biopiracy." To comply with the spirit of the CBD and the FAO's "International Seed Treaty," Canadian patent law should require applicants to disclose the origins of biological materials that are part of their claimed inventions. Canadian patent law should also mandate the equitable sharing of the benefits arising from the utilization of traditional knowledge and genetic resources from other countries.

On the copyright front, Canada would do well to introduce a full fair use provision – one that would amend the current Copyright Act so that the list of fair dealing rights would be illustrative rather than exhaustive. In transposing international law into domestic statutes, it should aggressively adopt a "Canadianized" version of the WIPO Internet treaties by, for example, establishing protection both for and from technological protection measures. Canadian leaders should also heed the advice of the Supreme Court of Canada, by facilitating a robust public domain through a freeze on copyright term extension.

Canada had a seat at the table during the TRIPs negotiations as part of a group known as "the Quad." Despite their presence, Canadian officials said little and played a minor role at best in designing the new international intellectual property paradigm. Years later, as intellectual property policy assumes even greater importance, Canada has an opportunity to atone for its previous silence by implementing forward-looking intellectual property policies that will serve as models for developed and developing countries alike.

NOTES

1 The World Intellectual Property Organization was established as a specialized agency of the United Nations in 1967.
2 Technically, some of these complaints came after TRIPs (e.g. in Canada's case), but the US has used the Section 301 bullying strategy as part of a larger pattern of bullying. Had Canada not been a NAFTA signatory, it would have been seen by the US as a TRIPs opponent. Furthermore, Canada's membership in the "Quad" was a result of US pressure.
3 Including Columbia, Peru, Australia, Bahrain, Chile, the Domincan Republic, Israel, Jordan, Malasia, Morocco, Oman, Panama, Korea, Singapore, South Africa, Thailand, and the United Arab Emirates. See <http://www.ustr.gov/Trade_Agreements/Bilateral/Section_Index.html.> "TRIPs-plus" means that bilateral agreements require parties to meet the standards of the TRIPs Agreement "plus" provide additional stronger or longer intellectual property protection.

REFERENCES

Acheson, Keith, and Christopher Maule. 2001. *Much Ado About Culture: North American Trade Disputes*. Ann Arbor: University of Michigan Press.

Benkler, Yochai. 2006. *The Wealth of Networks*. Yale, CT: Yale University Press.

Canada. 2004. *Canada's international trade in services – 2004*. Catalogue no. 67-203-XIE, March. Ottawa: Statistics Canada. Available at: <http://www.statcan.ca/english/freepub/67-203-XIE/0000467–203-XIE.pdf>

– 2006a. *Culture goods trade: Data tables*. Catalogue no. 87-007-XIE, June. Ottawa: Statistics Canada. Available at: <http://www.statcan.ca/english/freepub/87-007-XIE/87-007-XIE2007001.pdf>

– 2006b. *Culture services trade: Data tables*. Catalogue no. 87-213-XWE, March. Ottawa: Statistics Canada.

Coulter, Moureen. 1991. *Property in Ideas: The Patent Question in Mid-Victorian Britain*. Kirksville, MS: Thomas Jefferson University Press.

Commission on Intellectual Property Rights. 2002. *Integrating Intellectual Property Rights and Development Policy: Report of the Commission on Intellectual Property Rights*. London: Commission on Intellectual Property Rights. Available at: <http://www.iprcommission.org/graphic/documents/final_report.htm>. Last accessed 24 July 2007.

de Beer, Jeremy. 2005. "Constitutional Jurisdiction Over Paracopyrights." In *In the Public Interest: The Future of Canadian Copyright Law*, edited by Michael Geist. Toronto: Irwin Law.

Drahos, Peter. 1997. "States and Intellectual Property: The Past, the Present and the Future." In *From Berne to Geneva: Recent Developments in International Copyright and Neighbouring Rights*, edited by David Saunders and Brad Sherman. Nathan, Queensland: Australian Key Centre for Culture and Media Policy.

– 2002. "Developing Countries and Intellectual Property Standard-Setting." *Journal of World Intellectual Property* 5, no. 5: 765–89.

– and John Braithwaite. 2002. *Information Feudalism*. New York: The New York Press.

Geist, Michael. 2004. "A Blueprint for a Better Copyright Law." *Toronto Star*, 8 August.

– 2005. "Avoiding a WIPO Wipeout." *Ottawa Citizen*, 26 October. Available at: <http://www.canada.com/technology/story.html?id=3736e537-1634-49eb-ac07-a10d177e4ee2>

– 2007. "We mustn't cave in to copyright bullying." *Toronto Star*, 23 April. Available at <http://www.thestar.com/article/206012>

Gervais, Daniel. 2002. "The Internationalization of Intellectual Property: New Challenges from the Very Old and the Very New." *Fordham Intellectual Property Media and Entertainment Journal* 12, no. 4: 929–90.

– 2003. *The TRIPs Agreement: Drafting History and Analysis*. 2nd ed. London: Sweet and Maxwell.

Handa, Sunny. 2002. *Copyright Law in Canada*. Markham, ON: Butterworths.

Knopf, Howard. 2006. "CRIA Spinning on the WIPO Treaties." *Excess Copyright*, 27 February. Available at: <http://excesscopyright.blogspot.com/2006/02/cria-spinning-on-wipo-treaties.html>

Koury Menescal, Andréa. 2006. "Changing WIPO's Ways? The 2004 Development Agenda in Historical Perspective." *Journal of World Intellectual Property* 8, part 6 (2005): 761–96.

Lametti, David. 2005. "Coming to Terms with Copyright." In *In the Public Interest: The Future of Canadian Copyright Law*, edited by Michael Geist. Toronto: Irwin Law.

Lehman, Bruce. 2007. General comments at *Musical Myopia, Digital Dystopia: New Media and Copyright Reform*. The Centre for Intellectual Property Policy and the Schulich School of Music, Montreal, 23 March.

Love, James. 2007. "Canada, US and Italy on [Access to Knowledge] in PCDA discussions." *Knowledge Ecology International*, 13 June. Available at: <http://www.keionline.org/index.php?option=com_jd-wp&Itemid=39&p=42>. Last accessed 24 July 2007.

Marchant, Ron, and Sisule F. Musungu. 2007. "Essential Elements of a WIPO Development Agenda: What Could Constitute Success?" *ICTSD Programme on Intellectual Property Rights and Sustainable Development*, June. Geneva: The International Centre for Trade and Sustainable Development.

Marrakesh Ministerial of April 1994. 1994. "Agreement on Trade-Related Aspects of Intellectual Property Rights." *Marrakesh Agreement Establishing the World Trade Organization*. Annex 1C, 15 April. Available at: <http://www.wto.org/English/docs_e/legal_e/27-trips.pdf>

Matthews, Duncan. 2002. *Globalizing Intellectual Property Rights: The TRIPs Agreement*. London: Routledge.

May, Christopher. 2007. *The World Intellectual Property Organization: Resurgence and the Development Agenda*. Abingdon, Oxon: Routledge.

Musungu, Sisule. 2007. "WIPO Development Agenda – As the dust settles, pondering what is in the agenda, whether it is success or hot air." *Thoughts in Colours*, 9 July. Available at: <http://thoughtsincolours.blogspot.com/2007/07/wipo-development-agenda-as-dust.html>. Last accessed 24 July 2007.

New, William. 2007. "In A 'Major Achievement', WIPO Negotiators Create New Development Mandate." *Intellectual Property Watch*, 18 June. Available at: <http://www.ip-watch.org/weblog/index.php?p=656&res=1280_ff>. Last accessed 24 July.

Savage, Luiza. "Meet NAFTA 2.0." *Macleans*, 13 September 2006.

Sell, Susan. 2003. *Private Power, Public Law. The Globalization of Intellectual Property Rights*. Cambridge: Cambridge University Press.

Vaver, David. 2000. *Copyright Law*. Toronto: Irwin Law.

World Intellectual Property Organization. 2005a. *IIM on Development Agenda for WIPO First Session Report*. IIM/1/6, 18 August.

– 2005b. *IIM on Development Agenda for WIPO Second Session Report*. IIM/2/10, 1 September.

– 2005c. *IIM on Development Agenda for WIPO Third Session Report*. IIM/3/3 16 September.

– 2007. *Development Agenda for WIPO*. Available at: <http://www.wipo.int/ip-development/en/agenda/>

9 Canada's Adventures in Clubland: Trade Clubs and Political Influence

ROBERT WOLFE

Unlike Groucho Marx, Canadians want to belong to any club that will have us as a member, and that turns out to be quite a few international clubs. It is axiomatic that a central objective of Canadian foreign policy is to *participate* in making decisions that affect the country directly, while having *influence* on decisions that affect the evolving structure of global governance. The political practice of multilateralism, however, is not an open-ended Athenian forum where every state can speak freely, expecting its views to be given serious consideration by all others. In the messy reality of global governance, Canada can only play a role by aggregating its efforts with other countries. The notion of "clubs" is one way to think about how that process works. It is an especially useful idea when studying the World Trade Organization (WTO), where the current Doha round of multilateral trade negotiations is characterized by a bewildering array of clubs with banal and whimsical names, from the G-4 through the Dirty Dozen and the Friends of Fish to the G-90. Canada is a great joiner, but many observers now wonder whether Canada is still a member of the best clubs in WTO "clubland."

It is common to see international organizations in themselves as "clubs," meaning places where insiders (certain states and selected officials of those states) know the rules, and outsiders (citizens, other states) are not welcome (Keohane and Nye 2001). Regional agreements can also be seen as clubs (Padoan 1997), and particular treaties can be seen as providing "club goods," in the sense of excludable goods available only to members of those clubs. Sometimes the term will be applied to a loosely structured body, like the Paris Club of creditor states, or to a set of countries with no structure at all, as in referring to the states possessing nuclear weapons as the nuclear club. There was a time when the WTO's predecessor, the General Agreement on Tariffs and Trade (GATT), could be seen as an exclusive club: only selected countries could be Contracting Parties, and only selected officials could penetrate its inner mysteries. The WTO, however, is no longer an exclusive club and Membership automatically implies participation in every formal WTO body.[1]

The Doha negotiations take place in Negotiating Groups for Agriculture, Services, Non-Agricultural Market Access (NAMA), Rules, Trade Facilitation, Environment and Trade-related Intellectual Property Rights (TRIPS), all under the supervision of the Trade Negotiations Committee. Only the largest WTO Members can monitor and participate in all the associated meetings in addition to the regular work in the roughly five dozen WTO bodies. The US does so easily. The 27 member states of the European Union (EU) are represented by the European Commission. Perhaps less than half a dozen more Members have the capacity to participate actively across the board, notably Canada and Japan. Other leading developed and developing countries participate more actively in some areas than others. And all countries must find ways to aggregate their efforts with others in clubs.

CLUBS IN THE WTO

I define a "club" as a group of nations united or associated for a particular purpose, a definition that purposely evokes a looser form of association than the common tendency to see informal groups of states working within international organizations as "coalitions" (Odell 2006b). These clubs are voluntary – no Member of the WTO has to join a club, nor must a given club accept the participation of any Member.

Clubs provide their members with an opportunity to learn about issues with like-minded colleagues; to coordinate positions for WTO meetings, whether plenary or restricted groups; to span the gaps between opposing clubs in bridge clubs; and to debrief on past meetings. Clubs often speak as a group, allowing members to expand support for each other's preferred issues. Clubs also engage in analytic burden-sharing in the preparation of common proposals. The most-structured clubs require high-level recognition in capitals, especially for subordinating national strategy to joint negotiating positions; they have formal coordination/decision-making procedures; sometimes meet at the ministerial level; and sometimes have sophisticated analytical support. The least-organized are loose consultative mechanisms at the technical or delegate level, often requiring authority from capitals, but they matter in the larger dynamics of building consensus and in solving substantive problems.

The many WTO clubs show differing patterns of membership because countries do not have a single preference schedule that can readily be aligned with those of other countries across all issues. In agriculture, for example, Canada's allies on issues affecting eastern dairy farmers are not the same as its otherwise closer allies on issues affecting western grain farmers. Clubs vary, therefore, on the extent to which members share a common agenda. In the Cairns Group, Canada and Australia agree on ending export subsidies but disagree on whether "sensitive products" (usually understood to include sugar, dairy and rice) should be exempted from liberalization obligations. Similar tensions are found in the G-20, where India and Brazil do not agree on the extent to which some "special products" (ones important for food security or rural development) should be exempt from new obligations. That club formed to advance their agriculture objectives – their divergent interests on industrial goods mean that in that area of the negotiations, only a rump is able to work together as the NAMA-11. In services, Canada is associated with "collective requests" on many issues, but it is a target of other requests. Offensive and defensive concerns form a complex pattern for most Members.

Clubs in the WTO also differ on their procedural characteristics, as do similar groups in the International Monetary Fund (Woods and Lombardi 2006). Some clubs will always be chaired by one Member but some will have a rotating chair. The influence of some clubs depends more on the institutional power discussed below than on its members share in world trade. Finally the members of clubs will differ in their diplomatic and analytic capacity: some delegations have more, and better, resources in Geneva and in capitals than others, which affects the effectiveness and influence of their clubs.

The clubs that seem such an important part of the institutional design of the Doha round have roots in earlier GATT rounds, indeed in long established multilateral practices going back to the League of Nations. The establishment of groups was part of the United Nations (UN) from the beginning and now voting blocs and clubs of all sorts are common (Smith 2006, 50, 77n). Unlike the UN system, electoral clubs as such do not play a role in the WTO, although some regional clubs do work together occasionally on political issues and in the process of reaching consensus on appointing the chairpersons of WTO bodies. Three sorts of clubs are relevant for WTO negotiations. Clubs based on a broad *common characteristic* (e.g. region or level of development) can influence

Table 9.1
GATT Clubs

Kennedy Round 1960s
US domination of small organization

Tokyo Round 1970s
EC-12, US domination
Quad emerges de facto (Canada)
G-77 focused on UNCTAD and NIEO not GATT

Pre-Uruguay Round
Annecy (US, EC, Canada, Japan, Switzerland)

Uruguay Round 1986–94
EC-15, US prominence
Quad (Canada)
Cairns Group (Canada)
Net Food Importers Group
de la Paix group (Canada)
Invisibles group (Canada)
G10 (Brazil, India in blocking role)
Group of 12 on Antidumping (failed bridge club)
Subsidies (US, EC, Canada)

---

many issues, including the round as a whole, but only weakly. Clubs based on a *common objective* (e.g. agricultural trade) can have a great deal of influence, but on a limited range of issues. *Bridge clubs* can be essential for breaking deadlocks, or managing negotiations, often by building bridges between opposed positions. In the Law of the Sea negotiations in the 1970s, they were called "compromise groups" (Buzan 1980). In the UN such clubs are called "contact groups," "negotiating groupings" (Smith 2006, 73–4) or "Friends of the chair" when they are formed to help the Secretary General in his efforts to resolve a specific conflict (Prantl and Krasno 2004). As will be seen in Table 9.2, they are also known under different names in the WTO.

I have not seen mention of clubs in histories of the first 15 years of the GATT, perhaps because the small number of Contracting Parties was sufficiently like-minded not to need the device. Inevitably the emergence of clubs in the GATT was a story about the slow pace of agricultural reform, and conflict between Europe and the US.

Agriculture was effectively exempted from the GATT in the 1950s, and little progress was made in the Kennedy Round of the 1960s, whose main purpose had been to assimilate the then new European

Economic Community's Common Agricultural Policy (CAP) to the rules of the system – an objective that was not met. Some major deals in that round began life in small meetings of the most significant participants – the so-called "bridge club" of the US, the European Community (EC, then with only six member states), the United Kingdom, Japan and Canada (Winham 1986, 65). I take my term for groups formed to break deadlocks from this early example. The US hoped that the Tokyo Round of the 1970s would achieve what the Kennedy Round did not, but the EC argued that agriculture should be negotiated separately from industrial products; the US, seeking maximum liberalization, insisted on treating agriculture like any other sector (Winham 1986, 95). The group that became known as the Quad (for Quadrilateral Group of Trade Ministers: US, EU, Japan, Canada) after the 1981 Ottawa G-7 Summit had already made a contribution to bridging differences in the closing stages of the Tokyo Round.

As in the Tokyo Round, the US was the main proponent of liberalization in the Uruguay Round, but this time it was joined by the newly formed Cairns Group. A group of developing countries with preferential access to EC markets were concerned that they would lose market access and a group of mostly African countries was concerned that liberalization would increase world prices of key imported food products (Croome 1995, 113). The EC and US retained their prominence in the negotiations, but a growing role was played by clubs, like the Quad, the Cairns Group, the de la Paix group (a north/south group that pushed for a broadly based agenda), the G-10 (with Brazil and India in a blocking role) and the Invisibles group, a little-known Bridge club.

In the Doha Round, launched in 2001, clubs have proliferated. Part of the explanation is based on institutional design factors – the many developing country Members have discovered that clubs are essential in an organization that never takes votes (the consensus rule) and where nothing is agreed until everything is agreed (the Single Undertaking). The clubs are influenced by the national characteristics of their members (Costantini et al. 2007), but they are also influenced by other clubs – the many new clubs formed around the time of the Cancún ministerial in 2003 had learned from the practices of the Cairns group, formed nearly two decades before. The list in Table 9.2 shows the common characteristic, common objective and bridge clubs as they existed in early 2007. Figure 9.1, originally prepared by the International Centre for Trade and Sustainable Development and modified by the WTO secretariat, shows the overlapping membership of the agriculture clubs. Some domains might have fewer clubs because in the current negotiations the chair holds most meetings in informal plenary; it may also be that clubs proliferate as more WTO Members take a more intense interest in a

Table 9.2
WTO Clubland in Early-2007

Common characteristic clubs
  G-90†
    ACP†
    African Group†
    LDCs†
  ASEAN†
  CARICOM†
  Small and Vulnerable Economies (SVEs)
  Recently Acceded Members (RAMs)
  Small Vulnerable Coastal States (SVCS)

Common purpose clubs
Agriculture
  OFFENSIVE COALITIONS
  Cotton-4†
  Tropical and Alternative Products Group
  Cairns Group (NS)†
  G-20 (s/s)†
  DEFENSIVE COALITIONS
  G-10†
  G-33†
  RAMs, SVEs

Non-agricultural Market Access (NAMA)
  NAMA 11†
  Friends of MFN
  Friends of Ambition in NAMA
  Hotel d'Angleterre
  RAMs, SVEs

Rules
  SCVS
  Friends of Fish
  Friends of Antidumping Negotiations (FANs)

TRIPS
  African Group
  "Disclosure" group of developing countries
  Friends of Geographical Indications
  Friends Against Extension of Geographical Indications

Services
  G-25
  ASEAN-1 (-Singapore)
  African Group, ACP, LDCs, SVEs

Table 9.2
WTO Clubland in Early-2007 (Continued)

Real Good Friends of GATS/Friends of Friends*

Friends of ... (plurilateral expert) groups: Audiovisual, **legal; Architectural/ Engineering/Integrated Engineering***; **Computer and related services;** Postal/Courier including express delivery; **Telecommunications; Construction and Related Engineering;** distribution; education; **Environmental service; Financial services***; **Maritime transport;** Air transport; logistics; energy; Services related to Agriculture, Cross-border services (Mode 1/2), Mode 3, Mode 4, MFN exemptions

Trade Facilitation
Core Group/W142 group
Colorado Group/W137 group

Environment
Friends of environmental goods
Friends of the environment and sustainable development

Textiles
International Textiles and Clothing Bureau (ITCB)

Bridge clubs
AGRICULTURE AND NAMA (principal antagonists):
G-4 (US EU Brazil, India)†
G-6 (add Australia, Japan)†
SERVICES
Enchilada Group
GENERAL (deadlock-breaking)
Oslo or Non-G-6
Quad
Dirty Dozen (Quad plus)
"senior officials" (25–30)
Mini-ministerials† (25–30)

Notes:
1. Canada belongs to groups in **bold**, and is the coordinator of * starred groups. † indicates groups that have met at ministerial level during the Doha Round.
2. For a glossary of agriculture groups, see (WTO 2006). The list in this document is based both on self-identified groups and on sets of Members that have submitted joint proposals at various stages of the negotiations. The Five Interested Parties (FIPs) has ceased meeting in that form, as has, therefore, the FIPs Plus. The agriculture Quint does not seem to have met for some time.
3. The Enchilada Group incorporates Members who once met as the Core Group and then the G-15.
4. Certain regional (common characteristic) groups apparently no longer actively coordinate in WTO except occasionally on electoral or political issues, such as observer status: ALADI, Andean Group, Arab Group, APEC, CEFTA, GRULAC, Islamic Group, Mercosur, OECS, SADC, SAPTA, SELA.
5. The once-prominent Like-Minded Group (LMG) has not been active for many years. The status of the "informal group of developing countries" is not clear.

Figure 9.1
Membership in Agricultural Clubs

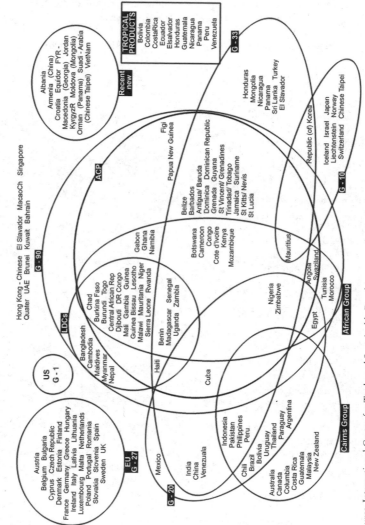

Source: International Centre for Trade and Sustainable Development and WTO Secretariat

particular domain. The services clubs are a special case. The more active members have always organized themselves in "Friends of" groups. These groups of experts do not include the WTO secretariat, and decide for themselves who can come to meetings. The list in Table 9.2 is based on the "collective requests" submitted in early 2006 under the plurilateral approach introduced in paragraph 7 of Annex C of the Hong Kong declaration (World Trade Organization 2005).

DECISION-MAKING AND CRITICAL MASS

At most 40 delegations are significant players in the negotiations, a reality mentioned again and again by senior members of the secretariat and by ambassadors, including from developing countries.[2] Agriculture is the area followed most closely, but at most 15 delegations really play a significant part (and the principal ideas come from less than 10). And yet the reality of the WTO is that consensus and the Single Undertaking require every member to understand and feel engaged in the negotiations. Reaching a consensus with 150 Members is not easy. The institutional design issue becomes structuring a process where the key players can get on with it, without losing touch with the interests of all the rest, and doing it in a way that builds confidence in the process and the results. Clubs are part of the solution.

The systemic public good of an open liberal multilateral trading system does not require collective supply by all 150 Members of the WTO, as long as the non-discrimination norms are respected. If the largest markets are open, the system will be open. And the necessary intellectual work of negotiating new rules need not involve all Members all the time. But how many Members are needed to provide systemic "critical mass"? The European Union (or EU, now with 27 member states) and the US are necessary but not sufficient for a deal. The idea of critical mass implies that the relevant process is of a sufficient size to be self-sustaining, whether it is a nuclear reaction or the wide diffusion of a social norm. Many applications in social science derive from Mancur Olson's work on the provision of collective goods. Whereas Olson's work is pessimistic on the possibility of cooperation, other scholars explore the circumstances under which a group of sufficient size can be created to supply public goods (Oliver and Marwell 2001).

Critical mass with respect to the WTO implies first that markets that represent a significant share of global production and consumption should help to supply the systemic public good, a form of *material power*. The public good of new rules also depends on acceptance by participants in the trading system that the rules themselves are appropriate and legitimate, which suggests that critical mass must have another dimension. The coercive power of the largest markets is limited now both by the emergence of other significant markets and by equally powerful symbolic and normative claims based on justice for developing countries, in general but especially for the poorest. In the Tokyo Round, developing countries could opt out of any aspect of the bargain, and their views could be ignored. But the WTO is now a Single Undertaking: once the shape of the package is agreed upon, final decisions are made on the package as a whole, not on the individual elements. Each participant must accept all the new obligations. That decision is inevitably made by consensus (meaning that nobody present objects). These two principles give every Member the ability to slow the process down, a form of *institutional power*, and developing countries are increasingly aware of that power in the WTO. They are also increasingly aware of the need to participate, because they will not be able to opt out of any of the new obligations, which has put stress on the ability of the WTO process to remain effective while becoming more inclusive and transparent.

Critical mass in the WTO, therefore, has two dimensions. When all issues are lumped together, and any Member can block consensus, institutional power must be joined to compulsory power to reach a successful outcome in negotiations. A bargain must satisfy those Members whose market weight is sufficient to give effect to the deal, but it must also satisfy those Members whose acquiescence is sufficient to give the deal legitimacy. Most matters will be settled informally because consensus forces actors to find a compromise when a vote is not available as a means to decide a controversy.

It is not surprising, therefore, that the real work is done in informal meetings of the various negotiating groups, in restricted meetings organized by the chair, or in bilateral sessions. Members talk at the Ministerial Conference every two years, in regular committees that meet two or three times a year and in the Negotiating Groups that meet every four to six weeks. They talk in hundreds of formal on-the-record meetings every year, and they talk in many hundreds more informal meetings, including "mini-ministerials" (Wolfe 2004). No organization with 150 Members can find consensus on sensitive matters like agricultural reform if all discussions must be held in public, in large groups, with written records. All Members must be in the room when the deal is done, but assembling the requisite critical mass requires smaller meetings.

WTO insiders understand the process as a series of nested "concentric circles." In the outer ring are official WTO meetings (mandated by the treaty or the rules of procedure); these plenary meetings are held only for the record. In the next circle are informal plenary meetings of a regular body, under its regular chair, held mostly for transparency purposes. The real work is done when the chair meets with a limited number of technical experts, or when s/he invites a small group of key players to explore selected issues. When these discussions reach an impasse, the traditional GATT response to negotiating difficulties now carried over to the WTO has been meetings of a restricted group of Members, usually known by the colour of the director-general's boardroom. The Green Room is therefore a real place, but the term also refers to a specific type of meeting, whether of ambassadors in Geneva or ministers at the biennial Ministerial Conference. The original Green Room practice reflected three negotiating realities: informality is vital; the largest Members, especially the US and the EU, must always be in the room; and other interested parties should be engaged in the search for consensus. Part of what the many clubs of Table 9.2 do is to create a claim that one of their number should represent them in the Green Room. Up to 30 Members often participate in Green Room meetings, and they are sometimes represented by two or more ministers or officials. While it is a large group for a negotiation, all key players plus all groups must be represented if it is to be *inclusive* and therefore legitimate. The members of the original Quad are always represented along with other leading traders, representatives of clubs, and coordinators of the regional groups. The process must also be *transparent* to other Members of the WTO. Representatives in the room must fairly articulate the views of their club, and must expeditiously and comprehensively report on the deliberations. Any results must also be fairly presented by the chairperson when s/he reports on the state of negotiations in plenary meetings, or when s/he drafts documents designed to attract consensus.

THE VALUE OF BRIDGE CLUBS

Bridge clubs are intended to play a coordinating role, but they are located outside the WTO concentric circles, since they are not chaired by the chairperson of the regular body, and the secretariat is often not invited. The utility of all restricted bridge clubs was questioned after the Doha negotiations were "suspended" in July 2006. A representative Green Room or mini-ministerial may be too large to provide leadership, and the old Quad will never return, but some new grouping may be needed to conclude the round. Such a new grouping may need to change either the *level* of participation or the *Members* involved.

The first approach is to try to bump thorny issues up to heads of government. Former Canadian Prime Minister Paul Martin was convinced that an informal meeting of leaders could make a major difference on issues like agricultural trade reform (Martin 2004). He received little support for the idea. Brazilian President Luiz Inacio Lula da Silva angled for months in 2005–6 to have a summit devoted solely to breaking the Doha logjam, but also received little support. In the event, on the margins of the St. Petersburg Summit in 2006, the G8 had a meeting with their five regular interlocutors (Brazil, India, China, Mexico and South Africa) but managed only to tell their trade ministers to get the job done. The ministers then failed. At the time of writing, there was little prospect that the similar injunction delivered at the 2007 meeting would be any more useful. The effort to engage leaders is based on what people think they remember about the G-7 Summit contributions to ending the Tokyo Round in 1978 and the Uruguay Round in 1993. In both cases, however, leaders did little more than ask the Quad trade ministers to meet in advance in order to present a report at the summit. Leaders can force coordination within their own government if the lack of such coordination is the obstacle to agreement, but leaders could not solve the agriculture problem from the top.

If changing the level does not help, changing the countries might. Part of the effort to re-start the round after the failed Cancún ministerial in 2003 was a process involving the principal antagonists on agriculture: the US and the EU, who are opposed to each other; and Brazil and India who are opposed both to each other and to the US and the EU. These four tried to sort things out as a "new Quad," (or G-4) and failed. In 2004, they included Australia, representing the Cairns Group, in what became known as the "five interested parties," or FIPs. They next included Japan, representing the G-10 (agricultural importers), in what became known as the G-6 – it met frequently, without success. The group did not meet at the ministerial or senior official level for many months after its spectacular failure to resolve the modalities conundrum in the summer of 2006. In early 2007, the G-4 countries are again engaged in quiet efforts to find a compromise, so far with no more success – and their efforts are not seen as legitimate even by the developing countries Brazil and India purport to represent because the process is not transparent and multilateral.

The G-6 failed as a bridge club in 2006 because they could not advance a systemic interest. The club contains the principal antagonists, but they are all publicly committed to their positions which make compromises difficult. The old Quad was more effective because one participant, Canada, was not a principal antagonist. Having listened to all the others, Canada was able to put possible compromises forward quietly among senior officials in a way that could advance the negotiations. Some negotiators think it is time, therefore, to change countries as well as the level at which Members are represented.

Two Uruguay Round events are precedents for changing the countries. The first is the "café au lait" process led by Switzerland and Columbia in 1986. Known as the de la Paix group after the hotel where they first met, this group advanced a compromise proposal on the arrangements and subjects for the Uruguay Round that was successful in part because the proponents shared not specific negotiating objectives but a commitment to the importance of the Round itself. The group was reconstituted in June 1988 with an informal proposal by seven countries (Australia, Canada, Hong Kong, Hungary, Korea, New Zealand and Switzerland) that helped energize the process (Croome 1995). Now a group of six WTO Members (Canada, Chile, Indonesia, Kenya, New Zealand and Norway) are trying something similar. Senior officials (not ministers) met in Oslo in October 2006 to discuss key issues blocking progress in the negotiations. None of the six belonged to the G-6, but they did represent many of the major clubs, north and south. Participants in the "non-G-6" or Oslo group have tried not to attract attention to themselves with their subsequent meetings on all aspects of the round, making it too early to assess the eventual contribution this bridge club might make.

WHERE IS CANADA IN WTO CLUBLAND?

This picture of power and influence in the WTO is remarkably complex. Some old hands who compare it to the simpler days of the Tokyo and Uruguay Rounds think the Canadian role is diminished. It should be apparent from Table 9.2, however, that the only current club to which Canada might once have expected to belong is the G-4. Is Canada's absence significant?

The current minority parliament both keeps the Canadian minister of international trade closer to home than some of his counterparts, and limits Canadian negotiators' public room to manoeuvre, but it is frequently said both in Geneva and in Ottawa that it is their quixotic support for supply management that has marginalized Canadian ministers. Politicians are tied in knots by the farm lobbies, as in November 2005 when the House of Commons after a full day of debate on agricultural trade policy gave unanimous approval to a motion instructing negotiators at the WTO's Hong Kong ministerial to seek increased market access abroad for agricultural exports while offering none at home in order to protect the supply management system (Canada 2005, 9960, 10017).[3]

All Canada's trading partners understand why in a minority parliament ministers will not risk even whispering that the likely Doha outcomes will be manageable for Canadian farmers, even if some adjustment will be needed (Gifford 2005). But that limits Canadian ability to build bridges on "sensitive products," as the trade minister admitted to a House of Commons committee earlier this year (Wilson 2007). As one Geneva ambassador told me privately, "Canadian ministers are not in the game." If material power were the whole story, this claim would be silly, but anything that affects a negotiator's credibility can affect other forms of power. It was awkward in April 2007 when Canada could join its Cairns Group colleagues in submitting a non-paper on tropical and alternative products, but could not sign on to the submission on sensitive products. It is hard to exert influence in favour of compromise if others know that you have promised your own domestic interests that you yourself will not compromise. But the main reason that Canada is not in the G-4 is because it is not a principal antagonist; we are not needed for a solution to the central blockage. On agriculture, other members only want us to reduce the restrictiveness of supply management and to end the export monopoly of the Wheat Board. Whatever the merits of those actions, they would make a trivial contribution to the overall Doha outcome. Similarly on trade in goods, Canada does not bring a lot of new trade to the table in market access negotiations because the country has relatively low levels of remaining protection as a result of NAFTA and the Uruguay Round.

It is neither surprising nor especially significant, therefore, that Canada is not in the G-4. It might become significant if the G-4 proves able to play a broader role, but so far it has not even been able to unblock the central obstacles to the round. Of more importance, Canada is still a valued player in many clubs, as shown in Table 9.2. Canada's well-respected ambassador in Geneva chairs the sensitive NAMA negotiations. He is supported by a staff of eleven professionals in Geneva, one of whom, for example coordinates the "Friends of Friends" club in services which manages the "collective requests" process. With its substantial number of trade policy professionals in Ottawa, Canada has been able, as the secretariat observed, to make contributions or proposals in a wide range of areas, including trade facilitation, agriculture, market access for non-agricultural goods, services, subsidies, anti-dumping and countervailing duties and intellectual property – a total of 70 documents in the trade negotiations series (TN) in the WTO Documents Online database between January 2003 and October 2006 (World Trade Organization 2007, para 37).[4] Few Members have made as substantial an analytic contribution to the negotiations. Canada is represented at all levels of the concentric circles in every area of the negotiations, from Green Room-type meetings (20–40 delegations) of ambassadors in Geneva and ministers at the Ministerial Conferences, through numerous mini-ministerials of trade and agriculture ministers to things like the Fireside Chats held by the chair of the agriculture negotiations, Enchilada talks held by the services chair, and of course the NAMA caucus, which the Canadian ambassador chairs. With respect to Bridge clubs, Canada has played a leading role in the Oslo group. The old Quad that met regularly from the end of the Tokyo Round in the 1970s through the lengthy Uruguay Round negotiations and to the early days of the WTO has not met at ministerial level since 1999. But it still meets informally among Geneva delegates, where Canada is useful as an intermediary and for its analytic capacity.

The jury is still out on whether clubs have helped or hindered the Doha round, which was still struggling when this chapter was written, but what we know is that decisions in any social context are taken, or at least shaped, by small groups. Less than 10 participants may be most efficient for decision-making, but effectiveness and legitimacy in the WTO often requires up to 30 Members in order to ensure that all perspectives are heard in the search for consensus. The list will differ by issue, but Canada is always present at that level in the concentric circles. However the round ends, and whatever form the next round takes, it is a safe assumption that decision-making will include some sort of Green Room-type meetings, and that clubs will be needed to ensure inclusive and transparent representation of all Members. Within the various domains of the WTO, it also seems probable that Members will find it easier to assemble the requisite critical mass by working together in clubs in an effort to manage the scale and complexity of the agenda. Finding a consensus on the management of a global trading system with 150 members with more set to join, is not going to get easier, but maintaining the Single Undertaking is vital. Canadians will continue to use clubs to advance the country's interests in this complex environment, playing a traditional analytic and bridge-building role.

NOTES

1 I capitalize Member when referring to the WTO, and not when referring to members of a club.
2 The WTO has 150 Members in May 2007. Counting the EU-27 as one, if 40 are more or less effective, that implies that roughly 80 Members are to varying degrees content to follow a lead set by others.
3 The opposition Bloc Québecois moved:
   That, in the opinion of the House, the government should give its negotiators a mandate during the negotiations at the World Trade Organization so that, at the end of the current round of negotiations, Canada obtains results that

ensure that the supply management sectors are subject to no reduction in over-quota tariffs and no increase in tariff quotas, so that these sectors can continue to provide producers with a fair and equitable income (Canada 2005, 1010).

The Conservatives (then in opposition in a minority parliament) moved: That the motion be amended by replacing all the words after "quotas" with "and also ensure an agreement that strengthens the market access of Canada's agricultural exporters so that all sectors can continue to provide producers with a fair and equitable income". (Canada 2005, 1530)

4 When less formal JOB documents are added, the number more than doubles – see WTO (2007b, Annex 1).

REFERENCES

Buzan, Barry. 1980. "'United We Stand ... ': Informal Negotiating Groups at UNCLOS III." Marine Policy 4 (3):183–204.

Canada. 2005. "Opposition Motion: World Trade Organization Negotiations." House of Commons Debates. Official Report. 38th Parliament, 1st Session. no. 155, 22 November. House of Commons. Available at: <http://canadaonline.about.com>

Costantini, Valeria, Riccardo Crescenzi, Fabrizio De Filippis and Luca Salvatici. 2007. "Bargaining Coalitions in the WTO Agricultural Negotiations." The World Economy 30, no. 5: 863–91.

Croome, John. 1995. Reshaping the World Trading System: A History of the Uruguay Round. Geneva: World Trade Organization.

Gifford, Mike. 2005. Can Canada's Supply Managed Dairy Industry Survive the Doha Round? Trade Policy Brief 2005–3, November. Ottawa: Canadian Agricultural Trade Policy Research Network. Available at: <http://www.uoguelph.ca/~catprn/PDF/TPB-05-03.pdf>

Keohane, Robert O. and Joseph S. Nye, Jr. 2001. "The Club Model of Multilateral Cooperation and Problems of Democratic Legitimacy." In Efficiency, Equity, and Legitimacy: The Multilateral Trading System at the Millennium, edited by Roger B. Porter, Pierre Sauvé, Arvind Subramanian and Americo Bevigilia Zampetti. Washington, DC: Brookings Institution Press, 264–94.

Martin, Paul. 2004. Prime Minister Paul Martin Speaks at the World Economic Forum On "The Future of Global Interdependence," Davos, Switzerland, 23 January. Privy Council Office. Available at: <http://www.pco-bcp.gc.ca/default.asp?Language=E&Page=archivemartin&Sub=speechesdiscours&Doc=speech_20040123_31_e.htm>

Odell, John S. 2006a. "Introduction." In Negotiating Trade: Developing Countries in the WTO and NAFTA, edited by John S. Odell. Cambridge: Cambridge University Press, 1–38.

– ed. 2006b. *Negotiating Trade: Developing Countries in the* WTO *and* NAFTA. Cambridge: Cambridge University Press.

Oliver, Pamela E, and Gerald Marwell. 2001. "Whatever Happened to Critical Mass Theory? A Retrospective and Assessment." *Sociological Theory* 19, no. 3: 292–311.

Padoan, Pier Carlo. 1997. "Regional Agreements as Clubs: The European Case." In *The Political Economy of Regionalism*, edited by Edward D. Mansfield and Helen V. Milner. New York: Columbia Unversity Press, 107–34.

Prantl, Jochen, and Jean Krasno. 2004. "Informal Groups of Member States." In *The United Nations: Confronting the Challenges of a Global Society*, edited by Jean E. Krasno. Boulder, CO and London: Lynne Rienner Publishers, 311–57.

Smith, Courtney B. 2006. *Politics and Process at the United Nations: The Global Dance*. Boulder, CO and London: Lynne Rienner Publishers.

Wilson, Barry. 2007. "Minister Maintains Stance on Supply Management." *Western Producer*, 8 March.

Winham, Gilbert R. 1986. *International Trade and the Tokyo Round Negotiation*. Princeton: Princeton University Press.

Wolfe, Robert. 2004. "Informal Political Engagement in the WTO: Are Mini-Ministerials a Good Idea?" In *Trade Policy Research 2004*, edited by Dan Ciuriak and John M. Curtis. Ottawa: Department of Foreign Affairs and International Trade (International Trade), 27–90.

Woods, Ngaire, and Domenico Lombardi. 2006. "Uneven Patterns of Governance: How Developing Countries Are Represented in the IMF." *Review of International Political Economy* 13, no. 3: 480–515.

World Trade Organization. 2005. *Doha Work Programme*. Ministerial Conference, Sixth Session. WT/MIN(05)/W/3/Rev.2, 18 December. Hong Kong: WTO.

– 2006. "Countries, Alliances and Proposals." *Agriculture Negotiations: Backgrounder*. Paper delivered to the WTO. 27 November. Geneva, Switzerland: WTO. Available at: <http://www.wto.org/English/tratop_e/agric_e/negs_bkgrndo4_groups_e.htm>

– 2007. *Trade Policy Review Canada: Report by the Secretariat –* CANADA. WT/TPR/S/179, 14 February. Trade Policy Review Body, World Trade Organization. Available at: <www.wto.org/English/tratop_e/tpr_e/s179-00_e.doc>

10 Canada and the Nuclear Club

TREVOR FINDLAY

"If Canada were a Great Power, its monopoly of the indispensable component of the atomic bomb [uranium] might put this country in a position to determine decisions as to the future use and control of the bomb, but as Canada is not a Great Power, her possession of uranium is perhaps more likely to expose her to embarrassment and difficulties."

C.S.A. Ritchie (1945)

The ultimate question to be addressed by this chapter is the extent to which Canada retains its presumed longstanding influence in nuclear non-proliferation issues as an original member of the nuclear non-proliferation "club" and the reasons for any changes that may have occurred in its standing and status. The traditional assumption has been that Canada's pioneering stances towards nuclear non-proliferation have afforded it tremendous moral, political and practical influence in the non-proliferation club that began to form in the 1950s and 1960s. After examining Canada's credentials for club membership the chapter will explore whether the country's presumed influence was always more imaginary than real and to what extent Canada has been and currently is able to leverage its membership.

BACKGROUND

Canada has traditionally been regarded as a prominent member of the nuclear non-proliferation "club." The club is a select group of mostly Western states that early in the nuclear era concluded that their security would not be enhanced by their acquisition of nuclear weapons and in fact might be harmed by such acquisition.[1] They thereafter committed themselves to pursuing nuclear non-proliferation and, as a necessary concomitant, nuclear arms control and ultimately (or at least rhetorically) complete nuclear disarmament.

Besides Canada, the original core members of the club are Australia, Austria, Finland, Ireland, Japan, New Zealand, the Netherlands,

Norway, Sweden and Switzerland. Since the end of the Cold War, new members have appeared: Germany, South Africa and (arguably) the entire expanding European Union (EU) stand as the most notable additions. Despite their status as nuclear weapon states (NWS), the Western nuclear powers – France, the United Kingdom and the United States – have also been close interlocutors with this group, depending on the issue and the government in power in each state at the time.

The "club" is completely informal and has no name. It has no regular meeting place, no regular meetings and makes no agreed policy pronouncements. Although from the 1970s to 1990s the club approximated the Barton Group of Western countries that met in Geneva and New York to coordinate their disarmament policies at the United Nations and related bodies, this group did not include the European neutrals – Austria, Sweden and Switzerland – and did include the Western NWS, so it cannot be considered to be identical to the non-proliferation club. The club is defined more by policy and behaviour than political geography. The broad characteristics of club members are set out in the following table, with individual national variations noted.

CANADA'S QUALIFICATIONS FOR CLUB MEMBERSHIP AND USE OF ITS LEVERAGE

Currently, Canada is a model citizen in respect of all of the criteria for club membership and has customarily attempted to leverage this to its advantage. There is, however, a complex, ever-changing and symbiotic relationship between club membership and leverage. As the non-proliferation regime has progressively tightened, often in reaction to crises that have threatened its integrity, like the 1974 Indian nuclear test or the discovery of Iraq's nuclear capabilities in 1990, so have the qualifications for membership. What looks like model non-proliferation citizenship in one era looks less than progressive in another. As the regime tightens, the ability to use one's leverage depends on keeping one's credentials current, which partly turns on using whatever leverage one has to further strengthen the regime. Hence membership of the non-proliferation club depends not just on passively joining up and complying with one's obligations, but also on promoting the strengthening of the non-proliferation regime by taking initiatives that in turn bolster one's credentials. This "double helix" effect has certainly been the Canadian experience.

Canada's case is made even more complicated by factors that have repeatedly demonstrated their potential for frustrating Canada's ability

Table 10.1
Qualifications for membership of the nuclear non-proliferation "club"

---

1   membership of and strong support for the International Atomic Energy Agency (IAEA)

2   membership of and strong support for the 1968 Nuclear Non-Proliferation Treaty (NPT)

3   an impeccable track record of compliance with the NPT, including early conclusion of a comprehensive safeguards agreement with the IAEA (non-compliance by the NWS parties to the NPT with their Article VI disarmament obligations tends to set them apart from the rest of the club on this point)

4   since 1997, conclusion, signature, ratification and implementation of an Additional Protocol to their comprehensive safeguards agreements in order to strengthen the safeguards regime

5   for club members that are also nuclear suppliers, the imposition of additional bilateral safeguards measures on importing states

6   active participation in NPT Review Conferences in seeking balanced outcomes, including insistence on the NWS complying with Article VI

7   membership of the nuclear export control groups, the Zangger Committee and Nuclear Suppliers Group (NSG)

8   signature and ratification of the 1996 Comprehensive Nuclear Test Ban Treaty (CTBT), a willingness to host monitoring stations and support for universalization of membership to permit entry into force

9   support for efforts to prevent the proliferation of ballistic and other missiles capable of delivering nuclear weapons, notably through the 1987 Missile Technology Control Regime (MTCR)

10   active participation in the First Committee of the UN General Assembly in sponsoring and supporting nuclear-related resolutions (here the US in particular tends to part company with the club, more than ever before under the current administration of George W. Bush)

11   membership of and active participation in the Conference on Disarmament (CD) in support of: a Fissile Material Cut-Off Treaty (FMCT); negotiations on Prevention of an Arms Race in Outer Space (PAROS) and for commencement of discussions (although not necessarily immediate negotiations) on nuclear disarmament (here again the US is the odd one out)

---

to leverage its undoubted non-proliferation credentials, at least at the level of political and diplomatic rhetoric. These are Canada's:

1   sometimes over-enthusiastic promotion of the peaceful uses of nuclear energy in pursuit of Canadian economic and commercial interests, notably the sale of uranium and Canadian Deuterium Uranium (CANDU) reactors;

2   membership of a nuclear alliance, the North Atlantic Treaty Organization (NATO), involvement in its nuclear planning and nuclear weapons deployments and the security benefits derived from sheltering under the US nuclear "umbrella";

3 failure to prevent India from using a CANDU reactor and Canadian fuel to produce nuclear weapons and the subsequent troubled Canada/India nuclear relationship; and

4 necessary deference to US preferences in the nuclear area when the US considers its national interests at stake.

The following sections will recount Canada's qualifications for club membership, the way that it has sought to leverage its membership to advance its policies and strengthen its membership further and the effects of the complicating factors on these efforts.

CANADA'S RENUNCIATION OF NUCLEAR WEAPONS

Canada was the first state capable of acquiring nuclear weapons to renounce the option. Tellingly, it did so without fanfare and even without formal government decision or announcement (Epstein 1985, 174–5). When it made its non-nuclear "non-decision" Canada not only had a latent technical and technological capacity to produce nuclear weapons, as a result of early trilateral cooperation with the British and Americans on what became the Manhattan and British bomb projects, it also had what were among the world's largest uranium deposits and at least an incipient capability to produce nuclear power reactors. During the Second World War Canada was the main supplier of uranium to the US and the UK. It had the only mill in North America for refining uranium ore and, along with the US and UK, built the first experimental reactor outside of the US at Chalk River near Ottawa. Canada was among the first countries to produce highly enriched uranium (HEU) and plutonium, the two alternative fissionable materials useful for making nuclear explosive devices. Indeed Canada supplied plutonium to the US nuclear weapons program from 1947 onwards. Thus from the 1940s to the 1960s, next to the UK and US, "Canada had greater knowledge of the scientific, technical and industrial aspects of atomic energy than any other country" (Epstein 1985, 173).

The fact that acquiring nuclear weapons never even entered Canadian heads, unlike those of other club notables like Australia, Sweden and Switzerland, seems to have added lustre to Canadian non-proliferation credentials. Canada not only avoided the act, it avoided the temptation. Epstein speculates that there was an assumption by the government of the day, led by Prime Minister Mackenzie King, that while Canada would increase its international prestige, influence and leverage by pursuing its advantages in regard to the peaceful atom, there were no advantages to be accrued from Canada acquiring nuclear weapons (Epstein

1985, 171). Indeed, to pursue the bomb might harm the promotion of peaceful uses in which Canada took such an early lead. Hence, not only was Canada not sacrificing anything it truly desired, it actually stood to materially benefit by doing so. This appears as a constant Canadian interpretation of its leverage potential in the nuclear non-proliferation field, but also one that has brought Canada grief.

CANADIAN MEMBERSHIP IN THE MULTILATERAL NUCLEAR ENERGY ORGANIZATIONS

Canada was an original and permanent member of the short-lived UN Atomic Energy Commission, established in December 1945. It had secured this position due to its role in the advent of nuclear weapons and its involvement in drawing up, along with the US and UK, the Three-Power Declaration of 15 November 1945 that had proposed the setting up of the Commission. Canada's strategic interests at that time were clearly to prevent a nuclear arms race between the US and the Soviet Union. Its geographical location between two nuclear hegemons left it vulnerable to devastation by nuclear accident or nuclear war. Canada, radically, favoured the outlawing of nuclear weapons, the destruction of all stocks or their transfer to the UN, essentially the earliest American proposal, known as the Baruch Plan.

In the Commission, Canada attempted not only to prevent a rupture between the two superpowers but to "emphasize the technical rather than the political approach to the control of atomic energy" (Epstein 1985, 174). This has also been a common theme of Canada's involvement in nuclear issues, apparently due to the belief that its technical capabilities would give it influence while permitting it to avoid political hot potatoes, particularly with the US. Some claim this reflects Canadian naiveté, while others see it as typical "middle power" conciliatory behaviour.[2]

When the UN Atomic Energy Commission collapsed, Canada played an active role in securing its replacement, the International Atomic Energy Agency. It was invited early in 1953 by the US, along with France and the UK, to help prepare the first draft statute for the agency (Barton 1997, 39). The organization was mandated to both control and, more importantly at the time, encourage and assist the development of nuclear energy for peaceful purposes, which suited Canadian objectives well. In 1957 Canada became an original member of the agency and a permanent member of its Board of Governors, a position that it retains today. Such was Canada's influence that a Canadian became the first director of nuclear safeguards at the agency (Barton

1997, 42) and it has since secured several key posts over the years.[3] As in the rest of the UN system, political and diplomatic influence translates into jobs which in turn may increase leverage.

According to nuclear critic Ron Finch, Canada's main motivation for being a part of the international nuclear organizations was the lure of profits from the peaceful uses of nuclear energy, promoted most enthusiastically in President Dwight D. Eisenhower's 1953 Atoms for Peace program. For Canada the benefits included "increased uranium development and the hope that this area would be opened up for private enterprise; expansion of the Canadian nuclear program; construction and manufacturing contracts for Canadian-owned companies; and the maintenance of good Canada-US relations, which were fundamental for the postwar Canadian economy" (Finch 1986, 76).

This is probably exaggerated. It is hard to see how Canada could have refrained from participating in the IAEA given its nuclear background and its multilateralist, middle power inclinations. Decisions to join international organizations are in any case usually made by foreign ministries on the simple grounds that every other self-respecting state is doing so; a conscious decision to stay out of (or leave) an international organization is of much greater import.

INVOLVEMENT WITH
THE NON-PROLIFERATION TREATY

Canada only formally renounced the bomb when it became a party to the NPT. In August 1969 it became the first country with the capability to produce nuclear weapons to ratify the treaty.[4] Canada had been active in promoting the concept of the NPT and in the negotiations that eventually occurred, and has undoubtedly always felt some ownership of the accord. During the negotiations, Canada:

attempted to persuade the non-aligned non-nuclear countries not to insist on too demanding commitments by the nuclear powers for far-reaching measures of nuclear disarmament, which it felt the nuclear powers would not be willing to make, thus jeopardizing the prospects for a treaty. On the other hand, it attempted to persuade the nuclear powers that they must make some concessions to the demands of the non-nuclear powers, such as, for example, to negotiate a comprehensive nuclear test ban. (Espstein 1985, 180)

This was typical Canadian use of its influence, seeking the middle ground and attempting to forge compromise in true "middle power" style. Canada was especially active in negotiations on Article VI concerning disarmament and Article IV on peaceful uses. In the subsequent

General Assembly debate on the treaty Canada rebutted arguments that the NPT would harm peaceful uses by pointing to its own experience in acquiring the full nuclear fuel cycle without acquiring the bomb, another favourite Canadian negotiating tactic – using its own experience as exemplar.

Canada has participated actively in all of the five-yearly NPT Review Conferences and has often been influential in efforts to secure successful outcomes through negotiated compromises. However these conferences have also revealed long-running complications in Canadian non-proliferation policy that limit its leverage.

At the 1985 Review Conference Canada joined Australia and Sweden, two of its closest (but more rumbustious) partners in the nuclear club, in pressing for comprehensive nuclear safeguards as a condition of supply. The Federal Republic of Germany (FRG), one of Canada's closest NATO allies, opposed the idea. This resulted in Ottawa, characteristically, suggesting a compromise to its own preferred outcome (Tucker 1986, 85).

At the 1995 Review Conference, Canada was crucial in securing the NPT's indefinite extension, again by seeking compromise, this time between non-nuclear weapon states which wanted to use their agreement to an extension to secure a binding commitment to nuclear disarmament measures (which Canada in theory strongly advocates) and the NWS, which opposed such a linkage.

As this search for compromise demonstrates, Canada, like other members of the non-proliferation club that shelter under the US nuclear umbrella, notably Australia, Japan and Germany, is hoisted on something of a petard in respect of the NPT. These states cannot divorce themselves entirely from nuclear weapons as long as they wish to retain their alliance with the US – witness how New Zealand was unceremoniously dumped from the Australia/New Zealand/US (ANZUS) Treaty when it refused entry to US warships suspected of carrying nuclear weapons. To call, as Canada does, for all NNWS, including those outside the umbrella, to forgo nuclear weapons forever is viewed by some of them, notably Brazil, India and Pakistan, as hypocritical.

Canada's acceptance from the 1960s through the 1980s of US nuclear weapons,[5] under a dual-key system, for use with Canadian aircraft and missiles based both in Canada and in Europe as part of NATO, also risked tarnishing its non-nuclear credentials. While the stationing caused controversy within Canada to the extent of helping bring down the Diefenbaker government in 1963,[6] the international damage was presumably contained as a result of Prime Minister Pierre Trudeau's announcement in 1968 that Canada would phase out the nuclear-capable systems as soon as equipment replacement permitted (this had occurred by 1984). Indeed, it is not clear that the outside world much noticed, with the exception of the puzzled Americans who were frustrated by Canadian delay in accepting the nuclear warheads. While Canada had laid itself open to further charges of hypocrisy, there is no evidence that other countries were tempted to openly voice doubts about Canada's non-proliferation *bone fides* and even less indication that Canada's international leverage in nuclear matters was affected. A key consideration is that during all this time there was little if any suggestion from any Canadian quarter that Canada should go one step further and acquire its own nuclear weapons.

One issue that did raise a brief flurry of international concern about Canadian nuclear non-proliferation credentials, including on the part of the US, was the suggestion in the late 1980s that Canada acquire nuclear-powered attack submarines from France or the UK to patrol its Arctic waters. Domestic opposition and international alarm was partly based on the poor example this would set to other countries of greater proliferation concern, like Brazil, that were seeking enriched uranium for submarine propulsion.[7] Luckily, Canada decided not to proceed before the issue damaged its credibility.

Canada did concur in the NATO dual-track decision in December 1979 to deploy Pershing II missiles in Europe while also engaging in the Intermediate-range Nuclear Forces (INF) disarmament talks (which Canada strongly supported). In 1983 Canada also agreed to permit testing of US cruise missiles over Canadian territory. The first tests took place in 1984, but the issue soon faded from public view. Neither case seems to have harmed Canadian non-proliferation credentials in the outside world.

Occasionally Canada has resisted US requests for involvement in nuclear-related alliance activity. In 1968 the Pearson government inserted a ballistic missile defence reservation clause in the renewal of the North America Air Defence (NORAD) Agreement saying it would not participate in any way in the active missile defence of North America. According to Tucker, arms control considerations in effect determined the course of Canadian defence policy on this issue, due to the perceived effects on US/Soviet nuclear arms negotiations and the non-proliferation regime (Tucker 1986, 86–7).[8]

Again, in May 1986 Canada criticized the American decision to disregard the limits set by the second Strategic Arms Limitation Talks (SALT II) treaty (Hampson 1987, 44). Some critics lambasted Canada for not being even more forceful and threatening to cancel (or review) Canada's agreement with the US on cruise missile testing. However, according to Hampson, such action might have jeopardized the free trade talks then underway with the US (Hampson

1987, 44); a case of potential leverage in the arms control area thus being sacrificed for potential economic gains.

In rhetoric, Canada has always strongly supported full implementation of Article VI of the NPT by the nuclear weapon states. But its leverage is limited: Trudeau's 1978 "nuclear suffocation" plan and his 1984 global peace initiative, involving whirlwind trips to various capitals to argue the case for nuclear disarmament, can be attributed to Trudeau seeing himself as potentially influential, rather than any attempt to leverage Canada's non-proliferation credentials. Indeed senior foreign affairs and defence officials viewed Trudeau's plan with "considerable reservations": "Such a solitary international mission by a Canadian public figure was unprecedented. The chances of a favourable outcome were minimal, and the risk of alienating Canada's allies and earning international and domestic ridicule considerable" (von Riekhoff and Sigler 1985, 58). Here was a case of a Canadian leader overselling Canada's (and his own) credentials in a doomed enterprise.

While Canadian links, past and present to nuclear weapons and nuclear deterrence make its advocacy of nuclear disarmament seem less genuine than that of neutral and non-aligned members of the non-proliferation club like Ireland and Sweden, which are outside of any nuclear umbrella and which have no nuclear weapon connections, it is at least arguable that NATO membership and alliance with the US give Canada entrée to an inner nuclear circle where its influence may be stronger. By comparison the Swedes can seem principled but ineffectual in their dealings with the NWS. And since the Irish and Swedes have already completely abjured nuclear involvement it could be argued that Canada, to the extent that it is serious about nuclear disarmament, is all the more admirable as it is actually risking its security by foreshadowing the loss of its nuclear umbrella, albeit in the distant future.

CANADA AND NUCLEAR SAFEGUARDS

Canada was initially uninterested in nuclear safeguards, designed to prevent diversion of fissionable material from peaceful uses to weapons, presumably lest they inhibit Canada's nuclear exports. However, Canada appears to have quickly concluded, like other nuclear exporters, that safeguards would actually facilitate its uranium and reactor exports by disassociating them from the bomb. Ottawa thus announced in 1965 that it would "require an agreement with the government of the importing country to ensure, with appropriate verification and control, that [Canadian] uranium is to be used for peaceful purposes only" (Finch 1986, 77). Such insistence on bilateral agreements acquiring the application of safeguards was, from the earliest days, at some material cost to Canada. France, for instance, already a nuclear weapon state, found such Canadian demands peremptory and refused in 1965 to sign such an agreement, thereby scuttling a deal to buy Canadian uranium.

It was Canada's nuclear relationship with a purported non-nuclear weapon state – India – that proved disastrous for Canada's original nuclear export policy and induced it to become one of the most robust supporters of nuclear safeguards. Swept up in the enthusiasm for peaceful nuclear technology stimulated by the US Atoms for Peace programme launched by President Eisenhower in 1953 and by the UN through several Atoms for Peace Conferences commencing in 1955, Canada provided India with a research reactor, the Canada-India Reactor (CIR)[9] under the British Commonwealth's Colombo Plan.[10] (It later became known as the CIRUS, when the US joined the project.) Despite the fact that the reactor was modelled on the NRX reactor at Chalk River that produced plutonium for the US bomb program, it was not subject to safeguards but only to a vague undertaking by the Indian government in April 1956 that it would "ensure that the reactor and any products resulting from its use will be employed for peaceful purposes only."

When in 1963 Canada agreed to provide India with a CANDU power reactor, this time under bilateral nuclear safeguards, India refused to accept the application of similar safeguards to CIRUS. "We knew that reactor was naked," a Canadian negotiator recalled. "Here was a chance to do something about it. But the commercial people kept saying that if we didn't give the Indians what they wanted, they'd get it elsewhere" (quoted in Pringle and Spigelman 1981, 377). India used the plutonium from CIRUS to produce the so-called peaceful nuclear device detonated under the Rajasthan desert in May 1974.

Even today it remains a puzzle as to why Canada pursued such nuclear prolificacy when it was obvious that India would thereby acquire the ability to produce nuclear weapons material, that its rivalry with China and Pakistan gave it strategic reasons to acquire the bomb and that its unwillingness to give more than vague peaceful use assurances and its opposition to the IAEA's prospective verification role as being "neo-colonialist" were suspicious.[11] India also had "world-class talent in physics, most notably Homi Babha, a Cambridge-educated scientist, the founder and prime mover of India's nuclear energy program" (Talbott 2004, 11) who had presided over the 1955 Atoms for Peace Conference. To be fair, no one, not even the Americans, suspected India's motives in 1956, and safeguards models were non-existent. Yet warning bells should have sounded when in 1958 India announced it would build a reprocessing plant to extract plutonium from CIRUS's spent fuel rods.

Canada's rationale for its nuclear largesse may have included "preventing the spread of communism," solidarity with a fellow Dominion of the old British Commonwealth and stealing a diplomatic march on the Americans, whose relationships with India were always troubled. But at least part of the rationale was undoubtedly a desire to kick-start Canada's nuclear export drive against stiff competition from other larger contenders, notably the Americans, the British and the French.

Canada aggressively pursued reactor sales with at least 24 other countries between 1945 and 1986, including Argentina, Taiwan, South Korea, Mexico, Romania and Finland (Finch 1986, 13). To maintain the Canadian nuclear industry and offset costs Atomic Energy Canada Limited was forced to compete with larger corporations from other developed countries by paying signficant agent fees and entering into improperly negotiated contracts (Finch 1986, 66). Scandal and public enquiries ensued. While this tarnished Canada's domestic nuclear industry and commercial reputation, it is not evident that it undercut Canada's influence in the non-proliferation club, since at least some other members were doing the same.

Paradoxically, though, the US at times had to constrain Canadian enthusiasm for peaceful uses. For example in the mid-1980s the US intervened to end talks between South Korea and Canada on a plan for Canada to extract plutonium from spent South Korean reactor fuel, apparently for the purpose of recycling it in a new power reactor Canada was to supply. Presumably the US feared South Korea acquiring plutonium extraction expertise (Spector 1988, 71).

After the Indian explosion in 1974 Canada tightened its non-proliferation policy considerably. First it denounced the idea of so-called peaceful nuclear explosions, removing a loophole that India had exploited. Second, it required IAEA safeguards on all Canadian exports of nuclear materials and technology. Third, all Canadian exporters were obliged to contact the government first before exporting. Fourth, there was to be a binding commitment to prior consent for transfers of Canadian origin material and technology to third countries. Fifth, Canada would insist on the right to apply fall-back safeguards on reprocessing and enrichment should IAEA safeguards fail to be applied for any reason. Finally, a binding commitment required the provision of adequate physical protection for Canadian-origin material.

A further tightening was announced on 22 December 1976, Canada becoming the first country to insist on comprehensive safeguards as a condition of supply.[12] Shipments to non-nuclear weapon states under future contracts would be restricted to those that ratified the NPT or otherwise accepted international safeguards on their entire nuclear program. Canada would terminate nuclear shipments to any non-nuclear weapon state that exploded a nuclear device.

Meanwhile Canada unsuccessfully attempted to negotiate new safeguards agreements with India and Pakistan. Two and a half years after the Indian explosion the Canadian government formally terminated nuclear cooperation with Pakistan, as it had already done with India. Safeguards agreements were meanwhile successfully negotiated with Argentina and South Korea, both potential CANDU customers.

Although damaging to Canada's non-proliferation credentials in the short term, the Indian explosion suggested Canadian gullibility rather than culpability. It also steeled Canada's nerve in redoubling its efforts in both the non-proliferation and disarmament fields, no doubt out of guilt but also in recognition of the fact that it could turn a bad situation to its own advantage and that of non-proliferation endeavours. Canada thus played a key role in establishment of the Nuclear Suppliers Group (NSG), an informal cabal of nuclear exporting countries that seeks to control the export of nuclear and dual-use technologies and techniques. (Canada was already an active member of the older Zangger Committee, also a group of nuclear exporting countries designed to control nuclear weapon-related exports.) In 1980 Canada became a founding member of the Group of 10 countries at the IAEA that committed themselves to promoting strengthened safeguards and even stronger export controls.[13]

Meanwhile, Canada's own comprehensive safeguards agreement, which the NPT requires state parties to conclude, entered into force on 21 February 1972, less than two years after the treaty itself entered into force on 5 March 1970. Canada was one of the first states to conclude and begin implementing an Additional Protocol which is designed to considerably strengthen nuclear safeguards. Its protocol was signed on 24 September 1998 and entered into force on 8 September 2000, three years after the model Additional Protocol was adopted by the IAEA Board of Governors. Canada was also one of the countries that signed the Convention on Nuclear Safety the day it was opened for signature, 20 September 1994, ratifying it just over a year later. As a country with at least one nuclear installation which has achieved criticality in a reactor core, Canada is among those whose ratification is required to bring the treaty into force. While signifying Canada's importance in civil nuclear power, this fact offers Ottawa no leverage potential; indeed such treaty requirements put pressure on Canada to ratify quickly, which is not always to the liking of the Canadian parliament or bureaucracy.

Although Canada has been strongly supportive of strengthened nuclear safeguards at the political level, the implementation body in Canada, the Canadian Nuclear Safety Commission (CNSC), has consistently complained that Canada's safeguards burden has been too great, especially given Canada's non-proliferation track record. The growth of the Canadian nuclear power industry and other peaceful uses of nuclear energy has made Canada, alongside Japan and Germany (and currently possibly Iran), one of the most thoroughly inspected country in the nuclear field. In part due to Canadian influence the IAEA in 1997 launched a so-called integrated safeguards program, which seeks to rationalize the successive layers of safeguards in states that have demonstrated full compliance over many years.[14] In 2005 Canada qualified for integrated safeguards, the second country with a large nuclear industry (after Japan) to do so (three of the most prominent members of the non-proliferation club, Australia, Japan and Canada were the first to qualify). Canada had pressed for such a program for both selfish national reasons and for multilateral ones. Integrated safeguards have not only lessened the financial and human resource burden on Canada, but they also permit scarce Agency verification resources to be redirected towards countries of real proliferation concern.

Here is a case where Canada was directly able to leverage its influence in the Board of Governors and in the non-proliferation community generally to achieve a net benefit to Canada, while also burnishing its proliferation credentials. Throughout the drawn-out process whereby the IAEA investigates whether a state qualifies for integrated safeguards, Canada was required to prove that it has consistently and fully complied with both its comprehensive safeguards agreement and the Additional Protocol. Canada's good behaviour on both counts was thus materially rewarded.

CANADIAN INVOLVEMENT IN NUCLEAR DISARMAMENT TALKS AND NEGOTIATIONS

From the outset Canada has also been continuously involved in all of the multilateral disarmament bodies. M.J. Tucker describes Canada as the "senior of [the non-nuclear] players" at the Stockholm and Geneva conferences (Tucker 1986, 81).

Canada has played an active role in the UN General Assembly's First Committee, which deals with international security resolutions, particularly relating to disarmament, since the UN's founding in 1945. It has also been a significant contributor to the work of the UN Disarmament Commission (UNDC) which is tasked with conducting studies of disarmament problems during its annual two to three week session. Both the First Committee and UNDC have universal UN membership, so Canada's role is not based on privileged access and special leverage but on a unilateral decision by Canada to be active and creative in both bodies.

But Canada has also been particularly influential in the narrower confines of the Western Group at the UN in New York and Geneva. In the 1970s Canada was crucially involved in establishing the Barton Group (named after then Canadian Ambassador William Barton) in New York, designed to permit France to participate in Western Group discussions of First Committee agenda items at a time when it was attempting to distance itself from perceived US domination of the Western alliance through NATO.[15] In addition, for many years the Barton Group in Geneva met at the Canadian mission to coordinate positions at the multilateral disarmament negotiations.

Unlike all other non-nuclear members of the non-proliferation club, Canada has been involved since 1945 in all of the limited membership multilateral disarmament negotiating bodies in all their permutations: the London Sub-Committee of the Disarmament Commission;[16] the Eighteen-Nation Disarmament Committee (ENDC); the Conference of the Committee on Disarmament; the Committee on Disarmament and the current Conference on Disarmament. In contrast to the First Committee and UNDC these bodies have been mandated to actually produce international treaties, among them the NPT itself, along with the CTBT and the 1997 Chemical Weapons Convention.

Canada is currently characteristically active in the CD, in particular in promoting negotiations on a Fissile Material Cut-Off Treaty (FMCT) and to prevent an arms race in outer space. In 1995 Canadian Ambassador Gerald Shannon succeeded in brokering what is widely regarded as the most balanced draft mandate for negotiations on an FMCT (containing an encapsulation of the scope of a future treaty that does not prejudice the position of any state on the issue). Canada's scope for influence beyond these activities is however entirely dependent on the CD commencing negotiations on any given item. Since it completed work on the CTBT in 1996, the CD has failed to begin negotiations on any of its agenda items and there is nothing Canada can do about it since the blockage comes from states with fundamental security interests at stake, notably China, India, Iran, Pakistan, Russia and the US. No amount of Canadian wordsmithing is able to budge such states from their positions.

Canada has also been willing, on occasion, to go outside the normal UN-endorsed multilateral forums to seek its arms control objectives (and not just in the case of the 1999 Ottawa Landmine Ban Convention). In the nuclear field this usually occurs at US invitation, but is undoubtedly in recognition of Canada's standing. In 1992, for instance, Canada joined the US and a select group of other Western states (France, Germany, Italy, Japan and the UK) in secret discussions aimed at establishing a regime for controlling transfers of equipment and technology that might contribute substantially to the development of unmanned nuclear delivery systems. This eventually became the Missile Technology Control Regime (MTCR) (Spector 1988, 36).

CANADA AND VERIFICATION

Especially in cases where political deadlock prevents negotiating progress, Canada has continued its self-imposed avocation of pursuing technical solutions, either with the goal of paving the way for political solutions or to ensure that when the political logjam breaks the technical obstacles have been resolved. Canada has specialized in verification, an invaluable contribution to debates that often focus on political issues in the absence of hard data about verifiability and technically feasible verification measures. This work has not been restricted to nuclear issues, such as seismic detection of underground nuclear tests, but also to verification in respect of biological and chemical weapons, conventional armed forces reductions and outer space. In 1982 Canada set up a Verification Research Unit in the Arms Control and Disarmament Division of the then Department of External Affairs and International Trade with an annual budget of C$1 million (Tucker 1986, 83). The unit produced widely admired research papers, held workshops and provided feedstock for Canadian delegations in various disarmament forums.[17] This activity continued until around 1996.

Apart from Finland and Sweden, Canada is probably the only non-nuclear weapon state ever to have undertaken such detailed, ongoing work on verification issues across the board. It undoubtedly paid dividends in raising Canada's profile, giving it a voice among both the NWS and NNWS and strengthening its negotiating hand. While the leverage thus gained was ultimately used in Canada's national interest, it also contributed to the international common weal by paving the way for technically-based compromises having the best chance of success in negotiations. Like Sweden, though, Canada simply chose to be active in this field: while it had some technical capacities to readily bring to the subject, so did most other Western countries which chose not to so specialize.

In addition to its technical contributions, Canada has, since November 1985, sponsored an annual or biannual resolution on verification in the UN General Assembly which invariably attracts consensus. In addition to keeping the verification issue before the Assembly, these resolutions have resulted in the establishment to date of three Groups of Governmental Experts to study the issue, with Canada in the chair.[18] The most recent was convened in 2006 and chaired by Canadian Ambassador John Barratt.

Such activities come at a price. As Tucker notes in respect of Canada, "the allocation of scarce public funds towards verification research, a disarmament fund and the operation of the Canadian Institute for International Peace and Security can be traced back to commitments made in multilateral fora" (Tucker 1986, 82).

CANADA AND NUCLEAR TESTING

In the 1950s Canada opposed a nuclear test ban treaty, favouring, as did the Americans, a "comprehensive disarmament agreement" rather than partial measures (Finch 1986, 77). However, as a result of growing public opposition to atmospheric nuclear testing in the 1960s Canada switched to strong support for a CTBT. US underground high-yield nuclear testing after 1963 on Amchitka Island in the Bering Straits, and Soviet testing at Novaya Zemlya, well north of the Arctic Circle, aroused Canadian political and public opposition. The government, responding to public protests, warned the US that it would be held responsible for any injuries to Canadians or damage to Canadian property from US tests and urged the Americans to reconsider.

Seeking a way to promote a test ban without alienating the US, Canada began assiduously contributing both diplomatic and technical expertise to the verification issue, since US opposition to a ban was partly predicated on fears that the Soviets would violate it by testing secretly underground. Canada began playing a key role in the Group of Scientific Experts in Geneva in studying seismic verification of the CTBT long before negotiations on a treaty began. The Canadian seismic facility at Yellowknife (originally established by the British in 1958), one of the most sophisticated in the world, enabled it to do so effectively. According to Bolt, like Sweden and Japan, "Canada wanted to have technical competence in seismological verification of a CTBT in order to wield some influence on test-ban matters" (Bolt 1976, 220). Here was a specific case of Canadian technical capability being used to increase its political leverage.

Canada signed the Partial Test Ban Treaty (PTBT) – which bans all nuclear tests except those conducted underground – on 8 August 1963 (the day that it was opened for general signature) and ratified it in January 1964. Unlike Australia, Canada had never seriously considered using nuclear explosives for peaceful purposes, such as in mining or geographical engineering [although there had been an abortive American proposal in 1960 to use them to release oil from the Athabasca tar sands (Findlay 1990, 18)], nor had it hosted nuclear tests by other states, so it was not giving up any option by abjuring such tests.

Canada's test ban policy, like Australia's, was not just a function of public opposition to testing and of technical expertise that could be parlayed into influence, but was crucially beholden to its "great and powerful friend," the United States. US test ban policy over the decades has swung wildly between idealistic enthusiasm and stubborn opposition. During the latter periods, of which there have been many more, Canada, like Australia, could do little more than seek compromises at the margins of UN resolutions and continue to make the verifiability case. For example, at the Second NPT Review Conference in 1980, Canada, in what was described as a "holding action," attempted to ameliorate nonaligned pressures on the US for an immediate CTBT by advocating the need for verification measures to be in place before the US and the Soviet Union could or should commit themselves to a CTBT (Tucker 1986, 85).

This incident illustrates another fundamental fact of Canadian nuclear non-proliferation diplomacy: it can wield significant influence when acting in concert with prevailing US views, especially in seeking continued strengthening of nuclear safeguards. However, when faced with immovable US national security interests, such as its opposition to radical nuclear disarmament measures or a curb on an arms race in outer space, Canadian policy grinds to a hortatory stop.

After participating actively in its negotiation, Canada was an original signatory of the CTBT on the day it was opened for signature and then quickly ratified it on 18 December 1998. Again, Canada's ratification is necessary to bring the treaty into force as, along with 43 other states listed in Annex 2 of the treaty, it is considered to be significant in the nuclear field and as having contributed actively to the treaty negotiations.

As part of the International Monitoring System for the treaty, Canada is designated to host three primary seismological stations, six auxiliary seismological stations, four radionuclide stations, a radionuclide laboratory, a hydroacoustic station and an infrasound station, making it one of the most significant contributors to CTBT verification. This is however at least partly a function of Canada's size and geographical location rather than its political influence and technical prowess. Canada is an active member of the Preparatory Commission for the Comprehensive Nuclear Test Ban Treaty Organization (CTBTO) in Vienna which is preparing for the treaty's eventual entry into force.

CANADA AND NUCLEAR ISSUES IN THE G8

In addition to all this activity and influence, Canada has on several occasions intervened to good effect on nuclear issues during summits of the world's leading industrialized countries.

During and after the 1995 Group of 7 (G7) summit in Halifax, Prime Minister Jean Chrétien was instrumental in the conclusion of a three-way memorandum of understanding between the G7, the EU and Ukraine on the closure of the devastated Chernobyl nuclear reactor. In this case Canadian influence may have been singular, since it maintained warm relations with Ukraine after being the first Western state to recognize its independence and due to the size of the Ukrainian diaspora in Canada.

Chrétien also intervened with the US and Russia in respect to the mixed oxide (MOX) nuclear fuel issue at the 1996 G7 meeting in Moscow on nuclear safety and security. He did this by offering, in principle, to consider using US and Russian weapons-grade plutonium to fuel Canadian CANDU reactors. While this ignited public and parliamentary opposition (including in Chrétien's own Liberal Party) the tests did go ahead at Chalk River.

After largely free-riding for the first decade after the Cold War (like most of its Western allies) on US efforts to deal with the Soviet nuclear legacy,[19] Canada successfully used its chairmanship of the Group of 8 (G8) in 2002 to good effect in helping initiate the Global Partnership Program at the Kananaskis Summit in Alberta. Consensus was reached partly due to Canada helping craft the six "principles" at the heart of the Partnership (see also Hay 2003, 10). Canada also greased the wheels of the agreement by pledging C$1 billion over ten years to help destroy the Soviet nuclear legacy of weapons, facilities and fissionable and other nuclear materials (see Canada 2006).

In all of these instances Canadian influence derived more from its membership in the G8 itself, its traditional intermediary skills and its chairmanship of particular summits rather than any special leverage deriving from its membership of the non-proliferation club. Nonetheless Canada's significant experience and expertise in nuclear matters helps it operate more effectively in the G8, especially in the more technical arena of the G8 nuclear working group, which in turn must help Canada redress some of the minnow status that it otherwise holds among such economic heavyweights. John Hay records that after the terrorist attacks of 11 September 2001 and an initially closer US-Russia relationship, Canada's role as a trusted third party in nuclear matters seemed less urgent and necessary (Hay 2003, 6). It remains to be seen whether the current cooling in US-Russia relations provides openings for Canadian nuclear diplomacy.

CANADA'S CURRENT LEVERAGE: STEADY STATE OR IN LONG-TERM DECLINE?

Influence and leverage are difficult to objectively assess. As Hay puts it, "National reputations are hard to measure, easy to exaggerate, and

readily lost. But it is at least plausible that skilled Canadian intervention from time to time has had a productive effect in multilateral set-
tings" (Hay 2003, 6). While this remains true, there is also at the very
least a perception internationally that Canada's ability to leverage its
membership in the "nuclear club" to achieve its policy objectives has
declined in the past couple of decades. This may simply be a reflection
of a general perception of a decline in Canada's global profile resulting,
inter alia, from its shrinking diplomatic service (Canada has the lowest
percentage of its foreign service officers stationed abroad of any Western country), its retreat from UN peacekeeping and its miserly and allegedly ineffective foreign aid program.

In the nuclear field there are however, some specific reasons for the
arguable decline in Canadian leverage and influence. The first is that as
membership of the UN and associated bodies like the CD has exploded,
Canada is no longer able to wield the "inside track" influence it once
did. The club is no longer exclusive. Canada no longer gets the same
chance to become a non-permanent member of the Security Council,
which now regularly deals with nuclear issues, especially since 9/11.
The single multilateral negotiating body has gone from the exclusive
London Sub-Committee of 6 to the 65-member CD. Canada has less air
time, it is more difficult to use Canadian influence to reach a consensus, and there are newly prominent participants with nuclear non-
proliferation credentials, notably South Africa and the Eastern Europeans.

The breakdown of the Cold War bloc structure and EU expansion has
also weakened Canada's role in matters nuclear. Once the 26-member
EU decides on a particular policy it is difficult for the non-EU Western
states to budge it. Canada is often forced to combine with Australia and
New Zealand in a CANZ grouping or with the addition of Japan (JCANZ)
as the only possible means of achieving strength in numbers.

Second, where once it was a favoured interlocutor of the British and
the Americans because of its early participation in the birth of nuclear
technology, the decline in the nuclear power industry since the 1970s
has meant that Canada's expertise and influence in this sector has seriously atrophied. Except as a uranium exporter, where it is among the
top three (after Australia and Kazakhstan), Canada's role in the peaceful nuclear industry no longer gives it the entrée it once did. Sales of the
CANDU reactor never reached expectations and there has not been a
sale since one to Romania in 2003.

A third reason is that Canada has let its diplomatic presence and
skills in the nuclear area atrophy. To be fair, this is partly due to the
fact that so little progress has been made in the past decade in negotiations in the CD that it is rightly perceived as luxurious to maintain a
large delegation in Geneva in anticipation of a resumption of serious

work. Canada does maintain a disarmament ambassador in Geneva, albeit one who must also attend to other UN matters.

Canadian disarmament delegations are also not receiving the research backing that used to make them so effective. The Department of Foreign Affairs and International Trade has abandoned its research capacity in the disarmament and non-proliferation field, including its Verification Research Unit, apparently due to budgetary considerations, combined with a misguided view that verification would no longer be required in the post-Cold War world. The establishment of the International Security Research and Outreach Program (ISROP) and the Canadian Centre for Treaty Compliance at the Norman Paterson School of International Affairs at Carleton University have partly remedied this situation, but neither has fundamentally redressed the department's own lack of in-house expertise.

A fourth reason for Canada's declining interest and influence in nuclear issues may be the "low-hanging fruit syndrome." The most immediately achievable steps have been taken. The CTBT, even though it involved a huge effort over many decades, has been concluded and now only awaits entry into force. Nuclear safeguards have been considerably strengthened since 1990. Apart from pressing and preparing for an FMCT, much of the work now involves seeking universalization of both the CTBT and Additional Protocol. The most important next steps – significant cuts in nuclear weapons – can only be taken by the nuclear weapon states themselves: Canadian advice and participation, along with that of other non-nuclear weapon states, is not welcome.

Related to this question of low-hanging fruit, Canada's initiation of and near-obsession with the Ottawa Landmine Convention absorbed Canadian diplomatic efforts, funding and resources, in the arms control field for several years during Lloyd Axworthy's term as Foreign Minister. While burnishing Canada's reputation in some quarters, Canada's peremptory setting of an urgent timetable for producing a treaty in record time may have harmed its reputation and influence in the arms control arena generally.

Finally, Canada has been remarkably uninvolved in the major challenges to the nuclear non-proliferation regime the past couple of decades – from Iran, Iraq, North Korea and Libya, either because it has not been invited or because it has deliberately chosen not to inject itself. While this is perhaps because of its defining experience with India, it may also reflect a Canadian conflict-avoidance disposition, a desire to stay out of the difficult cases in favour of pressing on issues with widespread international support and little likelihood of alienating anyone. Hence Canada has not been part of the six-party talks that have sought a resolution of the North Korean nuclear issue. It was not even part of Korean Peninsula Energy Development Organization (KEDO), the consortium that was intended to provide relatively proliferation-resistant nuclear reactors to North Korea in return for nuclear disarmament. The lack of Canadian interest is the more surprising given its strategic interest in the North Pacific and the fact that it could be the victim of an errant North Korean nuclear missile test or actual nuclear strike on the US.

Similarly Canada has not been part of the effort to lead Iran back into the non-proliferation fold: this effort has been dominated by the EU Three (Germany, France and the UK), along with the permanent five members of the UN Security Council. Perhaps Canada feels that it plays enough of a role in the IAEA Board of Governors on these issues to relieve it of obligations beyond that.

In the Iraq case Canada was so uninterested that, apart from providing veteran verification expert Ron Cleminson as a member of the College of Commissioners (the governing body) of both the UN Special Commission (UNSCOM) and the UN Monitoring, Verification and Inspection Commission (UNMOVIC), the Canadian role was minimal. It provided relatively few inspectors compared to Australia, France, the UK and the US. Canada was also not part of the trilateral Australia/UK/US inspection effort after the coalition invasion of Iraq in April 2003, presumably because it opposed the war. In the Libyan case the UK, US and IAEA took exclusive jurisdiction over the disarmament process.

The most powerful brake on Canadian leverage in the nuclear non-proliferation area is undoubtedly its relationship with the United States: there is a case to be made that Canada can only truly act significantly in the nuclear area if the US provides a window for it to do so. During the administration of George W. Bush, which has spurned multilateralism in favour of unilateral and bilateral efforts, Canada has struggled to find that window. While promoting the strengthening of nuclear safeguards and cooperative threat reduction is easy, as the US also supports this, Canadian efforts to advance agenda items out of favour with the US get nowhere. An ill-fated attempt in 2005 by Canadian CD Ambassador Paul Meyer to promote the establishment of General Assembly working groups on disarmament issues to bypass the deadlock in the CD was summarily quashed by Washington.

A TEST CASE OF CANADIAN INFLUENCE: THE US-INDIA NUCLEAR DEAL

Canada currently faces a potentially excruciating dilemma in formulating policy towards the nuclear cooperation agreement with India that the Bush administration has been seeking to finalize for the past two years. It presses many of the buttons that Canadian nuclear non-proliferation policy has sought to leave unpressed for many decades.

The agreement seeks an exemption for India from the agreed NSG export guidelines which ban nuclear exports to non-NPT states (India is one of only three such states, the others being Israel and Pakistan, with North Korea's status in some dispute). Canada holds the fate of the agreement in its hands in the sense that the NSG operates by consensus. Currently there appears to be no firm decision as to which way Canada will move. Presumably there is strong pressure from the US (and India) for Canada to refrain from opposing the deal in the NSG, while other members of the non-proliferation club, such as Australia and Sweden, are urging caution about rewarding India in a way that might undermine the NPT.

This is an especially difficult issue for Canada, not just due to its past involvement with the Indian nuclear program, but because the widely touted global nuclear energy revival hints of a reversal of fortunes for the Canadian nuclear industry in India and elsewhere. Although Canada's first response to the US-India deal was to issue a vague statement declaring its desire for resumed peaceful nuclear commerce with India, the government has declined to flesh this out. Unexpectedly, Canada's nuclear industry does not appear to be lobbying the government. Canada's decision will be a signal, either way, of its commitment to the sanctity of the NPT. Ottawa appears at this stage to be adopting a wait-and-see attitude, which may be the wisest current course given that opposition to the deal in the US Congress and Indian Parliament may yet kill it without Canada having to choose sides. But should the deal be finally concluded Canada will be forced to decide.

CONCLUSION

Canada is the longest standing member of the non-proliferation club of any non-nuclear weapon state. Its credentials for club membership in terms of treaty membership and compliance, diplomatic activism and creativity are impeccable. Along with other members of the Western alliance it has struggled to reconcile its non-proliferation club membership with other responsibilities and allegiances, most notably in respect of NATO membership and its proximity to and complex relationship with the United States. Canada's early involvement in matters nuclear has brought it both entrée to and influence in the non-proliferation club that goes well beyond what might be expected for its size and international heft in general. Its role in purveying nuclear materials and technology have, however, compromised its non-proliferation credentials, most notably in its unfortunate dealings with India. This has in turn, however, reinforced Canada's determination to prevent further nuclear proliferation and strengthened its hand in acting as an honest broker. Canada, like Sweden, has also as a matter of deliberate decision favoured technical contributions, especially in the area of verification, that have consequently increased its credibility and influence.

Whether Canadian leverage as a result of its continuing active membership of the nuclear non-proliferation club remains potent is a moot point. Although there is a perception abroad that Canadian diplomatic influence has generally declined, in the arcane area of arms control and disarmament, Canadian diplomacy continues to be visible and creative, although notably with less research backing than used to be the case. A test of Canadian non-proliferation resolve and influence will come if the US/India nuclear cooperation agreement is ever finalized: that issue represents a confluence of all of the challenges to Canadian policy over the past 60 years of the nuclear age.

NOTES

1 Leonard Beaton, one of the earliest writers on nuclear non-proliferation, argued in 1966 for "the organization of a self-conscious group of leading nonnuclear powers (Canada, Germany, Japan, India and Sweden for a start) ..." (Beaton 1966, 127).

2 See the works of Kim Richard Nossal and/or Andrew F. Cooper for extensive commentary on Canada's middle power role.

3 Most recently, Tariq Rauf in the Department of External Relations and Mark Gwozdecky as spokesperson for the director-general.

4 Canada signed the treaty 22 days after it was opened for signature on 1 July 1968.

5 The agreement on stationing of nuclear weapons was reached on 16 August 1963. The systems involved were: Canadian Bomarc anti-bomber missiles at two bases, in Ontario and Quebec; Genie air-to-air rockets on CF 101 (Voodoo) aircraft assigned to NATO but based in Canada; tactical nuclear weapons aboard CF 104 (Starfighter) aircraft in Europe; and Honest John surface-to-surface tactical missiles. Only the Voodoo aircraft were dual capable.

6 Through a motion of non-confidence in parliament.

7 Since British nuclear submarines use American technology, Washington's approval was needed before the UK could bid on the deal (Spector 1988, 323). Fears derived from a provision in comprehensive nuclear safeguards agreements that permits nuclear material for "non-proscribed military purposes" (non-explosive uses) to be removed from safeguards (see Article 14, the Structure and Content of Agreements between the Agency and States Required in Connection with the Treaty on the Non-Proliferation of Nuclear Weapons (INFCIRC/153, International Atomic Energy Agency, Vienna, 1972).

8　The clause was removed in the 1981 NORAD renewal agreement.

9　The US supplied the required heavy water that Canada was unable to.

10　Ron Finch notes that following the Second World War "Canadians were exposed to a barrage of propaganda which presented the dawn of the nuclear age in a generally positive light" (Finch 1986, 25).

11　Canada on several occasions even intimated that it was ready to present its own draft treaty in order to speed up negotiations.

12　Donald Jamieson, secretary of state for external affairs, House of Commons, 22 December 1976.

13　The other members are Australia, Austria, Denmark, Finland, Ireland, the Netherlands, New Zealand, Norway and Sweden.

14　For further information on integrated safeguards see Boureston and Feldman (2007).

15　From a personal conversation with William Barton (2007).

16　This met from 1945–47 and involved only Canada, France, the Soviet Union, the UK and the US.

17　The unit's work included a series of publications that were produced between 1985 and 1996 on arms control and verification issues. See < http://www.dfait-maeci.gc.ca/arms/menu-en.asp>

18　For details of the three verification panels see Grossman-Vermaas (2005).

19　Between 1992 and 2002 Canada contributed just C$120.3 million for the Canadian program in Central and Eastern Europe, the bulk of it (C$97 million) to Ukraine rather than Russia (quoted in Hay 2003, 2).

REFERENCES

Barton, William H. 1997. *"The IAEA as I remember it." International Atomic Energy Agency: Personal Reflections*. Vienna: IAEA.

Beaton, Leonard. 1966. *Must the Bomb Spread?* Harmondsworth: Penguin.

Bolt, Bruce A. 1976. *Nuclear Explosions and Earthquakes: The Parted Veil*. San Francisco: W. H. Freeman and Company.

Boureston, Jack, and Yana Feldman. 2007. "Integrated nuclear safeguards: development, implementation, future challenges." *Compliance Chronicles* 4, January. Ottawa: Canadian Centre for Treaty Compliance.

Canada. 2006. *Global Partnership Program: Making a Difference*. Department of Foreign Affairs and International Trade. Available at: <www.globalpartnership.gc.ca>

Epstein, William. 1985. "Canada." In *Nonproliferation: The Why and The Wherefore*, edited by Jozef Goldblat. London: Taylor & Francis, for SIPRI.

Finch, Ron. 1986. *Exporting Danger: A History of the Canadian Nuclear Energy Export Programme*. Montréal-Buffalo: Black Rose Books.

Findlay, Trevor. 1990. *Nuclear Dynamite: The Peaceful Nuclear Explosions Fiasco*. Sydney: Brassey's Australia.

Grossman-Vermaas, Rita. 2005. *The 1990 and 1995 United Nations Expert Panels on Verification: history, assessment and prospects for the 2006 panel*. Ottawa: Canadian Centre for Treaty Compliance. Available at: <http://www.carleton.ca/cctc/>

Hay, John. 2003. "Canada." In *Protecting Against the Spread of Nuclear, Biological and Chemical Weapons*, edited by Robert J. Einhorn and Michèle A. Flournoy. Washington DC: The Center for Strategic and International Studies.

Hampson, Fen Osler. 1987. "Arms control and East-West relations." In *Canada Among Nations 1986: Talking Trade*, edited by Brian W. Tomlin and Maureen M. Molot. Toronto: James Lorimer & Company.

Pringle, Peter and Spigelman, James. 1981. *The Nuclear Barons*. New York: Avon Books.

Ritchie, C.S.A. 1945. "Control of the Atomic Bomb by the United Nations Organization." 8 September. Ottawa: Department of External Affairs.

Spector, Leonard S. 1988. *The Undeclared Bomb: the Spread of Nuclear Weapons 1987–1988*. Washington DC: Carnegie Endowment for International Peace.

Talbott, Strobe. 2004. *Engaging India: Diplomacy, democracy and the bomb*. Washington DC: Brookings Institution Press.

Tucker, M.J. 1986. "Canadian Security Policy." In *Canada Among Nations 1985: The Conservative Agenda*, edited by Maureen Appel Molot and Brian W. Tomlin. Toronto: James Lorimer & Company.

von Riekhoff, Harold and John Sigler. 1985. "The Trudeau Peace Initiative: the politics of reversing the arms race." In *Canada Among Nations 1984: A Time of Transition*, edited by Brian W. Tomlin and Maureen Molot. Toronto: James Lorimer & Company.

PART THREE
The North American Game

11 The US Competitive Liberalization Strategy: Canada's Policy Options

CAROL WISE

By 2008, the North American Free Trade Agreement (NAFTA) will have accomplished its main objectives. A level of some 99 per cent of goods and services (in sectors covered by NAFTA) will flow duty-free between Canada, Mexico and the United States, and the explicit goals of increasing trade and foreign investment in North America will have been met within the next year. Yet, at least from the standpoint of Canada and Mexico, NAFTA has fallen short of its original expectations on the regional integration front. At least three shortcomings come to mind.

First, despite the stipulation of Article 24 of the General Agreement on Tariffs and Trade (GATT); that a preferential trade agreement such as NAFTA must remain open to new members, there has been no major initiative for further accessions since the formal launching of NAFTA in 1994. Second, while all three members initially colluded in the decision to forego the creation of strong regional institutions, ironically, this factor has prevented NAFTA from evolving into a more compelling regional project (Bélanger 2007; Studer 2007). The lack of a sound institutional framework has, in other words, hampered progress in key issue areas (such as migration, energy, regional infrastructure, and border security) that are intrinsic to the integration process but have instead been treated as externalities. And third, Canada's efforts to counter-balance US dominance over NAFTA through the broader 34-member hemispheric accord, or Free Trade Area of the Americas (FTAA), have been patently thwarted (Daudelin 2007; Mace 2007).

Nevertheless, from the Canadian perspective on NAFTA, the cup is arguably more than half-full. Since 1997, and long before the current oil price boom, Canada has been the fastest growing G8 economy, registering a fiscal surplus for most of this time period; net public debt has been reduced by nearly 30 per cent of gross domestic product (GDP) and, in stark contrast to the US fiscal situation, Canada's public pension and healthcare systems are on basically sound footing. Foreign investors are now soaking up Canadian assets, consumer spending is at record levels, and unemployment has just hit a 33-year low (*Economist* 2007a). When compared with Mexico, Canadian policy-makers have also been more effective in negotiating NAFTA-plus conditions with the US in the realm of border security, among others.

Although Canada's dependence on the US market continues, and the asymmetries in US-Canadian relations remain, over the duration of NAFTA this relationship has also become more mutual. For example, Canada accounts for most of the growth of US trade over the past two decades and is now its single most important trading partner. In 2004, US exports of goods and services to Canada exceeded its combined exports to Mexico and Japan, the second and third largest export markets for the US Yes, Canadian merchandise export dependence on the US has increased from 75.8 per cent of total exports to 82 per cent in 2006, but the US has also come to rely heavily on the long-term growth and stability of the Canadian economy. Apart from being the largest supplier of energy to the US market, Canada is now an essential partner in the cross-border production of auto components, automobiles, and metal products.

With NAFTA fading as a main reference point for public and private actors in North America, this chapter offers an assessment of Canada's options moving forward as seen through the lens of US foreign economic policy choices and trends. Until the collapse of the FTAA negotiations in 2005, the broadly held expectation was that NAFTA would eventually be superseded by a larger and more encompassing hemispheric integration scheme, one in which Canada had played a strong leadership role in crafting and rightfully envisioned itself as a major player. The lapse of the 2005 deadline for the completion of the FTAA without significant progress in reaching an agreement, as well as the North-South stalemate that has stalled the Doha Development Round at the World Trade Organization (WTO) since mid-2006, confirms that neither of these specific venues can be counted on in the near future. In light of these developments, there appear to be at least two interrelated clouds on the horizon for Canada.

First, is the US strategy of competitive liberalization, which has consisted of the negotiation of a patchwork of bilateral deals in the 2000s with "like-minded trading partners" in tandem with its pursuit of the FTAA. Some have convincingly argued that it was this parallel US strategy that ultimately derailed the FTAA negotiations (Zabludovsky and Gómez Lora 2007). After all, why should the small countries of Central America and others like Colombia, Panama, and Peru stick with the FTAA negotiations when the US is simultaneously dangling the carrot of more immediate market access via a bilateral treaty? While the US Congress has yet to approve all of these accords, their finalization has become increasingly certain with the exception of Colombia, which the Congress tabled indefinitely in July 2007 (*Economist* 2007b).

Once in place this emerging network will firmly re-establish what Canada has sought all along to prevent: the deeper consolidation of the US as the trade and investment hub of the hemisphere, and the relegation of Canada as just another spoke, albeit an important one. This, presumably, is one good reason for Prime Minister Stephen Harper's (2007) recent policy shift toward "hemispheric re-engagement," including the pursuit of stronger trade and investment ties with Canada's own "like-minded" Latin American partners.

Second, despite public pronouncements to the contrary, and akin to Mexico and the US, Ottawa seems to have no cohesive economic strategy toward China (Jiang 2006). Yet, in contrast with its two NAFTA partners who are struggling against fierce Chinese competition under conditions of high export similarity, Canada's rich natural resource base affords it the leeway to carve out a more complementary pattern of economic exchange with China. This would be similar to the Chilean-Chinese economic relationship, where the two countries have signed a bilateral free trade agreement (FTA) based on China's demand for Chile's raw material exports (copper and wood pulp) and Chile's importing of lower value-added industrial goods from China (Wise and Quiliconi 2007).

Sawchuk and Yerger (2006) have aptly shown that China has penetrated Canadian markets in these same low value-added industrial sectors (leather, footwear, clothing, electrical lighting, etc), but on the export side Canada has yet to step up to the plate and exploit these potential complementarities for two-way trade with China. Increasingly, with the US and China now the number one and two top exporters to Canada, respectively, Canada's overall competitiveness will not depend so fully on its productivity gains in relationship to the US. China now matters for Canada's competitiveness calculations, which both continue to lag behind those of the US and face further downward pressure, with China expanding assertively into a broad range of economic activities in Canada. While difficult export similarity indices have driven Mexican and US policy responses into a state of complete disarray with respect to China, there is no reason for Canada to follow suit. Rather, Canadian policy-makers have a real, if unexploited, chance to capitalize on these complementarities.[1]

Although I would assign equal weight to the importance of these two issues for Canada, space limitations allow for a detailed look at just one or the other. As such, this chapter will focus on the first challenge, the US strategy of competitive liberalization in the 2000s, and what this implies for Canada. I start with a brief review of Canada's performance under NAFTA and identify pending economic reform tasks in light of Canada's continued need to bolster its levels of productivity and competitiveness; from there follows a definition of the incipient "Regional-12" bloc that is now emerging in the hemisphere as a direct result of the US competitive liberalization strategy; in light of the analysis, I conclude with some comments on Canada's policy options moving forward.

CANADA'S PERFORMANCE UNDER NAFTA: PENDING REFORM TASKS[2]

The tenth anniversary of NAFTA was met with numerous academic and policy assessments, most of which judged its success or failure according to the growth of intra-bloc trade and investment flows, the net employment effects on each member country, and the accompanying distributional impacts (Hufbauer and Schott 2005, 22–36; Lederman, Mahoney and Servén 2005). In brief, these analyses found that total intra-bloc merchandise trade had grown by more than 200 per cent and that the stock of foreign direct investment (FDI) had increased several-fold from its pre-NAFTA levels. On the downside, labour markets and wage trends had turned increasingly uncertain for some types of occupations and skills sets and distribution had somewhat worsened across North America. Canada held its place as the NAFTA country with the lowest Gini coefficient and hence the most equitable pattern of income distribution, but underpinning this trend was an increase in inequality between the eastern and western parts of the country. For example, the gap between per capita GDP in Quebec and the rest of Canada now approached 60 per cent, while oil-rich Alberta's per capita gains soared off the chart (Boyer 2007).

As a result of these mixed findings, NAFTA's tenth anniversary reviews ranged from mildly favourable to outright negative (Audley et al. 2003; Weintraub 2004). The continued lack of enthusiasm or consensus over NAFTA's purpose and impacts reflects the gulf between the wishful theoretical thinking and the concrete empirical asymmetries that underpinned its launching back in the early 1990s. It was expected that over time the elimination of barriers to the free flow of goods, capital, and services within the preferential trade area would enable all three countries to better capture the benefits of regionalism (scale economies related to greater specialization, increased technological

Table 11.1
Growth Rates in North America

	United States		Canada		Mexico	
Year	GDP	PCGDP	GDP	PCGDP	GDP	PCGDP
1980	(0.2)	21,000	1.3	16,539	9.2	3,282
1990	1.7	26,141	0.2	19,229	5.1	3,187
1995	2.7	27,404	2.8	20,117	(6.2)	2,637
1997	4.5	30,096	4.2	21,287	6.8	4,165
1998	4.3	31,357	4.1	20,402	5.0	4,068
1999	4.1	32,870	5.5	21,677	3.6	4,958
2000	4.2	34,445	4.6	23,537	6.6	5,799
2001	0.3	35,163	1.5	23,048	(0.3)	6,326
2002	3.5	36,033	4.3	23,535	0.7	5,956
2003	4.9	37,423	5.2	27,403	1.3	5,878
2004	0.7	39,722	6.5	31,030	4.4	6,478
2005	3.6	41,917	3.0	34,028	3.0	6,771
2006	3.2	43,883	2.9	35,568	3.0	6,937

Notes: GDP: annual percent growth of real GDP; PCGDP: per capita GDP in US$
Source: International Financial Statistics (IFS), Washington, DC.

capabilities, and a more rapid and efficient deployment of those endowment factors for which Mexico has a comparative advantage), and trigger a dynamic process of income convergence between the three members (Sachs and Warner 2005).

The fact that NAFTA has yet to measure up to this buoyant scenario in some respects vindicates the doubters of neoclassical trade theory, who are still quick to note the impediments to realizing these conventional assumptions (Mosley 2000; Wade 2004). The obstacles would include, for example, institutional weaknesses, barriers to competition, sizeable skill deficits, technological drawbacks and infrastructure inadequacies – especially in the way of pre-9/11 infrastructure. These shortcomings have plagued all three members to varying degrees, but are especially debilitating for a developing economy like Mexico's. Yet even Canada, with its leg-up as a G8 country, has lagged in this regard. As the data presented in Table 11.1 suggest, Canada's purchasing power per capita remains about 81 per cent of that of the US; Canadian productivity and investment ratios are similarly behind (Sharpe 2006; Hurwitz and Marett 2007).

But the data also lend equivocal support to the champions of neoclassical analysis in the sense that both Canada and Mexico have converged toward the more highly developed US standard in terms of broad macroeconomic performance – inflation, interest rates, aggregate growth, and, in the case of Mexico since 1995, exchange rate stability. The indisputable successes in the macroeconomic realm include Mexico's ability to radically reduce inflation and interest rates to levels already achieved by Canada and the US, and its successful shift from a fixed to a floating currency regime in the wake of the 1994 peso crisis (Wise 2007a). Given Canada's tighter pre-existing pattern of integration with the US and its G8 status at the outset of NAFTA, its macroeconomic performance has been even more impressive. Of particular interest is the performance of the Canadian dollar under NAFTA, which has been highly volatile in historic terms, but has also recently recovered all the ground lost and more, relative to the US dollar since NAFTA entered into force. While some of Canada's uninterrupted growth has been due to the luck of high commodity prices since 2001, it is also policy-induced.

As the country's longstanding mercantilist policies had virtually imploded by the 1980s (Hart 2002), Canadian policy-makers met the challenge of heightened competition from the US market by executing a major fiscal overhaul and deep structural reforms through the 1990s. Although these bold moves were understandably anathema to most Canadians at the time, they are now paying off. Again, since 1997 Canada has been the fastest growing G8 economy, registering a fiscal surplus for seven consecutive years, and its net public debt has been reduced by nearly 30 per cent of GDP.

The current gap between Canada's sound macroeconomic performance and its less dynamic microeconomic returns is reflected in Table 11.2, where Canada continues to lag behind on most of the competitiveness indicators listed in the table. A 2005 report from the Institute for Competitiveness and Prosperity in Toronto notes that Canadians have simply not been "as successful as their US counterparts in creating value from our labor, intellectual, physical, and natural resources." The tackling of this tenacious gap (e.g., tax incentives that spur rather than deter investment; increased ties between R&D, universities, and private initiative; and the application of more advanced technology to the production of goods) emerged as one of the policy commitments made by winning conservative candidate, Stephen Harper, in Canada's January 2006 federal elections.

As Table 11.2 shows, from 1990 to 2005 Canada more than doubled its proportion of high-tech exports as a percentage of GDP. However, other key measures of competitiveness, such as the number of patents granted and R&D spending as a per cent of GDP, reflect a pattern of

Table 11.2
Competitive Inroads

		United States	Canada	Mexico
High Tech Exports (% GDP)	1990	33.0%	13.0%	8.2%
	2000	33.0%	18.6%	22.4%
	2005*	22-34%	29.0%	19.6%
R&D% GDP*	1996	2.5%	1.7%	0.3%
	2001	2.8%	2.3%	0.3%
	2002	2.7%	2.0%	0.4%
	2003	2.7%	2.0%	0.4%
	2004	2.7%	2.0%	0.4%
	2005	3.1%	2.0%	0.4%
Patents Granted	1999	153,487	13,778	3,899
	2000	157,496	12,125	5,519
	2001	166,038	12,019	5,479
	2005	143,806	13,060	8,098
Internet Users (per 1,000)	1994	49	25	0.4
	2001	551	512	36
	2005*	630	520	181
Productivity (output/hour) Index 1993 = 100	2000	145.8	125.8	145.9
	2001	149.9	121.9	144.8
	2002	161.3	124.8	154.0
	2003	171.6	126.2	159.2
	2004	177.0	132.8	168.2
	2005	185.9	137.6	170.7
	2006	192.5	138.3	176.1

Sources: World Trade Organization; International Labour Organization; INEGI Database, "Productividad de la mano de obra en diferentes países," Available at: <http://www.inegi.gob.mx/est/contenidos/espanol/rutinas/ept.asp?t=mano4&c=477>; * OECD Statistics by Country and World Bank Country Profiles, Available at: <http://devdata.worldbank.org/external/CPProfile.asp?SelectedCountry=MEX&CCODE=MEX&CNAME=Mexico&PTYPE=CP>

running in place. The implication of these seemingly contradictory trends is that most of Canada's export gains in technology-intensive goods are related to cross-border production and intra-industry trade with the US But by far the most serious challenge that stands out in Table 11.2 is the mediocre productivity gains that Canada has registered in the NAFTA era. Mexico's productivity growth rates easily surpassed those of Canada during this time period, while those of the US literally exploded. While Mexico trailed in the number of internet users and the ratio of R&D to GDP, this too supports the assumptions of neoclassical trade theory: Mexico did better at increasing productivity than increasing R&D because its comparative advantage is in labour, not science.

Relative to Mexico however, Canada is just the reverse – capital abundant and labour scarce – and the puzzle remains as to its inability to put this capital to more productive and innovative use. Despite registering a favourable increase in high tech exports and holding the line on R&D as a percentage of GDP, why haven't Canada's gains worked to boost its standing on international competitiveness indicators? If anything, Canada has slid in the rankings of the World Economic Forum's Global Competitive Index, dropping from 13th place in 2005 to 16th place in 2006 (WEF 2006). Certainly there is no shortage of answers to this question, which can be confirmed by just a quick browse through the rich array of research reports and policy prescriptions generated by academia, both public and private sector analysts, and Canada's network of policy think tanks.

Doubly puzzling, at least for those who subscribe to the importance of domestic institutions as a main explanation for economic performance (Rodrik 2003), is Canada's higher scores on four of the five main institutional indicators in the World Bank's Governance Matters Database (see Table 11.3) – voice and accountability, control of corruption, rule of law, and government effectiveness (Lederman et al. 2005: 41). Although Canada comes out behind the US on the measure of regulatory quality, the differences are marginal. Again, if Canadian institutions are every bit as efficient and transparent as those of the US, and way out ahead of Mexico's, why the lag in Canada's overall productivity and competitiveness indicators?

As with any reform gap, North and South alike, the answers tend to be more complex than the original question. In Canada's case, the bottleneck appears to lie in the breach between the candid and prescriptive insights offered up in the literature on Canadian economic policy and performance, and the constellation of political coalitions, special interests, and regional factions that have succeeded over time – intentionally or not – in perpetuating this low-productivity status quo. To put this differently, the parameters of public policy debate in Canada still seem

Figure 11.1
Mexico's Institutional Gap, with Respect to Canada and the US

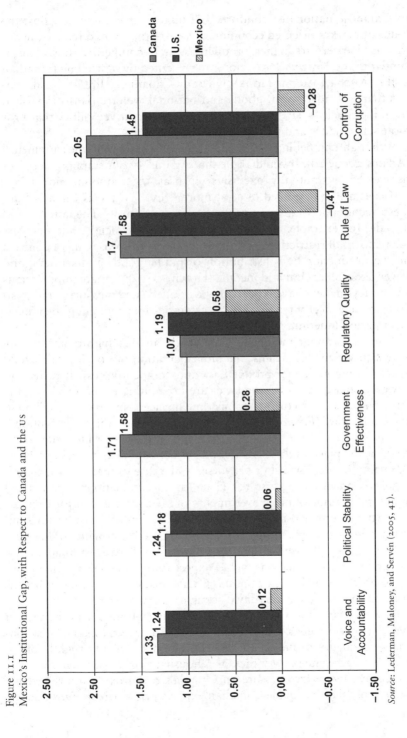

Source: Lederman, Maloney, and Servén (2005, 41).

to juxtapose nationalist comforts and quality of life issues against the kinds of market-oriented economic measures that would reduce the numerous barriers to higher productivity and competitiveness. This is similar to the *Fire and Ice* dichotomy presented by bestselling Canadian author Michael Adams (2004), whereby Canadian "fire" (liberal politics that prioritize social goods and national welfare) is distinguished from the much "icier" US *zeitgeist* (neo-conservative politics that promote self-reliance and market-based competition).

Although compelling as an exercise in "social value measurement" (Adams 2004, 20), I would argue that Adams' two metaphors need not be treated as mutually exclusive: just as US economic policy approaches are in dire need of a lot more "fire," so too is Canada's domestic economic strategy in need of a bit more "ice." The latter would include, for example, the reduction of inter-provincial trade barriers, the removal of restrictions on labour mobility, the loosening of controls on the production and distribution of public goods and services, and lower taxes on capital and income (Howitt 2007). Canadian politicians and policy-makers have repeatedly postponed such measures, and in so doing have exacerbated market uncertainties by prolonging the adjustment period indefinitely.

Arguments about the need to preserve Canada's high quality of life have also weighed in against the implementation of policies that would directly promote higher productivity and competitiveness. It turns out, however, that delays with the latter are now biting into progress on the former. According to the Economist Intelligence Unit's widely cited quality of life index (*Economist* 2005), in 2005 Canada ranked 5th internationally on per capita GDP rates, but 14th on quality of life indicators – versus a 2nd place ranking for the US on per capita GDP and 13th place on quality of life. For better or worse, in the case of the US these figures readily confirm the extent to which the accumulation of individual wealth takes pride of place over quality of life concerns. But for Canada, where the reverse is ostensibly the rule, the quality of life indicator similarly trails the country's ranking on per capita GDP. If quality of life were truly a trade-off for the 20 per cent differential between Canadian and US per capita GDP, then one would expect Canada's quality of life ranking to at least equal that of the US. Canadians, it seems, are getting less fire than the country's everyday discourse otherwise suggests.

Pressures for reform on the domestic front will mount in the face of these lackluster trends in Canadian per capita growth, income distribution, and quality of life measures. The bloom is already slightly off of Canada's aggregate growth rate, as a housing market slump in the US is exercising downward pressure on Canada's real growth and the strong Canadian dollar has made Canadian exports pricier (*Economist* 2007c).

Although perhaps still politically incorrect for many Canadians to posit reform solutions in market terms, recent economic history has shown that steady increases in productivity and competitiveness are the most direct route for addressing these prosperity concerns (Rodrik 2003).

As for NAFTA's potential here, it seems safe to say that it has delivered its punch in terms of the role that enhanced levels of trade and investment can play in catalyzing further microeconomic change for both Canada and Mexico. In fact, because of the institutional limitations that all three members agreed to at the outset (Bélanger 2007; Studer 2007), NAFTA has basically been frozen in place in so many respects and is sorely out of date when it comes to tackling today's structural challenges.

As Stephen Clarkson writes about in his chapter in this volume, there has been a renewed trinational effort to address these difficult microeconomic realities in the form of a parallel initiative – the Security and Prosperity Partnership of North America (SPP) in March 2005,[3] which was followed a year later by the creation of the North American Competitiveness Council (NACC) as part of this same process. However, these recent gestures mainly prescribe rather than mandate more coordinated policy approaches for enhancing productivity and competitiveness in North America, and each piles on new tasks with no concrete organizational mechanisms or significant financial allotments for implementing them (Wise 2007a). As such, it is clear that neither Canada nor Mexico can rely on these trinational attempts to reinvigorate NAFTA on a thinly crafted parallel track.

In both cases, solutions to hard microeconomic problems will have to come from policy stealth, political statecraft, and institutional innovation on the home front. As the following section suggests, external venues like the emergent US-led Regional-12 grouping can deliver some new trade and investment gains at the very margins; but it is doubtful that something like a Regional-12 can be counted on to trigger the execution of bold domestic economic reforms to the extent that NAFTA did in the early 1990s. In the case of Canada, where the domestic political economy is still in need of further fine-tuning, policy-makers are more or less on their own in the quest to more evenly and dynamically promote the nation's prosperity.

THE US COMPETITIVE LIBERALIZATION STRATEGY: WHAT A "REGIONAL-12 GROUPING" MIGHT MEAN FOR CANADA[4]

The rise and fall of the proposed 34-member FTAA is a woeful tale of cause, effect, and ultimately, sabotage. Although launched by the Clinton administration back in 1994, the subsequent 8-year refusal of the US Congress to renew the "fast-track" negotiating authority (now called Trade Promotion Authority, or TPA) – which is necessary for the US executive to fully honour commitments made at any trade negotiating table – clearly hampered the FTAA process. But there were other problems as well. As early as 1998 at the Summit of the Americas trade ministerial meeting in San José, Costa Rica, the FTAA countries agreed to a "single undertaking" strategy that proved to be perhaps *the* Achilles Heel for the negotiations. This essentially extended a de facto veto to each participant, such that the pace and scope of the FTAA negotiations could basically be set by the slowest moving reformers amongst the group.

Additional tensions obviously arose, such as the final standoff in 2003 between the US and Brazil over the timing and extent of concessions to be made between issues on the "old" (market access, agriculture, industrial goods) and "new" (services, investment, intellectual property rights) trade agendas. At any rate, once the George W. Bush administration finally obtained TPA from the Congress in August 2002, the Office of the US Trade Representative (USTR) moved quickly to make up for lost time. In its eagerness to restore US credibility and commitment to international trade negotiations the Bush team, led by USTR Robert Zoellick, launched its bilateral competitive liberalization strategy. At once, the US sought to counter the unfavourable "single undertaking" mode that had so burdened the FTAA and to ramp up its leadership role in the Doha Round. Ostensibly, these bilateral deals would complement ongoing negotiations at the regional and multilateral levels, and help pry loose the collective action bottlenecks that had threatened the timely completion of these larger agreements.

Alas, as of 2006, the US had concluded bilateral FTAs with Australia, Bahrain, Central America-Dominican Republic (DR), Chile, Jordan, Morocco, and Singapore. It also began, or is still in the process of finalizing, another long list of bilateral deals including those with: Ecuador, Malaysia, Panama, Peru, the Southern Africa Customs Union, and Thailand. Hindsight now shows that the US competitive liberalization approach has indeed modified the incentives for countries to participate in regional and multilateral trade negotiations, however, it has done so in just the opposite direction! Prior to the adoption of this new US strategy, small countries within Latin America or elsewhere had accurately perceived that the FTAA or Doha were the only ways to secure guaranteed access to the US market. With the 2002 policy shift, any number of small countries successfully scrambled to negotiate bilaterally with the US.

At least for the time being, just the fact that the US has signalled its willingness to move ahead on multiple fronts seems to have dissipated the will for smaller and poorer countries to pay the disproportionately higher costs of negotiating more lengthy and cumbersome trade agreements within these larger fora. And now, with the collapse of Doha and the FTAA, as well as the low probability of renewed US commitment on either front until after the 2008 presidential elections, there is growing momentum in Washington toward the consolidation of some of these bilateral deals in the Americas into a "seamless" regional bloc. Although Zoellick (2007) has taken over as president of the World Bank, the former USTR clearly articulated this proposal in a *Wall Street Journal* opinion piece in January 2007:

This year President Bush and the Democratic-led Congress should launch a new Association of American Free Trade Agreements (AAFTA). The AAFTA could shape the future of the western hemisphere, while offering a new foreign and economic policy design that combines trade, open societies, development and democracy. In concert with successful immigration reform, the AAFTA would signal to the Americas that, despite the trials of war and Asia's rising economic influence, US global strategy must have a hemispheric foundation ... George W. Bush enacted FTAs with Chile, the five states of Central America and the Dominican Republic. He also completed FTAs with Colombia, Peru and Panama. If Congress passes these agreements, the US will finally have an unbroken line of free trade partners stretching from Alaska to the tip of South America. Not counting the US, this free trade assembly would comprise two-thirds of both the population and GDP of the Americas.

Let me comment, first, on the pros and cons of Zoellick's proposed scheme, which even amidst the distraction of the current presidential election cycle is evolving as the de facto US strategy for the Americas; and, second, I'll address the possible implications of all this for Canada. Table 11.3 portrays the status of those FTAs that are now in place within the western hemisphere. What unites all of these countries, of course, is that each has completed or is in the process of completing an FTA with the US

Of note is the absence of the Mercosur (Southern Cone Common Market) countries – Argentina, Brazil, Paraguay, and Uruguay, and pending associate member Venezuela – precisely because this group has not been able to come to terms with the US within Doha or the FTAA negotiations on how to best combine the items on the "old" and "new" trade agenda. So, another distinguishing feature of the Regional-12 is that each and every one of its prospective Latin American members had already secured preferential access to the US market in one way or another (e.g., the Caribbean Basin Initiative; the Andean Trade and Preference Act, and so on) and all are obviously looking to defend this foothold.

Table 11.3
FTAs within the Western Hemisphere

	Free Trade Agreement	Enter into Force
1	Central America, Dominican Republic – US	2006
2	Canada – Central America	In process**
3	Chile – US	2003
4	Canada – Costa Rica	2002
5	Central America – Chile	2002***
6	Mexico – El Salvador, Guatemala and Honduras	2001
7	Chile – Mexico	1999
8	Mexico – Nicaragua	1998
9	Canada – Chile	1997
10	Costa Rica – Mexico	1995
11	Canada – Mexico – US	1994
12	Central American Common Market (Costa Rica, El Salvador, Honduras, Guatemala and Nicaragua)	1960
13	Mexico – Bolivia	1995
14	Mexico – Columbia – Venezuela (dropped out in 2006)	1995
15	Chile – Andean Countries	ACE****
16	Andean Community	1997
17	US – Panama	In process*
18	US – Andean Countries	In process*

Notes: * Concluded negotiation, legislative approval pending; ** Advanced negotiation;
*** In process, enter into force of the agreement between Chile and three Central American
countries: Guatemala, Honduras and Nicaragua; **** Bolivia (1993), Columbia (1994),
and Ecuador (1995).
Source: Zabludovsky and Gómez Lora (2007).

Table 11.4 summarizes a proposal by Jaime Zabludovsky (a former
NAFTA negotiator for Mexico and chief negotiator for the FTA between Mexico and the EU) and Sergio Gómez Lora (2007), which
depicts the additional FTAs that would need to be completed in order
to effectively weave together this hypothetical Regional-12 bloc. As
they note, Canada, Chile, El Salvador, Guatemala, Honduras, Mexico,
Nicaragua, and the US have in one way or another established FTAs
amongst themselves, amounting to twelve mini-free trade zones in all.
The US is still seeking to finalize FTAs with Peru and Ecuador, while
Canada and Central America are in the advanced stages of negotiating an FTA.

Table 11.4
FTAs Necessary to Create a Sub-regional Free Trade Zone of 12 Countries

Mexico – Dominican Republic
Mexico – Ecuador
Mexico – Peru
Chile – Dominican Republic
Central America – Andean countries
Panama – Andean countries, Canada and Mexico
Canada – Dominican Republic
Canada – Andean countries

Source: Zabludovsky and Gómez Lora (2007).

To move this plan forward, Mexico would have to negotiate with the same Andean countries that are now in the process of completing bilateral FTAs with the U.S; the Dominican Republic, which has negotiated an FTA with the US as part of the Central American Free Trade Agreement (CAFTA), would have to negotiate FTAs with Chile, Canada, and Mexico; Panama would need to complete FTAs with Canada, Mexico, and the Andean countries; and Canada, as shown in the bottom line of Table 11.5, would need to similarly negotiate with the Andean countries.[5] This, in effect, would complete the so-called Regional-12 scheme. Until Harper's July 2007 visit to Latin America, which included Barbados, Chile, Colombia, and Haiti, Canada's political will to pursue such a venture was rather dubious, as Harper's foreign policy efforts had heretofore focused somewhat narrowly on Afghanistan. In what seems to be a broadening of horizons, the prime minister has now declared the government's intentions to re-engage with the western hemisphere, the first steps being to wrap up a Canada-Central America-DR agreement, to negotiate new FTAs with Colombia, Peru, and to call for an FTA between Canada and the Caribbean.

Ottawa, it appears, is anticipating the still-implicit Regional-12 grouping and is moving assertively to stake out its claim along side the US in these hemispheric markets. But what's really at stake here for Canada? As Daudelin (2007), Mace (2007) and others have recently reminded us, despite Canada's championing of the FTAA right up to the dying end, its trade ties with these Latin American and Caribbean countries are still insignificant. For example, Daudelin (2007, 19) notes that Canada's "total trade with the region has grown by 500 per cent since 1990, to reach almost C$50 billion in 2006. Much of the growth is accounted for by imports, which grew six-fold over that period, while exports tripled to reach C$12 billion ... beyond Mexico, there has been little progress over the past fifteen years." Even within NAFTA, Canada's exports to Mexico were C$4 billion in 2006, a figure that barely accounts for 1 per cent of Canada's total exports.

The growth of Canadian FDI in Latin America over the past decade has overshadowed the expansion of trade, but most of these gains have been concentrated in those Southern Cone countries that are not factored into the Regional-12 proposal for reasons discussed earlier. Borrowing again from Daudelin's (2007, 18) estimates, of the total C$83 billion stock of Canadian FDI that was registered in 2005, Argentina, Brazil and Chile together accounted for around C$18.2 billion, while Mexico accounted for an additional C$3.1 billion. The remaining and by far largest stock of Canadian FDI (some C$60 billion) in 2005 was tucked away in tax havens in the Caribbean. In light of these combined trade and investment trends, and notwithstanding Harper's July 2007 good will trip to Latin America, the structural logic for Canada's re-entry into the hemispheric game based on sizeable trade and investment flows is not all that compelling.

Back in the early-1990s Canada's decision to become a hemispheric broker was driven by the notion that the FTAA would come to fruition, that it would do so in tandem with the completion of a new trade round at the WTO, and that these victories would enable Canada to secure deeper regional and international commitments around the "new" trade agenda, in particular. What a difference a decade makes: the failure to achieve these lofty goals is reason enough for the Canadian electorate to shirk at the notion of yet another hemispheric project as embodied in the Regional-12 proposal. However, just as Mexico's insistence on negotiating an FTA with the US in 1990 prompted Canada to enter into the NAFTA negotiations for fear of slipping in its prized access to the US market under the 1989 Canada-US Free Trade Agreement, so too does the prospect of a Regional-12 scheme raise this spectre. Surely the ongoing hub-and-spoke quagmire, the forever nagging asymmetries in Canada-US relations, and the chronic fear of opportunities lost factored in to Harper's decision to venture south this year (see *Economist* 2007a).

But more to the point, the US, by having corralled the region's smaller and weakest members – the trade equivalent of a "coalition of the willing" – into its bilateral competitive liberalization strategy, is quietly laying down a regulatory framework for a large part of the hemisphere that nicely accommodates US preferences and interests but not necessarily those of Canada. "Given the weight of the US in the region, it is highly probable that the nature and scope of these FTAs will become the model for economic relations across the hemisphere. The Canadian government will then have to adjust and adapt its preferences to conform to this evolving pattern" (Mace 2007, 114).

This raises two essential concerns: first, while Canada's trade and investment profile in Latin America may be underwhelming at this point in time (reality check: Canadian assets in the US are worth C$214 billion, and C$119 billion in Europe as a whole), Canadian businesses are not looking to lose any market share in the region. It is for this very reason that Mexico's enthusiasm for a Regional-12 grouping is picking up by the day (Zabludovsky and Gómez Lora, 2007). This is due to the increased competition that Mexico now confronts on both ends of the American bilateral FTAs – in the US market from other Latin countries who have gained access; and in those same Latin markets as a result of the heightened competition from US exports.

To a lesser extent, Canada faces this same dilemma; without committing to a Regional-12 scheme it will become increasingly tough to maintain even the currently modest nature of Canada-Latin American ties, let alone increase the flow of trade and investment from Canada to the region. A second concern for Canada is that which partially prompted its staying power within the FTAA process: the quest to establish a sound regulatory framework to govern the new trade agenda in the hemisphere (services, competition policies, investment). As services now account for almost 70 per cent of Canadian GDP, and the preservation of Canadian FDI shares in the region is clearly a concern, the ability of the US to basically craft its own regulatory framework and preferences into the Regional-12 scheme cannot be good news for Canadian businesses. As in the case of NAFTA, fear of exclusion seems to have already prompted a more proactive stance on the part of the Harper government.

There are other pragmatic reasons for Canada to spring into action on this front. For example, the Regional-12 model could serve as a badly needed catalyst for streamlining NAFTA's antiquated rules of origin and for further reducing the thick web of administrative barriers that continue to burden North American markets. This, in turn, would help to promote greater specialization and harmonization of trade and production norms across a broader geographical swath (i.e. the Regional-12 bloc). A much smaller number of actors at the negotiating table (12 versus the 34 countries at the FTAA), as well as the fact that the countries involved (see Tables 11.3 and 11.4) have already made a basic commitment to trade liberalization and regional integration, suggests a higher probability for constructive collective action.

In its own way, a Regional-12 group could constitute at least one path back toward tackling the tough new trade issues that have held up the FTAA from the standpoint of the Mercosur bloc, as well as the old market access issues (agriculture, industrial goods) that precipitated the collapse of the Doha negotiations in mid-2006. Make no mistakes, without the bigger Latin American countries like Brazil, Argentina, and Venezuela, the dynamic trade and investment gains from this strategy would be modest. Its appeal would be as a lever for getting back down to business in spurring higher trade and investment flows on the regional integration front, but in such a way that Canada is still very much a present and active player in this process.

Finally, I would argue that the political viability of formalizing this Regional-12 strategy would hinge largely on Canada's willingness to truly step back into the hemispheric fray. As confirmed by the public protests and street demonstrations that met President Bush along every stop in his March 2007 Latin American tour, US-Latin American relations in the 2000s have been nothing short of a disaster. This is obviously a world apart from the cordial reception and professional rapport with which Harper was received four months later on his tour of this same region. The tragic failures of Bush's foreign policy record (Iraq, Afghanistan, the Middle East, and so on) are such that this outgoing administration is under intense pressure to deliver something positive in this realm. In lining up to negotiate bilateral FTAs with the US, its hemispheric partners have basically held their noses and acted in their own rational interests to defend existing levels of US market access which are vitally important to the economic well-being of their own populations. This, in itself, falls far short of a foreign policy "success" from anyone's perch, Washington's astute political spin notwithstanding.

In line with my opening comments about an increase in mutual dependence between Canada and the US, the plain truth is that for the US to make any credible inroads on something like a Regional-12 grouping, it would need to act in concert with Canada. In this spirit, I conclude here by quoting a recent opinion piece by former prime minister Joe Clark (2007, 3–4), which offers a sensible justification for Canada's revamping of its hemispheric strategy:

There will always be arguments that Canada has only a minor influence in Latin America, so should not concentrate there. Indeed, a more generalized version of that view argues that a country Canada's size has not much influence anywhere, and so should be content with a relatively passive foreign policy, tucking ourselves into Washington's skirts, or tut-tutting those who actually enter the arena. On the contrary. Canada's mediating skills and reputation for balance are unusually pertinent in this era of cultural conflict and shifting power. That is specifically the case in Latin America and the Caribbean, when Washington's credentials are in decline, and Canada's experience as an economy, a federation, a democracy and a neighbour are relevant and respected.

CONCLUDING THOUGHTS

For the past decade, Canada has been on an indisputable roll. However, this chapter cautions that it would be premature for the nation to sit back and rest on these laurels. As the US learned the hard way with the onset of economic recession in the early-2000s, the business cycle is alive and well, and not just a relic of an earlier industrial era, as some had argued. With its own economic excesses now peaking in the form of historically high debts, deficits and a simmering housing crisis, the US is surely due for an adjustment that goes far beyond the limp efforts that Washington has made thus far in the way of fiscal reform and the curbing of rampant spending.

While the predictable contagion from another US downturn is certainly grounds for Canada's adoption of a more competition-oriented economic reform strategy, there is also the question of Canada's need to fully exploit its incredibly rich endowments. One critical example emerges in the under-tapped Canada-China economic relationship, which is another story for another time. For the purposes of this chapter, important is the 20 per cent gap in per capita GDP between Canada and the US; the growing national disparities in relative income gains; and a surprisingly lukewarm dataset on Canada's quality of life indicators when subjected to an international comparison – all of these trends suggest that much more could be done to deliver the country's macro-economic miracle to the wider population.

At the same time, Canada's economic performance could be more miraculous still, were politicians and policy-makers to draw up their ideological blinders and tackle some of the most glaring obstacles to economic dynamism (e.g. inter-provincial trade barriers, restrictions on labour mobility, controls on the production and distribution of public goods and services, and burdensome taxes on capital and income). For all the ongoing contemplation amongst Canadian academics and intellectuals concerning Canada's diplomatic place in the world (see Cohen 2004), I would argue that the question of its economic advancement merits at least proportionate attention. Canada's progress in the NAFTA era has been such that it is gradually gaining the fame of a small, open economy that is very much on the move; my hunch is that herein lies equal, if not more, possibilities for securing the international foothold, respect, and prestige that much of this diplomatic literature on Canada cries out for.

Some of Canada's success over the past decade certainly has to do with NAFTA-induced restructuring and the country's having hit the commodity lottery in the 2000s; but the long-running boom is also a tribute to an earlier round of risk-taking and tenacity on the part of the country's leaders. The various indicators reviewed in this chapter confirm that it is now time to take this restructuring project to the next level. At this point, the answers appear to lie more in the domestic realm, where the political incentives for economic reform are in need of basic realignment. Canada's sophisticated economic institutions are clearly an asset for undertaking another round of reforms to foster higher productivity and competitiveness, but again, the political incentives have somehow got to be reversed.

On the foreign economic policy front, there are also some secondary gains to be made via the option that I have reviewed here: deeper integration with an incipient Regional-12 grouping in the western hemisphere. Given the small size of the countries involved, and the fact that Canada's investment ties are strongest with the Mercosur bloc – the one sub-region that is excluded from this plan – it is doubtful that Canada's formalization of its participation in a Regional-12 grouping would yield the kinds of investment returns that Harper laid expectations to publicly during his July 2007 Latin American tour.

However, a Regional-12 group could very well provide the impetus for streamlining the worst and most antiquated vestiges of NAFTA (rules of origin and other administrative barriers at the border), as well as the opportunity for Canada to proceed further on new trade agenda items like services and investment in the hemisphere. Despite the periodic fretting in Ottawa about heightened economic reliance on the US market and the need to diversify its international ties, there is a kind of poetic justice to this current juncture in Canada-US relations: the US, for all the reasons stated in this chapter, would have serious difficulties proceeding on its own in the hemisphere without Canada's "mediating skills and reputation for balance" (Clark 2007). For those Canadian commentators looking to beef up the country's middle power status, a Regional-12 group may seem too small a step, but moving forward it could well prove a strategic one.

NOTES

The author thanks Katherine Baldwin, Marcela Lopez, and Victor Meza for their able research assistance in the completion of this chapter, as well as the Center for International Studies at the University of Southern California for funding these researchers.

1 This was a dominant theme in discussions that took place at the *3ʳᵈ Canada-China Economic Cooperation Conference: Energy and Beyond*, hosted by the China Institute, University of Alberta, Edmonton, 20–22 June 2007.

2 The first few paragraphs of this section, as well as Tables 1–5, borrow from Wise (2007a).

3 The SPP report submitted by the Ministers and Secretaries of the Economic, Security, and Foreign Policy areas of Canada, Mexico, and the US, to the three national leaders was published in June 2005. Available at: <http://www.usembassycanada.gov/content/can_usa/spp_ottawa_report.pdf>

4 The background context for this section draws from Mace (2007), Wise (2007b) and Zabludovsky and Gómez Lora (2007).

5 Chile rejoined the Andean Community of Nations (CAN by its Spanish acronym) as an associate member on June 8, 2007 after a thirty-year hiatus. Given that Canada and Mexico each has a separate FTA with Chile, and that each are in need of negotiating further with CAN for the completion of the Regional-12 group, these pre-existing deals with Chile could help to facilitate this process.

REFERENCES

Adams, Michael. 2004. *Fire and Ice*. Toronto: Penguin Group Canada.

Audley, John, et al. 2003. *NAFTA's Promise and Reality*. Washington, DC: Carnegie Endowment for International Peace.

Bélanger, Louis. 2007. "An Unsustainable Institutional Design: Incompleteness and Delegation Deficit in NAFTA." In *Regionalism and the State: NAFTA and Foreign Policy Convergence*, edited by Gordon Mace. Aldershot, UK: Ashgate.

Boyer, Marcel. 2007. "Quebec's Disappointing Economic Performance in the Last 25 Years." *Economic Note* (May). Montreal: Montreal Economic Institute.

Clark, Joe. 2007. "Op-Ed: For a Bolstering of Canada's Leadership in the Americas," *Focal Point* 6, no. 6 (July-August): 2–4.

Cohen, Andrew. 2004. *While Canada Slept: How We Lost our Place in the World*. Toronto: McClelland and Stewart.

Daudelin, Jean. 2007. "Canada and the Americas: A Time for Modesty." *Behind the Headlines* 64, no. 3 (May): 1–29. Toronto: Canadian International Council.

Economist. 2007a. "Harper Steps Out," 12 July. Available at: <http://www.economist.com/world/la/displaystory.cfm?story_id=9481429>

– 2007b. "Saying No to Free Trade," Briefing. *Economist Intelligence Unit*, 18 July.

– 2007c. "Canada Forecasts," Country Briefing. *Economist Intelligence Unit*, 11 July. Available at: <http://www.economist.com/countries/Canada/profile.cfm?folder=Profile-Forecast>

– 2005. "Quality of Life Index." In *The World in 2005*. Economist Intelligence Unit. Available at: <http://www.economist.com/media/pdf/QUALITY_OF_LIFE.pdf>

Harper, Stephen. 2007. "Canada's Renewed Engagement in the Americas," Address by the Prime Minister to the Chile-Canada Chamber of Commerce. Santiago, Chile, 17 July. Available at: <http://www.pm.gc.ca/eng/media.asp?id=1759>

Hart, Michael. 2002. *A Trading Nation: Canadian Trade Policy from Colonialism to Globalization*. Vancouver: University of British Columbia Press.

Howitt, Peter. 2007. "Innovation, Competition and Growth: A Schumpeterian Perspective on Canada's Economy." *Commentary*, no. 244 (April). Toronto: C.D. Howe Institute.

Hufbauer, Gary, and Jeffrey Schott. 2005. NAFTA *Revisited*. Washington, DC: Institute for International Economics.

Hurwitz, Stephen A., and Louis J. Marrett. 2007. "Financing Canadian Innovation: Why Canada Should End Roadblocks to Foreign Private Equity." *Commentary*, no. 244 (forthcoming). Toronto: C.D. Howe Institute.

Jiang, Wenran. 2006. "Meeting the China Challenge: Developing a China Strategy." In *Canada Among Nations 2006: Minorities and Priorities*, edited by Andrew F. Cooper and Dane Rowlands. Montreal & Kingston: McGill-Queen's University Press, 251–68.

Lederman, Daniel, William F. Mahoney and Luis Servén. 2005. *Lessons from* NAFTA *for Latin America and the Caribbean*. Palo Alto, CA and Washington, DC: Stanford University Press and the World Bank.

Mace, Gordon. 2007. "The FTAA Stalemate: Implications for Canadian Foreign Policy." In *Requiem or Revival? The Promise of North American Integration*, edited by Isabel Studer and Carol Wise. Washington, DC: Brookings Institution Press, 108–23.

Martin, Roger L. 2005. "Foreword." In *Realizing Canada's Prosperity Potential*. Report presented to the World Economic Forum, Annual Meeting, January. Available at: <http://www.competeprosper.ca/images/uploads/davo5.pdf>

Mosley, Paul. 2000. "Globalisation, Economic Policy, and Convergence." *World Economy* 23, no. 5 (May): 613–34.

Rodrik, Dani, ed. 2003. *In Search of Prosperity: Analytical Narratives on Economic Growth*. Princeton: Princeton University Press.

Sachs, Jeffrey, and Andrew Warner. 1995. "Economic Convergence and Economic Policies." NBER *Working Paper*, no. 5039 (February). Cambridge, MA: National Bureau of Economic Research.

Sawchuk, Gary and David Yerger. 2006. "With Whom Does Canada Compete at Home?" PRI *Working Paper*, no. 27 (August). Ottawa: Policy Research Initiative.

Sharpe, Andrew. 2006. "Lessons for Canada from International Productivity Experience." CSLS *Research Report*, no. 2006–02 (October). Ottawa: Centre for the Study of Living Standards.

Studer, Isabel. 2007. "Obstacles to Integration: NAFTA's Institutional Weaknesses." In *Requiem or Revival? The Promise of North American Integration*, edited by Isabel Studer and Carol Wise. Washington, DC: Brookings Institution Press, 53–75.

Wade, Robert. 2004. "Is Globalization Reducing Poverty and Inequality?" *World Development* 32, no. 4 (April): 567–89.

WEF. 2006. "Global Competitiveness Index Rankings and 2005 Comparisons." *Global Competitiveness Index*. Davos: World Economic Forum. Available at: <http://www.weforum.org/pdf/Global_Competitiveness_Reports/Reports/gcr_2006/gcr2006_rankings.pdf>

Weintraub, Sidney. 2004. "Trade, Investment, and Economic Growth." In *NAFTA's Impact on North America*, edited by Sidney Weintraub. Washington, DC: Center for Strategic and International Studies, 3–20.

Wise, Carol. 2007a. "Great Expectations: Mexico's Short-lived Convergence under NAFTA," *CIGI Working Paper*, no. 15 (January). Waterloo: The Centre for International Governance Innovation.

– 2007b. "No Turning Back: Trade Integration and the New Development Mandate." In *Requiem or Revival? The Promise of North American Integration*, edited by Isabel Studer and Carol Wise. Washington, DC: Brookings Institution Press, 1–23.

– and Cintia Quiliconi. 2007. "China's Surge in Latin American Markets: Policy Challenges and Responses," *Politics and Policy* 35, no. 3 (September): 410–38.

Zabludovsky, Jaime, and Sergio Gómez Lora. 2007. "Mexico, the FTAA, and Perspectives for Hemispheric Integration." In *Requiem or Revival? The Promise of North American Integration*, edited by Isabel Studer and Carol Wise. Washington, DC: Brookings Institution Press, 91–107.

Zoellick, Robert. 2007. "Happily Ever AAFTA." *Wall Street Journal*, 8 January, A17.

12 Manoeuvring within the Continental Constitution: Autonomy and Capacity within the Security and Prosperity Partnership of North America

STEPHEN CLARKSON

When inviting colleagues to contribute to this volume, its editors asked us to address several interrrelated issues concerning Canada's international room for manoeuvre, given its high levels of "North Americanization" in a context in which "the multilateral trade system remains functional but is unable to progress, the UN is stuck ... and the OAS never took off." In this chapter, I would like to explore a provisional answer to these questions by considering a possible new institution of continental governance, the Security and Prosperity Partnership of North America (SPP). "Provisional" because the SPP was only born in 2005. "Possible" because it is still not clear whether this new continental baby's cranium will harden and its organs will grow into a viable being.

DEFINITIONS

To proceed with the analysis in a situation characterized by tremendous political indeterminacy, I must first define my terms. To have "room for manoeuvre" presumes an *objective* context which, while presenting some *constraints*, also offers some *opportunities* for action. Implicit also in the notion is a *subjective* situation in which actors have both *consciousness* of this context and the *will* to exploit these opportunities. Applying this notion of manoeuvrability to the dynamics of North America's political economy, it follows that an unstable dialectic relationship connects these objective and subjective factors: what alters the subjective reality for one factor (one capital's change in political leadership affecting its political consciousness and will) can transform the objective constraints facing a partner country's political leadership.

Here, my concern is to assess the SPP's significance in enhancing and/ or constricting Canada's room for manoeuvre. Although we have legions of relevant actors – dozens of governmental institutions, thousands of businesses, and a civil society with incalculable diversity – I will radically simplify the analysis by focusing on the federal government's executive, bureaucracy, and legislature, plus the business community's principal spokesmen. Civil society in all its complexity will be relegated to the sidelines.

Since the editors have added the concept of autonomy to the list of issues they want their book to address, I will distinguish three more ideas before proceeding. First, I will restrict "sovereignty" to the legalistic issue of a state's formal right – as recognized by the international community – to constitute itself as a political actor on the world stage and to make agreements that derogate elements of its sovereignty when signing treaties with other sovereign states. I will use "autonomy" when referring to a jurisdiction's ability to achieve what it wants within its own territory. This leaves "capacity" to refer to a state's ability to achieve what it wants beyond its borders. Typically, trade agreements reduce the autonomy of a state, when it agrees to abandon specified discriminatory policies that favour its own firms, but increase its capacity since these corporations gain greater freedom to operate in the economies of its fellow signatories who have given up some of their discriminatory powers.

ANALYTICAL FRAMEWORK

Scholarly discussion of Canada's room for manoeuvre has long been bedevilled by the international relations discipline's adoption of conceptual systems developed in hegemonic powers which have few autonomy problems. Categorizing Canada as a "middle power" or "principal power" conveys a sense of potency measured along a one-dimensional power differential between it and the United States or between it and other players overseas. If Canada's diplomatic capacity cannot adequately be understood simply in terms of its position within the global power hierarchy, Innisian political economy can be equally misleading. Analyses of Canada as irretrievably hamstrung from the first colonial moment of its staple-trading insertion into global markets see the country's economic, social, political, cultural and military integration in North America as an omelette that cannot be unscrambled and that leaves it without any meaningful capacity for independent action.

My own preference is to approach this analytical quagmire by introducing the concept of "constitution" whose descriptive handles offer an alternative, arguably better grip on a constantly shifting, extraordinarily complex reality. Constitutions have long been recognized as seminal elements in the construction of the modern nation state. After all, they define citizens' rights and establish the norms, rules and institutions – executive, legislature, bureaucracy, courts and coercive agencies – which set the parameters for every political system. Whether written down in the form of a published document which is elaborated and amended by subsequent judicial interpretations (as in the United States) or whether produced more incrementally by conventions that have evolved over the centuries (as in the British case), constitutions are overwhelmingly understood to be domestic documents that structure a state's institutions and political processes.

Great Britain in the nineteenth century and the United States in the twentieth century may be ideal types for understanding the Westphalian state in its – respectively – unitary or separation-of-powers modes but, as imperial powers in their heydays, they do not help understand the myriad smaller states that, like Canada, have always been subject to some external control and never solely constituted by their own internal processes.

CANADA'S EXTERNAL CONSTITUTION UNDER BRITISH RULE: FORMAL BUT DIMINISHING

While the British North America (BNA) Act is generally understood to have comprised Canada's constitution until its "patriation" in 1982, the important point for this conceptualization is that it did not define Canada's entire legal regime. In some important respects, Canada grew up with the colonial version of what I call an "external" constitution, whose mandate diminished over the decades.

Norms. Ottawa established its own military and naval forces, but their deployment in action remained an imperial prerogative. When Parliament in Westminster changed the British Empire's norm of peace into the norm of war, the Dominion was *ipso facto* at war: Canada was engaged in hostilities with Germany the moment that London declared war on the Kaiser in 1914.

Rules. Initially, Westminster retained the executive function of negotiating and signing treaties on Ottawa's behalf and the legislative function of ratifying them – typically with the United States. On more than one occasion, it literally shaped Canada's contours – giving up vast territories to Yankee control without the nominally autonomous Canadian politicians' having a say in the matter. Although a foreign service was established when Canada's Department of External Affairs was founded in 1909, it was only with the Statute of Westminster in 1931, when the Dominions were declared to be autonomous members of the British Commonwealth, that the Canadian government formally assumed control over its foreign relations.

Rights. Canadians remained British subjects until after World War II and had the right – most often used by the provinces when contesting federal-government measures – to take appeals of certain types of legal cases for final resolution by the Judicial Committee of the Privy Council in Westminster.

Institutions. Canadian federalism's entire institutional corpus was defined by the British North America Act, with one notable exception: the ultimate function of deciding appeals in disputed cases remained in the hands of the Judicial Committee of the British Privy Council – until the Supreme Court of Canada became the court of last resort for judicial appeals in 1949.

Amendment. The last, and symbolically most powerful, element of Canada's legal order that remained in its external constitution was the power to amend the domestic constitution – the rules for changing the rules. This power of constitutional amendment, the ultimate symbol of national sovereignty, only shifted from Canada's external to its internal constitution in 1982 when the British parliament passed a resolution to incorporate in the BNA Act the amending formula, which Prime Minister Pierre Trudeau had negotiated with the provinces. In a legalistic sense Canada had become fully sovereign, but by this time Canada's external constitution had a far more powerfully American table of contents.

CANADA'S EXTERNAL CONSTITUTION WITHIN THE US IMPERIUM: INFORMAL BUT INCREASING

If we accept the view that a constitution can also be made up of unwritten conventions which, when practised over time, gradually gain the status of behaviour governing rules, then we can recognize how Canada's third imperial power relationship fostered a different – because largely informal – external constitution. While constantly evolving, the conventions of the US-Canada relationship defined certain rights and incorporated norms and rules, and, in some cases, actual institutions.

Norms. Civil servants and politicians responsible for managing the relationship between two highly unequal but closely allied states during the Cold War came to agree that Canada should not overtly criticize American foreign policy. As a *quid pro quo*, the United States was not to bully Canada, by acting unilaterally as it tended to do with Mexico. This norm was actually elaborated into a doctrine dubbed "quiet diplomacy" to indicate that Canadian-American conflicts were to be mediated to the extent feasible by bureaucrats who would consult in advance about all issues, but behind closed doors in order to keep political tensions – and touchy politicians – at bay (Merchant and Heeney 1971).

Rules. Equally unwritten, but generally respected was the rule of thumb that individual conflicts being dealt with on the bilateral agenda should not be linked but dealt with on their own merits. Occasionally Washington threatened reprisals in case Ottawa implemented a measure it opposed, but in general the no-linkage rule applied.

Rights. While constitutional rights are normally associated with citizens, corporations are no less interested in their entrepreneurial prerogatives. When the Liberals' notorious National Energy Program was announced in the budget of October 1980 as a series of measures designed to repatriate control over the Canadian oil and gas sectors, US transnational corporations protested that their Fifth Amendment property rights had been violated. The enormous pressure that the administration of Ronald Reagan consequently exerted over Ottawa was based on the notion that, by their very presence in the Canadian economy, US corporations had acquired rights not to have the value of their assets diminished.

Informal institutional realities. Canada's position in the immediate periphery of the US sphere of dominance created institutional realities that were manifested largely on an ad hoc and occasional basis. For the purposes of this analysis, they can be documented according to the main functions of the conventional constitutional order – legislative, executive, bureaucratic, coercive and judicial.

Legislative, executive and bureaucratic. On some Canadian policy issues of major concern to the United States' government and business, US executive, administrative and corporate players have periodically contributed to Canadian rule-making. When, for instance, the Progressive Conservative government of John Diefenbaker set up a commission to design a national strategy for the petroleum industry, the major American oil companies along with the US Department of State took a direct part in the advisory process. Strongly influencing the public's consciousness, the political institutions and the political agenda, it is not surprising that the transnational corporations (TNCs) effectively wrote the Diefenbaker government's National Oil Policy of 1961 which split the petroleum economy in two: western Canadian oil would be exported to supply the northwestern US, while oil for eastern Canada would be imported from the TNCs' overseas holdings.

Such regular provincial-state meetings as the conclaves between the New England governors and eastern Canadian premiers or those of the Pacific Northwest Economic Region are the tip of another iceberg which permits an executive, legislative and bureaucratic presence for bordering states in the processes of provincial governments impinging on their autonomy. By the same token, these gatherings give the Canadian provinces greater capacity to influence their US neighbour's policies.

Coercive. Beyond a common commitment to resisting the threat of Soviet aggression during the Cold War, a well-recognized norm governed Canada's defence relationship with the United States. "Defence against Help" was shorthand for Ottawa being obliged to establish defence forces and doctrines to the satisfaction of the Pentagon. The clear understanding was that if Canada did not finance the military structures and adopt the tactical orientation deemed necessary in Washington, American forces would do the job, but on their own terms. Canadians take this coercive diminution of autonomy for granted without noticing its constitutional significance.

Judicial. When it came to actual conflicts between the two governments, their resolution was, with one notable exception, achieved through the normal diplomatic processes of intergovernmental negotiation so cannot be seen as having a constitutional function. The obvious exception is the International Joint Commission (IJC), which had a mandate to resolve binational conflicts over boundary waters. The IJC brings us to the formally institutionalized parts of Canada's external constitution within the US imperium.

Formal institutions. During the Keynesian era, some important bilateral institutions were set up to provide more robust regulatory frameworks for managing major common issues. The North America Aerospace Defence Command (NORAD), established in 1957, is the most visible and lastingly significant of those institutions that formally incorporated an aspect of the hegemon's decision-making system into the northern periphery's polity. Involving as it did Canada's principal coercive power – US-made nuclear weaponry – on an issue in which Washington had a paramount interest, NORAD can be seen as a prototype for North America's asymmetrical institutions in which a reduction in real autonomy for the periphery was nominally offset by its increased capacity to affect the Pentagon's policies through Canadian personnel participating in NORAD's joint command.

Although it is the commonly used reference, the Canada-US Automotive Products Agreement (Auto Pact) of 1965 was not the first economic integration agreement which introduced an externally controlling element in a Canadian policy area. The Defence Production Sharing Arrangements of 1957 and an agreement on free cross-border trade in agricultural equipment were precursors of further economic integration by formal agreement. The Auto Pact was economically more consequential because it transformed one of Canada's biggest, nationally organized, tariff-protected industries into a continentally rationalized sector that guaranteed a minimum level of Canadian production in US-owned assembly plants.

Amendment. Norms get violated and rules get broken. On 15 August 1971, under a balance of payments strain caused by its war in Vietnam, President Richard Nixon detached the US dollar from the price of gold and imposed a surcharge on all imports. This unilateral act produced shockwaves round the world, but closer to home it was seen as a cataclysm. That "Nixonomics" had not been the subject of *quiet,* behind-closed-doors consultations broke the conventions that had developed. Washington had unilaterally amended the bilateral relationship's parameters, both reducing Ottawa's capacity to influence American decision-makers and increasing its autonomy over its own affairs – a point that President Nixon made when addressing the Parliament of Canada in 1973.

While NORAD and the Auto Pact can be seen as formal increments to Canada's growing US-centred external constitution, they paled in comparison with the major innovations in continental and global governance that were to follow. Once the Keynesian paradigm of economic development by national industrial strategies gave way to the neo-conservative approach to growth through transborder market liberalization, a new generation of global economic governance institutions emerged which explicitly introduced significant external components to their signatories' legal orders.

CANADA'S EXTERNAL CONSTITUTION UNDER CONTINENTAL AND GLOBAL ECONOMIC GOVERNANCE

By signing the Canada-United States Free Trade Agreement (CUSFTA) in 1989, the North American Free Trade Agreement (NAFTA) in 1994, and the World Trade Organization (WTO) in 1995, Canada took on norms, rules, rights and, in a few cases, institutional requirements that added formal and formidable components to its already considerable external constitution.

Norms. NAFTA and the WTO established principles such as *National Treatment* that do not have to be incorporated into Canada's domestic legislation to be binding. For example, no Canadian law requires federal or provincial or municipal governments to treat foreign-owned furniture companies at least as well as they treat Canadian-owned furniture firms. But since the trade agreements extended the national treatment principle from goods to investments and even to services, if any federal or provincial or municipal government discriminates in favour of a nationally or provincially owned firm, the government of Canada is now liable to legal attack by another state belonging to NAFTA or the WTO that deems one of its companies in Canada to have suffered unequal treatment.

Rules. Reflecting Washington's concern that Ottawa might reintroduce nationalist energy policies, CUSFTA prohibited it from pricing petroleum sold at home below the price charged for oil exported to the United States. Other rules prevented Ottawa from screening foreign takeovers below a much higher minimum firm size than had been (autonomously) established by Parliament and so had to be changed by CUSFTA's implementation legislation.

Rights. The only "citizens" whose rights in Canada were expanded under NAFTA were corporations based in the US or Mexico. NAFTA's Chapter 11 created a judicial process that gave non-Canadian NAFTA corporations the power to take the federal and any provincial or municipal governments to international commercial arbitration in cases of alleged expropriation. This corporate power to overturn the legislative outcomes of national political debates about the desirable regulatory regime to secure the citizenry's health or safety shows how the external constitution reduces the autonomy of domestic government (Levin and Marin 1996, 90). (The WTO did not create similar rights for its members, but corporations based overseas could use Chapter 11 by setting up branches in North America.)

Institutions. Neither NAFTA nor the WTO impinged directly on the Canadian executive, legislative, or administrative function. However, the quasi-judicial rulings of their dispute settlement processes have the same kind of rule-making function as do domestic courts.

NAFTA's Chapter 19 established dispute-settlement panels that may be invoked when a partner state challenges a domestic anti-dumping or countervailing-duty determination. Since appeals of these protectionist rulings are displaced from the domestic judicial system to supranational review, this innovation can be seen as an external addition to the Canadian judicial system with dual implications for its autonomy and capacity. On the one hand, Chapter 19's dispute-settlement panels reduced domestic judicial autonomy. But the limits to the counterpart increase in Canadian capacity were demonstrated by the long-running dispute over softwood lumber in which neither NAFTA's nor the WTO's dispute-settlement mechanism managed to discipline American protectionism.

In a clear example showing how the external constitution reduces domestic autonomy, the United States government successfully used WTO adjudication to invalidate the policy architecture that the federal government had put in place over several decades to buttress the domestic magazine industry in the face of overwhelming US dominance of the Canadian periodicals market (Magder 1998).

NAFTA's Chapter 11 withdrew even more autonomy from Canada's domestic judicial order, the power to review government actions. Instead of using national courts to protest governmental measures which they consider injurious to their corporate interests, American and Mexican firms can now invoke Chapter 11's provisions to activate binding international commercial arbitration. By the same token, Chapter 11 augments Canada's capacity to challenge US legislative and regulatory behaviour.

In its own terms, Chapter 11's privatization of judicial power represented a substantial reduction of domestic autonomy. But this contingent subordination of Canadian public policy to the transborder business strategies of US corporations was overshadowed, as an addition to the external constitution, during two phases following the catastrophe of 11 September 2001. First came a series of bilateral agreements in which Canada responded to American concerns by adjusting its security measures. Most recently is the unexpected deepening of North America's institutional structure that was triggered by the contradiction between the impediments to border crossings (that resulted from Washington's antiterrorism preoccupations) and the pressure for easy transboundary flows (that had been intensified by NAFTA).

THE PARADIGM SHIFT
TO BORDER SECURITY

The immediate lesson taught by Washington's unilateral border blockade on 11 September 2001 was confirmation that NAFTA had provided Canada with no executive capacity to affect American policy relating to transborder economic issues. The NAFTA Trade Commission did not meet to review the US government's invocation of national security to constrict border crossings. Nor was a North American summit convened to review the United States' unnegotiated shift to a new policy paradigm in which, as immortalized by the American ambassador to Canada, "security trumps trade" (Cellucci 2003), with security understood territorially as preventing any dangerous item or person from crossing an American border (see Galloway 2003). But in a matter of days, once the realities of interdependence had American TNCs raising a storm in Washington about the interruption of their continentally integrated production chains, Washington found itself negotiating with the periphery to establish new modalities for the secure passage of goods and people across its two land borders. In other words, while corporations had been restructuring their production and distribution systems continentally, North America had developed no governmental capacity beyond traditional intergovernmental relations.

Already during the presidency of Bill Clinton, Ottawa had negotiated agreements with Washington to improve both the security and infrastructure of the Canadian-American border, but the US government had not been particularly interested in Canada's high-tech approach to erasing many of the common border's barriers. Following 9/11, the United States suddenly paid close attention to what it had previously dismissed. The resulting 30-point Smart Border Plan signed by Homeland Security Advisor Tom Ridge and Minister of Foreign Affairs John Manley in Ottawa on 12 December 2001 appeared to represent a massive loss of autonomy on Canada's part for having accepted the Americans' security agenda. But since many of these 30 points, such as the FAST and NEXUS technologies to speed pre-cleared shipments and pre-screened business travelers across the border, had been made in Canada, the agreement actually signaled that Ottawa's capacity had increased and, along with it, that of the Canadian business community which was pressing hard for viable border-security solutions.

Considerable changes to the federal government's institutional structure (the creation of a new Department of Public Safety and Emergency Preparedness and the military reorganization of a Canada Command), significant tightening of measures to impede terrorist networks (increasing the number of countries whose citizens would require visas to enter Canada and the Anti-Terrorism Act itself), major investment in improving border infrastructure (highway improvements, personnel increases), strengthening security services (budget increases for the Canadian Security and Intelligence Service and the Royal Canadian Mounted Police) could all be interpreted by some civil society groups as evidence of drastically infringed autonomy of a Canadian state bowing to US pressure. But for the general public which accepted the terrorist threat as genuine, for politicians who supported Washington's commitment to a war on terrorism, and for the government's defence and security agencies which yearned for more engagement with their American counterparts, all these actions were so many manifestations of Canada acting in its own interests, albeit in parallel with the United States.

The Canadian government did not have enough capacity to dissuade Washington from taking such further unilateral initiatives as requiring passports for American travellers returning to the United States. But in working out joint initiatives such as Integrated Border Enforcement Teams, Canadian capacity was significant. As witnessed in other issues where the United States exerted its superior capacity, such as its demand that Canadian airlines share their passenger data, domestic autonomy suffered. Canadians had to get used to being prevented from boarding a domestic flight or having United Parcel Services (UPS) refuse to deliver a package between two points within Canada because their names had turned up in an American antiterrorist databank. In short, Canada's external constitution had been rejigged by the two executive branches to give themselves extra discretion to have their officials work together seamlessly, despite national borders.

THE SECURITY AND PROSPERITY PARTNERSHIP OF NORTH AMERICA

Ironically enough, a historic move to deepen trinational regulatory cooperation in North America was born in the White House at the very moment – March 2003 – when the Bush administration's anger with its neighbours was at its most intense.

The election of Vicente Fox and George Bush – two very conservative, on-their-sleeve-Christian, former neighbouring-state governors – had ushered in an unusual blooming of Mexico-US friendship, but the bonhomie had rapidly chilled when the government of Mexico had expressed scant solidarity with the Americans after the attacks of 11 September 2001 and failed, even rhetorically, to support their retaliation against the Taliban in Afghanistan. Washington had not expected the Mexicans to stymie its military plans in Iraq by opposing it in the Security Council where they held a temporary seat. It was equally disappointed by Canada's efforts during the early months of 2003 to rally allies at the United Nations to delay the American attack on Baghdad.

Notwithstanding the public discord due to their resisting the US president's determination to achieve regime change in Iraq, the March meeting at 1600 Pennsylvania Avenue with senior officials from the Fox and Chrétien governments came to the conclusion that border bottlenecks caused by US security concerns should no longer be allowed to jeopardize the transboundary flows of goods and people that were the life blood of the three highly integrated economies and so crucial to their hopes for future global competitiveness.[1] Security might trump trade in theory but it should not jeopardize prosperity in practice.

The formalization of this executive consensus took another two years to gestate. The continent's three leaders met formally in March 2005 for the first time in over a decade to address a North American agenda. As a consequence of their central agencies' diligence plus the very public urgings of the US Council on Foreign Relations-convened Independent Task Force on the Future of North America (Council on Foreign Relations 2005), Presidents Bush and Fox and Prime Minister Paul Martin signed on 23 March a document of uncertain legal status called the "Security and Prosperity Partnership of North America."

Galvanized by their leaders' commitment and by a tight, three-month deadline to produce an action plan, officials dealing with border security, transportation, agriculture, energy and economic policy in each of the three governments started a process of consultation in order to insert policy content into the SPP. Yet, content did not necessarily mean coherence. The measures proposed for the transportation sector were cobbled together on the telephone and by e-mail without their authors ever getting together for a meeting. In the hope that inclusion under the SPP umbrella might extract government funding, officials took projects off their shelves and bulked up the text. As a result, when ministers from the three countries met in Ottawa in June 2005 to announce the SPP's work plan, their shiny trilingual document looked something like an intergovernmental version of a Sears catalogue – some 300 proposals for regulatory changes that were to square the post-9/11 circle: achieve the highest possible level of border security for North America while facilitating the smoothest possible transboundary flows of people and commerce (SPP 2005).

Understandably, there was little public discussion of these proposals and still less general comprehension of their significance. For one thing, outsiders had no way of telling the difference between meaningless measures (initiate dialogue to identify issues in moving toward a trilateral agreement on expanding air transportation), trivial projects (improve transparency and coordination in energy information, statistics and projections) and powerful proposals (greater economic production from oil sands). For another, there was no trinational authority that could monitor progress on a continental basis. Within each federal government, authority could shift from one body to another. In Mexico, the Secretaría para la Gobernación took charge originally, but later ceded authority to Relaciones Exteriores. In Canada, control was originally censored in the Privy Council Office but was later decentralized. In Washington, the National Security Council had little authority other than speaking in the president's name. Real power was in the Department of Homeland Security and Commerce. Nor was there any indication explaining where money would come from to pay for these initiatives. Disinterested observers were not the only ones to voice their doubts. Highly interested businesses whose production chains traverse the Canadian-US and/or Mexican-US borders were happier that action was being promised than with the actual program or the all-bureaucrat process by which it had been made.

NORTH AMERICAN COMPETITIVENESS COUNCIL

Dismayed that a wide range of regulatory issues were being discussed without their having been consulted, business representatives from the three countries decided they needed to reconnect with the politics of continental integration, an issue to which they had only thrice paid serious attention – during the negotiation of the two free trade agreements and in the immediate aftermath of 11 September. UPS invited a few dozen business leaders from the three countries to its transportation hub in Louisville, Kentucky early in 2006 to discuss the problem of border barriers which were a huge concern to its courier business. Under the spectre of growing competition from China, many American businesses were reconsidering how to reduce their production costs in North America. Slowed down by the highly intrusive security demands of US border controls and impeded by inadequate highway infrastructure, transborder shipment delays had created significant transaction costs for many American TNCs which had located entities of their production chains around the continent. They were ready to consider getting directly involved in SPP.

One meeting led to another. Sixty business leaders met two months later in Washington under the joint auspices of the Council of the Americas and the US Chamber of Commerce. By then a consensus had emerged that the SPP should be formally monitored and activated by business participation in a separate but related institution.

When on 31 March 2006, the newly elected Canadian Prime Minister Stephen Harper managed to get himself invited to what had been scheduled as a Mexico-US summit in Cancún, the trilateral conclave was able to mark the SPP's first anniversary by three further decisions. The leaders accepted one of the Council on Foreign Relations 2005 task force's recommendations by agreeing to meet on an annual basis. Next, they reduced the June action plan into five more manageable priorities: strengthening competitiveness, emergency management, avian and human pandemic influenza, energy security and smart, secure borders. Then, with a handful of big business leaders whom they had brought to Cancún, they established a North American Competitiveness Council (NACC) that was to plug the three corporate communities directly into their governments' trilateral consultation process.

Institutionally speaking, these three innovations promised to change the face of North American governance. Whereas there had been no meeting of the three countries' leaders between September 2001 and March 2005, there was now to be a yearly North American summit that would address common concerns. While easy to dismiss as yet another occasion for mediatized photo opportunities, such a regular get-together could have substantial potential. For one thing, a regular trilateral pow-wow would put the US president on a par with the periphery's two heads of government, intrinsically reducing the power asymmetry between the former and the latter who, ipso facto, would get regular access to the White House. For another, each impending tri-national summit would energize the senior reaches of each country's executive, impelling them to insist that, lower down the bureaucratic chain of command, their own officials cooperate with their counter-parts in the other two countries in order to put together an agenda. Once completed, the meetings' decisions would produce a new action program that would drive subsequent governmental actions and foster further bilateral or trilateral cooperation among officials and business. Their resulting achievements would, in turn, have to be evaluated as the basis for their next meeting's agenda.

More intriguing by far was the NACC's insertion into the three coun-tries' institutional order. Its first meeting in Washington in August 2006 was attended by Mexican and Canadian business representatives appointed by their heads of government. Because the United States executive cannot appoint an advisory body without congressional approval, NACC's American members had been selected by the US Chamber of Commerce and the Council of the Americas. During the session, the governments' participants asked the trilateral corporate leaders to tell them what they were doing wrong. US Secretary of Com-merce Carlos Gutierrez urged the newborn Council to stimulate visible and rapid government action by focusing their advice on the short term. Picking the low hanging fruit, they should produce recommenda-tions that the three executives could implement quickly and easily with-out having to open the Pandora's box otherwise known as legislative authorization, which would involve their elected politicians in debating the measures or voting budgetary allocations.

Three priority areas – border security, energy integration and regu-latory harmonization – were selected. Responsibility for proposing solutions on each subject was delegated to one country's business leadership. Since nine of the ten business leaders whom Harper had invited were members of the Canadian Council of Chief Executives (CCCE), it was hardly surprising that the Prime Minister's Office (PMO) asked the CCCE, still run by the veteran free-trade lobbyist, Tom d'Aquino, to be the Canadian secretariat for the NACC and take charge of drafting its recommendations for border-security and trade-facilitation measures.

Mexico City's business participation was almost as predictable. The voice of Mexican capitalism was offered to those business *Camaras* that were most involved with exports. Not having the policy-analysis capac-ity of Canadian or American business groupings, these business associa-tions lodged the secretariat for the Mexican side of the NACC in a small think tank dedicated to promoting economic competitiveness, the Insti-tuto Mexicano para la Competitividad (IMCO). IMCO's delegated task for the NACC was to propose measures to bolster North American competitiveness and security in the energy sector.

In contrast with its two sets of corporate interlocutors who worked hand in glove with their governments, the NACC's US participants kept their distance from the Bush administration, which was rapidly losing credibility, and organized their own participatory process. The US Chamber of Commerce communicated its mandate – proposals for transborder regulatory harmonization – to its entire membership, inviting any company which so desired to take a seat at its NACC advisory table. Intense discussions involving company CEOs with their US competitors and Mexican or Canadian counterparts were orchestrated jointly by the US Chamber and the Council of the Americas. By November, the three secretariats had produced draft proposals which were circulated to their corporate cousins for comment and revision.

The results of these negotiations were made public at NACC's next formal gathering, which took place in Ottawa on 23 February 2007. On that day, representatives from each country's business community presented their 51 detailed recommendations to an impressive trinational ninesome: the US Secretaries of State, Condoleezza Rice; Commerce, Carlos Gutierrez; and Homeland Defence, Michael Chertoff; the Mexican Secretaries of External Relations, Patricia Espinosa; the Economy, Eduardo Sojo; and the Interior, Francisco Ramírez Acuña; the Canadian Ministers of Public Safety, Stockwell Day; Industry, Maxime Bernier; and Foreign Affairs, Peter MacKay (North American Competitiveness Council 2007). Not only had NACC created a continental business trialogue at the highest level, it had given this three-headed corporate powerhouse direct access to a new North American cabinet subcommittee. It was of slight import that this step towards more formalized continental governance had given the Canadian business community privileged access to its own national executive and bureaucracy, an intimacy it had long enjoyed. It was a much more dramatic innovation to grant Canadian business institutionalized access within the Washington beltway, promising greater capacity for corporate Canada. More significant still, the NACC presented the corporate and political leadership from the United States and Mexico with similar access in Ottawa. This would presumably have major effects on the Canadian government's autonomy in areas where the three business communities and the other two governments agreed on what actions should be taken.

On issues where Ottawa, Mexico City, and their respective business communities are in agreement, the continental periphery might gain new purchase in the American capital, increasing Canadian clout there. Regularized interactions with Mexican officials can also be expected to buttress a Canada-Mexico relationship that was born of NAFTA and, following some years on life support, was revivified after September 2001 and formalized in 2004 with the establishment of the Canada-Mexico Partnership which had been designed to give more content to this fragile third continental bilateral.

At a time when neoconservatism is fighting a rear-guard action globally and hemispherically, NACC's creation represents a further deterritorialization and marketization of North America's political processes which strengthen their isolation from environmental, labour and socio-political concerns. Should this corporate forum survive and grow, it will mark a notable addition to Canada's external constitution, empowering a muscular form of transborder, increasingly trilateral governance in which big business has greatly increased rights of access. In its present form, this new continental institution is carefully insulated from Canada's civil society organizations and the democratically elected institutions defined by the country's internal constitution – Parliament and the provincial governments – and can be amended at the pleasure of the participating leaders.

Beyond its institutional novelty, the SPP's impact in creating new norms and practices for Canada's legal order is likely to be modest for the immediate future. Its normative banner could be inscribed with such slogans as "Security Shall not Trump Trade" or "Trialogue Beats Dialogue." Since its programmatic thrust focuses on measures that can be implemented quickly and without legislative approval (for instance, the preparation for handling medical emergencies and natural disasters and the harmonization of certain minor standards in the periphery with those of the United States), immediate changes in Canadian rules will be limited.

Continuing engagement in the NACC by the three business communities will depend on their evaluation of the governments' response to the February 2007 action program. Should the experiment be deemed a success so that the Partnership subsequently becomes more ambitious, its longer term impact on the domestic legal order in Canada could become much more intrusive.

In the medium term, SPP remains an uneasy relationship within and between the three member states. Within each federal government, the fit between security and economic agencies remains awkward:

1 In Mexico City, the prosperity dossier is far more securely rooted in the governmental structure since the same generation of technocrats that had negotiated NAFTA is still staffing the working groups and driving the process of economic policy development. On the security side, the Centro de Investigación y Seguridad Nacional (Center for

Intelligence and National Security) is a young institution with little power to do much more than try to get the various agencies involved in security and intelligence to pull together. Having initially refused to sign off on the SPP, the Secretariat of External Relations is now taking on the role of lead department for managing it.

2 In Ottawa, the shift from the narrow focus of the Smart Border Agreement to the multi-dimensional SPP was accompanied by a parallel institutional evolution. The Smart Border initiative was negotiated and implemented on the Canadian side by John Manley when he was deputy prime minister operating in the Privy Council Office from where he was able to interact directly and continually with his American alter ego Tom Ridge in the White House. Political and administrative control of the Canadian side of the SPP has been moved down the bureaucratic hierarchy to two associate deputy ministers (ADMs), one in the Department of Public Safety, the other in the Department of Industry, with the Department of Foreign Affairs and International Trade having an overall coordinating function – hardly a structure for effective action.

3 But the SPP's greatest public administration problem lies in Washington where the bureaucratic nightmare known as the Department of Homeland Security (DHS) jealously guards its control of security issues. Unlike Ottawa, where the centralization characteristic of parliamentary government ensures close collaboration between the ADMs responsible for the prosperity and security portfolios, little can be done to have DHS compromise its goal of impermeable American land borders by making concessions on the altar of economic competitiveness

For Ottawa's prime concern – its relationship with Washington – the SPP created an important consultative process with which it hoped to revitalize the institutionally moribund NAFTA. But the promise of continuing dialogue leading to successful cooperation over many specific issues lost some of its allure in May 2007 when DHS Secretary Michael Chertoff broke off talks to establish a pilot project on land pre-clearance at the Fort Erie-Buffalo crossing. Although the two-year-long negotiations had been premised on the principle that the agreement would respect the laws of the country hosting the pre-clearance area and although fingerprinting is only mandatory in Canada for those charged with a crime, Chertoff insisted on US officials in Fort Erie being able to require these biometrics even of those US-bound travellers who decided at the last minute not to cross the border. Despite tremendous political and corporate support for a land pre-clearance system similar to the long-established facilities in major Canadian airports, Chertoff's decision showed how difficult it was to pass from the SPP's prosperity rhetoric to the practical problem of getting Homeland Security to modify its security obsession. Despite endorsement by the Council of Foreign Relations task force and enthusiastic support in the NACC's February 2007 report, the project's failure brought into question the SPP's ability to trump security with smoother-flowing trade.

Between Canada and Mexico, a growing commonality of interest around border issues is rewriting a long history of mutual ignorance. The difficulty each government has dealing with Washington has made it easier working with the other peripheral state on the many different SPP agenda items.

CONCLUSION

Canada operates simultaneously in two interacting worlds. In its multilateral sphere, it is located in the mid to higher ranks of the global hierarchy – neither so weak that it can exert no capacity abroad nor so strong as to operate autonomously from international influence at home (Clarkson and Cohen 2004, 1–11). As a middle power with a necessary interest in a liberal multilateral order (see Cooper et al. 1993), it must take its international obligations very seriously, not the least because they may offer it room for manoeuvre.

In its continental sphere, it has to confront the reality of its location in the United States' backyard and defence perimeter. Given that the major constraints in Ottawa's objective context are the multifarious interests of its generally hegemonic, sometimes imperialistic, often isolationist neighbour, this analysis has shown that the new Security and Prosperity Partnership of North America needs to be understood as the present iteration of a long-standing relationship whose constitutionalization has altered significantly over the decades, each change affecting Ottawa's room for manoeuvre. Hence the SPP creates a double-edged operating framework.

On the one hand, it officially gives subjective recognition to the continent's basic political reality: nothing proceeds that the United States does not want to happen. Ottawa can only pursue its own economic objectives by first meeting US security requirements. Accepting as context the United States' security fixation, the SPP provides a framework within which the reduction of Canadian autonomy resulting from US pressure can be managed and perhaps mitigated. On the other hand, the SPP's annual heads-of-government summits create new capacity for the Canadian government by legitimizing its voice in a number of key Washington agencies whose policies directly and significantly affect Canadian interests.

Trilateralizing formerly bilateral issues will also affect the continent's power dynamic. Ottawa has long resisted being identified with the United

States' other territorial neighbour, lest its relationship with Washington be contaminated by congressional fears of illegal immigrants and narcotraffic. Assuming the continental baby's cranium hardens and its organs develop, the SPP and NACC could herald the end of North America's two dyadic relationships operating disconnectedly. The Western Hemispheric Travel Initiative requiring American citizens to have secure identity documents when coming back to the United States has caused both Mexico and Canada to lobby together and with their American allies on this issue. To the extent that American policy designed to counteract problems at the Mexican border apply to Canada, Canadian autonomy will be negatively affected. To the extent that Canada and Mexico together exert more power over the continental giant, their capacity is increased and their power asymmetry is offset. And as they act together, the imbalance in North America's third bilateral relationship diminishes.

If a country's room for manoeuvre is subjectively determined by the will of its leadership to act, only time will tell how capable the PMO turns out to be in exploiting the SPP arrangement. In the meantime, we can conclude with some certainty that Canadian big business has pulled off another coup by inserting itself through the NACC into the government processes of all three countries while their elected politicians and civil societies are pushed further to the political sidelines.

NOTES

1 This analysis is based on confidential interviews carried out in Mexico City in 2006 and 2007 (primarily in the Secretariats of External Relations, Agriculture, Transport, and the Economy), in Washington in 2006 and 2007 (in the Mexican and Canadian embassies, the National Security Council and Department of Commerce as well as with officers in the US Chamber of Commerce, the Council of the Americas, and the Canada-US Business Council), and in Ottawa in 2007 (in the Departments of Public Safety and Foreign Affairs and International Trade and the Canadian Council of Chief Executives).

REFERENCES

Cellucci, Paul. 2003. Address by the US Ambassador to Canada at the Economic Club of Toronto, 25 March.
Clarkson, Stephen, and Marjorie Griffin Cohen. 2004. "Introduction: States under Siege." In *Governing under Stress: Middle Powers and the Challenge of Globalization*, edited by Stephen Clarkson and Marjorie Griffin Cohen. London: Zed Books, 1–11.

Cooper, Andrew F., Richard Higgott, and Kim Richard Nossal. 1993. *Relocating Middle Powers: Australia and Canada in a Changing World Order.* Vancouver, BC: UBC Press.

Council on Foreign Relations. 2005. "Building a North American Community: Report of an Independent Task Force."

Galloway, Gloria. 2003. "US Rebukes Canada." *Globe and Mail,* 26 March.

Levin, Richard C., and Susan Erickson Marin. 1996. "NAFTA Chapter 11: Investment and Investment Disputes." *Law and Business Review of the Americas* 83, no. 2: 90.

Magder, Ted. 1998. "Franchising the Candy Store: Split-Run Magazines and a New International Regime for Trade in Culture." *Canadian-American Public Policy* 34 (April).

Merchant, Livingston T., and A.D.P. Heeney. 1965. "Canada and the United States – Principles of Partnership." *Department of State Bulletin,* 2 August.

North American Competitiveness Council. 2007. *Enhancing Competitiveness in Canada, Mexico, and the United States: Private-Sector Priorities for the Security and Prosperity Partnership of North America.* Initial Recommendations of the North American Competitiveness Council. February.

Security and Prosperity Partnership of North America (SPP). 2005. "Report to Leaders." 27 June. Available at: <http://www.spp.gov/report_to_leaders>

13 CDA_USA 2.0:
Intermesticity, Hidden Wiring and Public Diplomacy

COLIN ROBERTSON

In January 2009, there will be a new administration in the White House and a new opportunity for Canada's leadership to be ready with an agenda that reflects a well-considered Canadian strategy towards the United States. The 2008 presidential election is about change rather than continuity, and the current focus on national security means that foreign policy is getting significant attention. Candidates for both parties are voicing their support for the importance of friends and allies and this presents an opportunity. January 2009 also marks the 20th anniversary of the implementation of the Canada-US Free Trade Agreement (FTA). Although the FTA, and its successor, the North American Free Trade Agreement (NAFTA), have served Canadians well by creating a trade-led prosperity, the new post-9/11 emphasis on "security" has halted the slow but steady gains of the post-FTA and NAFTA period. The time is right to comprehensively assess the American relationship and take it to a new level of sophistication – to CDA_USA 2.0, in the lingo of our times.

Ours is an "intermestic" relationship. In the American context, diplomacy – like politics – must be "local" to succeed. We already do diplomacy differently in the United States with continued innovation in our approach to Congress and with the states. An American strategy will oblige coordinated plans for both the "home" and "away" games. It will oblige recognition of the value of the "hidden wiring" of relationships – especially those at the province-state level.

Creating and implementing a strategy that takes the relationship to the next level – 2.0 – will be a challenge but we have many advantages, including the fact that Americans like Canadians. Too often, we fail to turn this to our advantage. We also forget that on almost any issue there will be more Americans who think like Canadians than there are Canadians.

The real challenge to progress lies at home. The latent anti-Americanism that Jack Granatstein defines as our secular religion presents a challenge that will require political will and national leadership.[1] Anti-Americanism ultimately holds us back and contributes to what Andrew Cohen (2007) calls the "Unfinished Canadian."

The "burden of primacy" that America carries in global affairs means that the initiative for improving the Canada-US relationship has to come from the Canadian side. Setting out an agenda for change that takes us beyond the FTA and NAFTA will require collaborative political leadership between levels of government in Canada, and an "intermestic" campaign waged with equal vigour on both sides of the border to remind Canadians why America matters to us, and to remind Americans why we matter to them. "Intermestic" is the right term because our geographic propinquity and economic interdependence has created a relationship that defies the traditional. The arrangements we have developed to manage our co-tenancy of the upper half of North America defy the classifications of domestic or international. It is a partnership where the "hidden wiring" of state-province and associated relationships play an increasingly important role.

We begin the process by deciding what it is we want from the United States, while "branding" Canada as a reliable ally and vital partner – demonstrating visibly the American jobs we sustain with our markets and the energy we supply to them to heat their homes and fuel their industry. The changes caused by new media and technology and a renewed preoccupation with national security requires continued evolution in how we practise diplomacy in the United States. Recognizing the differences in the American system of government, we need to devote particular effort to Congress, not only because of the potential harm its legislative actions can do to Canadian interests, but because at the local and state level is where pernicious ideas take root.

THE CHALLENGE OF PROPINQUITY

Concern over national security is exacerbated by anxiety about the continuing, large flow into the United States of economic migrants from Mexico and Latin America. For Americans, the border has become critical to keeping out both "illegals" – who allegedly take their jobs and keep wages low – and terrorists. In the popular mind, "border" means the walls, wires and armed guards with dogs that characterize the border with Mexico. For some politicians and bureaucrats, the instinct is to adopt a similar approach to the 49th parallel, regardless of the differences. To treat Canada "differently," I was often told during my diplomatic career, ran the risk of discriminating against Mexico. Neither Democrats nor Republicans want to risk offending the Latino vote. The rapidly growing Latino community brings with it significant political and cultural implications. At 40 million, the Latino population has eclipsed African Americans as the largest "minority" group in the United States.

Since Roosevelt embraced Mackenzie King, successive US administrations have recognized that America "needs" a strong Canada to protect its northern border, and today our role as the biggest source of imported energy is increasingly appreciated for its strategic value to the American economy. During the Cold War we were the first line of defence against Soviet missiles and bombers and bilateral cooperation was enshrined through the North American Aerospace Defense Command (NORAD), the BOMARC Missile Program and our assent to test cruise missiles. Today, we actively screen against another threat – terrorism, with resulting close complicity (sometimes overzealous) between our law enforcement agencies.

The legacy of Iraq is likely to leave many Americans wary of foreign engagements and more inclined to disengage from world events. Iraq only reinforces the increasingly popular attitude that America "should mind its own business," that the world "doesn't like us, doesn't want us and doesn't need us ... so why are we there?"[2] That attitude is creating an America that wants its borders fenced and guarded. Those who want a reduced American role may rejoice, but a retreating America will leave the world more vulnerable, more exposed to terrorism and more fragile and dangerous.

The debate over immigration has sharpened the nativist instinct. Those who argue that the "lock-down" on the southern border should also include the border with Canada come from both the left and the right and have a voice in Congress. We've even had "Minutemen" from Arizona try to incite some of our southern border neighbours to action but their scaremongering failed to incite the sensibly sceptical burghers of Vermont. Nonetheless, we have a problem.

The "Millenium Bomber," Ahmed Ressam, and the myth that some of the 9/11 terrorists came from Canada have had an enduring effect in legislation such as the Western Hemisphere Travel Initiative that already requires Canadians entering the United States by air and, in early 2008 those crossing by land, to have a passport or the equivalent. It may yet be undone through pressure from American communities, at the border and in tourism destinations, lobbying their legislators that the security requirements are unnecessary, likely to be ineffective and are already hurting their local economies. Their efforts have already convinced authorities to relent on passports for children crossing by land.

Visible discontent about the effects of globalization and the loss of jobs in traditional manufacturing, especially around Detroit's auto industry, is also giving rise to another wave of protectionist sentiment. Fuelled by populist demagoguery (watch CNN's Lou Dobbs for a live demonstration) it finds an increasingly sympathetic ear in a Congress once more under the control of the Democrats who are beholden to the unions whose money and votes are conditional on "labour" friendly legislation.

While China is the main target, Canadian interests will be affected, directly and as collateral damage. An activist approach, aimed at creating a positive attitude with Americans towards Canadians and the Canada brand, is essential. Some legislation – perhaps increased country-of-origin labelling of food and other products – will inevitably become law and make it even more important for Americans to view the Canada brand positively. We should take a page from the marketing efforts of New Zealand on lamb and Australia on wine and aim to make products like Canadian beef and salmon "premium" brands. We need to recognize that such promotion requires a permanent campaign and that it must begin with a focus on Congress.

CONGRESS, ADVOCACY, AND PUBLIC DIPLOMACY

Shortly after I joined the Foreign Service, Marcel Cadieux, who had served as Canadian ambassador in Washington, told a group of us junior officers that the best way to improve Canada-US relations would be to effect a change in the American constitution. Cadieux spoke half in jest – commentators were writing of the reassertion of Congress against the "imperial presidency" in the wake of Watergate. Cadieux's irritation with the American system of government was the result of the failed East Coast Fisheries Agreement that he had negotiated with the Carter Administration. It collapsed when the senior senator from the smallest state, Claiborne Pell, refused to bring it forward to ratification because of opposition from a few hundred Rhode Island scallops fishermen who were unhappy with their quotas. Pell was exercising his prerogative as chair of the Senate Foreign Relations committee, underlining forcefully the constitutional separation of powers and the checks and balances that distinguish the American system from our own.

Recognition that the legislative branch counted in foreign policy, especially in the negotiation of treaties, and that presidential administrations could not be counted on to deliver Congress" approval, changed the way Canada did diplomacy in the United States. Junior officers were dispatched to half a dozen consulates with congressional relations as part of their package and as ambassador (1981–1989), Allan Gotlieb began to walk the halls of Congress "lobbying" on behalf of Canadian interests. This marked a paradigm shift in the conduct of Canadian diplomacy.[3]

The focus on advocacy and Congress has only increased. Encouraged by the provincial premiers, Prime Minister Martin created an Advocacy Secretariat within the Embassy that brought congressional outreach, public affairs, state-province and federal-provincial relations under the same umbrella with a mandate to "further Canadian interests in the United States" (Canada 2004).

Looking at contentious issues, acid rain, beef, and lumber, always lumber, in each case the source of our problem is not the White House, but a Capitol Hill representing sectional interests or a local industry. Resolution requires defining the issue not as a Canada-US problem, but as an American challenge with American interests at stake and then finding American advocates and allies whose efforts to win public support for the cause can be supported. Success depends on the campaign for hearts and minds. If our perspective is seen as representing the "people's will," then a deal – inevitably negotiated through the Executive Branch with congressional support – is doable.

THE HIDDEN WIRING:
ALL POLITICS IS LOCAL

The binding that holds the relationship together is complex. Most attention focuses on the "visible wiring" – the relationships of prime minister and president, members of their cabinets, ambassadors and diplomats. Tone at the top does indeed matter, not least because of its effect in conditioning public opinion (see Martin 1982) but a growing strength of the relationship and an element that provides the anti-freeze when there is frost at the summit, is the "hidden wiring" of cross-border relationships: between leaders and legislators at the national, state-province, county and municipal levels; and between civil servants, business, labour, service clubs and sports teams.

The new "Canada caucus" in Congress has its counterpart in the parliamentary "border caucus." The Canada-US inter-parliamentary group at the national level is mirrored at the state and provincial level by legislators who participate in the national and regional conferences of state legislators and state governments.

The province-state dimension is particularly important (see Roberts 2006). It is in dealing with the intermestic that the "hidden wiring" works best: rivers that flow north and south, nurses and teachers who live in one country and work in the other, cows that are born in America, fattened in Canada and then slaughtered in the United States. The institutions that have developed around them are important and should be cultivated. Western governors and premiers meet annually as do eastern premiers and New England governors. The most integrated and successful arrangement, in the Pacific North West region, includes both legislators and civil servants. Taking place beyond the headlines, the emphasis is on creating and sustaining personal relationships, discussing shared problems and resolving the contentious and challenging. The attention is less policy-focussed and more about the practical aspects of intermesticity: compatible highway codes, access at ports of entry, flooding and water diversion, pesticide use and the migration of wildlife. The agenda also reflects their constitutional responsibilities for trade and resources, a fact sometimes overlooked by those who would apply the foreign policy override to all they survey.

Provinces have long engaged both lawyers and lobbyists to work on their behalf on meat and potato issues and provincial tourism campaigns are often delivered through American media. Formal provincial presence in the United States continues to expand through a web of agreements and undertakings with provinces and their offices, whether stand-alone or co-located, as with, for example, Alberta in the Washington Embassy, and Ontario in the New York Consulate General, magnifying the Canadian footprint.[4]

Furthermore, the synergies of partnership – when the different levels of government work together in a "Team Canada" effort – have been illustrated time and again, through, for example, the Team Atlantic Canada missions of prime minister and premiers, or through events that focus on a particular province. A notable example of a province-focussed event that advanced national interests was the ten-day exposition of Alberta and Canada – with an emphasis on energy, held on the Smithsonian Mall for two weeks around Canada Day and the fourth of July in 2006. Prime Minister Harper made his first official visit to Washington the next week and the atmosphere created by the Alberta-inspired events contributed positively to setting the right tone for the prime ministerial visit.

While I was in Los Angeles, we focussed our Canada Day events on a province, inspired by the example of former American Ambassadors Blanchard and Giffin, who put the emphasis on different American states at their Independence Day events. On Canada Days from 2001 to 2004, provincial trade missions led by premiers (consecutively, Alberta's Ralph Klein, British Columbia's Gordon Campbell, Manitoba's Gary Doer and Nova Scotia's John Hamm) anchored events that created a momentum that contributed to an increase in trade and investment.

While the national government creates frameworks and broad policy initiatives, the provincial and state governments are often best situated to practically advance their commercial, trade and investment interests. I saw this time and again – in New York, when provincial finance ministers came down to Wall Street to discuss their bond ratings, and in California, when the most successful trade missions were those led by provincial premiers and their ministers. The Team West Canada mission, led to Los Angeles by then Prime Minister Chrétien, opened doors. However, the follow-through, the most important part in creating and sustaining relationships, occurred at the provincial and often municipal level. The impetus behind opening an office in Tucson, Arizona, for example, stemmed largely from the partnership between the life sciences industries in Ottawa and Tucson and the political will the cities' two mayors brought to the process.

DOING DIPLOMACY DIFFERENTLY

I made over 300 calls on Capitol Hill during my Washington tour of duty. I remember in my early days, after speaking to our issue of the day using the approved talking points, an exasperated aide interrupting to say: "What is it you Canadians want? You look and sound like us but we talk differently. What is it that you want? You're worse than the Chinese!" He concluded with the classic Capitol Hill rejoinder: "What is your *ask?*"

He was right. Congressional offices receive an average of 20 calls a day; if you want to be remembered you need to be clear about your purpose. We adjusted our approach and developed new tools including a "map" that graphically outlined for each state the relationship between jobs and trade with Canada. Thanks to our improved analytical tools we could pinpoint individual districts and talk about jobs created by Canadian investment in a meaningful sense. Like politics, all trade is local.

The most significant improvement we made in our lobbying effort came when I began to make my calls accompanied by one of my senior military colleagues. The uniform of the Canadian Armed Forces, coupled with their personal stories about service abroad with American Forces, did more to advance our cause on issues like beef, lumber and water diversion than all of our well-reasoned arguments on the issue. Members of Congress and their staff were highly appreciative of our front-line involvement in Afghanistan and visibly sympathetic towards the casualties we are taking there. They would openly draw a link between our performance on security and our "ask" on trade.

With security at the top of the American agenda, we started by reminding Americans of active Canadian military engagement in support of peacekeeping and, increasingly, peace-making. We pointed out that we are an ally; that our border is secure and that America can continue to rely on Canada in the war against terrorism. Afghanistan is the most visible proof of our commitment to the war on terror. While understood by the administration and the Pentagon, our contribution is insufficiently appreciated by Congress and most Americans. There is a continuing requirement for proactive advocacy on our part.

Our common and enduring efforts at the border and in defence of the North American homeland make for a compelling story. There is the practical law enforcement cooperation of the RCMP and FBI and other police agencies as well as our intelligence sharing. On the defence side, there is NORAD and the growing "interoperability" of our forces on land, air and sea. We responded to the tectonic shift in American attitudes towards security after 9/11 with a series of policy initiatives. The most important has been the Smart Border Accord, an instance when the adjective was taken to heart and with subsequent effect. Unfortunately, its successor initiative, the Security and Prosperity Partnership (SPP), has become moribund and it will require significant political will to rouse it from its zombie-like state (for an in-depth view of the SPP, see Clarkson in this volume).

Advocacy in this new diplomatic paradigm draws more from the hardball of American politics than the niceties of *Satow's Guide to Diplomatic Practise*. It's more about outcomes and performance than means and process. Our targets are not fellow diplomats but rather journalists and politicians, lobbyists and legislators. And we are as likely to advance the Canadian cause at a tailgate party or hockey game as at the opera or symphony. Being able to talk the intricacies of baseball, football and basketball with Americans is a significant advantage.

Marketing is vital. When the Canadian Forces took up primary duty in Afghanistan in February 2006 we commissioned billboards in Washington subways that unabashedly illustrated our "boots on the ground" to drive home to Americans that we are active partners in the war on terrorism.

The tools of the trade are also different with websites like CanadianAlly.com and online networks like Connect2Canada rather than diplomatic notes. Using the web we built virtual communities that knew no borders. We started with the academic community – monitoring their research and then spotlighting it through electronic newsletters called *Think Tank Watch* and *Canada Watch*. Grants to those who wanted to study Canada were made conditional on their research having practical application to our interests.

Our most significant innovation was harnessing, on a national level, the power of our expatriates – those whom Jeff Simpson (2000) has dubbed our "star-spangled Canadians." The conventional approach had been to shun expatriates as canapé eaters and drinkers of cocktails. But this ignored their potential as our eyes and ears in the community and their capacity to open doors for us.

We built on the California experience. There, my entrée into Silicon Valley came largely through the bright young engineers and computer whizzes – graduates of Waterloo and other Canadian universities who'd been "sucked in" to use the Ross Perot expression, by jobs in Silicon Valley. We enticed them into our Digital Moose Lounge and sustained them with cases of Moosehead, Canadian and Blue and offered them Aero Bars and Smarties at social events like hockey games, picnics and the Terry Fox run. In Hollywood, we took it a step further and gave it an overtly commercial objective through the creation of our virtual Talent Guide of Canadians working in the Industry – canadiantalentla.com. The studios use it to employ the Canadian "talent" necessary to take advantage of our content incentives.

We took this approach to the national level with the strong encouragement of Ambassador Frank McKenna, whose "war room" approach to issues only improved our game, especially in the campaign that resulted in jointly addressing the threat to aquatic resources in the Red River basin posed by the Devils Lake diversion project in North Dakota. Connect2Canada, launched on Canada Day 2005, is aimed at Canadians living in the United States and gives members a single portal to regular and targeted updates of news and information from tourism to tax – it now even includes podcasts. In growing the network, we partnered with Canadian universities to reach out to American alumni as well as our Canadian studies programs. Today Connect2Canada has a "membership" of nearly 35,000. The goal is to reach 100,000.

Connect2Canada has proven its worth time and again. A legislator in Utah tells his local paper that "the terrorists had come in from Canada' and thanks to a member in Utah we were able to correct, oblige retraction and publicize within hours. Within hours of the arrests of the Toronto 17,[5] we distributed Prime Minister Harper's statement and our key messages to the Connect2Canada community and through another tool, Congress Plus, to every congressional office both in Washington and in the district.

A colleague once asked: "What can 30,000 Canadians do that 200 diplomats cannot?" The answer is, "a lot."

NEXT STEPS

Convincing Canadians that we need to move forward, once again, the relationship with the United States will require political leadership by the prime minister, premiers and mayors. Framing will be important and, in addition to economic arguments, it will offer an opportunity to positively present federal-provincial cooperation for the common good in the same fashion as the successful Chrétien "Team Canada" trade missions. Canadians like to see their different levels of governments working together.

We require a pro-active campaign that reminds Canadians that our prosperity derives from trade and investment. Premiers and provincial legislators should play an important role as they more readily appreciate the realities of local trading relationships. Business and labour leaders need to make common cause in reminding their employees and brothers and sisters in the labour movement that a considerable portion of their pay cheques depends on access to the American market, a fact all can appreciate even though views will naturally vary widely on how best to turn it to Canada's advantage.

1) Political Leadership

Political will is essential for success and it starts at the top. The asymmetry of the relationship means that prime ministers must prod presidents to achieve action and results. Domestic dialogue on the American relationship will be lively and coloured by distrust and animosity towards the Bush administration. In parliament, there are those in each party whose natural instinct is to oppose anything involving the United States. We can count on the cultural literati to sound the alarm on whatever they perceive to be a threat to sovereignty or cultural independence. The Afghan campaign, especially in Quebec, has resurrected fears of foreign military entanglements. All of this will require attention. Sifting, digesting, and giving political coherence to this strategy should be the work of a Task Force with a deadline of the next Inauguration (January 2009) and with the political weight to gather attention and effect change. Our academic/research community – universities and think tanks – should also be studying the relationship and preparing the intellectual capital that policy-makers rely upon. Leadership of the task force will be important and in the tradition of Rowell-Sirois and Laurendeau-Dunton, should be co-chaired by high-profile appointees from widely different political backgrounds.

Considerable homework has already been done by our leading think tanks.[6] The goal of the task force should be to recommend policies that create and sustain the wealth of Canada for continued investment in education, healthcare and instruments of sovereignty including our diplomatic service and armed forces. The scope of study should be wide, a root and branch look including standards and services, labour mobility, rail, roads and ports, environment and security. There is a need to address, for example, the challenges around trade, investment and competition policy including the fears of a "hollowing out" of Canadian head offices. The globalization of the Canadian economy, the deepening integration and interdependence with the United States, has implications that must be spelled out in terms that are meaningful locally. This means that we need the facts on the linkage between American-generated jobs and trade and investment in Canada – by region, by province, by city, by constituency and sectorally. I have already mentioned the Canadian Embassy's tool (nicknamed GOCART), that uses data from the Commerce Department and commercial sources to measure Canadian investment in the US using Statistics Canada and other data. A similar tool could be applied to American investment in Canada. Our domestic homework needs to be set against an equivalent study of Canadian interests in the United States and this offers an opportunity to deepen linkages between Canadian and American learning institutions and create a new knowledge network. Canadian universities have created first-class research centres devoted to the study of Europe, Latin America, Asia and the Pacific. We should use the opportunity that would arise from the work required by the Task Force to create centers dedicated to the study of the United States.[7]

2) Keep it Simple

We should go first for that which is easy to achieve so as to show early success, putting at the top of the list those items that only require regulatory or administrative approvals and that can be implemented quickly. Change always exacerbates public anxiety around standards and sovereignty and we must show how change in fact can bring discernible improvements.

We need to develop a shared description of the issues and a joint language so that the public in both countries can easily participate in the discussion. The vocal minority of critics will always trump the silent majority. To secure and maintain domestic support in both countries will require a sustained public education and outreach campaign.

In focussing on outcome, we should encourage symmetry and complementarity in approach, rather than harmonization and duplication. One approach does not fit every situation. As Allan Gotlieb has observed, we have a "multiplicity of instruments" at our disposal and we should apply them as you would use a "Swiss army knife," in the felicitous phrase of Bob Wolfe.[8] The most enduring and successful arrangements are binational, like NORAD, then bilateral. Rules should be designed to keep the playing rink free of debris and to threaten penalties, but their application should be rare and the emphasis should be on keeping the game going. Canadians will have to recognize that the US occasionally will exercise their right to the "trap door" exemption. It's not fair but we must get over it and keep our eyes on the puck. More rules are no panacea: anything requiring congressional approval will take forever and risks being held hostage to stuff that has nothing to do with the agreement. Lastly, US Treasury Secretary Jim Baker's advice to his team – "prepare, prepare, prepare" – has particular relevance to Canadians when negotiating with Americans. The United States usually doesn't pay attention until the third period when they put their A-team onto the ice and try to change their play-book. That's when preparation pays off.

3) Team Canada Redux

We should take a Team Canada Inc. approach in recognition of the "intermesticity" of the relationship, and use the "hidden wiring," that kilt of connections that sustains our shared space. But the concept must be taken to a new level through regular and ongoing trade and investment missions, involving provincial and municipal governments, as well as labour and business organizations. Some continuity could be brought to the process through annual "State of the Relationship" conferences executed regionally in partnership with business and labour. Business involvement, in particular, is essential and must target national, local and regional organizations, including the membership of Chambers of Commerce and the Canadian Manufacturers and Exporters as well as the Canadian Council for Chief Executives. Their partnership helped win support for the FTA and NAFTA. Their absence from the field sealed the "sad and melancholy" fate of the Multilateral Agreement on Investment (see Dymond 1999).

4) It's Security, Stupid

It is critical that we continue to make investments in our own security, particularly in the North. This is a currency that Americans understand. We pay little "rent" to defend ourselves in North America. The "interoperability" with American forces that characterizes our air and naval cooperation should for instance be applied to our land forces as well, as we are doing in Afghanistan and through relief missions as in East Timor.

Foreign diplomats often make the mistake of assuming that because traditional diplomacy requires the State Department to be their primary interlocutor on foreign policy and relations with the Administration it is, therefore, the principal player in the determination of American national security policy. They fail to understand that making national security policy is a bit like playing Star Trek chess – it occurs at various tables on different levels. What Eisenhower described as the military-industrial complex of the United States includes players like the National Security Council, Congress, the Pentagon as well as the defence industries. The Pentagon is critical, especially when America is at war. For Canadian industry it is also the source of significant contracting opportunities and Canada has long been the single largest foreign source of these contracts. In the "long, twilight" war on terror campaign, the Pentagon trumps the State Department. Diplomatic activity should respond accordingly.

5) Being There

In the smorgasbord of American politics, you can always identify like-minded groups or individuals and develop allies, regardless of party. As I mention above, on almost any issue there will be more Americans who think like Canadians than there are Canadians. But you have to be there and so we need to develop a presence in every state by the summer of 2008 in order to have an impact on the election that year. We could start by hiring expatriates working out of their homes, using the internet and telephone and through affiliation with local chambers of commerce. Their mandate would be to market and promote Canada and, by targeting legislators, to create a strong positive image of Canada as friend, ally and partner.

In the American system, local and state governments play a critical role in the progress of legislators. Unlike Canadians, Americans seem to expect their leadership to do their apprenticeship at the local/state level. Four of the last six presidents were governors. The leading presidential candidates for 2008 include the wife of a former governor, a state legislator, a former mayor and a pair of former governors. Ten former governors now sit in the Senate. Most of the new members in the current Congress served in local levels of government. Bringing American legislators to Canada should be an ongoing project. And, as members often remarked when I was on the Hill, make time for building camaraderie on the golf course, or for what Americans particularly enjoy in Canada, fishing and hunting. The "hidden wiring" counts and these networks should be a key part of the Canadian strategy towards relations with the United States.

A similar strategy should be followed on the business front, through the development of a network of state or regional-based private sector business associations to support trade relations. An excellent model is the Canada-Arizona Business Council. The national network could be built in affiliation with the superb Canada America Business Council.

Our own narrow diplomatic work should also be better adapted to the task, with an "American" stream within the Foreign Service that would complement the current functional streams – political/trade/aid/immigration. Recruitment should shift from the current guild mentality to that of a franchise, a service open to an all talents approach and different kinds of experience. It should allow for lateral entry, including for head of mission positions, from all levels of government, as well as business and academe.

Cultural diplomacy should also be broadened to recognize the value of popular entertainment in advancing the "Canada Brand" in the United States. For a model, look to the "Upper North Side" campaign waged in New York City. A "Think Big" strategy is needed – what about having Shania Twain perform aboard a Canadian frigate in San Diego or Norfolk harbour? Or a colour guard of returned Afghan veterans from the Princess Patricia Canadian Light Infantry when the Blue Jays play in Yankee Stadium?

The American public policy process is open and in continual churn and American think-tanks are the place where the political parties seek new ideas and sustenance. The think-tanks also provide a home for the "administration in waiting." More Canadians should be there, cultivating relationships and actively participating in the American debate, especially on issues of trade and security. We could take more advantage of opportunities like the Woodrow Wilson Center's Canadian program. Canadian political parties should emulate the example of the German conservative movement who has attached a scholar to the Heritage Foundation.

CONCLUSION

"Place, standing and perspective," coupled with Canadian sensitivity and sensibility, mean that when we're on game, we have the privilege, as observed by John Holmes (1981) – that most astute practitioner and observer of Canadian foreign policy – "to tell our best friends when their breath is bad" (see also, Holmes 1970; 1976). Geographic propinquity gives us "place," especially in terms of the American preoccupation with national security. The diversity of our population and especially the networks we gain through immigration gives us "standing" on the major developments of our time, like the rise of China and India. Our global diplomatic service also gives us a different "perspective," especially on places like Cuba, that we can bring to the table.

The American Revolution, or War of Independence (perspective is everything) created two nations. For too long, selective interpretations of Canadian-American relations have portrayed Canada as unequal or subjugated. This mindset has held us back from engaging the Americans as partners and mutual beneficiaries in the bounty of our shared geography. It took nearly three quarters of a century for us to exorcise the ghosts of Laurier's 1911 defeat on free trade but the political courage of Brian Mulroney has rewarded Canada with prosperity and security. We need to now exorcise the insecurity around our identity. It will begin by describing ourselves by what we are: a people that celebrates diversity within pluralism; a people that accommodated itself to our vast land and harsh climate through innovation in transportation and communication; a people with a flourishing cultural literacy and a sense of humour. And when pressed by serious threat – fascism, communism and now terrorism – we stand up and pay in blood.

The Peace Arch separating Blaine, Washington from Douglas, British Columbia proclaims we are "children of a common mother." Similar yet different. Through effort and design, Canadians have created a privileged place on the top half of North America. Played effectively, our relationship with the United States gives us a unique influence as interpreter of America to the world and to America on the world.

Allan Gotlieb's *Washington Diaries,* magisterially insightful on the conduct of Canadian diplomacy with the United States, contains this reflection, penned after he'd met with Richard Darman, then senior assistant to Ronald Reagan.

"I keep thinking of what Darman said to me the other day as I was leaving his office. 'You know, for us in the White House, there is good news and bad news. The bad news is that Reagan really can't say no to the Canadians. The good news is that you guys are too stupid to realize it.'"

"The sad reality," wrote Gotlieb (1991), "is he's right."[9]

Plus ça change? Not if we profit from experience and prepare for the future.

NOTES

The views in this essay are personal. They reflect 30 years in the Canadian foreign service drawing on four tours of duty in the United States as well as experience in Ottawa that included participation in the teams that negotiated the Canada-US Free Trade Agreement and NAFTA.

1 Jack has spoken often of anti-Americanism as our secular religion as in, for example, Granatstein (2003).
2 See the excellent continuing work done by the Pew Foundation and the survey work by the Chicago Council on Foreign Relations; see also Kohut and Stokes (2006).

3 The most comprehensive account of the conduct of Canadian diplomacy in Washington and beyond the beltway is contained in Allan Gotlieb's (2006) superb memoir, *Washington Diaries 1981–89*. Gotlieb wryly observes that his approach to Congress was vastly different from that of his predecessor, Arnold Heeney. For more on ambassadorial diplomacy and Congress see also the Washington chapters in Derek Burney's (2005) memoir *Getting it Done*.

4 John Higginbotham, and others at the Canadian Centre for Management Development, began cataloguing the hundreds of agreements between us states and Canadian provinces in 2004. Some of the most relevant work can be found in, Heynen and Higginbotham (2004) and Mouafo et al (2004).

5 In June of 2006, police arrested 17 Toronto residents (12 adults and 5 youths), seizing three metric tons of ammonium nitrate and assorted bomb-making materials (BBC News 2006). The media have labeled the group of suspected terrorists the "Toronto 17."

6 Alex Moens (2007) of the Fraser Institute argues, "Rather than approach each trade-related issue on a piecemeal basis, our government should be working with the us to reach a comprehensive agreement on security measures and a shared border to ensure we have continued access to the us market." Glenn Hodgson of the Conference Board has argued that the development of more integrated North American supply chains essentially ended after 2000 and that now is the time for a FTA II (see Hodgson and Triplett 2007). But the best start ing point for solid research on the trade dimension of the next steps is the work of Michael Hart (who holds the Simon Reisman Chair) and Bill Dymond both at the Canadian Center for Trade Policy and Law at Carleton University.

7 The Metropolis project on immigration, a joint effort of the Social Sciences and Humanities Research Council and Citizenship and Immigration Canada, now in-volving all levels of government and partners in 20 participating countries is a good example of an effective network that brings together experts around the world.

8 Allan Gotlieb has used the expression on various occasions, but it is most simply spelled out in his contribution to Griffiths (2000). In his 23 April 2003 article in the Toronto Star, my former colleague Bob Wolfe, now Queen's University pro-fessor, advanced the Swiss Army knife approach to diplomacy.

9 I kept a copy of *I'll Be With You in a Minute, Mr. Ambassador* on my desk at home and at the office – it remains the best single guide to conducting diplo-macy in the United States.

REFERENCES

BBC *News*. 2006. "Canada charges 17 terror suspects." 4 June. Available at: <http://news.bbc.co.uk/2/hi/americas/5044560.stm>.

Burney, Derek. 2005. *Getting It Done: A Memoir*. Montreal and Kingston: McGill-Queen's University Press.

Canada. 2004. "Prime Minister Announces Details of Secretariat at Washington Embassy." News Release, Canadian Embassy in the United States, Washington, DC, 29 April.

Cohen, Andrew. 2007. *The Unfinished Canadian: The People We Are.* Toronto: McClelland and Stewart.

Dymond, William A. 1999. "The MAI: A Sad and Melancholy Tale." In *Canada Among Nations 1999: A Big League Player?* edited by Fen Osler Hampson, Michael Hart, and Martin Rudner. Don Mills, ON: Oxford University Press.

Gotlieb, Allan. 1991. *I'll Be With You in a Minute, Mr. Ambassador: The Education of a Canadian Diplomat in Washington.* Toronto: University of Toronto Press.

– 2006. *Washington Diaries: 1981–1989.* Toronto: Random House.

Granatstein, Jack. 2003. "The Importance of Being Less Earnest: Promoting Canada's National Interests through Tighter Ties with the United States." Benefactor's Lecture, C.D. Howe Institute, 21 October.

Griffiths, Rudyard, ed. 2000. *Great Questions of Canada.* Toronto: Stoddart Publishers.

Heynen, Jeff, and John Higginbotham. 2004. *Advancing Canadian Interests in the United States: A Practical Guide for Canadian Public Officials.* Ottawa: Canadian School of Public Service. Available at: <http://www.csps-efpc.gc.ca/Research/publications/pdfs/p127_e.pdf>

Hodgson, Glenn, and Jack E. Triplett. 2007. "Canada-US Competitiveness: The Productivity Gap." *One Issue, Two Voices* 7 (June). Washington, DC: Canada Institute, Woodrow Wilson International Center for Scholars.

Holmes, John W. 1970. *The Better Part of Valour: Essays on Canadian Diplomacy.* Toronto: McClelland & Stewart.

– 1976. *Canada: A Middle-Aged Power.* Toronto: McClelland & Stewart.

– 1981. *Life with Uncle: The Canadian American Relationship.* Toronto: University of Toronto Press.

Kohut, Andy, and Bruce Stokes. 2006. *America Against the World: How We Are Different and Why We Are Disliked.* New York: Times Books.

Martin, Lawrence. 1982. *The Presidents and the Prime Ministers – Washington and Ottawa Face to Face: The Myth of Bilateral Bliss, 1867–1982.* Toronto: Doubleday Press.

Moens, Alex. 2007. *Canadian-American Relations in 2007: Recent Trouble, Current Hope, and Future Work.* Vancouver, BC: Fraser Institute.

Mouafo, Dieudonné, Nadia Ponce Morales, and Jeff Heynen, eds. 2004. *Building Cross-Border Links: A Compendium of Canada-US Government Collaboration.* Ottawa: Canadian School of Public Service. Available at: <http://www.csps-efpc.gc.ca/Research/publications/pdfs/p128_e.pdf>

Roberts, Kari. 2006. *A Continental Divide? Rethinking the Canada-*us *Border Relationship*. NEXT West Discussion Paper, July. Calgary: Canada West Foundation.
Simpson, Jeffrey. 2000. *Star-Spangled Canadians: Canadians Living the American Dream*. Toronto: HarperCollins Publishers.

14 Canadian Environmental Policy in a North American Context: Manoeuvring Toward Mediocrity

DEBORA L. VANNIJNATTEN

If there is a particular policy area in which one might have expected to see clear evidence of convergence in North America in the post-NAFTA (North American Free Trade Agreement) era, it would be environmental policy. As levels of economic integration in North America have increased, the rational desire (and political pressure) on the part of business to see the same kinds of regulations applied across borders has deepened. Moreover, attempts to develop and consolidate a coordinated "North American" environmental regime have intensified, with these efforts building on a long history of well established relationships on both the Canada-US and US-Mexico borders. What's more, citizens of the three North American countries have shown considerable support for government action to address environmental problems, particularly more recently.

Contrary to these expectations, however, convergence has not been the only or even the foremost trend in the environmental policy realm. Instead, the picture is much more complex. While there has been some convergence of goals in Canada-US (and in some cases, trilateral) environmental policy over the past decade or so at both the federal and sub-federal levels of government, the policy instruments employed by the two countries have differed. So, while Canadian environmental policy on the surface has come to look more like the American in terms of its stated goals, the way that we have gone about solving environmental policy problems in reality has been quite distinct. This Canada-US distinctiveness in policy instrument choice – and, specifically, the reluctance of Canadian governments, national and provincial, to impose stringent regulations or to experiment with market-based incentives – is one explanation why Canada has so often come up short in actual outcomes, relative to the US. Just recently, there are signs of a convergence in policy instrument choice at the sub-federal level, likely as a result of pressure from activist state neighbours. Yet, Canada retains considerable environmental policy room for manoeuvre – and has thus far used it to be decidedly mediocre.

CONVERGENCE: METHODOLOGICAL CLARITY

There is an active debate about the extent to which policies "converge," not only within national political systems but also across borders. In this sense, "convergence" refers to the coming together of two or more discrete entities or phenomena *over time* (Banting, Hoberg and Simeon 1995). This definition emphasizes that, in order to demonstrate convergence, the phenomena in question must have been more dissimilar in earlier periods than they are now. By contrast, arguing that two or more phenomena are "similar" requires only that the researcher show the ways in which these phenomena are alike, at a specific point in time. In this vein, an argument for policy "divergence" requires demonstrating that phenomena are moving away from each other. When neither convergence nor divergence can be observed, one can conclude only that the phenomena continue to be "distinct."

Clarity is also required when addressing the phenomena that are being studied. "Policy" is far too vague a term for meaningful study (i.e., determining whether convergence or divergence is occurring) and one must be more specific. This chapter will distinguish between policy goals, policy instruments and policy outcomes. Policy goals refer to the stated or expected ends of government commitments, as when Canada's federal government agreed to achieve a 6 per cent reduction in greenhouse gas (GHG) emissions below 1990 levels, on average, during the 2010–12 period under the terms of the Kyoto Protocol. Policy instruments refer to the actual means or devices that governments have at their disposal to achieve policy goals (Howlett and Ramesh 2003, 87). Regulation, subsidies, taxation and voluntarism are all examples of policy instruments. In the case of Canadian climate change policy, the federal government has relied mainly on voluntary industry action to reduce GHG emissions, rather than imposing emissions cuts through regulation, or by instituting some sort of taxation on emissions or an equivalent "cap-and-trade" emissions trading regime which would create an incentive for reduction. Environmental policy outcomes can refer to, among other measures, the amount and concentration of pollutants released into air, water or land by industrial and other facilities. Environmental policy goals, instruments and outcomes are thus separate phenomena, each of which can be observed over time for signs of convergence, divergence or continuing distinctiveness.

Policy instrument choice is probably a better indicator of a government's level of commitment to achieving its policy goals than the stated goals themselves. Certainly, a policy goal adopted by government provides a signpost for business and societal actors in terms of future political and policy directions. Yet, policy goals may not be adhered to (Canada's Kyoto goal is an obvious example here) or the stated goals may not provide a true picture of what government wishes to achieve with its policy. It is the actual policy instrument(s) chosen to implement that goal which provides more insight into government aims and commitment. For example, a willingness to incur the political and material costs associated with regulation, or with taxing environmentally unfriendly behaviour, indicates a higher level of commitment on the part of government actors to environmental protection than does a voluntary "challenge" issued to industry to change their environmental behaviour. So, while Canada may have agreed to its Kyoto goal internationally, at home its reluctance to develop an ambitious regulatory and/or market-based regime to achieve GHG reductions over the short and medium term gives us more insight into its commitment to address climate change.

And, the effectiveness of the policy in terms of achieving its environmental goals rests in large part on the instruments chosen to achieve those goals. A sizeable literature on the use of voluntary approaches in Canadian environmental policy, for example, indicates that while such instruments may be less costly for business, they have been largely ineffective in achieving pollution reductions (Gibson 1997; Harrison and Antweiler 2003). Regulations tend to place a higher burden on industry but fare better in terms of environmental outcomes. Some analysts argue that it is tax or market-based incentives (i.e., using the price mechanism) that are likely to be most effective in reducing pollution, although Canada has had relatively little experience with such instruments (McKitrick 1997; Ekins 1999).

Finally, it is important to separate methodologically the search for environmental policy convergence at the federal and sub-federal levels. Much of the literature which has compared Canadian and American environmental policy has focused primarily on the federal level relationship (Hoberg 1992; 2002; Hoberg, Banting and Simeon 2002). More recent studies have acknowledged the importance of sub-federal governments both as key environmental policy actors within their own federal systems (VanNijnatten 2003) and as environmental diplomats, working with their counterparts across the border (VanNijnatten 2006a). American states and Canadian provinces have considerable leverage in the environmental policy-making realm.[1] Studies of the American states have demonstrated a willingness to devote increasing resources to environmental protection (Brown 2001), to undertake innovations in terms of environmental policy approaches and instruments (Kraft and Scheberle 1998; Parisien and Wollenberg 2001; Marcus, Geffen and Sexton 2002; Rabe 2002), and to forge ahead in issue areas that are clearly of national or international concern, such as climate change (Rabe 2004) and air pollution (VanNijnatten 2004). Analysts of Canadian environmental policy are less optimistic about the activities of the provinces, as the highly decentralized environmental protection regime, along with the economic dependence of most provinces on natural resource development and federal reluctance to enter related policy arenas, has contributed to a tendency towards "buck-passing" rather than competitive innovation (Harrison 1996). However, individual provinces show signs of innovativeness on particular environmental issues; for example, Nova Scotia is on the cutting edge in solid waste management, and British Columbia has been a leader on both solid waste reduction and air quality.

And, at the same time that states are gaining ever more environmental policy latitude and provinces are becoming more adept at using the latitude they already possess, these sub-federal governments are also interacting more frequently with one another across the international border. In fact, this thickened network of cross-border ties at the sub-federal level has become *the* primary locus of environmental policy activity along the Canada-US border (VanNijnatten 2006b). While national governments have undertaken little in the way of new initiatives over the past decade, aside from updates/additions to existing bilateral agreements and memoranda of understanding for research collaboration and information sharing, there have been numerous institutional and policy innovations at the regional cross-border level, as discussed in more detail below.

THE FORCES OF (AND ARGUMENTS FOR) CONVERGENCE

There are numerous good (one might even say obvious) reasons to expect that we would see a convergence of environmental policy in North America. First, as economic interactions within North America increase, it is anticipated that this would have an impact on government policy choices. The United States and Canada conduct the world's largest bilateral trade relationship; in 2006, total merchandise trade between Canada and the US exceeded US$533.7 billion (Ferguson 2007). The US-Mexico trade relationship is not far behind in terms of scope and significance. Perhaps more to the point, there have been increases in intra-regional and intra-sector trade, which indicate the emergence of a more interdependent continental economy. At the sub-federal level, trade and economic relations have also become closer, particularly between neighbouring states and provinces. Here, not only is the level of trade increasing, but provinces and states also exchange a much broader range of goods than was previously the case (Policy Research Initiative 2006). Given these indicators of economic integration, business is likely to favour – and to press for – a harmonization of regulatory and policy approaches. And, indeed, we have seen prolonged discussions in Canada regarding the need for regulatory harmonization between Canada and the US in order to avoid, proponents argue, the undue costs incurred by firms that must comply with differing domestic and American regulations. Considerable discussion and research has focused on discovering those areas where regulatory differences between Canada and the US have significant impacts on trade, innovation and investment (Jacobs 2006; Ndayisenga and Blair 2006).

Such trade statistics and discussions of regulatory harmonization have ignited a vociferous debate about whether the pressures generated by economic integration must necessarily lead to policy convergence. In other words, as barriers to trade between two or more nations are removed (where imports/exports increase, firm and sectoral interactions become more interlinked across borders, cooperation on trade infrastructure is enhanced, and national economic interests become more similar), is it the case that the autonomy of governments to make distinctive policy choices is constrained in related areas like environmental and social policy? John McDougall, author of *Drifting Together: The Political Economy of Canada-US Integration*, answers a resounding "Yes." McDougall (2006, 25) argues that, as a result of decades of economic convergence between Canada and the US, "Canada is already engaged in a process of policy harmonization with the US that amounts to political integration by stealth." He notes that this trend has been enhanced in the post-9/11 era as Canadian officials make policy concessions in order to preserve access to the American market. Other studies, based on detailed empirical comparisons of policy, show a more nuanced picture in terms of the relationship between economic integration and policy convergence. Hoberg, Banting and Simeon (2002), in their study of national-level policy convergence in the social and environmental policy realms, argue that Canada "retains far more capacity for distinctive policy choices than many people believe," although environmental policy is seen to be somewhat more vulnerable than social policy in this respect. VanNijnatten and Boychuk (2004), in their inquiry into the relationship between economic integration and policy convergence at the sub-federal level, found only limited support for the contention that convergence may be occurring alongside higher levels of economic integration in the environmental policy field since 1995.

Second, recent attempts to develop and solidify environmental policy collaboration across borders within North America have also encouraged the convergence hypothesis. There has been an increase in political cooperation on environmental problems across borders at the trilateral level, bilaterally (Canada-us, us-Mexico) and within cross-border regions at the sub-federal level. With the signing of the North American Agreement on Environmental Cooperation (NAAEC) and the inclusion of environmental clauses in the NAFTA itself in the early-1990s, some environmental observers expected that a North American environmental regime would develop. The NAAEC and NAFTA provided a set of norms and rules intended to guide public and private environmental action, and a new institution, the North American Commission for Environmental Cooperation (CEC), was put in place to help establish a framework for continent-wide collaboration and, in certain circumstances, act as an environmental watchdog. To address environmental degradation on the us-Mexico border, a Border Environment Cooperation Commission was established alongside NAFTA and the NAAEC in order to promote and certify "environmental infrastructure" projects, which would then be funded by a new North American Development Bank. An Integrated Border Environmental Plan was also formulated to better coordinate existing initiatives as well as foster fresh projects on remediation and air quality. On the northern border, the us-Canada Air Quality Committee joined the venerable International Joint Commission as a bilateral environmental steward.

With the newly created trilateral framework and the system of existing and enhanced bilateral institutions and processes, it would seem that the building blocks were being put in place for a "top-down" North American environmental regime. Yet, perhaps the most interesting – and unexpected – phenomenon since NAFTA has been the development of increasingly dense sub-federal and cross-border regional organizational linkages along the Canada-us border, and to a lesser extent on the us-Mexico border. A succession of studies has found that, not only are state-province agreements becoming more numerous, they also have become increasingly formal, being based on written documents rather than implicit understandings or verbal commitments, and they have undergone institutional sprawl as initiatives proliferate

Table 14.1
Top 20 State-Province Pairs by Number of Environmental Linkages, 2005
(Increase in Linkages since 1980)

Pair	Total	Pair	Total
BC-WA	22 *(450%)*	QC-VT	12 *(100%)*
ON-MI	17 *(240%)*	NB-ME	12 *(100%)*
ON-MN	16 *(220%)*	AB-MT	11 *(175%)*
QC-NY	15 *(276%)*	AB-ID	11 *(267%)*
ON-NY	13 *(160%)*	QC-PA	11 *(267%)*
ON-WI	13 *(225%)*	ON-IN	11 *(120%)*
ON-OH	13 *(160%)*	ON-IL	11 *(120%)*
BC-ID	13 *(225%)*	AB-WA	11 *(267%)*
ON-PA	13 *(117%)*	BC-MT	11 *(267%)*
BC-OR	13 *(225%)*	BC-CA	11 *(175%)*

Source: VanNijnatten (2006a)

(Munton and Kirton 1996; Sanchez-Rodriguez et al. 1998; VanNijnatten 2003). A more recent study conducted by this author (VanNijnatten 2006a) provides detailed information on sub-federal environmental interactions in North America, indicating that a significant portion of state-province agreements and cooperative mechanisms are multilateral and cluster regionally. Table 14.1 shows both the number of linkages among state-province pairs, the percentage increase in the number of linkages since 1980 (in brackets) and the tendency toward regional clustering. Both this study and a burgeoning case study literature on sub-federal and cross-border environmental ties shows that multilateral, regional cooperation is deepening rapidly in the Northeast and Pacific Northwest regions, is ongoing in the Great Lakes and is getting started among Plains states and provinces.

Third, given the asymmetries in economic might, pollution levels and technical capacity between Canada and the US, one would expect Canada to follow the American lead in the environmental policy arena. Indeed, policy observers have coined the term "California Effect" to describe the influence of populous, innovative regions in the US which spur action elsewhere, including in Canada, largely because of their economic strength. One earlier example of this phenomenon has been the continent-wide spread of higher automobile emission standards first imposed by California. As California constitutes 10 per cent of the US automobile market, industries subject to that state's standards have responded by incorporating these into their manufacturing practices in other jurisdictions, including Canada. It would now appear that California is once again setting the environmental agenda, this time with regard to climate change and GHG emissions.

Finally, environmental concern on the part of Canadians, Americans and Mexicans has been a feature of the post-NAFTA period, thereby creating a common popular push for action. Studies comparing levels of environmental concern in Canada and the US have indicated that Canadians and Americans are quite similar with respect to environmental ethics (Boucher 2004, 19). Other authors have shown that complementary trends in public opinion in Canada and the US with respect to environmental degradation have encouraged action on the part of both governments at similar points in time (Harrison 2002; Hoberg 2002). In Mexico, public concern about the environment has been high, particularly with regard to air and water pollution, and the Mexican public is strongly in favour of including environmental standards in trade deals (World Public Opinion 2007).

Looking region-wide, in the mid-1990s Inglehart, Nevitte and Basanez (1996) found a high level of concern about environmental degradation and support for transboundary cooperation on the part of citizens of the three North American countries to address this degradation. Using the World Values Survey data, the authors show that, when asked about social policy integration, residents of Canada and the US (but not Mexico) expressed considerable reluctance with respect to the integration project itself. However, when asked whether they would support integration if "it meant that we could deal more effectively with environmental issues," clear majorities in each country answered "Yes" (Inglehart, Nevitte and Basanez 1996, 145–6). Though it would be difficult to argue that environmental concerns have been a top priority for North American citizens, particularly post-9/11, they have certainly remained on the agenda. And, there is also some evidence to suggest a recent increase in environmental concern on the part of citizens of all three countries (Angus Reid 2006; MIT 2006; CIDE and COMEXI 2004).

NATIONAL ENVIRONMENTAL POLICY:
CONTINUING DISTINCTIVENESS
WHERE IT MATTERS

At the national level of government, there has been some convergence of policy goals, although continuing distinctiveness in policy instrument choice in Canada and the US has left a deeper imprint. Certainly, national environmental agendas in the two countries have tended to be very broadly similar over time. Both administrations committed themselves to the goals associated with "sustainable development" after the release of the Brundtland Commission report in 1987, although the more ambitious "sustainability" approach – which places greater emphasis on the maintenance of ecological processes and functions over time and less emphasis on economic development – is making inroads in both countries. Beginning in the 1970s, the two countries began to build "first generation" environmental policy regimes, which focused on setting specific pollution standards for point sources (i.e., factories) at end-of-pipe. In most cases, Canadian legislation addressing pollution in specific media (air, water, soil) came a few years after American legislation (VanNijnatten 1999). By the 1990s, both countries were ruminating on the need to move toward "Next Generation" environmental policies that would address both point and nonpoint source (e.g., pesticide use) pollution problems and adopt a source reduction approach, i.e., prevent pollution in the first place (Canada 1999; Kettl 1998; Knopman and Fleschner 1999).

Canada and the US have also achieved considerable bilateral success, largely due to a similarity of perspective in terms of what should be achieved. For example, the 1999 renegotiation of the Pacific Salmon Treaty, difficult and conflict-ridden though it was, resulted in policymakers in both countries placing a much higher priority on the conservation of fish stocks, even to the short-term detriment of domestic fishing interests (see Pacific Salmon Commission 2007). The 2000 Ozone Annex to the Canada-United States Air Quality Agreement constituted a high-profile recognition that Nitrogen Oxide (NOx) was linked to transboundary smog formation and, more controversially in the US context, that power plants were the major culprit (VanNijnatten 2003). As a consequence, clear NOx reduction targets were set for each government. Efforts are now underway to include an additional annex to the agreement dealing with particulate matter, a move which reflects a bilateral consensus that this is the next pollutant requiring action. Various iterations of the Great Lakes Water Quality Agreement also suggest a common trajectory in terms of focus and goals, from the first version which directed binational attention to the problem of phosphorous over-enrichment, to the 1978 amendments which highlighted the need for toxic substance regulations, and through to the 1987 Protocol which focused on ecosystem health through more collaborative Remedial Action Plans and Lakewide Management Plans. The Great Lakes Water Quality Agreement is currently under review by the two governments, and a thorough-going debate is underway about how the two countries should use the agreement to address outstanding and increasingly complex problems.

Moreover, the shared perspective gained through bilateral cooperation on environmental problems has been transferred into the international area. For example, there has been conscious coordination of Canadian and American positions in international negotiations on successive Long Range Transboundary Air Pollution protocols on NOx, Sulfur Doixide and Persistent Organic Pollutants. Climate change has also seen considerable cooperation. From early discussions on the Framework Convention on Climate Change to negotiations on the Kyoto text, Canada and the US sought to coordinate their positions. Although the post-ratification environment saw diplomatic divergence, there has nevertheless been considerable Canada-US cooperation on climate-related projects at the operational level in the past and this co-operation has continued (Macdonald et al. 2004). And as the G8 leaders gathered in Germany in June 2007 to discuss, among other things, climate change, the Canadian and American positions seemed complementary in terms of their more moderate, intensity-based approach to GHG reductions.

There has also been some convergence in policy goals trilaterally, and the CEC figures prominently in such efforts. The CEC has a mandate "to promote trinational cooperation for sustainable development, conservation and environmental protection" through the provision of "tangible services, in the form of activities and outputs" (Mumme and Duncan 1996). Though it has limited resources, the CEC has provided these "tangible services" by supporting the formulation of Regional Action Plans, conducting and publicizing research on particular environmental problems, and supporting capacity-building efforts, particularly in Mexico. In all of these activities, the CEC aims to bring government officials, scientific and technical experts as well as societal interests together in order that they may gain a common understanding of environmental problems and share best practices with respect to taking action on these problems.

North American Regional Action Plans (NARAPs) are developed for selected persistent and toxic substances that are considered to be a top priority in the parties' (Canada, the United States and Mexico) common desire to address national and regional concerns associated with the sound management of chemicals. Existing NARAPs focus on "big bad" chemicals such as lindane, dioxins and furans, mercury, Polychorinated-Biphenyls (PCBs), and Dichloro-Diphenyl-Trichloroethane (DDT). Each NARAP has emerged out of an extensive consensus-building process, which begins with a trilateral, collaborative evaluation of the threats posed by a candidate pollutant and then results in a "decision document" outlining recommendations regarding the possible need for action (CEC 2007a). After further public consultation, the decision document is forwarded to the North American Working Group on the Sound Management of Chemicals, a group of key officials from all three countries, which may recommend trinational action via a NARAP. The resulting NARAP generally aims to reduce ambient levels of the pollutant and sets out a series of actions to support reduction efforts, including creating comparative databases, improving scientific understanding, conducting pilot projects (often in Mexico), encouraging voluntary actions by stakeholders and sharing best practices.[2] The three countries are also expected to submit specific action plans which will guide their reduction efforts at home.

Article 13 of the NAAEC allows the CEC Secretariat to prepare a research report for Council on any matter within the scope of its annual work program, and it has paid particular attention over the years to the problem of air pollution in North America. An early, high-profile study in the 1990s focused on transboundary flows of air pollutants. The study highlighted the controversial role of electric power plants in the generation of emissions, associated human health impacts, the decline of government funding for tracking and reducing pollutants, and the need for collaborative action (CEC 1997). This study was quite likely influential in Canada-US discussions of the Ozone Annex to the Canada-United States Air Quality Agreement (VanNijnatten 2003) and encouraged further study of air pollution on the US-Mexico border. The CEC then undertook to study the environmental effects of rapid changes in the electricity systems of Canada, Mexico, and the US, namely the opening of electricity markets to competition. This study again highlighted the role of the electricity sector in terms of air emissions and alerted governments to the large number of power projects being planned near international borders that were likely to affect the well-being of the public and the environment in neighbouring countries (CEC 2002). As part of its work on the environmental impacts of the electricity sector, the CEC has also conducted research into the possibility of establishing a multipollutant emissions trading regime within North America (Russell 2002). All of this work has served to set out an agenda for addressing air emissions in North America, particularly from power plants, and to highlight the need for common goals.

Winfield (2003) has shown how the CEC managed to successfully combine its capacity-building and networking objectives in its work on North American Pollutant Release and Transfer Registries (PRTRs), specifically in helping to put in place such a registry in Mexico. A PRTR is an environmental database or inventory of potentially harmful releases (generally from point sources such as factories) to air, water and soil, often including wastes transferred for treatment and disposal from the site of their production (OECD 2007). Data are provided by the facility to government, which can then track the generation, release and fate of various pollutants over time. The data are also made available to the public, which encourages the reporting industries to reduce their pollutant releases. The American Toxic Release Inventory (TRI) was the first PRTR introduced into North America in 1986, with the Canadian National Pollutant Release Inventory (NPRI) introduced some years later, in 1992. Although the two inventories are not identical in terms of the number of substances covered (the American TRI requires reporting on a broader range of substances), there is considerable overlap, enough that comparisons can be made. The CEC, in one of its more controversial projects, initiated a *Taking Stock* series which reports annually on comparative Canadian and American pollutant releases and transfers. The CEC also made the development of a PRTR in Mexico a priority and facilitated the emergence of a continental policy network, consisting of governmental, non-governmental, industrial and academic sectors from Canada, Mexico and the US to support this initiative (Winfield 2003). After years of collaboration, the first national inventory in Mexico, focusing on air emissions, was made public.

If one were to look no further than stated policy goals, it might be concluded that environmental policy convergence in North America has occurred, particularly between Canada and the US. On a range of environmental issues, from air pollution to toxic substance management to fisheries management, Canadians and Americans seem to have adopted similar policy goals. Even with respect to climate change, where observers often point to the Canadian decision to ratify the Kyoto Protocol and the American decision not to as the major environmental policy difference between the two countries, Canadian and American policy goals have been similar: a focus on both reducing emissions intensity rather than actual emissions and increasing domestic oil and gas exploration and supply rather than aggressively pursuing energy alternatives. However, a closer look at policy instrument choice shows a different trajectory, and the cases of air quality policy and climate change policy can be used as illustrations.

As noted above, Canada and the US agreed to reduce pollutants linked to the formation of ground-level ozone (smog), NOx as well as volatile organic compounds (VOCs), in the 2000 Ozone Annex to the Canada-United States Air Quality Agreement. Under the terms of the Annex, a national Pollution Emission Management Area (PEMA) was created in each country (rather than one which covered the transboundary pollution management area), creating two defined geographic areas within which reductions from emissions sources would have to be made. Each country then chose how the required reductions would be achieved within their PEMA. On the American side, states located within the US PEMA were subject to a federal NOx regulation, specifying that seasonal NOx emissions could not exceed specified limits or "budgets" (Canada 2002). Federal regulations on motor vehicles, fuels and off-road vehicles, as well as specific sources of VOCs, were also implemented at the state level. Moreover, as of 2002, a NOx Budget Trading Program was established for the US PEMA, whereby the Environmental Protection Agency (EPA) used the regulated NOx reduction target as a "cap" (the level of pollution that would be tolerated) and then created allowances to develop a pollution-trading market among NOx emission sources regulated under the cap.

While the US has used a regulatory regime supplemented by a market-based cap-and-trade program to reach its pollution emission targets within its PEMA under the terms of the Ozone Annex, the Canadians have gone about pursuing reductions within their PEMA in a quite different manner. There is no federal regulation imposing the NOx reduction target. Instead, because the provinces are, for the most part, responsible for regulating point sources of air pollution, extensive negotiation and consultation between the national and provincial levels of government with respect to a reduction response has taken place in the Canadian Council of Ministers of the Environment (CCME). Here, provinces and the federal government negotiate "Canada-wide standards" (CWS) as equals. The CWS for NOx, developed in 2000, is to be met by all provinces by 2010, although it exists under the auspices of an intergovernmental agreement and is thus not legally binding on any jurisdiction. Moreover, provinces choose their own targets and instruments to achieve the CWS. For example, Ontario aims to achieve a 45 per cent reduction of NOx and VOC emissions from 1990 levels using a variety of policy instruments. Initially, the province's implementation plan relied on instruments that did not actually require hard emission reductions, such as the Drive Clean Program for automobiles, a program to promote environmental training among dry cleaners; and a reporting and monitoring program for large emissions sources (Canada 2002). More recently, the Ontario government has put in place an Emissions Trading Registry which places a cap on emissions from the electricity sector (Ontario 2007a).

The situation is similar with respect to climate change policy. Here, the Canadian federal government has relied almost exclusively on non-regulatory instruments for encouraging GHG emissions reductions. In particular, the federal government has adopted a three-pronged strategy: distributing science and technology funds to encourage investment in low-emission environmental technologies; enhancing investment conditions (in a limited fashion) for renewable energies, particularly wind, using the tax system; and exhorting other sectors of society and other levels of government to undertake emissions reductions (VanNijnatten 2002; VanNijnatten and Macdonald 2003; Macdonald et al. 2004). With respect to the latter, a Voluntary Challenge Registry (now known as the Climate Change Voluntary Challenge and Registry) was established in the mid-1990s to encourage industry, business and governments to develop and implement voluntary action plans for reducing their GHG emissions. As it became clear that this approach was not working, the Liberal government undertook large-scale negotiations with various industry sectors, such as oil and gas and automotive, purportedly in an attempt to set up "convenants" with these industries, under which they would agree to achieve sector-wide reduction targets. This "large final emitter system" never materialized, however. Only negotiations with the automotive sector yielded anything, namely a nonbinding memorandum of agreement.

In the United States, a different picture emerged. Like Canada, it currently has no national legislation requiring action to reduce greenhouse gases. However, multiple bills mandating GHG reductions have been introduced in Congress, some even making it to a floor vote. Furthermore, the clearer federal regulatory mandate in the US case contributes to action and innovation in other ways. Stringent requirements under existing legislation, particularly the Clean Air Act, have given proponents of climate change action cause to push for mandatory federal action. For example, ten states, the District of Columbia, and New York City successfully sued the federal EPA for failing to adopt strong emission standards to reduce GHG emissions from new power plants across the nation (Sherman 2007). In addition, the federal government has provided considerable support to states to undertake GHG reductions, as part of their regional capacity-building efforts and regardless of the official position taken by successive administrations. The 1990 State and Local Climate Change Program, the 1992 Energy Policy Act and the 1990 Clean Air Act Amendments each provided incentives, albeit in different ways, for states to rethink their orientation toward greenhouse gases and conventional energy sources, and to put in place the technical and policy processes which would enable them to act on this "rethinking" (Rabe 2007).

SUB-FEDERAL ENVIRONMENTAL POLICY: CREEPING CONVERGENCE?

At the sub-federal level, it is also possible to make an argument for goal convergence in particular issue areas of environmental policy and in particular cross-border regions. Perhaps no issue is as illustrative of the scope and importance of cross-border regional cooperation as climate change. Considering the global scope of the climate change challenge, this is somewhat paradoxical. Yet the most ambitious initiative in North America has originated with the Conference of New England Governors-Eastern Canadian Premiers (NEG-ECP), which adopted a transboundary Climate Change Action Plan in 2001 committing its members to reduce GHG emissions to 1990 levels by 2010, ten per cent below 1990 levels by 2020 and to ultimately decrease emissions to levels that do not pose a threat to the climate. Complementary goals under the Plan include the establishment of a regional standardized GHG emissions inventory, reducing GHG emissions, particularly in the electricity and transportation sectors, and achieving higher levels of conservation. Environmental policy statements and activities in those states and provinces that are members of the NEG-ECP bear the imprint of the Climate Change Action Plan, though some more than others. Certain states have formally incorporated the NEG-ECP goals in legislation or action plans, while other jurisdictions have undertaken reduction activities in line with the suggested implementation actions laid out in the action plan (NEG-ECP 2006). More recently, all governors and premiers reaffirmed their commitment to the Climate Change Action Plan emission reductions goals during a press conference at the June 2006 annual NEG-ECP conference.

Further west, the Dakotas, Iowa, Minnesota, Manitoba and Wisconsin have launched an initiative called "Powering the Plains" (PTP), which brings together top elected and government officials, utility industry executives, agricultural producers and renewable energy advocates "to develop and implement strategies, policies, initiatives and projects in energy and agriculture that add value to the region's economy while reducing the risk of climate change and other environmental concerns" (Great Plains Institute 2007). The PTP is working on an integrated energy strategy which builds on the region's comparative advantages in renewable and carbon-neutral technology, such as alternative energy development (i.e., wind, biomass, and hydroelectricity), hydrogen production from renewable and carbon-neutral sources, environmental credit trading (renewable and carbon credits), and carbon sequestration in prairie soils and wetlands. Participating jurisdictions have a consensus agreement to develop regional scenarios for reducing CO_2 emissions 80 per cent from 1990 levels by 2050, and are developing a "regional energy transition roadmap" to help achieve this long-term goal (Great Plains Institute 2007).

In the Pacific Northwest, British Columbia, Washington, Oregon and California have been discussing integrated transportation systems based on environmentally friendly technology as well as renewable energy generation for some time. An agreement recently signed by British

Columbia and California formalizes an earlier commitment to create, in cooperation with Oregon and Washington, a "hydrogen highway" that runs from British Columbia to Baja California in Mexico. Fuelling stations would be built along the way, so that by 2010 a hydrogen-powered vehicle could easily travel that route (Hainsworth 2007). Perhaps more importantly, the agreement also commits California and British Columbia to cap and reduce GHG emission to 1990 levels by 2020 and to work on the development and implementation of clean technologies. This reduction initiative is occurring under the auspices of the broader Western Regional Climate Action Initiative, an agreement initially on the part of Arizona, California, New Mexico, Oregon, Utah and Washington to combat climate change by identifying ways to collectively reduce GHG emissions in the region. The agreement has gained popularity across the border, as British Columbia and now Manitoba have joined.

Goal convergence is also discernible in other environmental issue areas, such as mercury pollution reduction, the focus of another NEG-ECP Action Plan beginning in 1998 (NEG-ECP 1998). And, states and provinces in the Great Lakes region – working through the Great Lakes Commission and other collaborative organizations – have adopted common objectives with respect to dealing with aquatic nuisance species and coastal wetlands. In the Pacific Northwest, considerable effort has focused on joint initiatives with respect to transboundary air quality and ecosystem health in the Puget Sound-Georgia Basin area.

There has certainly been distinctiveness in terms of policy instrument choice at the sub-federal level, in ways that mirror differences at the federal level. However, one might argue that there are more recent signs of a "creeping convergence" in this regard. US states which are participating in the NEG-ECP's Climate Change Action Plan were from the beginning of the program much more likely to adopt regulatory targets for GHG reductions, energy conservation, alternative energy generation and tailpipe emissions (New England-Eastern Canada Coalition 2006). And, almost immediately, states undertook to establish a Regional Greenhouse Gas Initiative (RGGI) emissions trading system in the US Northeast. By contrast, eastern Canadian provinces were more likely to rely on voluntary "challenges" to encourage industry emissions reductions, negotiated emissions reductions agreements with industry which were not binding, as well as public education programs to encourage energy conservation. There was initially little in the way of regulated emissions reductions or alternative energy mandates.

However, this is changing. Prince Edward Island passed a Renewable Energy Act in December of 2005, which requires utilities to acquire at least 15 per cent of electrical energy from renewable sources by 2010.

And, there are plans to substantially increase this mandate. Quebec has formulated a comprehensive 2006–12 Action Plan for climate change that includes a hydro carbon levy, new tailpipe emission standards, alternative energy targets and reduction targets for various industrial sectors. New Brunswick has also released a five-year plan to reduce greenhouse gases that mandates more green power generation, encourages greater use of public transit, and establishes programs to help residents become more energy efficient (Canadian Press 2007). Ontario, for its part, has committed to doubling the installed capacity of renewable energy sources by 2025, has set targets for energy conservation and Premier Dalton McGuinty has signalled Ontario's interest in joining the RGGI (Ontario 2007b).

And, climate change policy is not the only area where convergence seems to be occurring. A recent study has found that there is clustering among the six New England states and the five eastern Canadian provinces with respect to policy instruments advocated in the NEG-ECP Mercury Action Plan (VanNijnatten and Boychuk 2006). Among the six states, clustering is very much in evidence; each have endorsed the reduction target; and, those states with air emissions sources tagged in the Action Plan (utility boilers, incinerators, etc.) have, for the most part, adopted limits more stringent than federal standards. There is also some clustering in terms of mercury-containing product restrictions, disposal objectives and notification requirements among New England states. The Atlantic provinces also have endorsed the NEG-ECP target and have adopted some mercury policy instruments that are consistent with the Mercury Action Plan, although they have not been quite as active as New England states. Atlantic provinces, like states, have been most active in regulating point sources associated with atmospheric mercury releases, and they have also adopted similar disposal and notification requirements.

MANOEUVRING TOWARD MEDIOCRITY: ENVIRONMENTAL POLICY OUTCOMES IN CANADA

All told, there is some evidence to suggest that convergence with respect to policy instrument choice may be gradually occurring at the sub-federal level. However, significant differences remain. And, even though there has been considerable agreement on environmental policy goals at the federal level, Canadian and American authorities have employed different policy instruments. In light of even the cursory examination provided here, it is difficult to argue that policy convergence is the most significant trend in the environmental policy realm. Canada retains, at least in this policy field, considerable room for manoeuvre in the North American context. This may provide some indication of the durability of domestic political and institutional forces as well as policy legacies, as Hoberg, Banting and Simeon (2002) have suggested. Indeed, although national climate legislation is likely to be passed in both countries, the proposals being debated are in keeping with earlier policy instrument preferences; while Americans are discussing an ambitious cap-and-trade scheme, the Canadian government continues to favour a more moderate, negotiated approach to achieving reductions in emissions intensity across various industrial sectors.

Certainly, it would seem that Canada has not used its room for manoeuvre to become an environmental policy leader or innovator. The reluctance of Canadian authorities to employ stringent command-and-control, or even market-based instruments, to achieve environmental ends, and their over-reliance on less coercive instruments such as voluntary initiatives and government spending or tax incentives, seems to have contributed to an overall less impressive record in addressing environmental degradation than is the case in the U.S, which has a stronger tradition of employing regulation and innovative market-based instruments such as emissions trading. It is impossible for us to conclude, given other variables in play, that a certain policy approach and/or instrument can consistently influence environmental outcomes, which are notoriously difficult to measure. However, it seems likely that the tendency of Canadian governments, federal or sub-federal, to *encourage* rather than *compel* pollution reduction bears some relationship to what can be achieved on the environmental policy front.

If we look to available pollution measures, we can see some evidence of this. Pollution data for Canada are hard to find; American agencies have been collecting, analyzing and publishing data under the terms of national air and water quality regulatory requirements for some time now. This has not been the case in Canada. However, in terms of toxins and air pollutants, we do have some bases for comparison. One of the most widely cited comparisons of Canadian and American emissions is the CEC's annual *Taking Stock* reports. The 2005 report found that, for example, Canadian facilities are responsible for 42 per cent of lead air emissions despite only accounting for 5 per cent of total reporting facilities. On average, Canadian facilities released lead into the air at a rate 13 times greater than their American counterparts (Ostroff 2005). In addition, with respect to total air emissions, Canada's emissions increased 8 per cent versus a US decrease of 21 per cent. Moreover, important work by Harrison and Antweiler (2004) shows that, after controlling for the scale of economic activity, releases of criteria air contaminants in Canada are several times higher than in the US.

With respect to climate change, neither the Canadian nor American track-records are particularly impressive. They are not *the same*, however. As Rabe (2006) notes,

Canadian greenhouse gases climbed 25 per cent between 1990 and 2004 whereas American emissions grew 14 per cent during this period. Sectoral comparisons suggest significantly lower American rates of emission growth over the past decade from electricity generation, industrial activity, and methane release from landfills … Using the metric of "carbon intensity," the ratio of greenhouse gas emissions per unit of gross domestic product, American carbon intensity declined 17 per cent during the 1990s as opposed to only 10 per cent in Canada.

Rabe also points out that the US outperformed Canada in this respect even though it experienced higher rates of economic growth than Canada during the 1990s. Thus, even without a national mandate for GHG reduction, pollution reduction requirements related to other federal legislation, along with new state regulatory initiatives, have enabled the Americans to make more progress on the climate change front. It remains to be seen whether recent provincial policy moves that adopt a more "American" regulatory approach to imposing emissions reductions – perhaps coupled with a national reduction mandate – can reverse the decidedly mediocre record of Canadian climate change policy.

NOTES

1 It should be noted here that the role of US states and Canadian provinces is not identical vis-à-vis environmental policy-making and implementation. States must operate within a context of "regulatory federalism," wherein they retain primary responsibility for implementing an increasing range of environmental requirements, though many of these requirements are set at the national level. In Canada, the federal environmental protection framework is more decentralized, regulatory authority for most pollution sources are the preserve of the provinces, and power resides in provincial capitals or intergovernmental forums where the federal government is merely one player at the table.
2 For more information on what is included in a North American Regional Action Plan, see the Mercury example, as reported by the CEC: <http://www.cec.org/programs_projects/pollutants_health/smoc/merc134.cfm?varlan=english#5>

REFERENCES

Angus Reid. 2006. "Canadians Rank Environmental Concerns." *Angus Reid Global Monitor,* 15 September. Available at: <http://www.angus-reid.com/polls/index.cfm/fuseaction/viewItem/itemID/13148>

Banting, Keith, George Hoberg, and Richard Simeon, eds. 1997. *Degrees of Freedom: Canada and the United States in a Changing Global Context.* Montreal and Kingston: McGill-Queen's University Press.

Brown, Steven R. 2001. *States Put Their Money Where Their Environment Is,* 1 April. Washington, DC: Environmental Council of the States.

Canada. 1999. *Moving Up the Learning Curve: The Second Generation of Sustainable Development Strategies.* Ottawa: Office of the Auditor General. Available at: <http://www.oag-bvg.gc.ca/domino/cesd_cedd.nsf/html/c9dec_e.html>

– 2002. *Canada-United States Air Quality Agreement: 2002 Progress Report.* Appendix B, Air Quality Report – Ozone Annex. Ottawa: Environment Canada. Available at: <http://www.ec.gc.ca/cleanair-airpur/CAOL/air/qual/2002/appendixb_e.html>

– 2006. *North American Linkages Briefing Note: Canada-US Relations and the Emergence of Cross-Border Regions.* Ottawa: Government of Canada. Available at: <http://policyresearch.gc.ca/doclib/PRI%20BN%20eng.pdf>

Canadian Press. 2007. "N.B. government sets greenhouse targets." *Globe and Mail,* 8 June. Available at: <http://www.theglobeandmail.com/servlet/story/RTGAM.20070608.wnbclimate0608/BNStory/National/home>

CEC. 1997. *Continental Pollutant Pathways: An Agenda for Cooperation to Address Long-Range Transport of Air Pollution in North America.* Montreal: Commission for Environmental Cooperation (CEC).

– 2002. *Environmental Challenges and Opportunities of the Evolving North American Electricity Market.* Montreal: Commission for Environmental Cooperation (CEC).

CIDE and COMEXI. 2004. *Global Views 2004: Mexico Public Opinion and Foreign Policy.* Mexico City: Centro de Investigacion y Docencia Economicas (CIDE) and Consejo Mexicano de Asuntos Internationales (COMEXI). Available at: <http://thechicagocouncil.org/UserFiles/File/Global_Views_2004_Mexico.pdf>

Ekins, Peter. 1999. "European environmental taxes and charges: recent experiences, issues, trends." *Ecological Economics* 31, no. 1 (October): 39–62.

Ferguson, Ian F. 2007. "United States-Canada Trade and Economic Relationship: Prospects and Challenges." *CRS Report for Congress,* 18 May. Available at: <http://www.nationalaglawcenter.org/assets/crs/RL33087.pdf>

Gibson, Robert, ed. 1998. *Voluntary Initiatives and the New Politics of Corporate Greening.* Peterborough: Broadview Press. Great Plains

Institute. 2007. "Powering the Plains." *Great Plains Institute*. Available at: <http://www.gpisd.net/resource.html?Id=61>

Hainsworth, Jeremy. 2007. "California, B.C. sign agreement to reduce greenhouse gases." *The Associated Press*, 31 May. Available at: <http://www.sltrib.com/news/ci_6030433>

Harrison, Kathryn. 1996. *Passing the Buck: Federalism and Canadian Environmental Policy*. Vancouver: UBC Press.

– 2002. "Federal-Provincial Relations and the Environment: Unilateralism, Collaboration, and Rationalization." In *Canadian Environmental Policy: Context and Cases*, edited by Debora L. VanNijnatten and Robert Boardman. Don Mills: Oxford University Press, 123–44.

– and Werner Antweiler. 2003. "Incentives for Pollution Abatement: Regulation, Regulatory Threats and Non-Governmental Pressures." *Journal of Policy Analysis and Management*, 22, no. 3: 361–82.

– and Werner Antweiler. 2004. "Do Environmental Policy Styles Matter? Evidence from Canada and the United States." Conference paper for *The Annual Meeting of the American Political Science Association*, Chicago, 2–5 September.

Hoberg, George. 1992. "Comparing Canadian Performance in Environmental Policy." In *Canadian Environmental Policy: Ecosystems, Politics, and Process*, edited by Robert Boardman. Toronto: Oxford University Press.

– 2002. "Canadian-American Environmental Relations: A Strategic Framework." In *Canadian Environmental Policy: Context and Cases*, edited by Debora L. VanNijnatten and Robert Boardman. Don Mills: Oxford University Press, 171–89.

– Keith Banting, and Richard Simeon. 2002. "The Scope for Domestic Choice: Policy Autonomy in a Globalized World." In *Capacity for Choice: Canada in a New North America*, edited by George Hoberg. Toronto: University of Toronto Press, 252–99.

Howlett, Michael and M Ramesh. 2003. *Studying Public Policy: Policy Cycles and Policy Subsystems*. Don Mills: Oxford University Press.

Inglehart, Ronald F., Neil Nevitte and Miguel Basanez. 1996. *The North American Trajectory: Cultural, Economic and Political Ties among the United States, Canada, and Mexico*. New York: Aldine de Bruyter.

Jacobs, Scott, and Jacobs and Associates. 2006. "Regulatory Impact Analysis in Regulatory Process, Method, and Co-operation: Lessons for Canada from International Trends." *North American Linkages* no. 26 (June): 1–125.

Kettl, Donald F. 1998. "Environmental Policy: The Next Generation." *Environment and Energy Policy Brief* no. 37 (October). Washington, DC: The Brookings Institution.

Kirton, John. 1997. "The Commission for Environmental Cooperation and Canada-US Environmental Governance." *The American Review of Canadian Studies* 27, no. 3 (Autumn).

Knopman, Debra, and Emily Fleschner. 1999. "Second Generation of Environmental Stewardship: Improve Environmental Results and Broaden Citizen Engagement." *Progressive Policy Institute Briefing*, 1 May. Available at: <http://www.ppionline.org/ppi_ci.cfm?knlgAreaID=116&subsecID=150&contentID=767>

Kraft, Michael E., and Denise Scheberle. 1998. "Environmental Federalism at Decade's End: New Approaches and Strategies." *Publius: The Journal of Federalism* 28, no. 1 (Winter): 131–46.

Macdonald, Douglas, Debora L. VanNijnatten, and Andrew Bjorn. 2004. "Implementing Kyoto: When Spending is Not Enough." In *How Ottawa Spends 2004–2005*, edited by G. Bruce Doern. Montreal and Kingston: McGill-Queen's University Press.

Marcus, Alfred A., Donald A. Geffen, and Ken Sexton. 2002. *Reinventing Environmental Regulation: Lessons from Project XL*. Washington, DC: Resources for the Future Press.

Massachusetts Institute of Technology. 2006. "MIT survey: Climate change tops Americans' environmental concerns." News Release. 31 October. Available at: <http://www.eurekalert.org/pub_releases/2006–10/miot-msc103106.php>

McDougall, John N. 2006. *Drifting Together: The Political Economy of Canada-US Integration*. Peterborough: Broadview Press.

McKitrick, Ross. 1997. "Double Dividend Environmental Taxation and Canadian Carbon Emissions Control." *Canadian Public Policy* 23, no. 4 (December): 417–38.

Mumme, Stephen P., and Pamela Duncan. 1996. "The Commission on Environmental Cooperation and the US-Mexico Border Environment." *Journal of Environment & Development* 5, no. 2 (June): 203.

Munton, Don, and John Kirton. 1996. "Beyond and Beneath the Nation-State: Province-State Interactions and NAFTA." Conference paper for *The International Studies Association Annual Conference*, San Diego, April.

Ndayisenga, Fidèle, and Doug Blair. 2006. "Regulatory Expenditures and Compliance Costs: Verifying the Link Using US Data." *North American Linkages* no. 25 (May). Ottawa: Policy Research Initiative.

NEG-ECP. 1998. *Mercury Action Plan 1998*, June. New England Governors-Eastern Canadian Premiers (NEG-ECP). Available at: <http://www.epa.gov/NF/eco/mercury/pdfs/Mercury_Action_Plan.pdf>

– 2006. *2006 Report Card on Climate Change Action: Third Annual Assessment of the Region's Progress Towards Meeting the Goals of the NEG/ECP Climate Change Action of 2001*, August. New England

Governors-Eastern Canadian Premiers (NEG-ECP). Available at: <http://www.vpirg.org/pubs/documents/Scorecard2006-Final.pdf>

Ontario. 2007a. "About the Registry." *Ontario Emissions Trading Registry.* Toronto: Ministry of the Environment. Available at: <http://www.oetr.on.ca/oetr/about_registry.jsp>

– 2007b. "Ontario to Explore Joining Forces with US States on Climate Change Initiative." News Release. 30 March. Toronto: Ministry of the Environment. Available at: <http://www.ene.gov.on.ca/en/news/2007/033001.php>

Organization for Economic Cooperation and Development. 2007. "What is a PRTR?" *Environmental Directorate.* Available at: <http://www.oecd.org/document/58/0,2340,en_2649_34365_1913466_1_1_1_1,00.html>

Ostroff, Joshua. 2005. "Report flags lead emissions, small facilities." *TRIO: The Newsletter of the North American Commission for Environmental Cooperation* (Summer). Available at: <http://www.cec.org/trio/stories/index.cfm?ID=168&ed=15&varlan=english>

Pacific Salmon Commission. 2007. "The Pacific Salmon Treaty – 1985." *Pacific Salmon Commission.* Available at: <http://www.psc.org/about_treaty.htm>

Parisien, Lia, and Adam Wollenberg. 2001. *State Environmental Innovations 2000–2001*, 15 June. Washington, DC: Environmental Council of the States.

Rabe, Barry G. 2002. "Permitting, Prevention, and Integration: Lessons from the States." In *Environmental Governance: A Report on the Next Generation of Environmental Policy*, edited by Donald F. Kettl. Washington, DC: Brookings Institution Press, 14–57.

– 2004. *Statehouse and Greenhouse: The Emerging Politics of American Climate Change Policy.* Washington, DC: Brookings Institution Press.

– 2007. "Beyond Kyoto: Designing Policies to Reduce Greenhouse Gases in Competing Federal Systems." *Governance* 20 (July).

Russell, Douglas. 2002. *Design and Legal Considerations for North American Emissions Trading.* Montreal: Commission for Environmental Cooperation.

Sanchez-Rodriguez, R.A., K. von Moltke, S. Mumme, J. Kirton, and D. Munton. 1998. "The Dynamics of Transboundary Environmental Agreements in North America." In *Environmental Management on North America's Borders*, edited by R. Kiy and J.D. Wirth. College Station: Texas A&M University Press, 32–9.

Sherman, Mark. 2007. "Justices: EPA Can Control Car Emissions." *Associated Press*, 2 April. Available at: <http://www.sfgate.com/cgi-bin/article.cgi?f=/n/a/2007/04/02/national/w083222D54.DTL>

VanNijnatten, Debora L. 1999. "Participation and Environmental Policy in Canada and the United States: Trends over Time." *Policy Studies Journal* 27, no. 2: 267–87.

– 2002. "Renewable Energy and the Liberal Policy Agenda: Continuity in the Third Mandate?" In *How Ottawa Spends 2002–2003: Innovation for Whom?* edited by G. Bruce Doern. Don Mills: Oxford University Press.

– 2003. "Analyzing the Canada-United States Environmental Relationship: A Multi-Faceted Approach." *The American Review of Canadian Studies* 33, no. 1 (Spring): 93–120.

– 2004. "Canadian-American Environmental Relationship: Interoperability and Politics." *The American Review of Canadian Studies* 34, no. 4 (Winter): 545–60.

– 2006a. "Towards Cross-Border Environmental Policy Spaces in North America: Province-State Linkages on the Canada-US Border." *AmeriQuests: The Journal of the Center for the Americas* 3, no. 1 (Special Issue). Available at: <http://ejournals.library.vanderbilt.edu/ameriquests/viewissue.php?id=7>

– 2006b. "The Constituent Regions of the Canada-United States Environmental Relationship." In *Canada and the US: Relationship at a Crossroads?* edited by George A. MacLean. Winnipeg: University of Manitoba Centre for Defence and Security Studies.

– and Douglas Macdonald. 2003. "The Clash of Energy and Climate Change Policies: How Ottawa Blends." In *How Ottawa Spends 2003–2004,* edited by G. Bruce Doern. Don Mills: Oxford University Press.

– and Gerard W. Boychuk. 2004. "Economic Integration and Cross-Border Policy Convergence: Social and Environmental Policy in Canadian Provinces and States." *Journal of Borderland Studies* 19, no. 1 (Spring): 37–58.

– and Gerard W. Boychuk. 2006. "Mercury Reduction in the Canadian Provinces: Interprovincial vs. Cross-border Policy Diffusion." Conference paper for *The 2006 Annual Meeting of the Canadian Political Science Association,* Canadian Political Science Association, Toronto, 6 June.

Winfield, Mark S. 2002. "The North American Commission for Environmental Cooperation: A Case Study in International Environmental Governance." Conference paper for *Globalization, Multi-Level Governance and Democracy,* Institute for Intergovernmental Relations, Queen's University, Kingston, ON, May.

– 2003. "North American Pollutant Release and Transfer Registries: A Case Study in Environmental Policy Convergence." In *Greening NAFTA: The North American Commission on Environmental Cooperation,* edited by D.L. Markell and J.H. Knox. Stanford: Stanford University Press, 38–56.

World Public Opinion. 2007. "International Publics Strongly Favor Labor and Environmental Standards in Trade Agreements." 21 March. Available at: <http://www.worldpublicopinion.org/pipa/articles/btglobalizationtradera/334.php?nid=&id=&pnt=334&lb=btgl>

Contributors

JEAN-CHRISTOPHE BOUCHER is a doctoral candidate in the Department of Political Science, Université Laval.

STEPHEN BROWN is associate professor at the School of Political Studies, University of Ottawa.

STEPHEN CLARKSON is professor of political economy, University of Toronto.

JEAN DAUDELIN is assistant professor at the Norman Paterson School of International Affairs, Carleton University.

JEREMY DE BEER is assistant professor in the Faculty of Law, University of Ottawa.

WENDY DOBSON is professor and director of the Institute for International Business, Joseph L. Rotman School of Management, University of Toronto.

TREVOR FINDLAY is director of the Canadian Centre for Treaty Compliance, associate professor at the Norman Paterson School of International Affairs, Carleton University, and senior fellow, The Centre for International Governance Innovation.

MICHAEL GEIST is associate professor in the Faculty of Law and Canada Research Chair of Internet and E-commerce Law, University of Ottawa.

TOM KEATING is professor in the Department of Political Science, University of Alberta.

CHRISTOPHER J. KUKUCHA is associate professor in the Department of Political Science, University of Lethbridge.

DANFORD W. MIDDLEMISS is professor in the Department of Political Science and director of the Centre for Foreign Policy Studies, Dalhousie University.

JOHN J. NOBLE is distinguished senior fellow at the Norman Paterson School of International Affairs, Carleton University and fellow at the Weatherhead Center for International Affairs, Harvard University.

COLIN ROBERTSON is president of the Historica Foundation of Canada.

STÉPHANE ROUSSEL is professor in the Department of Political Science and Canada Research Chair in Foreign and Canadian Defence Policy, Université du Québec à Montréal.

DANIEL SCHWANEN is chief operating officer and director of research at The Centre for International Governance Innovation.

DENIS STAIRS is professor emeritus in the Department of Political Science, Dalhousie University.

DEBORA L. VANNIJNATTEN is associate professor in the Department of Political Science, and program coordinator of the North American Studies Program, Wilfrid Laurier University.

CAROL WISE is associate professor at the School of International Relations, University of Southern California.

ROBERT WOLFE is professor at the School of Policy Studies, Queen's University.

Index